PENGUIN CLASSICS

SELECTED POEMS: PIERRE DE RONSARD

PIERRE DE RONSARD was born into a noble family of the Vendômois in 1524 and early in his life entered the French court as a page. In 1537 he visited Scotland in the retinue of James V's two successive French queens and stayed there until 1539. When a serious illness left Ronsard partially deaf, he was forced to abandon his plans for a military career and, temporarily withdrawing from court life, he went to study for a number of years under the humanist scholar Jean Dorat at the Collège de Coqueret. Here, with Jean-Antoine de Baïf, Joachim du Bellay and others, he formed a literary 'brigade', the Pléiade, one of whose aims was to restore the use of French as a literary language of equal value with Latin. This aim was to be achieved by imitating the genres and forms of Greek, Latin and Italian literature.

In 1550 Ronsard published his *Odes*, which gave France its first major works in the Pindaric style, and *Les Amours* (1552), a sequence of love poems addressed to 'Cassandre'. These works gained for him a great following and the patronage and support of King Charles IX and the royal family, as well as the admiration of Mary Stuart, who sent him a gift from prison. In 1555 and 1556 he published further collections of love poetry, the *Continuation des Amours* and the *Nouvelle Continuation*, as well as two books of *Hymns*.

During the Religious Wars in France, Ronsard produced, among other polemical poems, the *Discours des Misères de ce temps* (1562) and the *Remonstrance au peuple de France* (1563). After the disappointing reception of the first four books of his incomplete national epic, *La Franciade* (1572), and the death of Charles IX in 1574, Ronsard increasingly absented himself from court. He continued to write, however, and in 1578 published a new cycle of love poems, *Sonnets pour Hélène*. He died in 1585. Despite the widespread popularity he acquired during his lifetime, his poetry was largely forgotten over the next two hundred years. It was not until the nineteenth century that he was re-discovered and his position as the greatest French poet of his time recognized.

A graduate of Exeter University, where he was subsequently awarded a Ph.D. for his thesis on the poetry of the Pléiade, MALCOLM QUAINTON has been Professor of French Studies at Lancaster University since 1989. Author of *Ronsard's Ordered Chaos* (1980) and of a book on the Religious War poetry of Agrippa d'Aubigné (1990), he has also co-edited two collections of essays and published numerous articles and chapters in books on French Renaissance poetry and culture. He is currently editing the comedies of Jean-Antoine de Baïf, having published a critical edition of his selected poetry in 1970.

ELIZABETH VINESTOCK won an Exhibition to read Modern and Mediaeval Languages at Girton College, Cambridge, and subsequently studied at Lancaster University, gaining an MA with a dissertation on Agrippa d'Aubigné and a Ph.D. for research into the poetry of Ronsard's contemporary, Jean-Antoine de Baïf. She has published a number of articles on this poet and is currently engaged in writing a book on his *Poemes*. She teaches French at Lancaster University.

PIERRE DE RONSARD

SELECTED POEMS

With a prose translation, introduction and notes by
MALCOLM QUAINTON *and* ELIZABETH VINESTOCK

PENGUIN BOOKS

PENGUIN BOOKS

Published by the Penguin Group
Penguin Books Ltd, 80 Strand, London WC2R ORL, England
Penguin Putnam Inc., 375 Hudson Street, New York, New York 10014, USA
Penguin Books Australia Ltd, 250 Camberwell Road, Camberwell, Victoria 3124, Australia
Penguin Books Canada Ltd, 10 Alcorn Avenue, Toronto, Ontario, Canada M4V 3B2
Penguin Books India (P) Ltd, 11 Community Centre, Panchsheel Park, New Delhi – 110 017, India
Penguin Books (NZ) Ltd, Cnr Rosedale and Airborne Roads, Albany, Auckland, New Zealand
Penguin Books (South Africa) (Pty) Ltd, 24 Sturdee Avenue, Rosebank 2196, South Africa

Penguin Books Ltd, Registered Offices: 80 Strand, London WC2R ORL, England

www.penguin.com

First published 2002
1

Set in 10.5/12.5 pt PostScript Adobe Granjon
Typeset by Rowland Phototypesetting Ltd, Bury St Edmunds, Suffolk
Printed in England by Clays Ltd, St Ives plc

Contents

LE SECOND LIVRE DES AMOURS (LES AMOURS DE MARIE)

SUR LA MORT DE MARIE

LE PREMIER LIVRE DES SONNETS POUR HELENE

LE SECOND LIVRE DES SONNETS POUR HELENE

LES HYNNES

LES POËMES

EPITAPHES DE DIVERS SUJETS

DISCOURS DES MISERES DE CE TEMPS

LES DERNIERS VERS

Acknowledgements

We are grateful to the Research Committee of Lancaster University and to the British Academy for their financial support in funding the research for this book, and to the staffs of the British Library and Lancaster University Library for their generous help and practical advice.

We are deeply indebted to David Foster, who is a perfect illustration of the adage that all teachers are ultimately taught by their students: his regular presentations on Ronsard's verse during the course of his doctoral supervisions illuminated many obscure corners of Ronsard's text and maintained our momentum and enthusiasm for a challenging and outstanding poet. David also read portions of the text, and made many valuable comments and suggestions, for which he has our sincere thanks.

We can never adequately repay the debt we owe to Netta and to Gerald for their unflagging support, patience and encouragement. This book is jointly dedicated to them.

Chronology

	Ronsard	Literary Context	Historical Context
1524	Birth of Pierre de Ronsard at the manor of La Possonnière in the Vendômois.		François 1er is King of France. Defeated by the Holy Roman Emperor Charles V at Pavia, 1525, imprisoned until 1526.
1528		Castiglione, *The Book of the Courtier*.	
1530		Bembo, *Rime*. Sannazaro, *Rime*.	Foundation of the Collège de France.
1532		Machiavelli, *The Prince*. Ariosto, *Orlando Furioso*. Rabelais, *Pantagruel*. Marot, *L'Adolescence clémentine*.	Beginnings of the Reformation in England.
1533	Studies at the Collège de Navarre for 6 months.		Calvin adheres to Protestantism. Henry VIII becomes supreme head of the Church of England, 1533–4.
1534		Rabelais, *Gargantua*.	Decoration of Fontainebleau by Italian Mannerists Il Rosso and Il Primaticcio. Cartier discovers Canada, claims it for France.
1535		Bibles in French by Calvin and Olivetan.	Geneva adopts Reformed religion.

	Ronsard	*Literary Context*	*Historical Context*
1536	Page to the dauphin François (who dies in August) and then to Charles, duc d'Orléans, third son of the King.	Death of Erasmus. Calvin, *Institutio religionis christiani* (translated into French 1541).	Charles V invades Provence, but has to retreat. Franco-Scottish alliance. 1536–41, Michelangelo paints the *Last Judgement*.
1537	May: accompanies Madeleine of France to Scotland after her marriage to James V. After her death in July James V marries Marie, sister of the Guises, 1538.	French translation of Castiglione's *Book of the Courtier*.	
1538–9	Brief return to France, second short visit to Scotland.		
1540	Accompanies Lazare de Baïf on a diplomatic mission to the German princes. Then illness, onset of deafness.		Cellini (silversmith and sculptor) arrives in France.
1541		Secundus, *Opera*. Peletier translates Horace's *Art of Poetry*.	
1542			Death of James V. Accession of his daughter Mary Stuart, aged 6 days.
1543	Receives tonsure, enabling him to obtain benefices. This commits him to celibacy. (He never actually became a priest.)	French translation of Ariosto, *Orlando Furioso*.	Copernicus publishes book refuting geocentric conception of the universe.
1544	Studies for three years with Jean-Antoine de Baïf under Dorat in the home of Lazare de Baïf.	Scève, *Délie*. Death of Marot.	
1545	Meets Cassandre Salviati at court in Blois.	Pernette du Guillet, *Rimes*.	Council of Trent opens. It continues until 1563.
1546		Rabelais, *Tiers livre*.	Death of Luther.

	Ronsard	*Literary Context*	*Historical Context*
1547	Enters Collège de Coqueret, with Dorat as tutor. Publishes his first poem (in Jacques Peletier, *Œuvres poëtiques*).	Death of Lazare de Baïf. Du Bellay and Jean-Antoine de Baïf also studying at the Collège de Coqueret. Origins of the Brigade, later to become the Pléiade.	Death of François 1er; accession of Henri II (husband of Catherine de Médicis). Death of Henry VIII of England.
1548		Bèze, *Poemata*. Sébillet, *Art poëtique français*.	Mary Queen of Scots at the French court, betrothed to the future François II.
1549	Publishes individual poems in pamphlet form, including a poem celebrating the formal entry of Henri II into Paris.	Du Bellay, *Deffence et Illustration de la langue françoyse*; *L'Olive*. Tyard, *Erreurs amoureuses*. Bèze, *Abraham sacrifiant*.	Franco-Scottish alliance against England. Death of Marguerite de Navarre. Anglican Book of Common Prayer instituted.
1550	First four books of *Les Odes*, modelled on Pindar and Horace.	Du Bellay, *L'Olive* (enlarged edition).	Henri II retakes Boulogne from the English.
1551	Contributes to collection commemorating the death of Marguerite de Navarre.		
1552	*Les Amours* (known as *Les Amours de Cassandre*). Fifth book of *Les Odes*. Begins epic poem, *La Franciade*.	Baïf, *Les Amours de Méline*. Rabelais, *Quart Livre*.	Renewed hostilities between France and Charles V. Oct.1552–Jan.1553, François de Guise withstands siege of Metz by Charles V.
1553	*Le Livret de Folastries* published anonymously. Enlarged edition of *Les Amours* (with commentary by Muret).	Performance of Jodelle's *Cléopâtre captive*, first classical tragedy in French. French translation of Machiavelli, *The Prince*.	Mary Tudor (married to the future Philip II of Spain in 1554) restores Catholicism in England. Act later rescinded by Elizabeth I.

	Ronsard	Literary Context	Historical Context
1554	*Le Bocage*, drawing in part on pseudo-Anacreon.	Henri Estienne publishes a collection of poetry by pseudo-Anacreon.	
1555	*Les Meslanges* (also influenced by pseudo-Anacreon). *Continuation des Amours* (combined later with *Nouvelle Continuation* to form *Les Amours de Marie*). *Les Hymnes*.	Baïf, *L'Amour de Francine*. Nostradamus, *The Centuries*. Louise Labé, *Œuvres*. Philieul's French translation of Petrarch's *Canzoniere*.	Expedition of Villegagnon to Brazil.
1556	*Nouvelle Continuation des Amours. Le Second Livre des Hymnes.*	Belleau, verse translation of Anacreon's *Odes*.	Abdication of the Emperor Charles V. Philip II becomes King of Spain.
1557–9	Spends long periods at his family estate of La Possonnière. *Plaquettes* (pamphlets) of poems on public and political themes. Official court poet after death of Saint-Gelais, 1558. *Le Second Livre des Meslanges*, 1559.	Petrarchan songs and sonnets by Wyatt and Surrey published in *Tottel's Miscellany*, 1557, though written earlier. Du Bellay, *Les Antiquitez de Rome* and *Les Regrets*, 1558.	1557: French defeat at Saint-Quentin. 1558: Duc de Guise recaptures Calais from the English. Accession of Elizabeth I on death of Mary. 1559: Treaty of Cateau-Cambrésis with England. Marriage of Philip II to Elisabeth of France. Death of Henri II in a jousting accident. Accession of François II (marries Mary Queen of Scots 1558).
1560	First collected edition of the *Œuvres*, in 4 volumes: *Les Amours*, *Les Odes*, *Les Poëmes* and *Les Hymnes*.	Deaths of Du Bellay and Scève.	François II dies; Charles IX king under regency of Catherine de Médicis. Conspiracy of Amboise; signs of civil war.
1561			Colloque de Poissy (an unsuccessful attempt at religious reconciliation). Mary Queen of Scots returns to Scotland.

	Ronsard	Literary Context	Historical Context
1562	*Institution pour l'adolescence du Roy*, addressed to the young Charles IX. *Discours des Misères de ce temps*; *Continuation du Discours des Misères de ce temps*.		Massacre of Protestants at Vassy, provoking First War of Religion, 1562–3. Treaty of Hampton Court (between English and French Huguenots).
1563	*Remonstrance au peuple de France*; *Response aux injures et calomnies de je ne sçay quels Predicans . . . de Genève*.		Assassination of François de Guise.
1563–4	*Recueil des Nouvelles Poësies*, including the four seasonal hymns.	Birth of Shakespeare, 1564.	Death of Calvin in Geneva, 1564.
1565	*Elegies, Mascarades et Bergerie* based on court festivities of 1564. *Abbregé de l'Art Poëtique françois*. 1565–6, receives priories of Saint-Cosme and Croixval.	Belleau, *La Bergerie*.	
1567	Second collected edition.	Baïf, *Le Brave*; *Le Premier des Meteores*.	1567–8, Second War of Religion.
1568	Lawsuit against the dyer Fortin. Ill with fever intermittently until 1569.		Mercator's map of the world. 1568–70, Third War of Religion.
1569	*Le Sixiesme Livre et Le Septiesme Livre des Poëmes*.		Defeat of Calvinists at Jarnac and Moncontour; assassination of Condé.
1570		Baïf's Académie de Poésie et de musique.	

	Ronsard	Literary Context	Historical Context
1571	Third collected edition. Contributes to festivities in Paris in honour of Charles IX and his queen, Elizabeth of Austria.		
1572	*Les Quatre Premiers Livres de la Franciade*, unfinished national epic.	La Taille, *Saül furieux*; *L'Art de la tragédie*. Baïf, *Euvres en rime*, 1572–3.	August: St Bartholomew's Massacre of Protestants in Paris. 1572–3, Fourth War of Religion.
1573	Fourth collected edition.	Death of Jodelle. Desportes, *Premières Œuvres*.	
1574	Withdraws more and more from the court.	Baïf, *Etrénes de poézie fransoêze an vers mezurés*.	Death of Charles IX. Accession of Henri III. Fifth War of Religion, 1574–6.
1575	Contributes to the festivities for the Entry of Henri III to Paris.	Tasso, *Jerusalem Delivered*.	
1576		Baïf, *Mimes, Enseignemens et Proverbes*. Belleau, *Les Amours et nouveaux eschanges des pierres precieuses*.	Drake circumnavigates the world. Foundation of the Catholic League, led by Henri de Guise.
1577		Death of Belleau. D'Aubigné starts *Les Tragiques*.	Sixth War of Religion.
1578	Fifth collected edition, including *Sur la Mort de Marie*, *Sonnets pour Helene* and *Les Amours diverses*.	Du Bartas, *La Semaine*.	
1579	*Panegyrique de la Renommee*.	Spenser, *The Shepherd's Calendar*. Sidney writes *The Defence of Poesie*.	1579–80, Seventh War of Religion.
1580		Montaigne, *Essais*, Books I and II.	

	Ronsard	Literary Context	Historical Context
1581	Organizes celebrations of marriage of duc de Joyeuse with the Queen's sister.	Baïf, *Mimes, Enseignemens et Proverbes*, expanded edition. Sidney, *Arcadia*.	
1582		Sidney writes *Astrophel and Stella*.	Gregorian calendar introduced.
1584	Sixth collected edition.	Du Bartas, *La Seconde Semaine*.	Raleigh discovers Virginia.
1585	28th December, death of Ronsard.		1585–93, Eighth War of Religion.
1586	*Les Derniers Vers*. February, memorial service with oration by Du Perron.	Baïf, *Chansonnettes mesurées*.	
1587	Seventh collected edition, including Binet's biography of Ronsard.	Marlowe, *Tamburlaine*. Malherbe, *Les Larmes de St Pierre*. Tyard, *Discours philosophiques*.	Mary Queen of Scots executed by Elizabeth I.

Introduction

1. The Formation of the Poet and the Poet on Poetry

Pierre de Ronsard was born in 1524 at the manor of La Possonnière near Vendôme, the youngest of the four surviving children of Louis de Ronsard (1479–1544) and Jeanne Chaudrier (died 1545). Born and brought up in this family of the minor nobility in the Vendômois, Ronsard was never to forget the natural beauty of this area, and not only does he set some of his love poetry against his native countryside, but a number of his finest poems reveal a deep feeling for, and a sensitive observation of, Nature in all her moods. His father had fought in the Italian campaigns of Charles VIII and Louis XII (1494–1513) and had returned, like many of his fellow combatants, imbued with a love of Italian culture, a fact borne out by the manner in which he rebuilt the ancestral manor of La Possonnière after the wars in the more refined Italianate style, considered fashionable by the nobility of the period. Soldier, diplomat and cultivated gentleman with literary friends and protégés (among them the Grand Rhéto-riqueur poet Jean Bouchet, 1476–1557), Louis became the *maître d'hôtel* ('master of the household') to the sons of François 1ᵉʳ (king 1515–47). It was in fact he who accompanied the royal princes to Spain during the four-year period (1526–30) when they were held hostage by Charles V in exchange for the release of François, who had been captured during the disastrous French defeat at Pavia (1525).

After an early education in which Jean Bouchet and Jean de Ronsard (an uncle from whom Pierre was to inherit a considerable library on his death in 1535) no doubt played their part, the future poet was sent to the Collège de Navarre in Paris in 1533, where he spent an unhappy and unprofitable semester, returning to La Possonnière sometime in 1534. Whilst at the Collège Ronsard made the acquaintance of Charles de Guise, later Cardinal de Lorraine, who was to become a powerful and influential patron in future years. Destined by his father for a military and diplomatic career, Pierre was attached as a page to the king's eldest son, the dauphin François, shortly before the prince's death (1536). There is evidence to suggest that Ronsard was present both at the death and at the autopsy of the dauphin (it was suspected that François had been poisoned by an Italian servant acting on behalf of the Emperor Charles V), and it is possible that the poet's later preoccupation with human mortality and the passage of time can be traced to his encounter with death at such an impressionable age.

Ronsard now passed briefly into the service of Charles, Duke of Orleans (1522–45), the king's youngest son. Later in the same year (1536) he became page to Charles's sister, Madeleine de France, and in May 1537 he accompanied her to Scotland for her marriage to James V (this marriage formed part of France's foreign policy to strengthen an alliance with Scotland against the common enemy, England). After the death of Madeleine (July 1537), Ronsard remained in Scotland for the marriage of James V to another French princess, Marie de Guise (June 1538) – mother of Mary, Queen of Scots – returning to France via England later in the same year, where he rejoined the service of Charles, Duke of Orleans, at the Royal Stables, situated in what is now the Place des Vosges. After a second diplomatic visit to Scotland (1539), Ronsard accompanied the humanist scholar and diplomat Lazare de Baïf on an unsuccessful mission to Haguenau (1540) to elicit the support of German Lutheran princes for a resumption of hostilities against Charles V of Spain. Upon his return, first to Paris and then to La Possonnière in August 1540, a serious illness left Ronsard partially deaf and dashed all hopes of a military career. (Later Protestant polemic will maliciously claim that Ronsard's deafness and his illness of the late 1560s were manifestations of venereal disease caused by his promiscuous lifestyle at court.) It was probably during his convalescence in the beauty of the Vendômois, in the early 1540s, that Ronsard began seriously to write poetry both in French and Latin, some of which found its place in *Les Odes* and *Le Bocage* of 1550.

In March 1543 Ronsard and his father travelled to Le Mans, where the future leader of the Pléiade received the tonsure, which was a necessary first step towards a career in the Church. As a result of this, Ronsard's financial future was secured (in spite of his numerous protestations of poverty throughout his life): he now had access to rich ecclesiastic benefices and church livings in return for nominal celibacy, but without any of the onerous responsibilities of priesthood. Whilst in Le Mans he also had the first of several meetings with Jacques Peletier du Mans (1517–82), poet, philosopher, mathematician and translator of Horace's *Ars Poetica* (*Art of Poetry*, 1541), who encouraged Ronsard (as he later encouraged Joachim du Bellay) in his poetic ambitions, and who was to publish one of Ronsard's earliest odes in his *Œuvres poëtiques* of 1547.

Later in 1543 we find Ronsard frequenting the circle of humanists and men of letters who met at the Parisian house of Lazare de Baïf, and when a year later the Hellenist scholar Jean Dorat became the tutor to Lazare's son, Jean-Antoine, Ronsard shared his private lessons for a period of some three years. On the death of Lazare de Baïf (1547) Ronsard and Jean-Antoine enrolled as students at the Collège de Coqueret in Paris, where they were joined by Joachim du Bellay and where Dorat taught Greek and Latin literature. The intensive and encyclopedic humanist education they enthusiastically received from Dorat is well documented, and included close textual analysis and commentary on a wide selection of Greek and Latin authors as well as practical tuition in the art of writing poetry modelled on the example of ancient texts.

Thus was born in embryonic form the loose and flexible grouping of poets under the leadership of Ronsard who were known first as the Brigade and later as the Pléiade, and whose ideals were given their first coherent expression in the *Deffence et Illustration de la langue françoyse* (1549), a prose work published under Joachim du Bellay's name but almost certainly written in collaboration with Ronsard. Motivated by the nationalistic wish to emulate the example of Renaissance Italy, this early manifesto advocated the defence and renewal of French as a poetic language by means of a programme of linguistic, stylistic and metrical enrichment, and by a revitalizing process of imitation of ancient and Italian models. In subsequent years Ronsard was to return time and time again to define and refine his poetic principles, and a surprisingly large corpus of his verse is self-reflexive in that it focuses attention, either directly or indirectly, on its own processes and objectives, and in particular on definitions of the poet's mission and of the nature and function of poetry. By doing so, such poetic texts complement the numerous theoretical statements he and his fellow poets make in prose treatises and in prefaces to their collections of verse.

For Ronsard and the Pléiade, imitation does not exclude personal invention and creativity: rather, it supports and enhances them. In the same way as a bee assimilates pollen from diverse sources and transforms it into something personal and original (honey), so the poet nourishes and strengthens his own creative resources and individual voice by converting his fully digested reading into new text in a process that has been called *innutrition*. Poetic excellence, therefore, is determined by the manner in which a poet rejuvenates received material and personalizes a common stock of themes, images and stylistics inherited from Greco-Roman and Italian traditions.

Conscious of being innovators in that they were the first generation of poets to have assimilated the revival of classical scholarship and the richness of Italian Renaissance culture, Ronsard and his friends were dismissive of previous French poetry, associating it with frivolous court activity and with Ignorance, allegorized as a monster. Even Clément Marot, who was a precursor of the new movement in certain respects, was unjustly relegated to an outworn medieval tradition, as were the Grands Rhétoriqueurs, a group of poets writing between 1450 and 1530. Similarly, the genres of earlier French poetry were rejected in favour of models and forms from Italy (sonnet) and classical antiquity (ode, epic, elegy, eclogue, epigram, tragic and comic theatre).

Far from being a court pastime, poetry is seen by Ronsard as a sublime and noble art. Although he recognizes the importance of technique and craftsmanship (the numerous variants and the frequent revisions of his verse bear eloquent witness to this), Ronsard gives priority to inspiration, which is often equated, as in Platonic thought, with one of four 'divine furies'. In order to receive this divine 'madness' and to be worthy of it, the poet undertakes an initiation, which combines Christian and classical elements. Purified and inspired by bathing in the spring of Hippocrene in a ceremony reminiscent of Christian baptism, the virtuous poet joins the Muses and rustic divinities in a circular dance that symbolizes his integration into eternal natural cycles. Freed from ambition and envy, contemptuous of worldly wealth and material honours, the divinely inspired poet seeks the solitude of Nature, and pursues spiritual and intellectual activities in meditative seclusion.

Learned, virtuous and assured of immortality for himself and the subject of his verse, the inspired poet is given prophetic powers, and, as an intermediary between the gods and mankind, he becomes an interpreter of divine secrets and of the mysteries of the universe. (This idea that the inspired poet is a prophet or seer will reappear in the work of nineteenth- and twentieth-century French poets.) The poet, however, does not deliver his utterances in a straightforward and easily accessible manner, for poetry, defined by Ronsard as an allegorical theology, hides its truths under a mantle of poetic fictions (allegory, imagery, mythology, rhetorical figures), which have to be decoded and interpreted. Poetry, therefore, is designed to appeal to the reader's emotions and intellect, and, in Ronsard's early theoretical statements in particular, it is clear that his audience is intended to be cultured and erudite. Such an elevated conception of poetry and the adoption of the *doctus poeta* ('learned poet') ideal of Horace are accompanied by another Horatian theme, that of *odi profanum* ('I hate the common throng'). Scornful of the common mass of people, the poet is in turn misunderstood and even reviled by them, a theme that distantly prefigures the nineteenth-century idea of the *poète maudit* ('cursed poet').

Lest the present-day reader should be offended by such elitist and exclusive sentiments, it should be stressed that in practice Ronsard seeks compromises with his public throughout his career, and that many of his most beautiful and compelling poems are easily accessible to a wide audience. Moreover, Ronsard's poetry is not of one piece or of one style, for he consciously adheres to the classical principle of *varietas*. Reflecting the fluctuating variety and copiousness of Nature, the staggering diversity of his work is evident not only in his choice of models, forms and themes, but also in that of tone and register, for his verse moves between the three rhetorical styles (high, middle, low).

Most of these ideas on poetry and the poet's vocation are illustrated in the texts of this anthology, and these have been selected to demonstrate not only how such theoretical concerns cover a wide creative period and different poetic forms (including odes, love sonnets, elegies, hymns and poetic discourses), but also how they are voiced in a variety of significant and persuasive ways. Sometimes these self-reflexive matters are expressed overtly as direct statements or as explicit commentaries, as in 'À sa Muse' (64), in the autobiographical opening section of the 'Hynne de l'Autonne' (73), and in the extracts from the ode 'À Michel de l'Hospital' (55) and 'La Lyre' (75). On other occasions such preoccupations manifest themselves obliquely and allusively, and may require interpretation and a reading competence that comes from a developing familiarity with the wider corpus of Ronsard's work. Such poems include the ode 'Ô Fontaine Bellerie' (57), where the competent reader is invited to make a comparison between the animating and immortalizing power of poetry and the sounds, vitality and youthfulness of Nature. Similarly, in the 'Discours du Verre' (65) glass-blowing can be considered as a metaphor for inspiration and textual amplification, as well as for the aesthetic principle of diversity in unity. Even a passage in the scientific 'Hynne du Ciel' (72) associates cosmology with the aesthetic notion of *libre contrainte* (the balance of freedom and constraint, diversity and unity, abundance and measure), for what fascinates Ronsard is the manner in which the opposing movements of the planetary system are harmonized and perfectly choreographed within the all-embracing and eternal circular form of the outer sphere.

Finally, certain texts define poetic principles and writing strategies less by direct or allusive methods than by providing a practical demonstration of the process in question. 'L'Ombre du Cheval' (77), for example, is an elaborate metaphor for, and a concrete illustration of, the mimetic practices and the imaginative procedures by which text can be conceived and generated from almost nothing. Other poems – a sonnet from the *Sonnets pour Helene* (47) and the 'Cartel pour le combat à cheval' (66) – use the complex patterns of dance as an image for the creative principle of *libre contrainte*, whilst also providing an excellent example of how Ronsard on occasion reworks his texts after the manner of a palimpsest.

2. Ronsard the Love Poet

By common critical consent Ronsard is considered to be one of France's greatest love poets. However, although his amatory verse is the most accessible and best-known area of his prolific output, as present-day readers we may need to make certain mental adjustments if we are not to betray the intellectual and cultural context within which his love poetry was conceived, and if we are not to use evaluative criteria that are inappropriate and anachronistic. The most common assumption we must discard is the post-Romantic notion that creative excellence and originality are dependent on 'sincerity' and lived experience. Ronsard's three main collections of love poetry to Cassandre, Marie and Hélène are very different in tone and style, but they have in common the fact that they are addressed to women for whom Ronsard almost certainly had no deep affection, and the same is true for other women celebrated at different moments throughout his life (Sinope, Astrée, Genèvre). The three main love cycles are written, to a greater or lesser extent, within conventions, each with its well-defined themes, images, formulae and stylistics transmitted from classical and Italian traditions. In most cases the distinctive quality of a poem has little to do with the veracity of the 'love story' as described, but should be judged by the way received material is renewed and personalized by technical virtuosity, by subtle deviations or patterns of emphasis, and by complex and allusive processes of intertextual adaptation.

Although in the preface to *Les Odes* (1550) he had written scathingly of Petrarchist love poetry, which at that stage he considered inferior to the elevated manner of the ode, he was to modify his opinion, following the publication of successful sonnet sequences by his fellow poets Joachim du Bellay and Pontus de Tyard. Ronsard's first collection of love poems appeared in 1552. Written predominantly within the Petrarchist convention, this cycle of 183 decasyllabic sonnets, now commonly known as *Les Amours de Cassandre*, was accompanied by an appendix of musical settings by contemporary composers. In 1553 a second edition was published, minus the musical supplement but augmented by additional poems (including two alexandrine sonnets) and a commentary by Marc-Antoine de Muret. Inspired by Cassandre Salviati, the daughter of an Italian banker, whom Ronsard had met during a court entertainment at Blois in 1545, this collection was fundamental in establishing the sonnet cycle in French poetry, as well as in fixing the technical rules governing the regular French sonnet (see Glossary of Literary Terms, p. 319). Mediated through the thematic and stylistic conventions of Petrarchism, Ronsard's 'love' is that of a poet enamoured of an artistic ideal of beauty rather than of Cassandre as an individual (in this sense she remains a literary pretext). Even Cassandre's marriage in 1546 to Jehan Peigné, Seigneur de Pray, forms part of the literary 'story' in that Ronsard's unrealizable 'love' replicates the situation of Petrarch and Laura.

Nevertheless, within the convention, the personal presence and poetic authority of Ronsard are clearly felt. Not only does he often surpass his models by technical and artistic skill, by the crafting of sonnets of structural coherence and of richly allusive beauty, but he also convincingly renders the psychological and emotional complexities of love by highlighting its obsessions, anxieties and ambiguities. In addition, as an illustration of the manner in which Ronsard personalizes and extends his inherited material, a number of the selected poems draw attention to a tension between the spiritual idealism of the Petrarchist mode and a frustrated sensuality which reveals itself both across the collection as a whole and within individual poems (2, 4, 5).

If coherence operates at the level of individual texts by the networking of lexical, phonic and syntactic parallelisms and by dense patterns of circularity (2, 8, 11, 14, 17), unity is assured across the entire sequence by the repetition of a number of thematic and stylistic features. These include themes of metamorphosis and desire, of illness, wounding and healing, of prophecy and poetry, of hubris, punishment and self-destruction, and these are in turn supported by an abundance of mythological illustration (see below, section 5), and by images associated with eyes, light, mirrors, sun, water, climate, animals, war, portraiture and painting.

First constituted in the collected works of 1560, where it was accompanied by a commentary by Rémy Belleau, Ronsard's second book of love poetry – now generally referred to as *Les Amours de Marie* – has little in common with his first cycle to Cassandre. Comprised of two separate collections – the *Continuation des Amours* (1555) and the *Nouvelle Continuation des Amours* (1556) – and composed predominantly of alexandrine sonnets and *chansons* ('songs'), these poems, inspired by an unidentified country girl from the Anjou called Marie, represent a temporary abandonment of the spiritual idealism of Petrarchism for a more naturalistic conception of love, based not on fidelity and service but on realism and reciprocity of affection. At the same time the rejection of the erudite refinements of Petrarchism is supported by the adoption of a simpler style, a 'beau stile bas', which Ronsard associates with the manner of the Latin elegiac poets (Catullus, Ovid, Tibullus) and their neo-Latin imitators, and which had already been prefigured in his lighter poetry of *Le Livret de Folastries* (1553), *Le Bocage* (1554) and *Les Meslanges* (1555). What also characterizes the collection and gives it unity is the tone of playful and teasing intimacy (Marie is no longer the disdainful and unapproachable Petrarchist goddess, but a 'real' person), the recourse to conversational and dialogic techniques, the emphasis throughout on rustic settings and nature imagery, and an endearing atmosphere of freshness, youthfulness and sensual enjoyment.

In the fifth collected edition of 1578 a separate section entitled *Sur la Mort de Marie* was added to *Le Second Livre des Amours*. Ronsard borrows his title and frequent textual reminiscences from the second part of Petrarch's *Canzoniere* (*In morte de Madonna Laura; On the death of my lady Laura*), in which the Italian poet had mourned the death of Laura. It is now accepted that Ronsard composed this slender volume of thirteen sonnets and three longer poems on behalf of the Duke of Anjou (the future Henri III), whose mistress Marie de Clèves died in 1574, and that he appended it to his collection after the manner of Petrarch to suit his own artistic ends. It is in this part that one of Ronsard's best-known poems, 'Comme on voit sur la branche au mois de May la rose' (31), is found. Although rich in intertextual resonance – echoing both Ronsard's own verse and that of Latin and neo-Latin poets – this magnificent sonnet has no precise source, and the manner in which Ronsard breathes new life into a traditional comparison (flower/woman) and transcends death belongs uniquely to him.

It was partially to compete with the increasing popularity of Philippe Desportes, whose *Premières Œuvres* appeared in 1573, that Ronsard responded to the Italianate fashion of the court and included a new and distinctive cycle of Petrarchist verse in his 1578 collected edition. The two books of mainly sonnets (all in alexandrine metre) are addressed to a lady-in-waiting to Catherine de Médicis, Hélène de Surgères, who was something of a blue-stocking, renowned less for her beauty than for her virtue and intellect.

The *Sonnets pour Helene* is a composite and heterogeneous collection, characterized by internal inconsistencies and ruptures, ironies and surprises. It sets up expectations that it denies, patterns that it disrupts, in a reading process that demands constant mental adjustments and displacements. It introduces Petrarchist features that are subverted, Platonic elements that are openly rejected. Its unity and identity are further challenged by the way in which Ronsard transfers sonnets originally included in *Les Amours diverses* of 1578 to the *Sonnets pour Helene* in later collected editions (much to the annoyance of Hélène de Surgères herself!). Indeed, the often-quoted sonnet 'Le soir qu'Amour vous fist en la salle descendre' (47), which describes a dance as it fragments and reforms, loses shape and yet retains form and order within diversity, can be interpreted as an emblem, a paradigm, for our complex and ever-shifting experience of the sequence, as our reading hovers continuously between integration and fragmentation.

Nevertheless, certain recurrent thematic and stylistic features do give a fragile and provisional coherence to the collection. The first of these (discussed below, in section 5) involves the identification of Hélène with Helen of Troy; this manifests itself on two levels throughout the cycle and brings within its orbit other associated aspects, for example, the exploitation of the name Hélène, the interface between illusion and reality, an interest in sign systems (verbal and non-verbal). Other aspects woven into the texture of the collection provide further unifying links. The poignant awareness of old age, mingled with the realization that love and his advanced years are foolish bedfellows, recurs as an obsession, and gives increasing urgency to Ronsard's preoccupation with passing time and with the ways in which the poet seizes the present moment and perpetuates his name beyond the grave. The ever-present threat of the Religious Wars hangs over a number of poems and rejuvenates the Petrarchist association of love and war and the accompanying military metaphor. Unlike in the collections to Cassandre and Marie, where the natural world forms the backcloth to the 'love story', a number of the sonnets of the Hélène sequence are apparently rooted in the personal experiences and realities of court and urban life. And never far from Ronsard's mind is his central concern with poetry itself, with its nature and function, and especially with his own self-promotion and self-fashioning.

3. Ronsard the Scientific, Philosophic and Moral Poet

Although he is stereotypically associated with poetry of a lighter vein – with love, wine, nature and the pleasures of life – such a reductive assessment does a disservice to the way in which Ronsard fulfils his divine role as interpreter of the world's mysteries and discusses serious moral and philosophical questions about the relationship between man and the world he inhabits. On the scientific level Ronsard constructs a cosmology, best seen in the 'Hynne du Ciel' (72), which revolves around notions of flux and stability. His universe, very much that of his time, is a comforting and self-contained geocentric system, in which hierarchy and order are synonymous, and in which the regularity, rapidity and circularity of diurnal revolution and of planetary movement bear witness both to the eternity and beauty of the cosmos and to God's creative glory. In turn the universe is sustained by an infused World Soul and by a dynamic and fragile balance of opposing forces (a *discordia concors*) as illustrated by the superimposition of the four elements, by the harmonized diversity of heavenly motion, and by the division of the cosmos into extralunar and sublunar regions, the former enduring and perfect, the latter changeable and subject to decay.

The consequences for man of this scientific dimension are in turn explored by Ronsard, and a constant attempt is made not only to explain flux as a necessary aspect of a rational order, but also to integrate mankind into this pattern and to see him as a vital (if transient) factor of the cosmic structure, subject to identical processes and laws. However, it is not always easy to look beyond the fluctuating and disconcerting phenomena of the sublunar world and to perceive natural or divine order beyond occurrences which appear to be inexplicable and strange, arbitrary and irrational. 'Les Daimons' (71) is a case in point. On the one hand, the *hymne* is an encyclopedic summary of the origins and nature of d(a)emons; on the other, it reveals the superstitious credulity prevalent in the sixteenth century to which Ronsard himself is not wholly immune. However, throughout the poem, which is addressed to a bishop 'whose mind seeks to understand the Universe' (l. 1), Ronsard searches for causes and explanations, and aims to bring the fantastic and the disturbing within the reassuring realm of rational discourse, of familiar human experience and natural processes. Following Neoplatonic theories, rather than adhering to the traditional Christian belief which associated demons solely with diabolical practices, Ronsard sees d(a)emons as intermediaries between the divine and the human, as both good and evil, depending on their constitution (their proportions of spirit and bodily matter) and their dwelling place (their proximity to, or distance from, the Heavens). Similarly, he attempts to give a reasoned explanation for the materialization of d(a)emons and for their nightmarish apparitions, arguing that they are an externalization, a psychic projection, of our anxieties and obsessions. Again, some of the apparently mysterious and worrying activities of d(a)emons are traced by Ronsard to recognizable natural phenomena (earthquakes, atmospheric lights), whilst his several expressions of Christian orthodoxy throughout the text are one further method of bringing the unknown within familiar perceptions and within the laws of divine providence.

The same rationalizing processes are found in Ronsard's account of the disturbing and incongruous events of 'Le Chat' (76). Here the death of a servant, the destruction of a cherished laurel tree, a nightmare involving a cat, and Ronsard's illness, all form a pattern which is explained by an elaborate theory of universal signs and portents. This theory, which associates man and the natural world, has, at its centre, a pantheistic philosophy in which God and an infused World Soul are equated.

Within this general perspective of incorporating man into a universal order, and of seeking rational explanations and natural causation for the irrational events in the world, the concept of hubris provides a moral dimension to Ronsard's discussions, for excessive arrogance is invariably considered as a threat to the precarious cosmic and social stability. It is in the ode 'À Guy Pacate' (61) that Ronsard weaves together multiple Horatian reminiscences to form an original moral and philosophical commentary on human mortality and presumption. Associated with a series of archetypal examples of hubris, death and illness are envisaged as mechanisms to preserve the balance between macrocosm and microcosm, and to ensure that human beings do not transgress beyond the allotted limits of their condition, but remain firmly within their place in the hierarchical cosmic structure.

Far from considering death as a painful, irrational accident, as an absurdity which highlights man's contingency and negates the value of life, Ronsard intellectually justifies mortality as a moral and philosophical necessity, as an element of an equitable natural order. Existentialist anguish has little place in the poet's vision, and the horror of death, although compellingly evoked in the account of his own deathbed agony in *Les Derniers Vers*, is relatively rare in his work. More typically, as in the posthumously published elegy 'À Philippes Des-Portes, Chartrain' (69), Ronsard makes a sensualist's distinction between the active processes of life and the inactive and insentient state that follows death. In this poem, where religious inspiration is reduced to a minimum, he questions the Christian-Platonic notion that happiness resides in the soul's contemplation of God after death, and shows little enthusiasm for a soul which is passive and does not have the perfection associated with movement and action. More frequently, as in the ode 'De l'election de son sepulchre' (60), he prefers to evoke an afterlife which is emphatically classical and pagan, and in which death is described not as a brutal rupture, but as a continuation, in heightened form, of life's pleasures and active processes. Elsewhere, he transcends mortality by the intensity of creative and intellectual processes – by knowledge and poetry – or he distances himself from death by classical euphemisms which divert the mind, and which replace harsh realities with poetic fictions and natural, familiar images (30, 31, 60). Even though death looms so large in his work, Ronsard is justly celebrated as a poet of life.

4. Ronsard the Official and Political Poet

Given the system of patronage and the importance of the court as both audience and benefactor, it is only to be expected that a number of Ronsard's poems are official and circumstantial in nature. However, Ronsard's attitude to the court was ambivalent. On the one hand, he profited generously from benefices and patronage (he received, for example, the ecclesiastic livings of Saint-Cosme and Croixval in 1565–6); in return he fulfilled his official duties by commemorating the births, marriages and deaths of rich and powerful patrons (monarchs, princes, nobles, statesmen, prelates), and by responding to national events of military, social and political importance (royal entries, military victories, peace treaties). On the other hand, he periodically satirized the court and courtiers (44; 50, ll. 23–4; 82, ll. 403–8), and equated his poetic vocation with seclusion in nature and a rejection of worldly wealth and ambition. Indeed, during his severe illness (1568–9), and more frequently after the failure of his unfinished epic *La Franciade* (1572) and the death of Charles IX (1574), Ronsard spent lengthy periods away from court, where Desportes's star was in the ascendant.

Ronsard's ambivalence towards the court should not be seen as hypocrisy, but rather as the expression of a tension, at the very heart of the patronage system, between the practical necessities and expediency of public office and the ideal conditions conducive to creativity. In spite of these ambiguities and constraints – indeed, perhaps because of them – Ronsard frequently transcends the conventions and the mechanical formulae often associated with occasional verse. At the same time as it celebrates the victory of François de Guise over Charles V at Metz (1552–3), 'La Harangue de . . . François, duc de Guise, aux soldats de Metz' (74) is an inspired exercise in exhortatory eloquence, in demonstrative (eulogizing) rhetoric and myth-making. In an expanding frame of historical reference and nationalistic fervour, François's ancestry is traced back to the heroes of the Crusades, the main episodes of which are depicted, together with serpents and various mythological figures, on the armour he wears. The heightened realism of this *ekphrasis,* with its imaginative visual detail, is only one of the outstanding beauties of this text: equally impressive are the use of a specialized military lexicon and the persuasive energy of François's oration, which is structured on a simple, but emotionally charged, antithesis between valour and cowardice, honour and dishonour.

The 'Cartel pour le combat à cheval' (66) provides an illustration of Ronsard's participation, sometimes as both poet and artistic direc-tor, in court entertainments. As it nears its conclusion, the aesthetic ideal of *libre contrainte* assumes civic and political significance with the mention of Henri III and France, and the reader is reminded that such court festivities, with their emphasis on a symbolism of social order and discipline, were often organized as part of a process of reconciliation during the continuing Religious Wars.

It was, in fact, the first of the several Religious Wars which devastated France from 1562 to 1598 that provided Ronsard with the perfect opportunity to reconcile his official position as national poet with his private beliefs as a religious and political conservative. First constituted as a separate section in the second collected edition of Ronsard's works (1567), the *Discours des Miseres de ce temps* is dedicated to the regent Catherine de Médicis, and gathers together poems which, for the greater part, were originally published as individual pamphlets between 1560 and 1563. Although Ronsard advocates moderate internal reform to counter the corruption and abuses of the Catholic Church, he supports the monarchy and Catholicism as bulwarks of national stability against the disorder of theological innovation and the threat of religious schism. Alternately conciliatory and contentious, depending on the ebb and flow of events and on his oscillating support, now for Catherine's strategy of reconciliation and compromise, now for the repressive policies of the Guises, the *Discours* are marked by a variety of tones (lyrical, confessional, satirical, ironical, defamatory), by a range of dialogic techniques (appeals, invocations, rhetorical questions, patterns of conversation and debate), and by an impassioned eloquence which is patriotic, political and religious in inspiration.

Ronsard's religious position, like Montaigne's, is that of the fideist who places theological matters beyond human reason. He argues that human discourse does not have the power to discuss the ineffable nature of the divine, and that the Protestants' questioning of doctrine and their inquiry into divine mysteries are acts of hubris which challenge God's prerogatives. Opinion, allegorized as a monster, is described as presumptuous and socially divisive. Ronsard takes delight in pointing to the discrepancy between the theory and prac- tice of Protestantism, between the Reformers' acts of violence and desecration and the simplicity of faith of the early Christian Church, whose principles they claim to espouse. He debates theological dogma with them (for example, the sacrament of the Eucharist), and sees the doctrinal differences between the diversity of Protestant sects as proof of the error of the Reformed Church.

In turn the political and patriotic inspiration finds its most intense expression, firstly, in passionate appeals to French Calvinist theologians and military leaders (de Bèze, Louis de Bourbon-Condé, Odet de Coligny) to respect their homeland and make common cause by uniting with Catholics to wage war against the infidel Turk in a new crusade, and secondly, in a developed allegory of Mother France and in extended images of birth, maternity and matricide (80). It is a tribute to the persuasive and emotional intensity of the *Discours* that they left their thematic and stylistic marks on the subsequent polemical verse of Catholics and Protestants alike, and in particular on the epic poem *Les Tragiques* of the Calvinist Agrippa d'Aubigné (1552–1630).

5. Ronsard and Mythology

It has already been noted that mythology is one of several means used by Ronsard to cloak his profoundest truths and concerns under a 'fabulous mantle' (73, l. 82). Within such a perspective, mythology is a figurative language with which he explores and articulates those areas of human experience which are the most important to him. It should not surprise the reader, therefore, to learn that certain mythological narrative poems have been interpreted as parallels to matters of poetic theory and practice. 'La Mort de Narcisse' (67), for example, can be read as a self-reflexive text in the way that it suggests a tension and a problem of writing at the very heart of the Pléiade's humanist ideal. In a culture in which invention is synonymous with imitation, the wish to reflect and create the self, instead of reflecting and creating variations of texts by others, can be seen as a real and enduring concern for Ronsard.

However, although Ronsard himself gives an overtly symbolic interpretation of the birth of Pallas Athene in 'La Lyre' (75: a poem which makes copious use of fable and mythological figures – Apollo, Mercury, Bacchus – to support his commentary on poetry and the poetic mission), and although he encourages a metaphorical reading of the 'Hynne de Calays et de Zethés' (70) towards the end of the poem, nevertheless care should be taken not to reduce the richly allusive resonance of mythological references to one explicit and simplistic allegorical meaning.

Mythology is at the centre of Ronsard's imaginative world; it is one of his prime modes of figurative expression and it permeates all areas of his work. From his earliest collections he demonstrates an interest in mythological narrative poems which are fragmentary and episodic in nature and resemble miniature epics. 'La Defloration de Lede' (59) of 1550 has a simple linear narrative structure within which are inserted sensuous and picturesque descriptions, best illustrated by the evocation of the decorative paintings on Leda's basket, which occupies a large part of the second section of the text. Although it could be argued that mythology is essentially ornamental here, the scenes depicted on the basket provide an implicit commentary on the debate between the relative merits of poetry and painting which preoccupied Ronsard throughout his career, and which led him to conclude on the superiority of poetry's visual and expressive power.

Published six years later, the 'Hynne de Calays et de Zethés' (70) has a much more complex texture and employs more sophisticated narrative techniques. The narrative thrust is continually interrupted by embedded speeches, descriptions and developed images, whilst the wide temporal perspective involves frequent recalls of the past (flashbacks) and projections towards the future (prophecies). A simplistic allegorical reading of this magnificent and exuberant fragment along the lines proposed by Ronsard himself (the Harpies are equated with scavenging courtiers and the mythological heroes with steadfast philosophers) would limit the imaginative impact of this 'monstrous' text, and do a disservice to the fantastic realism which is one of its most impressive qualities.

In Ronsard's love poetry, too, mythology is rarely merely decorative and never gratuitous, in that it invariably contributes both to the thematic coherence of the cycle as a whole and to that of individual sonnets. Most of his mythological examples are inherited from Petrarchism and support traditional themes associated with love –

physical and mental suffering (Prometheus, Tantalus, Ixion, Sisyphus), presumption and punishment (Icarus), self-destruction (Actaeon), metamorphosis and desire (Jupiter), petrifaction and paralysis (Medusa). However, it is not so much what he borrows from the convention that is of prime importance, but *how* he organizes his mythological material for a poetic purpose within his sonnets by employing a wide range of structural and unifying principles. Sometimes a single myth is threaded through the entire sonnet in an overt and systematic fashion (3, 14). On other occasions, the mythological figure is not identified by name but by allusive associations operating throughout the sonnet's fabric below surface level, and, depending on the reader's frame of cultural reference and competence, these will result in varying degrees of understanding and poetic resonance (10, 17). Again, an explicit mythological reference may be limited on a first reading to the final tercet, or even the last line, but in the retrospective re-reading and re-adjustment that circularity occasions, earlier thematic and stylistic prefigurations appear, which suggestively signal the overt mythological pronouncement of the sonnet's closure (11). Finally, several myths which have common thematic and formal features may be embedded in the organization of the sonnet and foregrounded either by binary patterning (40) or by syntactical repetition at key points in the sonnet (2).

Since it is often the case that a number of myths are repeated across the love-sequence, these act as memory markers and as unifying elements. This strategy is in evidence in *Les Amours de Cassandre*, where Ronsard uses the legend of Cassandra of Troy and her associations with Apollo to support an ever-expanding and cumulative cluster of themes across the entire cycle, such as wounding and healing, poetry and prophecy. The same process reappears in a more complex and allusive manner in the *Sonnets pour Helene*, where the fused identities of Hélène de Surgères and Helen of Troy operate simultaneously on two levels throughout the collection. Besides the usual Homeric version of Helen's abduction by Paris and the resulting Trojan War, Ronsard also exploits an alternative version of the myth which guarantees Helen's virtue as innocent victim and faithful wife. According to this variant of the myth, it was a phantom

Helen that accompanied Paris to Troy, whilst the 'real' Helen was
transported to Egypt for the duration of the war to await the return
of her husband Menelaus. Ronsard could have read this alternative
version in Euripides' *Helen* (412 BC), a tragi-comedy which repro-
duces the legend of a phantom Helen to explore (as does Ronsard
throughout the sequence) the interplay between reality and illusion,
and to pinpoint a nexus of associated ideas (duplication and duplicity,
substitution and displacement, identity and naming, truth and fic-
tion). Ronsard's play on the name of Hélène (as opposed to her body),
his interpretation of linguistic and other signs and his preoccupations
with the literary principles of imitation and invention, with truth
and 'feigning' (fictionality), are also linked to the questions of the
status and nature of identity and reality posed by the alternative
Helen myth.

6. *The Art of Ronsard*

Readers not familiar with the technicalities of French verse may
prefer to look at the Glossary of Literary Terms and the pages
devoted to how to read French poetry (pp. 306–8) before commenc-
ing this section. For the purposes of clarity and convenience, in
the following pages techniques have been delineated and discussed
separately: however, in practice several stylistic and formal features
often operate in conjunction and in a mutually supportive fashion.
The quality of a poem is always the sum of all its parts.

We have already drawn attention to the remarkable diversity and
richness of Ronsard's work, to the range of its subject matter, formal
expression, tone and style. Throughout his career Ronsard constantly
re-invented himself, even within the prescribed conventions of love
poetry. The same poet who produced the elevated lyricism of the
Pindaric odes, the sublime rhetoric of *Les Hymnes*, and the persuasive
eloquence of the *Discours*, turned his hand with equal success to
light amatory and Bacchic verse, to lascivious kiss poems and to
bawdy poems like 'Gayeté' (78). The encyclopedic compass of his
verse can be said to reflect both the boundless enthusiasm of the

French Renaissance for comprehensiveness and innovation, and a curiosity about everything that concerned mankind and the rapidly changing world of the period.

This diversity is in evidence on the formal level too, and is well illustrated by Ronsard's *Odes*, where the multiplicity of stanza forms, rhyme schemes and versification patterns bears witness to his exploration of the rhythmical and musical possibilities of form and structure. Modelling his verse on the inconstant and variable perfection of Nature, Ronsard is, on the one hand, attracted to the copious and fluctuating diversity of Pindar, and to the freedom and 'errance' ('meandering') of pieces of indeterminate length and unprescribed formal structure (hymns, mythological narrative poems, elegies, poetic discourses). On the other hand, he is equally at ease within the constrained and tightly organized architecture of the sonnet, and he is rightly considered as one of the greatest exponents of this form, which he, more than any other individual poet, was responsible for establishing in early modern French poetry.

On occasion he constructs his sonnets on strong repetitive formulae located at the beginning of each quatrain and tercet (2, 4, 15), or at other important focal points (27). At other times, a developed simile (marked firmly by *comme* and *ainsi*) and/or a symmetrical patterning of quatrains and tercets provide the sonnet's foundation (8, 9, 18, 31). Elsewhere, inner structure is built on a grid of binary schemes, often antithetical in nature, or on a logical presentation of material (such as a narrative sequence of events) culminating in an epigrammatic last line, or in a final line of perfect balance and closure (11, 14). Other organizational principles may be at work within the sonnet, and these function either alone or, more frequently, in combinations that are jointly reinforcing. We have already commented on the manner in which mythology often contributes to the coherence of individual sonnets and of an entire cycle. Circularity is a favourite strategy used by Ronsard: at the closure of a sonnet, parallelisms and repetitions (of words, sounds, syntactical units, grammatical features, rhetorical figures) return the reader to the poem's opening, either directly or via intermediary elements located throughout the text. This process encourages a re-reading and a re-evaluation of the sonnet, and invariably reveals subtle networks across the poem which contribute to its unity.

Although seen at their most allusive and intense within the density of the sonnet form, the same structuring principles are also found within Ronsard's longer poems. At its most obvious, the circularity of 'Gayeté' (78), with its reiteration of apostrophes, exclamations and terms of endearment at the opening and closing of the text, is an ironic and playful subversion of the poem's initial innocent ecstasy. Similarly, aspects of circularity also become apparent from an attentive reading of the opening and closure of 'Les Daimons' (71: common Christian references and an emphasis on the novelty of Ronsard's enterprise) and of the 'Hynne du Ciel' (72: parallel Christian-Platonic notes).

In other contexts, semantic fields and lexical clusters function across entire poems, providing structural landmarks and strengthening coherence and identity. One of the unifying features of 'L'Ombre du Cheval' (77) is a vocabulary of deception, insubstantiality and absence, whilst the complex orchestration of 'La Lyre' (75) is underscored by an extended metaphor centred on birth, conception and motherhood. Financial terms are a recurrent aspect of the fabric of the elegy to Desportes (69), whilst the repetition of a vocabulary of numbers and counting makes a significant contribution to the inner structure of 'Elegie XIII' (68), in very much the same way that a lexicon of violence and weaponry supports the masonry of the *Continuation du Discours* (80).

The descriptive and visual qualities of Ronsard's verse are very much in evidence in the poems of this anthology, and these should be seen as his contribution to the long-standing debate concerning the rivalry between poetry and painting as to which is the pre-eminent art. In order to demonstrate the evocative power of poetry to feed the imagination and construct vivid pictures in the mind, Ronsard has frequent recourse to the painterly processes of *enargeia*, and nowhere more successfully than in his use of *ekphrasis*. However, his descriptive fragments of works of art are not merely decorative exercises in an epic tradition stretching back to Homer, for they are invariably integrated into the narrative thrust and the main thematic concerns of his poems. The splendid description of the musical instrument in 'La Lyre' (75) depicts scenes and mythological figures which are central to his commentary on inspiration and poetry, whilst the basket of Leda in 'La Defloration de Lede' (59) contains pictorial and sensuous elements which prefigure the later narrative (the rape of Leda). Similarly, the animating representation of François de Guise's armour in 'La Harangue' (74) is essential to the poet's processes of myth-making and to his promotion of national glory.

In other poems Ronsard's descriptions surprise the reader by their heightened and imaginative vision and by their surreal qualities. Because of their picturesque detail, their fabulous ingenuity and their evocative intensity, they engrave themselves on our memory and act as mnemonic signposts in our reading and recollection of the poem. Among the most memorable accounts are the cave of Auton and the figure of Maladie (73), the fluctuating shapes and metamorphoses of d(a)emons (71), and the physical decrepitude of Phineus and the descriptions of the warring soldiers, and of the bulls and the snake which guard the Golden Fleece (70).

Ronsard's graphic realism and his eye for observed detail also animate his imagery, which often comes from the activities and phenomena of nature. In the 'Hynne de Calays et de Zethés' (70) an extended sequence of some twelve similes amplifies the latter half of the poem, and, although these embedded images could be said to slow down the narrative momentum and defer completion, they enrich the *epyllion* with epic colouring and impress by their pictorial qualities, their inventiveness and their self-generating energy. The coherence and the persuasive power of the *Continuation du Discours* (80) are in large measure the result of two parallel sets of images, the one focusing on birth, maternity and matricide, the other on animals and insects. These twin sequences, structured throughout the poem, are brought together and culminate in the poignant allegory of a devastated Mother France, within which is embedded an extended Homeric simile of destructive caterpillars (ll. 335–56).

Attentive to the visual appeal of his verse, Ronsard is equally sensitive to its musical and phonic qualities. The close alliance of poetry and music was one of the objectives of the Pléiade, and the success of this aim can be measured in practice by the numerous musical settings of Ronsard's poetry, not only by leading Renaissance musicians but by nineteenth- and twentieth-century composers. The value of rhyme for Ronsard was determined by its acoustic, not visual, properties, and throughout his work he experimented with the phonic possibilities of a variety of rhyme schemes, as a reading of the odes in this anthology demonstrates. Towards the same musical purpose he and his fellow poets were instrumental in establishing the alternation of masculine and feminine rhymes as a convention of French poetry. The ode 'Bel aubepin fleurissant' (62) is one example among many of how he combines a rhythmical metre and stanza form (7,3,7,7,3,7), a regular rhyme scheme (*aabccb*) and an identical patterning of masculine and feminine rhymes (*mmfmmf*) within a symmetrical form conducive to musical accompaniment. Elsewhere end-rhyme, often supported by internal rhyme and assonance, is used to underscore the meaning and coherence of a poem or even of an entire collection. In a number of sonnets, for example, circularity and enclosure are strengthened by recurrent sound patterns, and especially by the way in which sonorities found in stressed positions in the final tercet recall the *a* and *b* rhymes of the quatrains (2, 11, 14, 17). In the 'Discours du Verre' (65), terminal rhymes, internal rhymes and assonance ('verre', 'vers', 'uni*vers*', 'di*vers*', '*ver*ité') unite with a multiplicity of words sharing the common [ɛR] sound not only to give the poem a phonic identity, but also to emphasize items of focal and semantic importance. The final poem of the five books of odes from the 1567 edition onwards – 'À sa Muse' (64) – provides an appropriate closure to the collection in a number of ways, none more significant than the manner in which the rhymes which resonate across lines 8–20 ('meilleure', 'meure', 'demeure'; 'Univers', 'divers', 'vers'; 'gloire', 'victoire', 'memoire') incorporate many of the principal themes of the collection as a whole (death, unity/diversity, poetry, immortality, glorious victories, memory).

Alliteration is rarely used by Ronsard in a gratuitous or purely ornamental manner; rather, it invariably mimes sense directly or

xl

draws attention to the words which carry the semantic burden of a line. The song of the nightingale ('Et ja le Rossignol doucement jargonné, / Dessus l'espine assis sa complainte amoureuse': 26) and the hissing of a snake ('Et sa langue en sifflant sible d'une voix telle, / Que les petits enfans se mussent sous l'aisselle': 70, ll. 633–4) are heard in the repeated sibilant sound [s] of the above lines, whilst the alliterative [k] pattern of the following quotation is designed to render the clattering noise of the avaricious Harpies: 'Tousjours d'un craquetis leur maschoire cliquoit, / Tousjours de palle faim leur bec s'entrechoquoit' (70, ll. 171–2). On the other hand, in the following two examples alliteration is primarily employed to good effect to accentuate and to link those words which are essential to meaning: 'Je voleray tout vif par l'Univers' (64, l. 10); 'Enchanté, je servis une vieille carcasse, / Un squelette seiché, une impudente face' (54, l. 10).

Rhythmical effects provide a further illustration of Ronsard's consummate artistry as a poet. Foregrounded by deviations from normal caesura positioning and by patterns of repetition and accumulation, rhythm in Ronsard's verse is almost always at the service of sense or of emotional appeal and compelling argument. By increasing the frequency of syllabic divisions within his lines, by dislocating the normal structure of the alexandrine with a variety of *enjambements* and internal caesura breaks, by repeating infinitives denoting movement in antithetical patterns, and by multiplying binary, ternary and anaphoric items, Ronsard fuses style and sense, form and content, in order to evoke the self-energizing rhythm of a dance or an equestrian ballet (47, 66). Similar rhythmical techniques are employed to depict a river in full spate (75, ll. 57–68) and the ever-changing shapes of d(a)emons (71, ll. 39–64). Elsewhere, and nowhere to better effect than in the polemical poetry of the *Discours des Miseres de ce temps*, an accumulation of rhetorical questions and repetitive formulae (especially anaphora) gives the verse its rhythmical energy, its emotional power and its persuasive force (80, ll. 145–66; 82, ll. 17–56, 325–39, 661–74). At the same time by an abundance of *enjambements*, by deviations from normal rhythmical measure and by a diversity of internal breaks and pauses, Ronsard skilfully avoids the obtrusiveness of terminal rhyme and the rigidity of repetitive rhythms into which mediocre poets can fall when writing a lengthy series of rhyming couplets.

It is not uncommon in Ronsard's verse for the foregrounding of words occasioned by deviations in rhythm to operate in conjunction with alliteration. In this line from a sonnet of *Les Derniers Vers* (83) describing his physical emaciation,

Decharné, denervé, demusclé, depoulpé,

the normal structure of the alexandrine (6+6 syllables) is divided into four trisyllabic words sharing common phonic and grammatical features (all are past participles). This, in turn, prefigures the tercets, both by parallelism ('despouillé', l. 9) and by antithesis (the patterning of four present participle constructions), and these elements contribute jointly to the unity of the sonnet. In the same way these lines from the 'Hynne de l'Autonne' (73)

Tu [the poet] seras du *v*ulgaire appellé *f*renetique,
In*s*ensé *f*urieux *f*arouche *f*antastique,
*M*au*s*sade *m*al-plai*s*ant: (ll. 61–3)

not only employ a list of adjectives (all of them trisyllabic) to good rhythmical effect, but use alliteration to stress those lexical items which are crucial to meaning. In addition, the absence of punctuation has an important role to play in bringing the epithets into closer contact and in accelerating the rhythm of the lines.

Deviations of any sort (lexical, phonic, syntactic, rhythmical, stylistic) heighten attention and cause surprise by departing from norms established either externally by poetic convention or internally by normative processes created by the poem itself. For Ronsard, as for Baudelaire (1821–67) and Apollinaire (1880–1918), surprise is a fundamental feature of poetic practice, and can be achieved in a number of different ways throughout his verse. It can take the form of homophonic or homonymic word play (especially in the *Sonnets pour Helene*), or of a sudden change of linguistic register caused by the unexpected introduction of a foreign word (73, l. 367) or of a neologism invented by Ronsard himself (9: 'Adoniser'). Again, surprise may result from the juxtaposition of disparate elements within a single poem (4, 5) or by the proximity of two discordant poems where the positioning has been chosen as an act of deliberate subversion (16, 17). Finally, as in this appeal to the Protestant leader de Bèze, surprise can result from an audacious and startling image:

> Ne presche plus en France une Evangile armée,
> Un CHRIST empistollé tout noirci de fumée,
> Qui comme un Mehemet va portant en la main
> Un large coutelas rouge de sang humain. (80, ll. 119–22)

After his death, Ronsard's poetry was largely forgotten for more than two centuries, victim of the classical reforms of Malherbe (1555–1628) and the sweeping condemnation of Boileau (1636–1711). After his 'rediscovery' in the nineteenth century, research has restored Ronsard to his just place in the history of French poetry, not only acknowledging his superlative achievement as a poet of love, wine and nature, but increasingly emphasizing the importance of his scientific, circumstantial, political and philosophical verse. Twentieth-century composers (Ravel, Poulenc, Milhaud, Lennox Berkeley) have been attracted to the harmonic quality of his verse, and musical settings of his poetry are readily available. His work influenced the Irish poet W.B. Yeats, and a selection of his poems was translated by Sylvia Plath. A number of editions of his poetry have been accompanied by the work of modern artists: Henri Matisse, for example, selected his favourite love poems and illustrated them with lithographs for a limited edition entitled *Florilège des Amours de Ronsard*, published in 1948 in the series 'Les Peintres du Livre'. Ronsard and his fellow poets of the Pléiade bequeathed a rich legacy to future generations. They established in French poetry many of the genres they inherited from Greco-Roman and Italian traditions, and were innovators in a diversity of poetic forms and in matters of metre, rhyme and versification. Above all, Ronsard redefined the nature and function of poetry, considering it a sublime and sacred art, and seeing in the mission of the poet an unparalleled dignity and a promise of immortal glory.

The Present Translation

The twin aims of this prose translation are to serve Ronsard by making his work accessible to a twenty-first century English-speaking public, and to enable readers who are unfamiliar with sixteenth-century French syntax, vocabulary and spelling to understand and appreciate his poetry as he wrote it. To serve these aims, what is wanted is a faithful translation (not necessarily literal), proceeding line by line where this is compatible with acceptable English structures. However, as the first priority must be to make the sense clear, it has sometimes been necessary to re-order convoluted sentences containing embedded clauses, inversions and unconventional word order imposed by the demands of metre or rhyme. Punctuation has been modified for the sake of clarity. At the same time, the requirements of the reader wishing to follow the French text are borne in mind, and where further explanation of the meaning is needed, help is given in the notes on the poems.

Presentation of *what* is said is only the first stage in translating. *How* it is said is of fundamental importance, especially in poetry. The challenge is not only to convey Ronsard's thought and vision, but to attempt simultaneously to represent his poetic voice, and his rich and ornamental style.

With these ends in view, we have tried to preserve the register and tone of the poems, to reflect the range from the high style of a Pindaric ode or a hymn to the low style of the lighter poetry. These are aspects of the work which can be transmitted in prose. However, poetic style is by its nature harder to render in prose. Alliteration can seldom be imitated exactly, but, where we cannot reproduce it, we attempt to convey a similar effect by using an alternative alliteration, sometimes at a different point in the sentence. Since vowel sounds (often emphasized by the morphology of verbs and adverbs, for example) are quite different in French and in English, assonance presents an even more demanding challenge. Ronsard's musicality can only be suggested. Devices that depend less on particular sounds, such as antithesis and anaphora, can be more effectively reproduced, and they help to give an impression of the rhythm of the verse. Figures such as metaphor and simile are translated literally for the most part, with notes to clarify any obscurity.

Word play was much admired in the sixteenth century, and is often impossible to translate. It figures most prominently in Ronsard's love poetry, for example, when he plays on the names of his mistresses. Attempts have been made to reflect these in the translation, but in some cases there is no feasible equivalent, and a note has to take on the task of elucidation.

An aspect of Ronsard's language which may trouble readers is the way in which general sentiments about the human race are invariably expressed in the masculine. This is characteristic of the period. Court, church and state offices were held by men, and it was overwhelmingly men who participated in public life. Generally the only women to have influence were members of the royal family or the aristocracy. That being so, it is not so surprising to find such statements, and they should be considered not as exclusive, but as inclusive of women. Although sometimes the translation avoids specifying gender, it would not accurately represent the original to do so on every occasion.

We have endeavoured by the precision of the translation to obviate the need for a lexical glossary and detailed notes of a linguistic nature.

The Language of the Text

Sixteenth-century French differs to some extent from the language in use today. Some words were then of a different gender (for example, *amour* was feminine), while others had a different meaning instead of, or in addition to, the modern one (for instance, *si* meant 'yet' or 'nevertheless' as well as 'if' and 'so'). As regards spelling, the reader must accept that it had not yet become fixed at the time of Ronsard, and that words are therefore not always spelt in the modern way, or even consistently (for an example of this inconsistency, see the general introduction to the Notes on *Les Hynnes*, p. 288). However, when read aloud words often become immediately recognizable, so that *je sçay* is clearly *je sais* and *nuict* is *nuit*. From these examples it will be seen that there are often extraneous letters, which do not appear in the modern spelling. Many patterns will quickly begin to appear familiar, such as imperfect verbs ending in *-ois*, etc., and *françois* for *français*. Before a consonant, *es* is found where we now have *ê* (*estre* for *être*) or *é* (*meschant* for *méchant*), and similarly *-as*, *-is*, *-os*, *-us* before a consonant may represent modern *â*, *î*, *ô*, *û* (e.g. *baston* for *bâton*, *isle* for *île*, *tost* for *tôt*, *couster* for *coûter*). One may find *ez* in place of *és* (e.g. *couchez* for *couchés*), or *eu* in place of *u* (e.g. *leu* for *lu*). Many words now ending in *-i* then ended in *-y*, as in *vray*. There are two other features that may disconcert the modern reader. Firstly, certain nouns may have an initial capital where such would not be the case in contemporary usage (e.g. 'Soleil', 'Lions'). Our translation reflects the French text in this respect. Secondly, the use of accents was infrequent and inconsistent in the sixteenth century, and words such as 'Helene', 'Nereides' and 'egal' appear without accents, although the pronunciation was similar to that of today.

Syntax was freer and looser than in modern French. For instance, a plural subject may be followed by a singular verb. Ronsard sometimes produces sentences which are incomplete or grammatically incorrect by modern standards, and this occasionally makes the sense difficult to grasp. In such circumstances our primary goal has been to make the meaning more explicit, even if it has meant departing from the original syntax.

Like the other poets of the Pléiade, Ronsard put into practice their theories about the enrichment of the vocabulary of French. They recommended creating neologisms, by borrowing from Greek or Latin, or combining two French words, or inventing diminutives; they revived old words, adopted dialect expressions, or drew on the language used in various crafts. (These words have not all survived into modern French, as a result of the purification of the language carried out by seventeenth-century classical grammarians and writers.) In addition, the Pléiade poets favoured the flexibility permitted by using one part of speech to fulfil the function of another; for example, adjectives and infinitives are used as nouns (e.g. *l'espais de la nue, le naistre*).

There is no book in English devoted specifically to the French language in the sixteenth century, but readers may usefully consult Wendy Ayres-Bennett's *A History of the French Language through Texts*. Fuller information, in French, is given in the book by Fragonard and Kotler. Both are listed in the 'Suggestions for Further Reading' below.

Suggestions for Further Reading

Editions of Ronsard

Œuvres complètes, ed. Paul Laumonier, completed by I. Silver and R. Lebègue, 20 vols. (Hachette, then Droz, then Didier, Paris, 1914–75)

Œuvres complètes, ed. Jean Céard, Daniel Ménager and Michel Simonin, Bibliothèque de la Pléiade, 2 vols. (Gallimard, Paris, 1993–4)

Selected Poems of Pierre de Ronsard, chosen and edited by Christine Scollen (Athlone, London, 1974, reprinted Bristol Classical Press, 1995)

Ronsard: I Poems of Love, II Odes, Hymns and Other Poems, selected and edited by Grahame Castor and Terence Cave (Manchester University Press, 1975–7)

The selections by Scollen and by Castor and Cave contain the French texts without English translations, but with critical apparatus in English.

Translations

Lyrics of Pierre de Ronsard, Vandomois, chosen and translated by Charles Graves (Oliver and Boyd, Edinburgh and London, 1967)

Sonnets pour Hélène, with English renderings by Humbert Wolfe (Allen and Unwin, London, 1972)

Poems of Pierre de Ronsard, translated by Nicholas Kilmer (University of California Press, 1979)

Theme and Version: Plath and Ronsard, ed. Antony Rudolf, with essays by Yves Bonnefoy, Audrey Jones and Daniel Weissbort (Menard Press, London, 1995)

Biographical Studies

Simonin, Michel, *Pierre de Ronsard* (Fayard, Paris, 1990)
Wyndham Lewis, D. B., *Ronsard* (Sheed & Ward, London, 1944)

There is no accurate, up-to-date biography of Ronsard in English. Wyndham Lewis's life of Ronsard is romanticized and dated, whereas Simonin's French biography is detailed and authoritative.

Critical Studies

Campo, Roberto, *Ronsard's Contentious Sisters. The Paragone between Poetry and Painting in the Works of Pierre de Ronsard* (University of North Carolina Press, 1998)
Cave, Terence (ed.), *Ronsard the Poet* (Methuen, London, 1973)
Fallon, Jean, *Voice and Vision in Ronsard's 'Les Sonnets pour Hélène'* (Peter Lang, New York, 1993)
Ford, Philip, *Ronsard's 'Hymnes'. A Literary and Iconographical Study* (Medieval & Renaissance Texts & Studies, Tempe, Arizona, 1997)
— and Gillian Jondorf (eds.), *Ronsard in Cambridge* (Cambridge French Colloquia, 1986)
Gadoffre, Gilbert, *Ronsard par lui-même* (Seuil, Paris, 1960, reprinted 1994)
Gendre, André, *Ronsard: poète de la conquête amoureuse* (La Baconnière, Neuchâtel, 1970)
— *L'Esthétique de Ronsard* (SEDES, Paris, 1997)
McGowan, Margaret M., *Ideal Forms in the Age of Ronsard* (University of California Press, 1985)

Ménager, Daniel, *Ronsard. Le Roi, le Poète et les Hommes* (Droz, Geneva, 1979)

Quainton, Malcolm, *Ronsard's Ordered Chaos: Visions of Flux and Stability in the Poetry of Pierre de Ronsard* (Manchester University Press, 1980)

Stone, Donald, *Ronsard's Sonnet Cycles: A Study in Tone and Vision* (Yale University Press, 1966)

Sturm-Maddox, Sara, *Ronsard, Petrarch and the 'Amours'* (University Press of Florida, 1999)

Wilson, Dudley, *Ronsard, Poet of Nature* (Manchester University Press, 1961)

General Historical, Linguistic and Literary Background

Ayres-Bennett, Wendy, *A History of the French Language through Texts* (Routledge, London and New York, 1996)

Castor, Grahame, *Pléiade Poetics: A Study in Sixteenth-Century Thought and Terminology* (Cambridge University Press, 1964)

Clements, Robert J., *Critical Theory and Practice of the Pléiade* (Harvard University Press, Cambridge, Mass., 1942, reprinted by Octagon Books, New York, 1970)

Cuddon, J. A., *A Dictionary of Literary Terms* (Penguin Books, London, 1982)

Forster, Leonard, *The Icy Fire: Five Studies in European Petrarchism* (Cambridge University Press, 1969)

Fragonard, Marie-Madeleine and Éliane Kotler, *Introduction à la langue du XVIe siècle* (Nathan, Paris, 1994)

Lewis, Roy, *On Reading French Verse: A Study of Poetic Form* (Clarendon Press, Oxford, 1982)

McFarlane, I. D., *A Literary History of France: Renaissance France 1470–1589* (Barnes & Noble, New York, and Benn, London, 1974)

Moss, Ann, *Poetry and Fable: Studies in Mythological Narrative in Sixteenth-Century France* (Cambridge University Press, 1984)

Prescott, Anne, *French Poets and the English Renaissance* (Yale University Press, 1978)

Radice, Betty, *Who's Who in the Ancient World* (Penguin Books, London, 1973)

Salmon, J. H. M., *Society in Crisis: France in the Sixteenth Century* (Methuen, London, 1979)

Weber, Henri, *La Création poétique au XVIᵉ siècle en France*, 2 vols. (Nizet, Paris, 1956)

Recordings

Antoine de Bertrand, *Amours de Ronsard*, Ensemble Clément Janequin (Harmonia Mundi, France, 1985): CD HMA 1901147

Chansons sur des poèmes de Ronsard, Ensemble Clément Janequin (Harmonia Mundi, France, 1994): CD HMC 901491

Note on the Texts

Our text reproduces that of the sixth collected edition of 1584. This choice has been dictated, firstly, by the fact that this was the last edition published before the death of Ronsard in 1585, and probably the last edition over which he exercised full authorial and editorial control. Secondly, the scholarly critical edition of his *Œuvres Complètes* (2 vols.) in the Bibliothèque de la Pléiade series, which is readily and conveniently available for consultation, is also based on the 1584 text. Like the Bibliothèque de la Pléiade edition, our selection respects the order, spelling and punctuation of the 1584 edition, and limits modifications to distinguishing between *i* and *j*, *u* and *v*, and to replacing the ampersand (&) by the word *et*. Closing guillemets (») at the beginning of a line are a convention used by sixteenth-century writers and printers to denote a maxim (*sententia*). In the translation we have rendered these by double quotation marks.

We have, however, made some adjustments to the text of 1584. Because of their interest, we have included a small number of poems which Ronsard chose to suppress and which did not figure in the 1584 edition (these poems – numbers 30, 78, 79 – are clearly signalled in the text as *pièces retranchées*, 'suppressed pieces'). In these cases, the text reproduced is that of the last collected edition prior to the poem's removal. In addition, we have selected some poems which were published posthumously (poems 53, 54, 69, 83–5), and our choice has been governed by the criteria referred to below. In the case of some of the longer poems it has not proved possible to reproduce the text in its entirety: we have, therefore, resorted to the use of extracts, a procedure which has enabled us to do justice to the diversity of Ronsard's poetry. Omitted passages have been signalled in the French text; they are also summarized in the Notes on those occasions when they are considered to be significant.

In order to facilitate reference to the poems for the purpose of illustration, we have numbered our selected poems with Arabic numerals. In the case of Ronsard's sonnets, which have no titles, we have followed the convention used by all modern editions, including that of the Bibliothèque de la Pléiade, and given Roman numbers to them.

Our aims in making our selection of texts have been, firstly, to represent the impressive variety and range of Ronsard's poetry across his entire poetic career; secondly, to include individual pieces of high poetic quality and intrinsic importance; and, thirdly, to choose poems which relate Ronsard to the contemporary context, be it socio-political, literary or historical.

SELECTED POEMS

LE PREMIER LIVRE DES AMOURS
(LES AMOURS DE CASSANDRE)

I (IX)

Le plus touffu d'un solitaire bois,
Le plus aigu d'une roche sauvage,
Le plus desert d'un separé rivage,
Et la frayeur des antres les plus cois,

Soulagent tant mes soupirs et ma vois,
Qu'au seul escart d'un plus secret ombrage
Je sens guarir ceste amoureuse rage,
Qui me r'afole au plus verd de mes mois.

Là renversé dessus la terre dure,
Hors de mon sein je tire une peinture,
De tous mes maux le seul allegement:

Dont les beautez par Denisot encloses,
Me font sentir mille metamorfoses
Tout en un coup d'un regard seulement.

THE FIRST BOOK OF LOVE POEMS
(TO CASSANDRE)

(IX)

The thickest part of a lonely wood, the steepest point of a forbidding rock, the wildest spot on an isolated shore and the fearsome aspect of the most silent caverns
    soothe my sighs and my lamentations to such a degree that it is only by seeking the solitude of a most secret shade that I feel I am being cured of this raging love, which is driving me mad in the most verdant months of my age.
    There, lying on the hard ground, I pull from my breast a painting, for all my sufferings the only relief;
    its beauties, with which Denisot has infused it, make me undergo a thousand metamorphoses all at once from a single glance.

3

2 (xx)

Je voudroy bien richement jaunissant
En pluye d'or goute à goute descendre
Dans le giron de ma belle Cassandre,
Lors qu'en ses yeux le somne va glissant.

Puis je voudroy en toreau blanchissant
Me transformer pour sur mon dos la prendre,
Quand en Avril par l'herbe la plus tendre
Elle va fleur mille fleurs ravissant.

Je voudroy bien pour alleger ma peine,
Estre un Narcisse et elle une fontaine,
Pour m'y plonger une nuict à sejour:

Et si voudroy que ceste nuict encore
Fust eternelle, et que jamais l'Aurore
Pour m'esveiller ne rallumast le jour.

(xx)

How I wish I could turn a rich yellow and rain down in a shower of gold drop by drop into the lap of my lovely Cassandre, as sleep is stealing into her eyes.

Then I wish I could change into a white bull to take her on my back, when in April she walks through a meadow of tenderest grass, a flower herself, ravishing a thousand flowers.

How I wish, in order to ease my pain, that I might be a Narcissus and she a fountain, so that I could plunge into it a whole night through at my pleasure;

and furthermore I wish that this night would last for ever, and that Aurora would never light up the day again and wake me up.

3 (XXXVI)

Pour la douleur qu'Amour veut que je sente,
Ainsi que moy Phebus tu lamentois,
Quand amoureux et banny tu chantois
Pres d'Ilion sur les rives de Xante.

Pinçant en vain ta lyre blandissante,
Fleuves et fleurs et bois tu enchantois,
Non la beauté qu'en l'ame tu sentois,
Qui te navroit d'une playe aigrissante.

Là de ton teint tu pallissois les fleurs,
Là les ruisseaux s'augmentoyent de tes pleurs,
Là tu vivois d'une esperance vaine.

Pour mesme nom Amour me fait douloir
Pres de Vandôme au rivage du Loir,
Comme un Phenis renaissant de ma peine.

(XXXVI)

On account of the pain which Love decrees that I feel, you, like me, Phoebus, used to lament, when lovesick and in exile you sang close to Troy on the banks of the Xanthus.

Plucking in vain your beguiling lyre, you enchanted rivers and flowers and woods, but not the beauty whose effects you felt in your soul, which inflicted on you a festering wound.

There with your pallid complexion you turned the flowers pale, there the streams became swollen with your tears, there you lived in vain hope.

For the same name as you, Love makes me suffer, close to Vendôme on the banks of the Loir, like a Phoenix reborn from my sorrow.

4 (XLIII)

Ores la crainte et ores l'esperance
De tous costez se campent en mon cœur:
Ny l'un ny l'autre au combat n'est veinqueur,
Pareils en force et en perseverance.

Ores douteux, ores pleins d'asseurance,
Entre l'espoir le soupçon et la peur,
Pour estre en vain de moy-mesme trompeur,
Au cœur captif je promets delivrance.

Verray-je point avant mourir le temps,
Que je tondray la fleur de son printemps,
Sous qui ma vie à l'ombrage demeure?

Verray-je point qu'en ses bras enlassé,
Recreu d'amour, tout penthois et lassé,
D'un beau trespas entre ses bras je meure?

(XLIII)

Now fear and now hopefulness is encamped in every part of my heart; neither the one nor the other is victorious in the battle, both equal in strength and in tenacity.

Now fearful, now filled with confidence, between hope, doubt and dread, in a vain attempt to deceive myself, I promise to set free my captive heart.

Shall I not see before I die a time when I shall pluck the flower of my lady's springtime, the lady who makes my life languish in the shadows?

Shall I not see myself clasped in her arms, spent with love, completely breathless and exhausted, dying a delightful death in her arms?

5 (XLIV)

Je voudrois estre Ixion et Tantale,
Dessus la roue et dans les eaux là bas,
Et nu à nu presser entre mes bras
Ceste beauté qui les anges égale.

S'ainsin estoit, toute peine fatale
Me seroit douce et ne me chaudroit pas
Non, d'un vautour fussé-je le repas,
Non, qui le roc remonte et redevale.

Voir ou toucher le rond de son tetin
Pourroit changer mon amoureux destin
Aux majestez des Princes de l'Asie:

Un demy-dieu me feroit son baiser,
Et sein sur sein mon feu desembraser,
Un de ces Dieux qui mangent l'Ambrosie.

(XLIV)

I wish that I was Ixion and Tantalus, on the wheel and in the waters down below, and that naked I was pressing her naked in my arms, this beauty who is the equal of the angels.

If it were so, all suffering inflicted by fate would seem sweet to me, and I would not care, not even if I were the prey of a vulture, not even if I were fated to push a boulder uphill and to see it roll down again.

Seeing or touching the roundness of her breast could change my destiny as a lover, raising me to the majesty of the Princes of Asia;

her kiss would make me a demi-god, and quenching my fire with my flesh against her flesh would make me one of those Gods who feast on Ambrosia.

6 (LII)

Avant qu'Amour du Chaos ocieux
Ouvrist le sein qui couvoit la lumiere
Avec la terre, avec l'onde premiere,
Sans art, sans forme estoyent brouillez les Cieux.

Tel mon esprit à rien industrieux,
Dedans mon corps, lourde et grosse matiere,
Erroit sans forme et sans figure entiere,
Quand l'arc d'Amour le perça par tes yeux.

Amour rendit ma nature parfaite,
Pure par luy mon essence s'est faite,
Il me donna la vie et le pouvoir,

Il eschaufa tout mon sang de sa flame,
Et m'agitant de son vol feit mouvoir
Avecques luy mes pensers et mon ame.

(LII)

Before Love opened the womb of inert Chaos, which was incubating light, together with the earth and with the primeval waters, the Heavens, without pattern and without form, were in a turbulent state.

Similarly, my spirit, utterly unoccupied, within my body of gross and heavy matter was wandering aimlessly without form and without any well-defined shape, when Love's bow pierced it with arrows from your eyes.

Love made my nature perfect, my being became pure through his agency, he gave me life and power,

he heated all my blood with his flame, and setting me in motion with his flight he made my thoughts and my soul move with him.

7 (LVIII)

Quand le Soleil à chef renversé plonge
Son char doré dans le sein du vieillard,
Et que la nuit un bandeau sommeillard
Mouillé d'oubly dessus nos yeux alonge:

Amour adonc qui sape mine et ronge
De ma raison le chancellant rempart,
Comme un guerrier en diligence part,
Armant son camp des ombres et du songe.

Lors ma raison, et lors ce Dieu cruel,
Seuls per à per d'un choc continuel
Vont redoublant mille escarmouches fortes.

Si bien qu'Amour n'en seroit le veinqueur
Sans mes pensers qui luy ouvrent les portes,
Tant mes soudars sont traistres à mon cueur.

(LVIII)

When the Sun, head thrown back, plunges his golden chariot into the bosom of old father Ocean, and night stretches over our eyes a drowsy blindfold soaked in oblivion,

thereupon Love, who is sapping, undermining and eroding the tottering rampart of my reason, sets off in haste like a warrior, arming his camp with shadows and with dreams.

Then my reason, and then that cruel God, constantly clashing in single combat as equals, continually multiply a thousand fierce skirmishes;

so much so that Love would not emerge victorious, were it not for my thoughts, which open the gates to him, so treacherous are my soldiers to my heart.

8 (LIX)

Comme un Chevreuil, quand le printemps détruit
Du froid hyver la poignante gelée,
Pour mieux brouter la fueille emmiëlée,
Hors de son bois avec l'Aube s'enfuit:

Et seul, et seur, loin de chiens et de bruit,
Or' sur un mont, or' dans une valée,
Or' pres d'une onde à l'escart recelée,
Libre, folastre où son pié le conduit:

De rets ne d'arc sa liberté n'a crainte
Sinon alors que sa vie est attainte
D'un trait meurtrier empourpré de son sang.

Ainsi j'alloy sans espoir de dommage,
Le jour qu'un œil sur l'Avril de mon âge
Tira d'un coup mille traits en mon flanc.

(LIX)

Just as a Roebuck, when spring shatters the piercing frost of cold winter, bounds out of its forest with the Dawn, the better to browse the honey-sweet foliage,

and in solitude and safety, far from hounds and noise, now on a hill, now in a valley, now beside a remote and secluded pool, frolics freely wherever his feet take him,

and, free, has no fear of net or bow, until the moment when his life is struck down by a murderous arrow stained red with his blood,

just so did I roam without anticipating any harm, on that day when an eye, in the April of my age, fired all at once a thousand arrows into my side.

9 (XCIV)

Soit que son or se crespe lentement,
Ou soit qu'il vague en deux glissantes ondes,
Qui çà qui là par le sein vagabondes,
Et sur le col nagent follastrement:

Ou soit qu'un noud illustré richement
De maints rubis et maintes perles rondes,
Serre les flots de ses deux tresses blondes,
Mon cueur se plaist en son contentement.

Quel plaisir est-ce, ainçois quelle merveille,
Quand ses cheveux troussez dessus l'oreille,
D'une Venus imitent la façon?

Quand d'un bonnet sa teste elle Adonise,
Et qu'on ne sçait s'elle est fille ou garçon,
Tant sa beauté en tous deux se desguise?

(XCIV)

Whether her golden hair curls gently, or whether it glides in two flowing waves, which, drifting now here, now there over her breasts, float playfully on her neck,

or whether her two rippling blonde tresses are caught in a knot richly ornamented with many rubis and many round pearls, my heart delights in its enjoyment.

What a pleasure it is, or rather what a marvel, when her hair, caught up above the ear, imitates the style of a Venus!

Or when, putting a cap on her head, she turns into an Adonis, and one cannot tell whether she is a girl or a boy, so ingeniously does her beauty disguise itself as both!

10 (CXX)

Franc de raison, esclave de fureur,
Je vay chassant une Fere sauvage,
Or' sur un mont, or' le long d'un rivage,
Or' dans le bois de jeunesse et d'erreur.

J'ay pour ma lesse un long trait de malheur,
J'ay pour limier un violent courage:
J'ay pour mes chiens, l'ardeur, et le jeune âge,
Et pour piqueurs, l'espoir et la douleur.

Mais eux voyans, que plus elle est chassee,
Plus elle fuit d'une course eslancee,
Quittent leur proye: et retournent vers moy

De ma chair propre osant bien leur repaistre.
C'est grand pitié (à mon dam je le voy)
Quand les valets commandent à leur maistre.

(cxx)

Unconstrained by reason, in thrall to mad passion, I am hunting a wild Animal, now on a mountain, now along a river, now in the forest of youth and delusion.

I have for my leash a long cord of misery, I have for my bloodhound a fierce determination; I have for my hounds ardour and youthful years, and for whippers-in, hope and suffering.

But they, seeing that the more hotly she is hunted, the more headlong is her flight, abandon their quarry, and turn back towards me,

even daring to feed the hounds on my own flesh. What a sorry state of affairs it is (as I see to my cost), when servants seize power over their master!

11 (CXXIX)

Di l'un des deux, sans tant me déguiser
Le peu d'amour que ton semblant me porte,
Je ne sçauroy, veu ma peine si forte,
Tant lamenter, ne tant Petrarquiser.

Si tu le veux, que sert de refuser
Ce doux present dont l'espoir me conforte?
Sinon, pourquoy d'une esperance morte
Me nourris-tu pour tousjours m'abuser?

L'un de tes yeux dans les enfers me rue,
L'autre plus doux, à l'envy s'esvertue
De me remettre en paradis encor:

Ainsi tes yeux, pour causer mon renaistre,
Et puis ma mort, sans cesse me font estre
Or' un Pollux, et ores un Castor.

(CXXIX)

Say one thing or the other, without so completely disguising from me how little love your appearance promises me; since my suffering is so strong, I cannot adequately express it, either in lamenting or in imitating Petrarch.

If it is what you want, what is the use of refusing to give me this sweet present, the hope of which gives me comfort? If it is not, why do you nourish me with a barren hope, and delude me constantly?

One of your eyes casts me into hell, the other, gentler, vies with it by striving to restore me to paradise again;

thus your eyes, by causing my rebirth and then my death, ceaselessly make me now into a Pollux, and now into a Castor.

12 (CXXXV)

Douce beauté, meurdriere de ma vie,
En lieu d'un cœur tu portes un rocher:
Tu me fais vif languir et desecher,
Passionné d'une amoureuse envie.

Le jeune sang qui d'aimer te convie,
N'a peu de toy la froideur arracher,
Farouche fiere, et qui n'as rien plus cher
Que languir froide, et n'estre point servie.

Appren à vivre, ô fiere en cruauté:
Ne garde point à Pluton ta beauté,
Quelque peu d'aise en aimant il faut prendre.

Il fault tromper doucement le trespas:
Car aussi bien sous la terre là bas
Sans rien sentir le corps n'est plus que cendre.

(CXXXV)

Sweet beauty, murderess of my life, in place of a heart you have a stone; you cause me, while yet alive, to languish and waste away, inflamed by an amorous desire.

The young blood that invites you to love has failed to pluck the coldness from you, who, savage and cruel as you are, like nothing better than to languish coldly, and to have no suitors.

Learn to live, O you who are fierce in your cruelty; do not keep your beauty for Pluto, we must take some small pleasure in love.

We must cheat death sweetly, because, furthermore, down there, beneath the earth, the body is without feeling and is no more than dust.

13 Stanses

Quand au temple nous serons
Agenouillez, nous ferons
Les devots selon la guise
De ceux qui pour louer Dieu
Humbles se courbent au lieu
Le plus secret de l'Eglise.

Mais quand au lict nous serons
Entrelassez, nous ferons
Les lascifs selon les guises
Des Amans qui librement   10
Pratiquent folastrement
Dans les draps cent mignardises.

Pourquoy donque, quand je veux
Ou mordre tes beaux cheveux,
Ou baiser ta bouche aimee,
Ou toucher à ton beau sein,
Contrefais-tu la nonnain
Dedans un cloistre enfermee?

Stanzas

When we are kneeling in the temple, we shall act like devout worshippers in the manner of those who, to praise God, humbly prostrate themselves in the most secret place in the Church.

But when we are entwined together in bed, we shall act like voluptuaries in the manner of Lovers who freely and wantonly indulge in a hundred frolics between the sheets.

Why then, when I want either to nibble your lovely hair, or to kiss your beloved mouth, or to touch your lovely breast, do you act like a nun enclosed within a cloister?

Pour qui gardes-tu tes yeux
20   Et ton sein delicieux,
Ton front, ta lévre jumelle?
En veux-tu baiser Pluton
Là bas, apres que Charon
T'aura mise en sa nacelle?

Apres ton dernier trespas,
Gresle, tu n'auras là bas
Qu'une bouchette blesmie:
Et quand mort je te verrois
Aux Ombres je n'avou'rois
30   Que jadis tu fus m'amie.

Ton test n'aura plus de peau
Ny ton visage si beau
N'aura veines ny arteres:
Tu n'auras plus que les dents
Telles qu'on les voit dedans
Les testes de cimeteres.

Donque tandis que tu vis,
Change, Maistresse, d'avis,
Et ne m'espargne ta bouche:

For whom are you reserving your eyes and your delicious breast, your forehead, your twin lips? Do you want to kiss Pluto with them, in the Underworld, after Charon has taken you into his boat?

In the end, when you are finally dead, in the Underworld, you will be emaciated and will have only a bloodless little mouth; and if after my own death I should see you in the abode of the Shades I would not acknowledge that you were once my mistress.

Your skull will no longer have any skin, and your face, which is now so lovely, will have neither veins nor arteries; you will have only teeth such as are seen in the skulls in cemeteries.

Therefore, while you are alive, Mistress mine, change your mind, and do not

Incontinent tu mourras, 40
Lors tu te repentiras
De m'avoir esté farouche.

Ah, je meurs! ah, baise moy!
Ah, Maistresse, approche toy!
Tu fuis comme un Fan qui tremble:
Au-moins souffre que ma main
S'esbate un peu dans ton sein,
Ou plus bas, si bon te semble.

begrudge me your mouth; very soon you will die, and then you will repent of once having been harsh to me.

Oh, I am dying! Oh, kiss me! Oh, Mistress mine, come closer! You flee like a quivering Fawn; at least allow my hand to play a little over your breast, or lower down, if you think fit.

14 (CLII)

Lune à l'œil brun, Deesse aux noirs chevaux,
Qui ça, qui là qui haut qui bas te tournent,
Et de retours qui jamais ne sejournent,
Trainent ton char eternel en travaux:

À tes desirs les miens ne sont egaux,
Car les amours qui ton ame epoinçonnent,
Et les ardeurs qui la mienne eguillonnent,
Divers souhaits desirent à leurs maux.

Toy mignottant ton dormeur de Latmie,
Voudrois tousjours qu'une course endormie
Retint le train de ton char qui s'enfuit:

Mais moy qu'Amour toute la nuict devore,
Depuis le soir je souhaite l'Aurore,
Pour voir le jour, que me celoit ta nuit.

(CLII)

Brown-eyed Moon, Goddess with the black horses, which turn you now here, now there, now high, now low, and, making only short-lived reappearances, pull your chariot through its endless labours,

my desires are not the same as yours, because the loves that pierce your soul and the passions which inflame mine long for different desires to ease their sufferings.

You, caressing your sleeper on Mount Latmus, would always wish for a slumberous motion to hold back the progress of your chariot as it speeds away;

but I, who am devoured by Love all night long, from evening onwards I yearn for the Dawn, so that I may see the light of day, which your night hid from me.

15 (CLX)

Or' que Jupin espoint de sa semence
Veut enfanter ses enfans bien-aimez,
Et que du chaud de ses reins allumez
L'humide sein de Junon ensemence:

Or' que la mer, or' que la vehemence
Des vents fait place aux grans vaisseaux armez,
Et que l'oiseau parmi les bois ramez,
Du Thracien les tançons recommence:

Or' que les prez et ore que les fleurs
De mille et mille et de mille couleurs
Peignent le sein de la terre si gaye,

Seul et pensif aux rochers plus segrets
D'un cœur muet je conte mes regrets,
Et par les bois je vay celant ma playe.

(CLX)

Now when Jupiter, excited by his virility, wants to engender his much-loved children, and when with the heat of his burning loins he inseminates Juno's moist womb,

   now when the sea, now when the wildness of the winds yields to great warships, and now when amid the wooded forests the bird renews her complaints against the Thracian,

   now when the meadows and now when the flowers with thousands upon thousands upon thousands of colours are painting the bosom of the earth so brightly,

   alone and pensive among the most secluded rocks I recount my sorrows with a mute heart, and through the woods I go, concealing my wound.

16 (CLXXII)

Je veux brusler, pour m'en-voler aux cieux,
Tout l'imparfait de mon escorce humaine,
M'éternisant comme le fils d'Alcméne,
Qui tout en feu s'assit entre les Dieux.

Ja mon esprit desireux de son mieux,
Dedans ma chair, rebelle, se promeine,
Et ja le bois de sa victime ameine
Pour s'immoler aux rayons de tes yeux.

Ô saint brazier, ô flame entretenue
D'un feu divin, avienne que ton chaud
Brusle si bien ma despouille connue,

Que libre et nu je vole d'un plein saut
Outre le ciel, pour adorer là haut
L'autre beauté dont la tienne est venue.

(CLXXII)

So that I can take flight to the heavens, I want to burn all the imperfections of my human vesture, making myself immortal like Alcmene's son, who, all ablaze, took his seat among the Gods.

Already my spirit, desirous of attaining its greatest good, is pacing rebelliously through my body, and already it is bringing the wood for its sacrificial victim to be immolated in the rays from your eyes.

O holy pyre, O flame nourished by a divine fire, may it come to pass that your heat burns my familiar outer skin so thoroughly

that free and naked I may fly with one single bound beyond the sky, to adore on high the other beauty from which your own has come.

17 (CLXXIII)

Mon fol penser pour s'en-voler plus haut
Apres le bien que hautain je desire,
S'est emplumé d'ailes jointes de cire,
Propres à fondre au rais du premier chaud.

Luy fait oiseau, dispost de saut en saut
Poursuit en vain l'objet de son martire,
Et toy qui peux et luy dois contredire,
Tu le vois bien, Raison, et ne t'en chaut.

Sous la clarté d'une estoile si belle
Cesse, Penser, de hazarder ton aile,
Qu'on ne te voye en bruslant desplumer:

Pour amortir une ardeur si cuisante,
L'eau de mes yeux ne seroit suffisante,
Ny l'eau du ciel, ny les flots de la mer.

(CLXXIII)

My foolish thought, in order to take flight to greater heights, seeking the perfect good that I desire in moments of high-mindedness, has feathered itself with wings attached with wax, which are likely to melt in the first rays of the hot sun.

Transformed into a bird, nimbly hopping and hopping, it pursues in vain the cause of its martyrdom, and you, who can and must oppose it, you see it all clearly, Reason, and take no heed.

Stop risking your wings, Thought, in the blazing light of such a beautiful star, lest we see you lose your feathers in flames;

to deaden such a burning ardour, the water from my eyes would not be sufficient, nor the water from the sky, nor the waves of the sea.

18 (CLXXIV)

Or' que le ciel, or' que la terre est pleine
De glas, de gresle esparse en tous endrois,
Et que l'horreur des plus froidureux mois
Fait herisser les cheveux de la plaine:

Or' que le vent qui mutin se promeine,
Rompt les rochers, et desplante les bois,
Et que la mer redoublant ses abois,
Sa rage enflee aux rivages ameine:

Amour me brusle, et l'hyver froidureux,
Qui gele tout, de mon feu chaleureux
Ne gele point l'ardeur qui tousjours dure.

Voyez, Amans, comme je suis traité,
Je meurs de froid au plus chaud de l'esté,
Et de chaleur au cœur de la froidure.

(CLXXIV)

Now when the sky, now when the earth is filled with ice, with hail widespread over
the whole area, and when the horror of the chilliest months makes the grasses of
the meadow bristle like hair,

   now when the wind, which prowls about mutinously, cracks the rocks and uproots
the woods, and when the sea, redoubling its roar, sends its surging rage on to the
shore,

   Love burns me, and chilly winter, which freezes everything, cannot freeze the
everlasting ardour of my hot fire.

   See, Lovers, how I am treated: I die of cold in the hottest part of the summer,
and of heat in the heart of coldness.

19 (CXCII)

Il faisoit chaud, et le somne coulant
Se distilloit dans mon ame songearde,
Quand l'incertain d'une idole gaillarde
Fut doucement mon dormir affolant.

Panchant sous moy son bel ivoyre blanc,
Et m'y tirant sa langue fretillarde,
Me baizottoit d'une lévre mignarde,
Bouche sur bouche, et le flanc sus le flanc.

Que de coral, que de liz, que de roses,
Ce me sembloit à pleines mains descloses
Tastay-je lors entre deux maniments?

Mon Dieu, mon Dieu, de quelle douce haleine,
De quelle odeur estoit sa bouche pleine,
De quels rubis, et de quels diamans?

(CXCII)

It was hot, and silky slumber was stealing into my dreaming soul, when the hazy shape of a sprightly phantom softly came to perturb my sleep.

Leaning towards me with her lovely white ivory, and offering me her flickering tongue, she kissed me repeatedly with her dainty lips, mouth upon mouth, and body upon body.

How much coral, how many lilies, how many roses, did I seem to fondle then with two caresses of my fully opened hands!

O God, O God, with what sweet breath, with what scent was her mouth filled, with what rubies, and with what diamonds!

20 (CXCIII)

Ces flots jumeaux de laict bien espoissi
Vont et revont par leur blanche valée,
Comme à son bord la marine salée,
Qui lente va, lente revient aussi.

Une distance entre eux se fait, ainsi
Qu'entre deux monts une sente égalée,
Blanche par tout de neige devalée,
Quand en hyver le vent s'est adouci.

Là deux rubis haut eslevez rougissent,
Dont les rayons cet ivoyre finissent
De toutes parts uniment arrondis:

Là tout honneur, là toute grace abonde:
Et la beauté si quelqu'une est au monde,
Vole au sejour de ce beau paradis.

(CXCIII)

These twin waves of thickly clotted milk ebb and flow over their white valley, just as on its shore the briny tide, which slowly ebbs, slowly rises also.

A space forms between them, exactly like a levelled pathway between two hills, which is white all over with drifted snow, when in winter the wind has dropped.

There two rubies standing erect gleam red, smoothly rounded on all sides, and their radiance puts the finishing touch to that ivory;

there all honour, there all grace abounds; and beauty, if there is any in the world, flies to the realm of this lovely paradise.

LE SECOND LIVRE DES AMOURS
(LES AMOURS DE MARIE)

21 Elegie à son livre

[...]
  Si quelque dame honneste et gentille de cœur
(Qui aura l'inconstance et le change en horreur)
Me vient, en te lisant, d'un gros sourcil reprendre
Dequoy je ne devois oublier ma Cassandre,[1]
Qui la premiere au cœur le trait d'amour me mist,
Et que le bon Petrarque un tel peché ne fist,
Qui fut trente et un an amoureux de sa dame,[2]
Sans qu'un autre jamais luy peust eschauffer l'ame: 40
Respons-luy je te pri', que Petrarque sur moy
N'avoit authorité de me donner sa loy,
Ny à ceux qui viendroyent apres luy, pour les faire
Si long temps amoureux sans leur lien desfaire.
  Luy-mesme ne fut tel, car à voir son escrit
Il estoit esveillé d'un trop gentil esprit
Pour estre sot trente ans, abusant sa jeunesse

THE SECOND BOOK OF LOVE POEMS
(TO MARIE)

Elegy to his Book

[...] If on reading you some virtuous and noble-spirited lady (who has a horror of inconstancy and change) should come frowningly to reproach me, saying that I ought not to have forgotten my Cassandre, who was the first to lodge love's dart in my heart, and adding that the worthy Petrarch did not commit such a sin, but continued to love his lady for thirty-one years without any other love ever being able to inflame his soul, give her this answer, I beg you, that Petrarch had no authority over me to impose his law on me, nor on those who came after him, to make them go on loving for so long without breaking their bonds.

He himself did not do so, for to judge from his writings he was animated by too lively a spirit to persist in his folly for thirty years, squandering his youth and his

Et sa Muse au giron d'une vieille maistresse:
Ou bien il jouyssoit de sa Laurette, ou bien
50 Il estoit un grand fat d'aimer sans avoir rien.
Ce que je ne puis croire, aussi n'est-il croyable:
Non, il en jouyssoit: puis la fist admirable,
»Chaste, divine, saincte: aussi l'amoureux doit
»Celebrer la beauté dont plaisir il reçoit:
»Car celuy qui la blasme apres la jouïssance
»N'est homme, mais d'un Tygre il a prins sa naissance.
Quand quelque jeune fille est au commencement
Cruelle, dure, fiere, à son premier amant,
Constant il faut attendre: il peut estre qu'une heure
60 Viendra sans y penser, qui la rendra meilleure.
Mais quand elle devient voire de jour en jour
Plus dure et plus rebelle, et plus rude en amour,
On s'en doit esloigner, sans se rompre la teste
De vouloir adoucir une si sotte beste.
Je suis de tel advis: me blasme de ceci,
M'estime qui voudra, je le conseille ainsi.

    Les femmes bien souvent sont cause que nous sommes
Volages et legers, amadouans les hommes
D'un espoir enchanteur, les tenans quelquefois
70 Par une douce ruse, un an, ou deux, ou trois,

Muse in the lap of an old mistress; either he did enjoy the favours of his little Laura, or else he was a great idiot to love without receiving any reward. That I cannot believe, nor is it credible. No, he enjoyed her; then he made her out to be worthy of admiration, chaste, divine and holy; after all, "a lover must celebrate the beauty from whom he receives gratification; for he who criticizes her after he has enjoyed her is not a man, but was born of a Tiger". When some young girl is at the beginning cruel, hard-hearted and merciless to her first lover, he must remain constant and patient; it may be that, without any action on his part, a time will come which will make her more amenable. But when she actually becomes day by day harder-hearted and more intractable, and harsher in love, one should retreat, without taking too much trouble to try to soften such a foolish creature. Such is my opinion; let anyone who wants criticize me or applaud me for it, but that is what I advise.

    Women are very often the reason why we are fickle and capricious, as they lead men on with a bewitching hope, sometimes by a charming ruse keeping them for a

Dans les liens d'Amour sans aucune allegeance:
Ce-pendant un valet en aura jouïssance,
Ou bien quelque badin emportera ce bien
Que le fidele amy à bon droit cuidoit sien.[3]
[. . .]

   Dy leur, si de fortune une belle Cassandre
Vers moy se fust monstrée un peu courtoise et tendre,
Et pleine de pitié eust cherché de guarir
Le mal dont ses beaux yeux dix ans m'ont fait mourir,
Non seulement du corps, mais sans plus d'une œillade
Eust voulu soulager mon pauvre cœur malade,
Je ne l'eusse laissée, et m'en soit à tesmoin
Ce jeune enfant ailé qui des amours a soin.[4]

   Mais voyant que tousjours elle marchoit plus fiere,
Je desliay du tout mon amitié premiere,   160
Pour en aimer une autre en ce païs d'Anjou,
Où maintenant Amour me detient sous le jou:
Laquelle tout soudain je quitteray, si elle
M'est comme fut Cassandre, orgueilleuse et rebelle,
Pour en chercher une autre, à fin de voir un jour
De pareille amitié recompenser m'amour,

---

year, or two, or three, in the bonds of Love without any relief; meanwhile a servant will enjoy their favours, or else some buffoon will carry off that prize which the faithful suitor rightly believed to be his. [. . .]

Tell them [those who criticize me] that if by good fortune a certain beautiful Cassandre had shown herself a little more gracious and tender-hearted towards me, and if, full of pity, she had sought to cure the sickness caused by her beautiful eyes, from which I have been suffering unto death for ten years, if she had wished to comfort my poor, sick heart, not even with her body, but simply with a look, I would not have left her; and let me call as my witness that young winged child who has charge of love affairs.

But seeing that she was growing ever more stony-hearted, I completely cast off my first attachment, to love another in this region of Anjou, where now Love holds me under his yoke; her, too, will I abandon immediately, if her behaviour towards me is like Cassandre's, haughty and rebellious, and I shall seek yet another, in order to see my love one day rewarded by an equal devotion, and to feel the affection of

Sentant l'affection d'un autre dans moymesme:
»Car un homme est bien sot d'aimer, si on ne l'aime.
   Or si quelqu'un apres me vient blasmer, dequoy
170   Je ne suis plus si grave en mes vers que j'estoy
À mon commencement, quand l'humeur Pindarique
Enfloit empoulément ma bouche magnifique:[5]
Dy luy que les amours ne se souspirent pas
D'un vers hautement grave, ains d'un beau stile bas,
Populaire et plaisant, ainsi qu'a fait Tibulle,
L'ingenieux Ovide, et le docte Catulle.
Le fils de Venus hait ces ostentations:
Il suffist qu'on luy chante au vray ses passions
Sans enflure ny fard, d'un mignard et doux stile,
180   Coulant d'un petit bruit, comme une eau qui distile.
Ceux qui font autrement, ils font un mauvais tour
À la simple Venus, et à son fils Amour.[6]
[...]

another being directed towards me; for "a man is very foolish to love, if he is not loved".

Now, if someone later should criticize me because my poetry is no longer so elevated as it was in the beginning, when the Pindaric spirit swelled my grandiloquent mouth extravagantly, tell him that love does not utter its sighs in poetry which is gravely elevated, but rather in a pleasing low style, simple and appealing, such as that used by Tibullus, the ingenious Ovid, and the learned Catullus. Venus' son hates those ostentatious displays; it is enough to sing one's passions truly, without bombast or affectation, in a sweet and charming style, which flows with a soft sound, like water trickling. Those who do otherwise do a bad turn to Venus, who is simple, and to her son Love. [...]

22 (11)

Marie vous avez la joue aussi vermeille
Qu'une rose de May, vous avez les cheveux
Entre bruns et chatains, frisez de mille nœuds,
Gentement tortillez tout autour de l'oreille.

Quand vous estiez petite, une mignarde abeille
Sur vos lévres forma son nectar savoureux,
Amour laissa ses traits en vos yeux rigoureux,
Pithon vous feit la voix à nulle autre pareille.

Vous avez les tetins comme deux monts de lait,
Qui pommelent ainsi qu'au printemps nouvelet
Pommelent deux boutons que leur chasse environne.

De Junon sont vos bras, des Graces vostre sein,
Vous avez de l'Aurore et le front et la main,
Mais vous avez le cœur d'une fiere Lionne.

(11)

Marie, you have cheeks as red as a rose in May, you have hair between brown and chestnut, coiled into a thousand curls, prettily twining right around your ears.

When you were small, a sweet little bee made its delicious nectar on your lips, Love left his arrows in your stern eyes, Peitho gave you a voice unmatched by any other.

You have breasts like two mounds of clotted milk, which swell round as apples, just as in early spring two buds enfolded in their sheaths swell round as apples.

Your arms are those of Juno, your breasts are those of the Graces, you have both the brow and the hand of Aurora. But you have the heart of a fierce Lioness.

23 (IV)

Le vingtiesme d'Avril couché sur l'herbelette,
Je vy ce me sembloit en dormant, un Chevreuil,
Qui çà qui là marchoit où le menoit son vueil,
Foulant les belles fleurs de mainte gambelette.

Une corne et une autre encore nouvelette
Enfloit son petit front d'un gracieux orgueil:
Comme un Soleil luisoit la rondeur de son œil,
Et un carquan pendoit sous sa gorge douillette.

Si tost que je le vy, je voulu courre apres,
Et luy qui m'avisa print sa fuite és forests,
Où se mocquant de moy ne me voulut attendre:

Mais en suivant son trac, je ne m'avisay pas
D'un piege entre les fleurs, qui me lia le pas:
Ainsi pour prendre autruy moy-mesme me fis prendre.

(IV)

On the twentieth of April, lying on the grass, I saw, so it seemed to me as I slept, a Roebuck, which was ambling here and there as the desire took him, trampling the lovely flowers with much prancing.

One horn and another, still newly budding, made his little brow swell with a charming pride; his round eyes shone like a Sun, and a chain hung beneath his downy throat.

As soon as I saw him, I wanted to give chase, and he, noticing me, took flight into the forests, where, mocking me, he declined to wait;

but as I followed his track, I did not notice a snare among the flowers, which trapped my feet. Thus, in trying to catch another, I was myself caught.

24 (IX)

Marie, qui voudroit vostre nom retourner,
Il trouveroit aimer: aimez-moy donc Marie,
Vostre nom de nature à l'amour vous convie.
À qui trahist Nature il ne faut pardonner.

S'il vous plaist vostre cœur pour gage me donner,
Je vous offre le mien: ainsi de ceste vie
Nous prendrons les plaisirs, et jamais autre envie
Ne me pourra l'esprit d'une autre emprisonner.

Il fault aimer, maistresse, au monde quelque chose.
Celuy qui n'aime point, malheureux se propose
Une vie d'un Scythe, et ses jours veut passer

Sans gouster la douceur des douceurs la meilleure.
Rien n'est doux sans Venus et sans son fils: à l'heure
Que je n'aimeray plus, puissé-je trespasser!

(IX)

Marie, if anyone wanted to rearrange your name he would find *'aimer'*, 'to love'; so love me, then, Marie, your name by its very nature invites you to love. Anyone who betrays Nature is not to be pardoned.

If you are willing to give me your heart as a pledge, I will entrust mine to you; in that way we shall grasp the pleasures of this life, and never will any other desire succeed in making my mind the prisoner of any other lady.

One must love something in the world, beloved. A person who does not love at all, unhappy creature, is creating the life of a Scythian for himself, and seeks to spend his days

without tasting the greatest sweetness of all sweetnesses. Nothing is sweet without Venus and without her son; when the time comes that I no longer love, let me die!

25 (x)

Marie, en me tanceant vous me venez reprendre
Que je suis trop leger, et me dites tousjours,
Quand j'approche de vous, que j'aille à ma Cassandre,
Et tousjours m'appellez inconstant en amours.

»L'inconstance me plaist: les hommes sont bien lours
»Qui de nouvelle amour ne se laissent surprendre:
Qui veult opiniastre une seule pretendre
N'est digne que Venus luy face de bons tours.

Celuy qui n'ose faire une amitié nouvelle,
A faute de courage, ou faute de cervelle,
Se défiant de soy que ne peut avoir mieux.

Les hommes maladifs ou mattez de vieillesse
Doivent estre constans: mais sotte est la jeunesse,
Qui n'est point esveillée et qui n'aime en cent lieux.

(x)

Marie, you scold me and reprimand me for being too fickle, and you always tell me, when I come near you, to go to my Cassandre, and you always call me inconstant in love.

I like inconstancy: "men are dullards indeed who do not let themselves be surprised by a new love". Anyone who obstinately lays claim to just one mistress does not deserve to have Venus do him favours.

He who dares not form a new relationship lacks heart or lacks wit, not having the confidence to think he could have something better.

Men who are sickly or stricken with age have to be constant; but foolish is the young man who is not spirited and who does not love in a hundred different places.

26 (XIX)

Marie levez-vous ma jeune paresseuse,
Ja la gaye Alouette au ciel a fredonné,
Et ja le Rossignol doucement jargonné,
Dessus l'espine assis sa complainte amoureuse.

Sus debout allon voir l'herbelette perleuse,
Et vostre beau rosier de boutons couronné,
Et vos œillets mignons ausquels aviez donné,
Hier au soir de l'eau d'une main si songneuse.

Harsoir en vous couchant vous jurastes vos yeux
D'estre plus-tost que moy ce matin esveillée:
Mais le dormir de l'Aube aux filles gracieux

Vous tient d'un doux sommeil encor les yeux sillée.
Ça ça que je les baise et vostre beau tetin
Cent fois pour vous apprendre à vous lever matin.

(XIX)

Marie, get out of bed, my young sleepyhead, already the merry Lark has carolled its song to the sky, and already the Nightingale, perched on a thorn bush, has sweetly trilled its lovesick lament.

Come on, get up, let's go and see the dew-pearled grass, and your lovely rose bush, crowned with buds, and your pretty carnations, which you watered yesterday in the evening with such a careful hand.

Last evening as you were going to bed you swore by your eyes to be awake before me this morning; but the sleep of Dawn, so delightful to girls,

enfolds you still, and seals your eyes in sweet slumber. Here, come here, so that I can kiss them and your lovely breast a hundred times, to teach you to get up early in the morning.

27 (XXVIII)

Vous mesprisez nature: estes-vous si cruelle
De ne vouloir aimer? voyez les Passereaux
Qui demenent l'amour, voyez les Colombeaux,
Regardez le Ramier, voyez la Tourterelle:

Voyez deçà delà d'une fretillante aile
Voleter par les bois les amoureux oiseaux,
Voyez la jeune vigne embrasser les ormeaux,
Et toute chose rire en la saison nouvelle.

Ici la bergerette en tournant son fuseau
Desgoise ses amours, et là le pastoureau
Respond à sa chanson, ici toute chose aime:

Tout parle de l'amour, tout s'en veut enflamer:
Seulement vostre cœur froid d'une glace extreme
Demeure opiniastre et ne veut point aimer.

(XXVIII)

You despise nature: are you so cruel as to refuse to love? See the Sparrows that display their love, see the young Pigeons, look at the Ringdove, see the Turtledove;

see the amorous birds fluttering hither and thither in the woods with quivering wings, see the young vine embracing the elms, and all things laughing for joy in the new season.

Here the young shepherdess, turning her spindle, gives voice to her loves, and there the young shepherd answers her song, here all things love;

everything speaks of love, everything wants to be fired by it; only your heart, cold with an extreme iciness, remains obstinate and refuses to love.

28 (XLIV)

Marie, baisez-moy: non, ne me baisez pas,
Mais tirez moy le cœur de vostre douce haleine:
Non, ne le tirez pas, mais hors de chaque veine
Succez-moy toute l'ame esparse entre vos bras:

Non, ne la succez pas: car apres le trespas
Que serois-je sinon une semblance vaine,
Sans corps desur la rive, où l'amour ne demeine
(Pardonne moy Pluton) qu'en feintes ses esbas?

Pendant que nous vivons, entr'aimons nous, Marie,
Amour ne regne point sur la troupe blesmie
Des morts, qui sont sillez d'un long somme de fer.

C'est abus que Pluton ait aimé Proserpine,
Si doux soing n'entre point en si dure poitrine:
Amour regne en la terre et non point en enfer.

(XLIV)

Marie, kiss me; no, don't kiss me, but draw out my heart with your sweet breath; no, don't draw it out, but out of each vein suck from me my whole soul so that it flows out in your embrace.

No, don't suck it out; for after my death what would I be except an empty phantom without a body, on the shore where love (forgive me for saying so, Pluto) does not engage in its frolics except in fantasy?

While we are alive, let's love each other, Marie; Love does not reign over the pallid troop of the dead, whose eyes are sealed in a long, ironbound slumber.

It's a lie that Pluto loved Proserpina, for such a sweet torment cannot penetrate such an unfeeling breast; Love reigns on earth and not in the Underworld.

29 Amourette

Or' que l'hyver roidist la glace épesse,
Réchaufon nous ma gentile maistresse,
Non acroupis pres le fouyer cendreux,
Mais aux plaisirs des combats amoureux.
Assison-nous sur ceste molle couche:
Sus baisez-moy, tendez-moy vostre bouche,
Pressez mon col de vos bras despliez,
Et maintenant vostre mere oubliez.

Que de la dent vostre tetin je morde,
10   Que vos cheveux fil à fil je destorde:
Il ne faut point, en si folastres jeux,
Comme au dimenche arrenger ses cheveux.

Approchez donc, tournez-moy vostre joue.
Vous rougissez? il faut que je me joue.
Vous sou-riez: avez-vous point ouy
Quelque doux mot qui vous ait resjouy?
Je vous disois que la main j'allois mettre
Sur vostre sein: le voulez-vous permettre?
Ne fuyez pas sans parler: je voy bien
20   À vos regards que vous le voulez bien.

Love Song

Now that winter is hardening the thick ice, let us warm ourselves up, my sweet mistress, not by crouching in front of the ash-strewn hearth, but with the pleasures of amorous combat. Let us sit on this soft couch; come here, kiss me, give me your mouth, clasp my neck with opened arms, and now forget your mother.

Let me nibble your breast with my teeth, let me uncoil your hair strand by strand; it's not necessary, for such frolicsome sport, to arrange your hair as you do on Sunday.

Come closer then, turn your cheek towards me. Are you blushing? I must have my fun. You are smiling; have you perhaps heard some sweet word that has delighted you? I was saying to you that I was going to put my hand on your breast; will you allow that? Don't run away without a word. I can see quite well from your glances

Je vous cognois en voyant vostre mine.
Je jure Amour que vous estes si fine,
Que pour mourir, de bouche ne diriez
Qu'on vous baisast bien que le desiriez:
Car toute fille encor' qu'elle ait envie
Du jeu d'aimer desire estre ravie.
Tesmoin en est Helene qui suivit
D'un franc vouloir Pâris qui la ravit.
   Je veux user d'une douce main forte.
Hà vous tombez: vous faites ja la morte.   30
Hà quel plaisir dans le cœur je reçoy:
Sans vous baiser vous mocqueriez de moy
En vostre lit quand vous seriez seulette.
Or sus c'est fait, ma gentille brunette:
Recommençon à fin que nos beaux ans
Soyent reschauffez de combats si plaisans.

that you really want it. I know what you want by looking at your face. I swear by Love that you are so sly that, even on pain of death, you would not say in words that I should kiss you, even though you wanted me to; for every girl, even if she longs for the game of love, desires to be ravished. Witness Helen, who of her own free will followed Paris, who ravished her.

I want to use a gentle force. Oh, you are swooning; you are already imitating death. Oh, what pleasure fills my heart; if I did not kiss you, you would mock me when you were all alone in your bed. Come now, it's done, my pretty little dark-haired girl; let's start again, so that our best years may be warmed by such delightful combat.

30 [VI: pièce retranchée en 1578]

Je vous envoye un bouquet, que ma main
Vient de trier de ces fleurs épanies,
Qui ne les eust à ce vespre cueillies,
Cheutes à terre elles fussent demain.

Cela vous soit un exemple certain
Que vos beautez, bien qu'elles soient fleuries,
En peu de tems cherront toutes fletries,
Et comme fleurs, periront tout soudain.

Le tems s'en va, le tems s'en va, ma Dame,
Las! le tems non, mais nous nous en allons,
Et tost serons estendus sous la lame:

Et des amours, desquelles nous parlons,
Quand serons morts, n'en sera plus nouvelle:
Pour-ce aimez moy, ce pendant qu'estes belle.

[VI: suppressed in 1578]

I am sending you a posy, which I have just selected with my own hand from these blossoming flowers; if they had not been gathered this evening, they would have fallen on the ground tomorrow.

Take this as a clear example that your beauties, although they are in full bloom, in a short time will wither away and fall, and, like flowers, will perish in an instant.

Time passes, time passes, my Lady; alas! not time, but we, we pass away, and soon we shall be stretched out beneath a tombstone;

and when we are dead, no more will be heard of the love we are speaking of; therefore love me, while you are still beautiful.

SUR LA MORT DE MARIE

31 (IV)

Comme on voit sur la branche au mois de May la rose
En sa belle jeunesse, en sa premiere fleur,
Rendre le ciel jaloux de sa vive couleur,
Quand l'Aube de ses pleurs au poinct du jour l'arrose:

La grace dans sa fueille, et l'amour se repose,
Embasmant les jardins et les arbres d'odeur:
Mais batue ou de pluye, ou d'excessive ardeur,
Languissante elle meurt fueille à fueille déclose.

Ainsi en ta premiere et jeune nouveauté,
Quand la terre et le ciel honoroient ta beauté,
La Parque t'a tuee, et cendre tu reposes.

Pour obseques reçoy mes larmes et mes pleurs,
Ce vase plein de laict, ce panier plein de fleurs,
Afin que vif et mort ton corps ne soit que roses.

ON THE DEATH OF MARIE

(IV)

Just as in the month of May we see on its stem the rose in its lovely youthfulness, in its first blooming, making the sky jealous by its vivid colour, when Dawn sprinkles it with her tears at break of day,

grace reposes in its petals as well as love, scenting the gardens and trees with fragrance; but, battered by rain or by excessive heat, languishing it dies, as petal after petal unfolds.

Likewise in your first youthful newness, when heaven and earth honoured your beauty, the Fates have killed you, and as dust you now repose.

For funeral offerings receive my tears and weeping, this bowl full of milk, this basket full of flowers, so that alive and dead your body is nothing but roses.

LE PREMIER LIVRE DES SONNETS
POUR HELENE

32 (III)

Ma douce Helene, non, mais bien ma douce haleine,
Qui froide rafraischis la chaleur de mon cœur,
Je prens de ta vertu cognoissance et vigueur,
Et ton œil comme il veut à son plaisir me meine.

Heureux celuy qui souffre une amoureuse peine
Pour un nom si fatal: heureuse la douleur,
Bien-heureux le torment, qui vient pour la valeur
Des yeux, non pas des yeux, mais de l'astre d'Helene.

Nom, malheur des Troyens, sujet de mon souci,
Ma sage Penelope et mon Helene aussi,
Qui d'un soin amoureux tout le cœur m'envelope:

Nom, qui m'a jusqu'au ciel de la terre enlevé,
Qui eust jamais pensé que j'eusse retrouvé
En une mesme Helene une autre Penelope?

THE FIRST BOOK OF THE SONNETS FOR HELEN

(III)

My sweet Helen, no, rather my sweet inhaling, you who coldly chill the heat of my heart, I draw from your virtues understanding and vigour, and your eyes lead me where they will at their pleasure.

Happy is the man who suffers the pains of love for a name that is so fateful, happy the grief, blessed the torment suffered on account of the power of Helen's eyes, no, not her eyes, but her star.

Name, bane of the Trojans, cause of my anguish, my virtuous Penelope and at the same time my Helen, who envelops my whole heart in an agony of love;

name that has swept me up to heaven from earth, who would ever have thought that I would have encountered in one and the same Helen a second Penelope?

33 (VI)

Dedans les flots d'Amour je n'ay point de support,
Je ne voy point de Phare, et si je ne desire
(Ô desir trop hardy!) sinon que ma Navire
Apres tant de perils puisse gaigner le port.

Las! devant que payer mes vœux dessus le bort,
Naufrage je mourray: car je ne voy reluire
Qu'une flame sur moy, qu'une Helene qui tire
Entre mille rochers ma Navire à la mort.

Je suis seul me noyant de ma vie homicide,
Choisissant un enfant un aveugle pour guide,
Dont il me faut de honte et pleurer et rougir.

Je ne sçay si mes sens, ou si ma raison tasche
De conduire ma nef: mais je sçay qu'il me fasche
De voir un si beau port et n'y pouvoir surgir.

(VI)

Amid the rolling seas of Love I have no protection, I can see no Beacon, and yet I desire nothing except (O desire that is too bold!) that my Ship, after so many perils, may reach the port.

Alas! before I can make my votive offerings upon the shore, I shall be shipwrecked and die, for I see only one blazing light shining over me, only one Helen who amid a thousand rocks is luring my Ship to death.

I am alone and drowning, the murderer of my own life, because I have chosen a child, a blind boy, as my guide, for which I must weep and blush with shame.

I do not know whether my senses or whether my reason is striving to steer my boat, but I know that it grieves me to see such a beautiful port and be unable to surge forward to enter it.

34 (ix)

L'autre jour que j'estois sur le haut d'un degré,
Passant tu m'advisas, et me tournant la veue,
Tu m'esblouïs les yeux, tant j'avois l'ame esmeue
De me voir en sursaut de tes yeux rencontré.

Ton regard dans le cœur, dans le sang m'est entré
Comme un esclat de foudre alors qu'il fend la nue:
J'euz de froid et de chaud la fiévre continue,
D'un si poignant regard mortellement outré.

Lors si ta belle main passant ne m'eust fait signe,
Main blanche, qui se vante estre fille d'un Cygne,
Je fusse mort, Helene, aux rayons de tes yeux:

Mais ton signe retint l'ame presque ravie,
Ton œil se contenta d'estre victorieux,
Ta main se resjouyt de me donner la vie.

(ix)

The other day when I was at the top of a flight of stairs, you caught sight of me as you were passing by, and, turning your gaze towards me, you dazzled my eyes, so deeply was my soul stirred by the shock of finding myself the focus of your eyes.

Your look penetrated my heart, my blood, like a flash of lightning when it rends the clouds; I turned hot and cold with an unremitting fever, mortally wounded by such a piercing look.

Then, if you had not in passing by made me a sign with your lovely hand, with your white hand, you who boast of being the daughter of a Swan, I would have died, Helen, from the rays from your eyes;

but your sign saved my soul, which had almost been snatched away; your eye was pleased to be victorious, but your hand rejoiced in giving me life.

35 (xix)

Tant de fois s'appointer, tant de fois se fascher,
Tant de fois rompre ensemble et puis se renouer,
Tantost blasmer Amour et tantost le louer,
Tant de fois se fuyr, tant de fois se chercher,

Tant de fois se monstrer, tant de fois se cacher,
Tantost se mettre au joug, tantost le secouer,
Advouer sa promesse et la desadvouer,
Sont signes que l'Amour de pres nous vient toucher.

L'inconstance amoureuse est marque d'amitié.
Si donc tout à la fois avoir haine et pitié,
Jurer, se parjurer, sermens faicts et desfaicts,

Esperer sans espoir, confort sans reconfort,
Sont vrais signes d'amour, nous entr'aimons bien fort:
Car nous avons tousjours ou la guerre, ou la paix.

(xix)

On so many occasions making peace, on so many occasions quarrelling, on so many occasions breaking with each other, and then making it up again; now denouncing Love and now extolling him, on so many occasions avoiding each other, on so many occasions seeking each other out;

on so many occasions revealing ourselves, on so many occasions concealing ourselves, now submitting to the yoke, now throwing it off, giving a promise and retracting it, these are signs that Love has struck close at our hearts.

A lover's volatility is the mark of a loving bond. Simultaneously feeling hatred and pity, swearing and forswearing, oaths made and unmade,

hoping without hope, comfort that is no comfort, if these are true signs of love, then we love each other deeply, for we are always either at war or at peace.

36 (XXII)

Puis qu'elle est tout hyver, toute la mesme glace,
Toute neige, et son cœur tout armé de glaçons,
Qui ne m'aime sinon pour avoir mes chansons,
Pourquoy suis-je si fol que je ne m'en delace?

Dequoy me sert son nom, sa grandeur et sa race,
Que d'honneste servage et de belles prisons?
Maistresse, je n'ay pas les cheveux si grisons,
Qu'une autre de bon cœur ne prenne vostre place.

Amour, qui est enfant, ne cele verité.
Vous n'estes si superbe, ou si riche en beauté,
Qu'il faille desdaigner un bon cœur qui vous aime.

R'entrer en mon Avril desormais je ne puis:
Aimez moy, s'il vous plaist, grison comme je suis,
Et je vous aimeray quand vous serez de mesme.

(XXII)

Since she is all winter, all sheer ice, all snow, and her heart armoured all around with icicles, since she loves me only so that she can receive my songs, why am I so foolish that I do not free myself from her?

What good to me is her name, her greatness and her ancestry, other than to provide honourable bondage and beautiful prisons? Beloved, my hair is not so grey that someone else would not take your place with a glad heart.

Love, who is a child, does not conceal the truth. You are not so grand, or so richly endowed with beauty, that you should scorn a true heart that loves you.

I cannot now return to the April of my life; love me, I beg you, grey-haired as I am, and I shall love you when you are in the same state.

37 (XXXIII)

Nous promenant tous seuls, vous me distes, Maistresse,
Qu'un chant vous desplaisoit, s'il estoit doucereux:
Que vous aimiez les plaints des tristes amoureux,
Toute voix lamentable et pleine de tristesse.

Et pource (disiez-vous) quand je suis loin de presse,
Je choisis vos Sonnets qui sont plus douloureux:
Puis d'un chant qui est propre au sujet langoureus,
Ma nature et Amour veulent que je me paisse.

Vos propos sont trompeurs. Si vous aviez souci
De ceux qui ont un cœur larmoyant et transi,
Je vous ferois pitié par une sympathie:

Mais vostre œil cauteleux, trop finement subtil,
Pleure en chantant mes vers, comme le Crocodil,
Pour mieux me desrober par feintise la vie.

(XXXIII)

While we were walking all alone, you said to me, Beloved, that a song did not appeal to you if it was sweet, that you liked the laments of sad lovers, any utterance that is doleful and filled with sadness.

'And for that reason,' you said, 'when I am far from the crowd, I choose the most mournful of your Sonnets; then my nature and Love urge me to find sustenance in a song that is suited to a melancholy subject.'

Your words are hypocritical. If you cared about those who have a sorrowing and stricken heart, I would awaken your pity in sympathy for me;

but your wily eyes, which are too slyly guileful, shed tears while singing my verse, like the Crocodile, the better to rob me of my life by deception.

38 (L)

Bien que l'esprit humain s'enfle par la doctrine
De Platon, qui le vante influxion des cieux,
Si est-ce sans le corps qu'il seroit ocieux,
Et auroit beau louer sa celeste origine.

Par les Sens l'ame voit, ell' oyt, ell' imagine,
Ell' a ses actions du corps officieux:
L'esprit incorporé devient ingenieux,
La matiere le rend plus parfait et plus digne.

Or' vous aimez l'esprit, et sans discretion
Vous dites que des corps les amours sont pollues.
Tel dire n'est sinon qu'imagination

Qui embrasse le faux pour les choses cognues:
Et c'est renouveller la fable d'Ixion,
Qui se paissoit de vent et n'aimoit que des nues.

(L)

Although the human spirit gives itself airs in the doctrine of Plato, who boasts that it is an emanation of the heavens, the fact is that without the body it would remain inert, and would extol its celestial origin in vain.

It is through the Senses that the soul sees, that it hears and that it imagines, it becomes activated through the good offices of the body; when incorporated in a body the spirit becomes inventive, and matter makes it more perfect and more admirable.

Now you love the spirit, and without thinking you say that love is defiled by the body. Such a claim is nothing but imagination,

which embraces what is false instead of things that are known, and it is like reliving the fable about Ixion, whose appetite was satisfied by mere air, and who fell in love with what was only cloud.

39 (LX)

J'attachay des bouquets de cent mille couleurs,
De mes pleurs arrosez harsoir dessus ta porte:
Les larmes sont les fruicts que l'Amour nous apporte,
Les soupirs en la bouche, et au cœur les douleurs.

Les pendant je leur dy, Ne perdés point vos fleurs
Que jusques à demain que la cruelle sorte:
Quand elle passera, tombez de telle sorte
Que son chef soit mouillé de l'humeur de mes pleurs.

Je reviendray demain. Mais si la nuict, qui ronge
Mon cœur, me la donnoit par songe entre mes bras,
Embrassant pour le vray l'idole du mensonge,

Soulé d'un faux plaisir je ne reviendrois pas.
Voyez combien ma vie est pleine de trespas,
Quand tout mon reconfort ne depend que du songe!

(LX)

Over your door last night I fastened bunches of flowers in a hundred thousand
colours, watered by my weeping; tears are the fruits that Love brings us, together
with sighs on our lips, and in our hearts suffering.

As I hung them up I said to them, 'Do not shed your flowers before tomorrow,
when my cruel lady comes out; when she passes beneath you, fall down so that her
head will be wet with the moisture of my tears.

I shall come back tomorrow. But if night, which ravages my heart, were to place
her in my arms in a dream, I would embrace the illusory apparition instead of the
real person,

and sated by a false pleasure I would not come back. See how full of death my
life is, when all my consolation depends solely on a dream!'

LE SECOND LIVRE DES SONNETS
POUR HELENE

40 (I)

Soit qu'un sage amoureux ou soit qu'un sot me lise,
Il ne doit s'esbahir voyant mon chef grison,
Si je chante d'amour: tousjours un vieil tison
Cache un germe de feu sous une cendre grise.

Le bois verd à grand' peine en le souflant s'attise,
Le sec sans le soufler brusle en toute saison.
La Lune se gaigna d'une blanche toison,
Et son vieillard Tithon l'Aurore ne mesprise.

Lecteur, je ne veux estre escolier de Platon,
Qui la vertu nous presche, et ne fait pas de mesme:
Ny volontaire Icare ou lourdaut Phaëthon,

Perdus pour attenter une sotise extrême:
Mais sans me contrefaire ou Voleur ou Charton,
De mon gré je me noye et me brusle moy-mesme.

THE SECOND BOOK OF THE SONNETS FOR HELEN

(I)

Whether a wise lover or whether a fool reads me, he should not be astonished, on seeing my greying head, if I sing of love: an old, smouldering log still conceals a germ of fire beneath grey ashes.

It takes a great effort to make green wood blaze up when you blow on it, while dry wood burns at any time without any blowing. The Moon was won by a white fleece, and Aurora does not disdain her old husband Tithonus.

Reader, I do not want to be a disciple of Plato, who preaches virtue to us, but does not practise it, nor a headstrong Icarus or a dull-witted Phaeton,

who perished because they attempted acts of extreme folly; but without imitating either the Flier or the Charioteer, of my own free will I am both drowning and burning myself.

41 (IX)

Ny la douce pitié, ny le pleur lamentable
Ne t'ont baillé ton nom: ton nom Grec vient d'oster,
De ravir, de tuer, de piller, d'emporter
Mon esprit et mon cœur, ta proye miserable.

Homere en se jouant de toy fist une fable,
Et moy l'histoire au vray. Amour, pour te flater,
Comme tu fis à Troye, au cœur me vient jetter
Le feu qui de mes os se paist insatiable.

La voix, que tu feignois à l'entour du Cheval
Pour decevoir les Grecs, me devoit faire sage:
Mais l'homme de nature est aveugle à son mal,

Qui ne peut se garder ny prevoir son dommage.
Au pis-aller je meurs pour ce beau nom fatal,
Qui mit toute l'Asie et l'Europe en pillage.

(IX)

Neither gentle pity nor sorrowful tears have given you your name: your Greek name comes from seizing, ravishing, killing, pillaging, carrying off my heart and mind as your wretched prey.

Homer amused himself by making up a fable about you, but I have written the true story. Love, to flatter you, has acted as you did in Troy, and kindled in my heart the fire that is insatiably devouring my bones.

The treacherous words you uttered when you were near the Horse, in order to deceive the Greeks, ought to have made me prudent, but man is by nature blind to his peril,

and cannot protect himself nor foresee his misfortune. If the worst comes to the worst, I shall die on account of this fateful name, which caused all Asia and Europe to be laid waste.

42 (XXVI)

Au milieu de la guerre, en un siecle sans foy,
Entre mille procez, est-ce pas grand' folie
D'escrire de l'Amour? De manotes on lie
Les fols qui ne sont pas si furieux que moy.

Grison et maladif r'entrer dessous la loy
D'Amour, ô quelle erreur! Dieux, merci je vous crie.
Tu ne m'es plus Amour, tu m'es une Furie,
Qui me rens fol enfant et sans yeux comme toy:

Voir perdre mon païs, proye des adversaires,
Voir en nos estendars les fleurs de lis contraires,
Voir une Thébaïde et faire l'amoureux!

Je m'en vais au Palais: adieu vieilles Sorcieres!
Muses je prens mon sac, je seray plus heureux
En gaignant mes procez, qu'en suivant vos rivieres.

(XXVI)

In the midst of war, in a century without faith, beset by a thousand lawsuits, is it not great lunacy to write of Love? They put handcuffs on lunatics who are not as raving mad as I am.

Submitting once more to the rule of Love when I am grey-headed and ailing, O what an error that is! You gods, have mercy, I beg of you. To me you are no longer Love, you are a Fury, turning me into a foolish and sightless child like you.

To see my country ruined, a prey to its enemies, to see the lilies of France on our standards in conflict, to see a Theban War and to play the lover!

I am going off to the Law courts; farewell, you old Witches! Muses, I am taking my bag of documents, and I shall be happier if I win my lawsuits than if I follow your streams.

43 (XXXII)

J'avois esté saigné, ma Dame me vint voir
Lors que je languissois d'une humeur froide et lente:
Se tournant vers mon sang, comme toute riante
Me dist en se jouant, Que vostre sang est noir!

Le trop penser en vous a peu si bien mouvoir
L'imagination, que l'ame obeissante
A laissé la chaleur naturelle impuissante
De cuire de nourrir de faire son devoir.

Ne soyez plus si belle, et devenez Medée:
Colorez d'un beau sang ma face ja ridée,
Et d'un nouveau printemps faites moy r'animer.

Æson vit rajeunir son escorce ancienne:
Nul charme ne sçauroit renouveller la mienne.
Si je veux rajeunir il ne faut plus aimer.

(XXXII)

I had been bled, and my Lady came to see me while I was languishing with a cold and lingering humour. Turning to look at my blood, all smiles, she said to me jestingly, 'How black your blood is!

Too much thinking has had the effect on you of stirring up your imagination, so that your obedient soul has left your natural heat powerless to digest, to nourish, or to fulfil its task.'

Cast off your beauty, and become a Medea; with healthy blood bring back the colour into my now wrinkled face, and with a second spring give me new life.

Aeson had his aged skin rejuvenated, but no spell could renew mine. If I want to be rejuvenated, I must stop loving.

44 (XLI)

Laisse de Pharaon la terre Egyptienne,
Terre de servitude, et vien sur le Jourdain:
Laisse moy ceste Court et tout ce fard mondain,
Ta Circe, ta Sirene, et ta magicienne.

Demeure en ta maison pour vivre toute tienne,
Contente toy de peu: l'âge s'enfuit soudain.
Pour trouver ton repos, n'atten point à demain:
N'atten point que l'hyver sur les cheveux te vienne.

Tu ne vois à ta Cour que feintes et soupçons:
Tu vois tourner une heure en cent mille façons:
Tu vois la vertu fausse, et vraye la malice.

Laisse ces honneurs pleins d'un soing ambitieux,
Tu ne verras aux champs que Nymphes et que Dieux,
Je seray ton Orphee, et toy mon Eurydice.

(XLI)

Leave Egypt, land of Pharaohs and land of slavery, and come to the Jordan; leave, I beg you, this Court with all this worldly pretence, your Circe, your Siren and your sorceress.

Stay at home and live in total liberty, be content with little, for time is slipping swiftly away. To find your peace, do not wait for tomorrow; do not wait until winter whitens your hair.

You see nothing at your Court but hypocrisy and suspicion; you see in one hour a hundred thousand twists and turns; you see virtue made false and evil-doing made true.

Leave behind those honours, which are full of ambitious concerns. In the country-side you will see only Nymphs and Gods; I shall be your Orpheus and you my Eurydice.

45 (XLII)

Ces longues nuicts d'hyver, où la Lune ocieuse
Tourne si lentement son char tout à l'entour,
Où le Coq si tardif nous annonce le jour,
Où la nuict semble un an à l'ame soucieuse:

Je fusse mort d'ennuy sans ta forme douteuse,
Qui vient par une feinte alleger mon amour,
Et faisant toute nue entre mes bras sejour,
Me pipe doucement d'une joye menteuse.

Vraye tu es farouche, et fiere en cruauté:
De toy fausse on jouyst en toute privauté.
Pres ton mort je m'endors, pres de luy je repose:

Rien ne m'est refusé. Le bon sommeil ainsi
Abuse par le faux mon amoureux souci.
S'abuser en amour n'est pas mauvaise chose.

(XLII)

During these long winter nights, when the slothful Moon drives her chariot round so slowly on her circular course, when the Cock so tardily announces the day, when the night seems like a year to the troubled soul,

I would have died of misery, had it not been for your shadowy shape, which comes to soothe my love by an illusion, and, nestling completely naked in my arms, sweetly deceives me with a specious joy.

The real you is fierce and pitilessly cruel; the false you can be enjoyed in the utmost intimacy. Beside your spectral image I fall asleep, beside it I find rest;

nothing is refused me. Thus kindly sleep deludes my lovesick pain by a false substitute. Deluding oneself in love is no bad thing.

46 (XLIII)

Quand vous serez bien vieille, au soir à la chandelle,
Assise aupres du feu, devidant et filant,
Direz chantant mes vers, en vous esmerveillant,
Ronsard me celebroit du temps que j'estois belle.

Lors vous n'aurez servante oyant telle nouvelle,
Desja sous le labeur à demy sommeillant,
Qui au bruit de mon nom ne s'aille resveillant,
Benissant vostre nom de louange immortelle.

Je seray sous la terre et fantôme sans os
Par les ombres myrteux je prendray mon repos:
Vous serez au fouyer une vieille accroupie,

Regrettant mon amour et vostre fier desdain.
Vivez, si m'en croyez, n'attendez à demain:
Cueillez dés aujourd'huy les roses de la vie.

(XLIII)

When you are very old, sitting in the evening by candlelight beside the fire, winding
and spinning wool, you will say, full of wonder, as you sing my verses, 'Ronsard
used to celebrate me in the days when I was beautiful.'

Then no maid of yours, on hearing those words, even if she is already half-asleep
from her toils, will fail to wake up at the sound of my name, and bless your name
with immortal praise.

I shall be beneath the earth and, a bodiless phantom, I shall be taking my rest in
the myrtle groves of the Underworld; you will be an old woman hunched over the
hearth,

lamenting my love and your cruel disdain. Live now, listen to me, do not wait
until tomorrow: pluck this very day the roses of life.

47 (XLIX)

Le soir qu'Amour vous fist en la salle descendre
Pour danser d'artifice un beau ballet d'Amour,
Vos yeux, bien qu'il fust nuict, ramenerent le jour,
Tant ils sceurent d'esclairs par la place respandre.

Le ballet fut divin, qui se souloit reprendre,
Se rompre se refaire, et tour dessus retour
Se mesler s'escarter se tourner à l'entour,
Contre-imitant le cours du fleuve de Meandre:

Ores il estoit rond ores long or' estroit,
Or' en poincte en triangle en la façon qu'on voit
L'escadron de la Grue evitant la froidure.

Je faux, tu ne dansois, mais ton pied voletoit
Sur le haut de la terre: aussi ton corps s'estoit
Transformé pour ce soir en divine nature.

(XLIX)

On the evening when Love drew you down into the ballroom to dance with exquisite art a beautiful ballet of Love, although it was night your eyes restored the day, so abundant were the beams of light they flashed across the room.

The ballet was divine, as time after time it resumed, separated, re-formed, and circling back and forth merged, parted and turned about and about, imitating the course of the river Meander.

Now it was round, now long, now narrow, now coming to a point; forming a triangle, in the shape of a flight of Cranes seen escaping from the cold season.

No, I'm wrong, you were not dancing, rather your feet were fluttering above the surface of the ground; for your body had been transformed for that evening into a divine essence.

48 (LVII)

De Myrte et de Laurier fueille à fueille enserrez
Helene entrelassant une belle Couronne,
M'appella par mon nom: Voyla que je vous donne,
De moy seule, Ronsard, l'escrivain vous serez.

Amour qui l'escoutoit, de ses traicts acerez
Me pousse Helene au cœur, et son Chantre m'ordonne:
Qu'un sujet si fertil vostre plume n'estonne:
Plus l'argument est grand, plus Cygne vous mourrez.

Ainsi me dist Amour, me frappant de ses ailes:
Son arc fist un grand bruit, les fueilles eternelles
Du Myrte je senty sur mon chef tressaillir.

Adieu Muses adieu, vostre faveur me laisse:
Helene est mon Parnasse: ayant telle Maistresse,
Le Laurier est à moy je ne sçaurois faillir.

(LVII)

Helen, who was weaving a beautiful crown of Myrtle and Laurel entwined leaf with leaf, called me by my name: 'See what I am giving you; you will be my writer, Ronsard, mine alone.'

Love, who was listening to her, thrust Helen into my heart with his piercing arrows, and appointed me as her Bard: 'Do not let such a fruitful subject paralyse your pen: the greater the subject matter, the greater your swan-like glory when you die.'

That is what Love said to me, striking me with his wings; his bow made a loud noise, and I felt the everlasting leaves of the Myrtle quiver on my head.

Farewell, Muses, farewell, your favours are forsaking me. Helen is now my Parnassus: with such a Mistress, the Laurel is mine and I cannot fail.

49 (LXV)

Je ne serois marry si tu contois ma peine,
De conter tes degrez recontez tant de fois:
Tu loges au sommet du Palais de nos Rois:
Olympe n'avoit pas la cyme si hautaine.

Je pers à chaque marche et le pouls et l'haleine:
J'ay la sueur au front, j'ay l'estomac penthois,
Pour ouyr un nenny un refus une vois,
De desdain de froideur et d'orgueil toute pleine.

Tu es comme Deesse assise en tres-haut lieu.
Pour monter en ton ciel je ne suis pas un Dieu.
Je feray de la court ma plainte coustumiere,

T'envoyant jusqu'en haut mon cœur devotieux.
Ainsi les hommes font à Jupiter priere:
Les hommes sont en terre, et Jupiter aux cieux.

(LXV)

I would not be sorry, if you were counting my sufferings, to count the steps of your staircase, which I have counted and recounted so often. You are housed at the top of the Palace of our Kings; even the summit of Mount Olympus was not so high.

At each step I lose my breath and my pulse races; sweat covers my brow, gasps rack my chest, all so that I can hear a firm no, a refusal, a voice utterly filled with disdain, coldness and haughtiness.

You are like a Goddess seated in a very high place. I am not a God who can climb up to your heaven. I shall voice my customary lamentation from the courtyard,

sending up to you on high my devoted heart. In the same way men direct their prayers to Jupiter: men are on earth and Jupiter in the heavens.

50 Elegie

Six ans estoient coulez, et la septiesme annee
Estoit presques entiere en ses pas retournee,[1]
Quand loin d'affection, de desir et d'amour,
En pure liberté je passois tout le jour,
Et franc de tout soucy qui les ames devore,
Je dormois dés le soir jusqu'au point de l'aurore.
Car seul maistre de moy j'allois plein de loisir,
Où le pied me portoit, conduit de mon desir,
Ayant tousjours és mains pour me servir de guide
Aristote ou Platon, ou le docte Euripide,[2]   10
Mes bons hostes muets, qui ne faschent jamais:
Ainsi que je les prens, ainsi je les remais.
Ô douce compagnie et utile et honneste!
Un autre en caquetant m'estourdiroit la teste.

    Puis du livre ennuyé, je regardois les fleurs,
Fueilles tiges rameaux especes et couleurs,
Et l'entrecoupement de leurs formes diverses,
Peintes de cent façons, jaunes rouges et perses,

Elegy

Six years had elapsed and the seventh year had almost completed its cycle, returning over its footsteps, when far removed from passion, desire and love I used to spend the whole day in total liberty and, free from all cares that devour our souls, used to sleep from evening until break of dawn. For, sole master of myself, I used to go at my leisure wherever my feet carried me, led by my wishes, always having in my hands, to serve as my guides, Aristotle, Plato or learned Euripides, my good, silent guests, who never displease; as freely as I pick them up, so freely do I put them down again. O sweet company, useful and honourable! Anyone else would numb my brain by prattling.

    Then, tiring of books, I would look at the flowers, their leaves, stems, side-shoots, their different varieties and colours, and the intermingling of their diverse shapes, painted in a hundred ways, yellows, reds and blues, unable to get my fill of marvelling

Ne me pouvant saouler, ainsi qu'en un tableau,
20 D'admirer la Nature, et ce qu'elle a de beau:
Et de dire en parlant aux fleurettes escloses:
»Celuy est presque Dieu qui cognoist toutes choses,
Esloigné du vulgaire, et loin des courtizans,
De fraude et de malice impudens artizans.

Tantost j'errois seulet par les forests sauvages
Sur les bords enjonchez des peinturez rivages,
Tantost par les rochers reculez et deserts,
Tantost par les taillis, verte maison des cerfs.

J'aimois le cours suivy d'une longue riviere,
30 Et voir onde sur onde allonger sa carriere,
Et flot à l'autre flot en roulant s'attacher,
Et pendu sur le bord me plaisoit d'y pescher,
Estant plus resjouy d'une chasse muette
Troubler des escaillez la demeure secrette,
Tirer avecq' la ligne en tremblant emporté
Le credule poisson prins a l'haim apasté,
Qu'un grand Prince n'est aise ayant prins à la chasse
Un cerf qu'en haletant tout un jour il pourchasse.[3]
Heureux, si vous eussiez d'un mutuel esmoy
40 Prins l'apast amoureux aussi bien comme moy,

at Nature and her beauties, as if they were in a picture; and I would say, as I addressed the blossoming flowers, "A man is almost God, if he knows all things", if he is removed from the common herd, and is far from courtiers, who are the shameless artisans of deceit and malice.

Sometimes I roamed all alone through the wild forests, over the rush-covered fringes of the painted river banks, sometimes among isolated and deserted rocks, sometimes through thickets, green home of the deer.

I loved the continuous flow of a long river, and the sight of billow after billow prolonging its course, and one wave joining another wave as it rolled on; and, leaning forward from the bank, I enjoyed fishing there, invading the secret domain of the scaly race, pulling with my line and carrying away all aquiver the unwary fish caught on the baited hook; and the delight I derived from this silent hunt was more intense than the pleasure a great Prince derives from capturing in the chase a stag that he has breathlessly pursued all day long. I would have been happy if, with a shared emotion, you as well as I had taken the amorous bait, which I alone

Que tout seul j'avallay, quand par trop desireuse
Mon ame en vos yeux beut la poison amoureuse.

    Puis alors que Vesper vient embrunir nos yeux,
Attaché dans le ciel je contemple les cieux,
En qui Dieu nous escrit en notes non obscures
Les sorts et les destins de toutes creatures.
Car luy, en desdaignant (comme font les humains)
D'avoir encre et papier et plume entre les mains,
Par les astres du ciel qui sont ses characteres,
Les choses nous predit et bonnes et contraires: 50
Mais les hommes chargez de terre et du trespas
Mesprisent tel escrit, et ne le lisent pas.[4]
Or le plus de mon bien pour decevoir ma peine,
C'est de boire à longs traits les eaux de la fontaine
Qui de vostre beau nom se brave, et en courant
Par les prez vos honneurs va tousjours murmurant,
Et la Royne se dit des eaux de la contree:[5]
Tant vault le gentil soin d'une Muse sacree,
Qui peult vaincre la mort, et les sorts inconstans,
Sinon pour tout jamais, au moins pour un long temps.   60
Là couché dessus l'herbe en mes discours je pense
Que pour aimer beaucoup j'ay peu de recompense,

swallowed, when in an excess of desire my soul drank the amorous poison from your eyes.

    Then, when the evening star brings darkness to our eyes, fixing my gaze on the sky I contemplate the heavens, where God writes for us in signs that are plain to see the fates and destinies of all creatures. For he, not deigning to take paper and pen and ink in his hands (as humans do), predicts for us by means of the stars in the sky, which are his symbols, events both good and adverse; but men, burdened with earthly dust and with death, despise such writings and do not read them. Now what helps me most to beguile my suffering is to drink long draughts of the waters of the fountain that boasts your beautiful name, and running through the meadows constantly murmurs your virtues, and calls itself Queen of the waters of this land: such is the value of the kindly care of a sacred Muse, who can vanquish death and the inconstant fates, if not for ever, at least for a long period. Lying there on the grass, thinking aloud, I reflect that I reap little reward for loving deeply, and that

Et que mettre son cœur aux Dames si avant,
C'est vouloir peindre en l'onde et arrester le vent:
M'asseurant toutefois qu'alors que le vieil âge
Aura comme un sorcier changé vostre visage,
Et lors que vos cheveux deviendront argentez,
Et que vos yeux, d'amour ne seront plus hantez,
Que tousjours vous aurez, si quelque soin vous touche,
70   En l'esprit mes escrits, mon nom en vostre bouche.
    Maintenant que voicy l'an septiéme venir,
Ne pensez plus Helene en vos laqs me tenir.
La raison m'en delivre, et vostre rigueur dure,
Puis il fault que mon age obeysse à Nature.

revealing one's heart so freely to Ladies is like trying to paint the waves and curb the wind; however, I reassure myself with the thought that when old age like a sorcerer has changed your face, and when your hair turns silver, and when your eyes are no longer frequented by love, you will still, if you have any feeling at all, have in your mind my writings, my name on your lips.

    Now that the seventh year is approaching, do not think, Helen, that you can keep me in your snares any longer. Reason sets me free, as does your harsh cruelty; moreover, my age is obliged to obey Nature.

51 (LXXV)

Je m'enfuy du combat, mon armee est desfaite:
J'ay perdu contre Amour la force et la raison:
Ja dix lustres passez, et ja mon poil grison
M'appellent au logis et sonnent la retraite.

Si comme je voulois ta gloire n'est parfaite,
N'en blasme point l'esprit, mais blasme la saison:
Je ne suis ny Pâris, ni desloyal Jason:
J'obeis à la loy que la Nature a faite.

Entre l'aigre et le doux, l'esperance et la peur,
Amour dedans ma forge a poly cest ouvrage.
Je ne me plains du mal, du temps ny du labeur,

Je me plains de moymesme et de ton faux courage.
Tu t'en repentiras, si tu as un bon cœur,
Mais le tard repentir n'amande le dommage.

(LXXV)

I flee from the battle, my army is routed; in my war against Love I have lost my strength and my reason; already the fifty years that have passed and already my greying hairs are calling me home and sounding the retreat.

If my glorification of you has not been fully accomplished as I wished, do not blame my willing spirit for that, but blame the season of my life; I am neither Paris nor faithless Jason: I am obeying the law that Nature has ordained.

Between bitterness and sweetness, hope and fear, Love has perfected this work of art in my smithy. I do not lament the pain, the time or the toil;

I lament over myself and your perfidious character. You will repent of it, if you are kind-hearted, but repentance that comes too late does not make amends for the injury.

SONNETS À DIVERSES PERSONNES

52 (LVII)

Je vous donne des œufs. L'œuf en sa forme ronde
Semble au Ciel, qui peut tout en ses bras enfermer,
Le feu, l'air et la terre, et l'humeur de la mer,
Et sans estre comprins comprend tout en ce monde.

La taye semble à l'air, et la glere feconde
Semble à la mer qui fait toutes choses germer:
L'aubin ressemble au feu qui peut tout animer,
La coque en pesanteur comme la terre abonde.

Et le Ciel et les œufs de blancheur sont couvers.
Je vous donne (en donnant un œuf) tout l'Univers:
Divin est le present, s'il vous est agreable.

Mais bien qu'il soit parfait, il ne peut egaler
Vostre perfection qui n'a point de semblable,
Dont les Dieux seulement sont dignes de parler.

SONNETS TO VARIOUS PEOPLE

(LVII)

I am giving you some eggs. An egg, with its round shape, resembles the Sky, which can enfold everything in its embrace, fire, air and earth, and the watery humour of the sea, and, without being encompassed, encompasses everything in this world.

The membrane resembles the air, and the fertile white resembles the sea, which is the source of all germination, and the yolk resembles fire, which animates everything; the shell like the earth has considerable weight.

Both Sky and eggs have a white surface. I am giving you the whole Universe (by giving an egg): the present is a divine one, if it is pleasing to you.

However, although it is perfect, it cannot equal your perfection, which has no parallel, and of which the Gods alone are worthy to speak.

53 [LX: pièce ajoutée en 1587]

Vous estes deja vieille, et je le suis aussi.
Joignon nostre vieillesse et l'accollon ensemble,
Et faison d'un hyver qui de froidure tremble
(Autant que nous pourrons) un printemps adouci.

Un homme n'est point vieil s'il ne le croit ainsi:
Vieillard n'est qui ne veut: qui ne veut, il assemble
Une nouvelle trame à sa vieille: et ressemble
Un serpent rajeuni quand l'an retourne ici.

Ostez moy de ce fard l'impudente encrousture,
On ne sçauroit tromper la loy de la nature,
Ny derider un front condamné du miroir,

Ni durcir un tetin desja pendant et flasque.
Le Temps de vostre face arrachera le masque,
Et deviendray un Cygne en lieu d'un Corbeau noir.

[LX: added in 1587]

You are already old, and so am I. Let us unite our old age and embrace it together, and out of a winter that shivers with cold let us make (as far as we can) a milder spring.

A man is not old if he does not think he is: no one is an old man if he does not want to be; if he does not want to be, he weaves a new strand into his old fabric, and resembles a rejuvenated snake when the year turns full circle.

Take off those brazen layers of make-up; it's no use trying to cheat the laws of nature, or to smooth the wrinkles of a forehead that is condemned by the mirror,

or to give back its firmness to a breast that is already sagging and flabby. Time will tear the mask from your face, while I shall become a Swan instead of a black Crow.

54 [LXI: pièce ajoutée en 1587]

Que je serois marry si tu m'avois donné
Le loyer qu'un Amant demande à sa Maistresse!
Alors que tout mon sang bouillonnoit de jeunesse
Tous mes desirs estoient de m'en veoir guerdonné.

Maintenant que mon poil est du tout grisonné,
J'abhorre en y pensant moy mesme et ma fadesse,
Qui servis si long temps pour un bien qui se laisse
Pourrir en un sepulchre aux vers abandonné.

Enchanté, je servis une vieille carcasse,
Un squelette seiché, une impudente face,
Une qui n'a plaisir qu'en amoureux transi.

Bonne la loy de Cypre, où la fille au rivage
(Embrassant un chacun) gaignoit son mariage,
Sans laisser tant languir un amant en souci.

[LXI: added in 1587]

How vexed I should be if you had given me the reward that a Lover asks of his Lady! When all my blood seethed with youth, all my desires were fixed on receiving that as my recompense.

Now that my hair is completely grey, I abominate, when I think about it, my foolishness and myself, who served for so long to gain a possession that is left to rot in a tomb, abandoned to the worms.

Bewitched, I served an old carcass, a desiccated skeleton, a brazen face, a person who takes no pleasure except in a swooning lover.

The custom of Cyprus was a good one, whereby a girl went along the shore (embracing all the men) and thus earned money for her dowry, and so did not leave a lover to languish so long in misery.

LES ODES

55 À Michel de l'Hospital, Chancelier de France

[...]

Strophe 11
Donne nous, mon pere, dit-elle,[1]
Pere, dit-elle, donne nous
Que nostre chanson immortelle
Passe en douceur le sucre dous:
Fay nous Princesses des montagnes,
Des antres, des eaux et des bois,
Et que les prez et les campagnes
S'animent dessous nostre vois:
Donne nous encor d'avantage
La tourbe des chantres divins,   350
Les Poëtes et les Devins,
Et les Prophetes en partage.

Antistrophe
Fay que les vertueux miracles
Des vers charmez et enchantez
Soyent à nous, et que les oracles
Par nous encore soyent chantez:

THE ODES

To Michel de l'Hospital, Chancellor of France

[...] *Strophe 11* 'Grant us, Father dear,' she says, 'Father,' she says, 'grant that our immortal song may surpass sweet sugar in its sweetness. Make us Princesses of the mountains, of the caves, the waters and the woods, and make the pastures and meadows come alive at the sound of our voices. Grant us especially as our birthright the further gift of the host of divine bards, the Poets and Seers and Prophets.

Antistrophe 'May we have as our own the miraculous powers of spellbinding, enchanted poetry, and furthermore may we be the ones to chant the oracles. Grant

Donne nous ceste double grace
De fouler l'Enfer odieux,
Et de sçavoir la courbe trace
360   Des feux qui dancent par les Cieux:
Donne nous encor la puissance
D'arracher les ames dehors
Le sale bourbier de leurs corps,
Pour les re-joindre à leur naissance.[2]

Epode
Donne nous que les Seigneurs,
Les Empereurs et les Princes
Soyent veus Dieux en leurs provinces,
S'ils reverent nos honneurs.
   Fay que les Rois decorez
370   De nos presens honorez
Soyent aux hommes admirables,
Lors qu'ils vont par la cité,
Ou lors que pleins d'equité
Donnent les loix venerables.

Strophe 12
À-tant acheva sa requeste,
Courbant les genoux humblement,
Que Jupin d'un seul clin de teste
Accorda liberalement.

us this double blessing, that we may tread underfoot the horrors of Hell, and understand the curving path of the fires that dance across the Heavens. Grant us also the power to pluck souls out of the filthy mire of their bodies, in order to restore them to their birthplace.

Epode 'Grant us that Lords, Emperors and Princes may be considered Gods in their domains, if they respect the honours due to us. Make the Kings, on whom we bestow our revered presents, worthy of admiration in the eyes of the people, as they pass through the city, or when, imbued with justice, they promulgate wise laws.'

Strophe 12 Thereupon, humbly kneeling, she concluded her request, to which Jupiter, with a single inclination of his head, beneficently acceded. 'If all the mortal

Si toutes les femmes mortelles
Que je donte dessous mes bras, 380
Me concevoyent des filles telles,
(Dit-il) il ne me chaudroit pas
Ny de Junon ny de sa rage:
Tousjours pour me faire honteux,
M'enfante ou des monstres boiteux,[3]
Ou des fils de mauvais courage,

Antistrophe
Comme Mars: mais vous troupe chere,
Que j'aime trop plus que mes yeux,
Je vous plantay dans vostre mere
Pour plaire aux hommes et aux Dieux. 390
Sus donques retournez au monde,
Coupez moy de rechef les flos,
Et là d'une langue faconde
Chantez ma gloire et vostre los:
Vostre mestier, race gentille,
Les autres mestiers passera,
D'autant qu'esclave il ne sera
De l'art aux Muses inutile.

women whom I seduce with my embraces conceived daughters such as these,' he said, 'I should not care about Juno or her fury: to shame me, she always bears me either limping monsters or evil-natured sons,

Antistrophe 'like Mars; but you, my beloved band, whom I love far more than life itself, I planted you inside your mother to delight both men and Gods. Arise then, return to the world, cleave once more the waves, and there with eloquent tongue hymn my glory and your renown. Your craft, O noble breed, will surpass other crafts, inasmuch as it will not be the slave of technical skill, which is of no use to the Muses.

Epode

Par art le navigateur
400   Dans la mer manie et vire
La bride de son navire:
Par art plaide l'Orateur,
Par art les Rois sont guerriers,
Par art se font les ouvriers:
Mais si vaine experience
Vous n'aurez de tel erreur,
Sans plus ma sainte fureur
Polira vostre science.[4]

Strophe 13

Comme l'Aimant sa force inspire
410   Au fer qui le touche de pres,
Puis soudain ce fer tiré tire
Un autre qui en tire apres:
Ainsi du bon fils de Latonne
Je raviray l'esprit à moy,
Luy, du pouvoir que je luy donne,
Ravira les vostres à soy:
Vous par la force Apollinée
Ravirez les Poëtes saints,
Eux de vostre puissance attaints
420   Raviront la tourbe estonnée.[5]

Epode 'Through technical skill the navigator at sea controls and pulls the reins of his ship; through technical skill the Orator pleads his case, through technical skill Kings become warriors, through technical skill artisans learn their trade; but you will not have the sterile experience of such an aberration, because my divine fury will suffice to perfect your erudition.

Strophe 13 'Just as the Magnet communicates its force to a piece of iron that comes into close contact with it, and then instantly this iron, which is attracted, attracts another, which attracts others after it, just so shall I ravish the spirit of Latona's noble son, while he in turn, with the power that I give him, will ravish your spirits; you, by the might of Apollo, will ravish the saintly Poets, while they, under the influence of your potency, will ravish the awestruck multitude.

Antistrophe

À fin (ô Destins) qu'il n'avienne
Que le monde appris faussement,
Pense que vostre mestier vienne
D'art, et non de ravissement:
Cest art penible et miserable
S'eslongnera de toutes parts
De vostre mestier honorable
Desmembré en diverses parts,
En Prophetie, en Poësies,
En mysteres et en amour,   430
Quatre fureurs qui tour-à-tour
Chatouilleront vos fantasies.[6]

Epode

Le traict qui fuit de ma main,
Si tost par l'air ne chemine,
Comme la fureur divine
Vole dans un cœur humain,
Pourveu qu'il soit preparé,
Pur de vice, et reparé
De la vertu precieuse.
»Jamais les Dieux qui sont bons   440
»Ne respandent leurs saints dons
»Dans une ame vicieuse.

Antistrophe 'So that (O Fates) it does not happen that the world mistakenly thinks your craft comes from technical skill and not from the ravishment of inspiration, this laborious, miserable technical skill will be far removed from all aspects of your honourable craft, which is divided into diverse parts, into Prophecy, Poetry, holy mysteries and love, four furies that each in turn will stimulate your imagination.

Epode 'The bolt that speeds from my hand does not travel through the air as fast as the divine fury flies into a human heart, provided that it is well prepared, free from vice, and adorned with precious virtue. "Never do the Gods, who are good, lavish their holy gifts on a wicked soul."

Strophe 14

Lors que la mienne ravissante
Vous viendra troubler vivement,
D'une poitrine obeïssante
Tremblez dessous son mouvement:
Et souffrez qu'elle vous secoue
Le corps et l'esprit agité,
À fin que Dame elle se joue
450 Au temple de sa Deité.
Elle de toutes vertus pleine,
De mes secrets vous remplira,
Et en vous les accomplira
Sans art, sans sueur ne sans peine.

Antistrophe

Mais par-sur tout prenez bien garde,
Gardez-vous bien de n'employer
Mes presens dans un cœur qui garde
Son peché, sans le nettoyer:
Ains devant que de luy respandre,
460 Purgez-le de vostre douce eau,
À fin que bien net puisse prendre
Un beau don dans un beau vaisseau:

Strophe 14 'When my ravishing fury reaches you and moves you vigorously, with a compliant spirit tremble under the effect of its stimulation; and allow it to stir your body and arouse your mind, so that it can reign in glory like a Queen in the temple of her Godhead. Abounding in all virtues, it will fill you with my secrets, and in you will bring them to fruition without technical skill, without sweat and without struggle.

Antistrophe 'But above all else, take good care, take care not to squander my presens on one whose heart still retains its sinfulness without first cleansing it. Therefore, before bestowing these gifts on him, purify his heart with your sweet water, so that, truly clean, it can receive a fine gift in a fine receptacle; and then,

Et luy purgé, à l'heure à l'heure
Tout ravi d'esprit chantera
Un vers en fureur qui fera
Au cœur des hommes sa demeure.[7]

Epode

Celuy qui sans mon ardeur
Voudra chanter quelque chose,
Il voirra ce qu'il compose
Veuf de grace et de grandeur: 470
Ses vers naistront inutis
Ainsi qu'enfans abortis
Qui ont forcé leur naissance:
»Pour monstrer en chacun lieu
»Que les vers viennent de Dieu,
»Non de l'humaine puissance.

Strophe 15

Ceux que je veux faire Poëtes
Par la grace de ma bonté,
Seront nommez les interpretes
Des Dieux, et de leur volonté: 480
Mais ils seront tout au contraire
Appellez sots et furieux
Par le caquet du populaire
De sa nature injurieux.

when it is purified, suddenly, suddenly, wholly rapt in spirit, he will sing inspired poetry that will dwell in the hearts of men.

Epode 'Anyone who, without my inspiring ardour, tries to sing something will find all he composes is bereft of grace and grandeur; his poetry will be brought forth as futilely as aborted children born before their time. "This shows in every case that poetry comes from God, and not from human power."

Strophe 15 'Those whom I elect to make Poets, in the grace of my goodness, will be called the interpreters of the Gods and their will; but conversely they will be termed foolish and mad by the back-biting populace, whose nature it is to revile.

Tousjours pendra devant leur face
Quelque Demon, qui au besoin
Comme un bon valet, aura soin
De toutes choses qu'on leur face.[8]

Antistrophe
Allez mes filles, il est heure
De fendre les champs escumeux:
Allez ma gloire la meilleure,
Allez mon los le plus fameux:
Vous ne devez dessus la terre
Long temps ceste fois sejourner,
Que l'Ignorance avec sa guerre
Ne vous contraigne retourner,
Pour retomber sous la conduite
D'un guide, dont la docte main
Par un effroy Grec et Romain
Tournera l'Ignorance en fuite.

Epode
À-tant Jupiter enfla
Sa bouche rondement pleine,
Et du vent de son haleine
Son bon esprit leur soufla.

490

500

Always around the Poets will hover some Daemon, who, when needed, will take care of everything that happens to them, like a good servant.

Antistrophe 'Go now, my daughters, it is time to cleave the foamy plains; go now, you who are my greatest glory, go now, my most celebrated renown; you will not stay long on the earth on this occasion, before Ignorance with its hostilities forces you to come back here again, before returning to earth once more, led by a guide whose learned hand will put Ignorance to fearful flight with Greek and Latin.'

Epode Then Jupiter filled his mouth round and full, and with the wind of his

Apres leur avoir donné
Le luth qu'avoit façonné
L'ailé courrier Atlantide,[9]
D'ordre par l'eau s'en-re-vont:
En tranchant l'onde elles font
Ronfler la campagne humide.[10]   510
[. . .]

breath he breathed his good spirit into them. After he gave them the lute that had been fashioned by the winged messenger, the grandson of Atlas, they set off in order through the water; and cutting through the waves they make the watery realm resound.

[. . .]

56 À sa Maistresse

Mignonne, allons voir si la rose
Qui ce matin avoit desclose
Sa robe de pourpre au Soleil,
A point perdu ceste vesprée
Les plis de sa robe pourprée,
Et son teint au vostre pareil.

Las! voyez comme en peu d'espace,
Mignonne, elle a dessus la place
Las las ses beautez laissé cheoir!
Ô vrayment marastre Nature,
Puis qu'une telle fleur ne dure
Que du matin jusques au soir!

Donc, si vous me croyez mignonne,
Tandis que vostre âge fleuronne
En sa plus verte nouveauté,
Cueillez cueillez vostre jeunesse:
Comme à ceste fleur la vieillesse
Fera ternir vostre beauté.

To his Mistress

Beloved, let us go and see if the rose, which this morning had unfurled her crimson gown to the Sun, has not lost this evening the folds of her crimson gown and her complexion that resembles your own.

Alas! See how in a short space of time, beloved, she has shed around her on the ground, alas, alas! her beauteous charms. O Nature, you are a truly unnatural mother, since such a flower lives only from morning until evening!

So, if you will trust me, beloved, while your age is blossoming in its most verdant freshness, gather, gather the bloom of your youth; just as it does to this flower, old age will blight your beauty.

57 'Ô Fontaine Bellerie'

Ô Fontaine Bellerie,
Belle fontaine cherie
De nos Nymphes quand ton eau
Les cache au creux de ta source
Fuyantes le Satyreau,
Qui les pourchasse à la course
Jusqu'au bord de ton ruisseau.

Tu es la Nymphe eternelle
De ma terre paternelle:
Pource en ce pré verdelet   10
Voy ton Poëte qui t'orne
D'un petit chevreau de lait,
À qui l'une et l'autre corne
Sortent du front nouvelet.[1]

L'Esté je dors ou repose
Sus ton herbe, où je compose,
Caché sous tes saules vers,
Je ne sçay quoy, qui ta gloire
Envoira par l'univers,
Commandant à la Memoire   20
Que tu vives par mes vers.

'O Fountain of Bellerie'

O Fountain of Bellerie, lovely fountain beloved of our Nymphs when your waters conceal them in the depths of your spring as they flee from the young Satyr who pursues them, chasing them right up to the brink of your stream.

You are the eternal Nymph of my ancestral land; see, therefore, in this fresh green meadow your Poet, who honours you with a little suckling kid, whose two horns are budding from its youthful brow.

In Summer I sleep or rest on your grassy bank, where, concealed beneath your green willows, I write something that will spread your glory through the universe, bidding Memory to let you live on in my poetry.

L'ardeur de la Canicule[2]
Ton verd rivage ne brule,
Tellement qu'en toutes pars
Ton ombre est espaisse et drue
Aux pasteurs venans des parcs,
Aux bœufs las de la charrue,
Et au bestial espars.

Iô,[3] tu seras sans cesse
Des fontaines la princesse,
Moy celebrant le conduit
Du rocher percé, qui darde
Avec un enroué bruit
L'eau de ta source jazarde
Qui trepillante se suit.

The fierce heat of the Dog days does not burn your green banks, because so deep and dense all around is the shade that you offer to the shepherds coming from the pastures, to the oxen weary from the plough, and to the straying cattle.

Rejoice! You will for ever be the princess of fountains, because I celebrate the stream issuing from the pierced rock, which with a gurgling sound spouts out the water of your babbling spring, which dances along unceasingly.

58 'J'ay l'esprit tout ennuyé'

J'ay l'esprit tout ennuyé
D'avoir trop estudié
Les Phenomenes d'Arate:[1]
Il est temps que je m'esbate,
Et que j'aille aux champs jouer.
Bons Dieux! qui voudroit louer
Ceux qui collez sus un livre
N'ont jamais soucy de vivre?

    Que nous sert l'estudier,
Sinon de nous ennuyer?   10
Et soin dessus soin accroistre
À nous, qui serons peut estre
Ou ce matin, ou ce soir
Victime de l'Orque[2] noir?
De l'Orque qui ne pardonne,
Tant il est fier, à personne.

    Corydon[3] marche davant,
Sçache où le bon vin se vend:
Fay refraischir la bouteille,
Cerche une ombrageuse treille   20
Pour souz elle me coucher:
Ne m'achete point de chair,

'My mind is thoroughly exhausted'

My mind is thoroughly exhausted from too much study of Aratus' *Phaenomena*; it is time I had some fun, and went out into the fields to play. Good Heavens! Who would want to praise those who, glued to a book, never have any interest in living?

What use to us is studying, except to exhaust us? And to pile care upon care on to us, who will perhaps become, either this morning or this evening, the victim of black Orcus? Orcus who is so pitiless that he does not pardon anyone.

Corydon, go on ahead, find out where good wine is on sale; chill the bottle, look for a shady arbour where I can recline; don't buy me any meat, because, however

Car tant soit elle friande,
L'Esté je hay la viande.

    Achete des abricôs,
Des pompons, des artichôs,
Des fraises, et de la crême:
C'est en Esté ce que j'aime,
Quand sur le bord d'un ruisseau
Je la mange au bruit de l'eau,
Estendu sus le rivage,
Ou dans un antre sauvage.

    Ores que je suis dispos
Je veux rire sans repos,
De peur que la maladie
Un de ces jours ne me die,
Je t'ay maintenant veincu:
Meurs galland, c'est trop vescu.

30

---

tasty it may be, I hate meat in Summer.

  Buy apricots, melons, artichokes, strawberries, and some cream – that's what I like in Summer, when, beside a stream, I eat to the sound of the water, stretched out on the bank, or in a lonely cave.

  Now while I am hale and hearty I want to laugh without stopping, for fear that one of these days illness may say to me, 'I have defeated you now: die, my merry friend, you have lived too long.'

59 La Defloration de Lede

Le cruel Amour veinqueur
De ma vie sa sujette,
M'a si bien escrit au cœur
Vostre nom de sa sagette,
Que le temps qui peut casser
Le fer et la pierre dure,
Ne le sçauroit effacer
Qu'en moy vivant il ne dure.

Mon luth qui des bois oyans
Souloit alleger les peines,   10
Las! de mes yeux larmoyans
Ne tarit point les fonteines:
Et le Soleil ne peut voir
Soit quand le jour il apporte,
Ou quand il se couche au soir,
Une autre douleur plus forte.

Mais vostre cœur obstiné,
Et moins pitoyable encore
Que l'Ocean mutiné
Qui baigne la rive More,   20

The Deflowering of Leda

Cruel Love, conqueror of my life, which is now subjected to him, has written your name so deep in my heart with his arrow that time, which can shatter iron and solid rock, would be unable to eradicate it and prevent it from surviving within me while I live.

My lute, which used to ease the sorrows of the listening woods, alas! fails to dry up the fountains of my weeping eyes; and the Sun, either when it is bringing the day, or when it sets in the evening, can see no other grief that is stronger.

Yet your heart, stubborn and less merciful even than the mutinous Ocean that

Ne prend mon service à gré,
Ains a d'immoler envie
Le mien à luy consacré
Des premiers ans de ma vie.

Jupiter espoinçonné
De telle amoureuse rage,
A jadis abandonné
Ciel, throne, femme, mesnage:
Car l'œil qui son cœur estraint,
30   Comme estraints ores nous sommes,
Ce grand Seigneur a contraint
De tenter l'amour des hommes.

Luy porté de son desir,
Naissant d'une flame esprise,
Se laissa d'Amour saisir,
Comme une despouille prise:
Puis il a bras, teste et flanc,
Et sa poitrine cachée
Sous un plumage plus blanc
40   Que le laict sur la jonchée.

washes the Moorish shores, does not welcome my devotion, but wants to sacrifice my heart, which has been dedicated to it since the earliest years of my life.

Jupiter, goaded by just such a madness of love, in times past abandoned heavens, throne, wife and home, because the eye that gripped his heart, as we ourselves are gripped, constrained that great Lord to experience the love of mortals.

He, driven by his desire, which was born of a kindled flame, let himself be seized by Love, like captured spoils; then he concealed arms, head, flanks and his breast beneath plumage whiter than milk curds on a bed of rushes.

En son col mit un carcan
Taillé d'artifice, où l'œuvre
Du laborieux Vulcan
Admirable se descœuvre.
D'or en estoyent les cerceaux
Piolez d'esmail ensemble:
À l'Arc qui verse les eaux
Ce bel ouvrage resemble.

L'or sur la plume reluit
D'une semblable lumiere,   50
Que le clair œil de la nuit
Dessus la neige premiere:
Il fend le chemin des cieux
D'un long branle de ses ailes,
Et d'un voguer spacieux
Tire ses rames nouvelles.

Comme l'aigle fond d'enhaut,
Ouvrant l'espais de la nue,
Sur l'aspic qui leche au chaud
Sa jeunesse revenue:[1]   60

Round his neck he placed a chain, artistically fashioned, where the handiwork of industrious Vulcan is wonderfully revealed. Its round bands were of gold, as well as being enamelled in many colours, for this beautiful work of art resembles the Rainbow that pours down water.

The gold gleams on the feathers with a light resembling the bright eye of the night shining on the first snow; he cuts a path through the skies with a long sweep of his wings, and, sailing in broad-winged flight, plies these new oars.

Just as the eagle, parting the thick clouds, swoops down from a height on the snake which licks its new skin in the warmth, restored to youthfulness, just so did

Ainsi le Cygne voloit
Contre-bas, tant qu'il arrive
Dessus l'estang où souloit
Jouer Lede sur la rive.

Quand le Ciel eut allumé
Le beau jour par les campagnes,
Elle au bord accoustumé
Mena jouer ses compagnes:
Et studieuse des fleurs
70   En sa main un panier porte
Peint de diverses couleurs,
Et d'histoire en mainte sorte.

Seconde Pause

Du haut du panier s'ouvroit
À longues tresses dorées
Une Aurore qui couvroit
Le ciel de fleurs colorées:
Ses cheveux vaguoyent errans
Souflez du vent des narines
Des prochains chevaux tirans
80   Le Soleil des eaux marines.[2]

the Swan fly down until he alighted upon the pool where Leda was in the habit of playing at the water's edge.

When the Sky had spread the lovely light of day across the countryside, she led her companions to play on the familiar banks, and, being intensely fond of picking flowers, she carried in her hand a basket painted with diverse colours and stories of many kinds.

Second Part

On the upper part of the basket there appeared, with long golden tresses, Aurora, who was strewing the sky with colourful flowers; her hair was floating about here and there, blown by the wind from the nostrils of the nearby horses, which were pulling the Sun up out of the waters of the sea.

Ainsi qu'au ciel fait son tour
Par sa voye courbe et torte,
Il tourne tout à l'entour
De l'anse en semblable sorte:
Les nerfs s'enflent aux chevaux,
Et leur puissance indontée
Se roidist sous les travaux
De la penible montée.

La mer est peinte plus bas,
L'eau ride si bien sur elle, 90
Qu'un pescheur ne ni'roit pas
Qu'elle ne fust naturelle:
Ce Soleil tombant au soir
Dedans l'onde voisine entre,
À chef bas se laissant cheoir
Jusqu'au fond de ce grand ventre.

Sur le sourci d'un rocher
Un pasteur le loup regarde,
Qui se haste d'approcher
Du couard peuple qu'il garde: 100
Mais de cela ne luy chaut,
Tant un limas luy agrée,
Qui lentement monte au haut
D'un liz au bas de la prée.

Just as he pursues his course in the sky along his curving, twisting path, he twines right round the handle in like fashion; the horses' sinews swell, and their untamed power stiffens with the exertion of the strenuous ascent.

The sea is painted lower down, and the water is rippling on it so convincingly that even a fisherman would not doubt that it was real; this Sun, setting in the evening, is slipping into the water nearby, letting himself plunge headlong into the depths of this great womb-like abyss.

On the brow of a rock, a shepherd sees the wolf as it hurries towards the cowardly flock he is watching over; but he does not care about that, so fascinated is he by a snail that is slowly climbing to the top of a lily down below in the meadow.

Un Satyre tout follet
Larron, en folastrant tire
La panetiere et le laict
D'un autre follet Satyre:
L'un court apres tout ireux,
L'autre defend sa despouille,
Le laict se verse sur eux
Qui sein et menton leur souille.

Deux beliers qui se hurtoyent
Le haut de leurs testes dures,
Portraits aux deux bords estoyent
Pour la fin de ses peintures.
Tel panier en ses mains mist
Lede qui sa troupe excelle,
Le jour qu'un oiseau la fist
Femme en lieu d'une pucelle.

L'une arrache d'un doy blanc
Du beau Narcisse les larmes,
Et la lettre teinte au sang
Du Grec marry pour les armes:

A very playful, thieving Satyr is playing the fool, and making off with another playful Satyr's bag and his milk; the one runs after the other in a great rage, the other defends his prize, the milk spills over them, and soils their chests and chins.

Two rams, which were butting each other with the tops of their hard heads, were portrayed on the two edges to complete the pictures. Such a basket did Leda, who outshone her companions, take in her hands, on the day that a bird made her a woman instead of a maiden.

One of the girls with her white fingers plucks the tears of handsome Narcissus, and the letter dyed with the blood of the Greek who was angry about the armour;

De crainte l'œillet vermeil
Pallist entre ces pillardes,
Et la fleur que toy Soleil
Des cieux encor' tu regardes.[3]

À l'envi sont ja cueillis
Les verds thresors de la plaine,   130
Les bassinets et les lis,
La rose, et la marjolaine:
Quand la vierge dit ainsi
(Laissant la rose odorante
Et la belle fueille aussi
De l'immortel amaranthe):

Allon troupeau bien-heureux
Que j'aime d'amour naïve,
Ouyr l'oiseau douloureux
Qui se plaint sur nostre rive.   140
Et elle en hastant ses pas
Court par l'herbe d'un pied vîte:
Sa troupe ne la suit pas,
Tant sa carriere est subite.

amid these pillagers the scarlet carnation turns pale from fright, and so does the
flower that you, Sun, are ever watching from the skies.

In a spirit of rivalry now are picked the green treasures of the meadow, buttercups
and lilies, rose and marjoram; then the maiden speaks these words (leaving the
fragrant rose as well as the lovely petal of the immortal amaranth):

'Let us go, happy band that I love with a sincere love, to hear the sorrowful bird
that is lamenting on our shore.' And she, quickening her steps, runs fleet-footed
over the grass; her band does not follow her, so rapidly does she dart away.

Du bord luy tendit la main,
Et l'oiseau qui tressaut d'aise,
S'en approche tout humain
Et le blanc yvoire baise:
Ores l'adultere oiseau
150 Au bord par les fleurs se joue,
Et ores au haut de l'eau
Tout mignard pres d'elle noue.

Puis d'une gaye façon
Courbe au doz l'une et l'autre aile,
Et au bruit de sa chanson
Il apprivoise la belle:
La nicette en son giron
Reçoit les flames secrettes,
Faisant tout à l'environ
160 Du Cygne un lict de fleurettes.

Luy qui fut si gracieux,
Voyant son heure opportune,
Devint plus audacieux
Prenant au poil la fortune:[4]
De son col comme ondes long
Le sein de la vierge touche,
Et son bec luy mit adonc
Dedans sa vermeille bouche.

From the water's edge she holds out her hand to the bird, and he, trembling with pleasure, approaches, human-like, and kisses the white ivory; now the adulterous bird frolics at the water's edge among the flowers, and now upon the water he swims very sweetly beside her.

Then seductively he curves both wings over his back, and with the sound of his song he tames the lovely girl; the simple child takes on to her lap the concealed flames of his passion, making a bed of flowers all around the Swan.

He, who had been so gentle, seeing a favourable opportunity, grew bolder, seizing fortune by the forelock; with his long, rippling neck he touched the maiden's breast, and then placed his beak inside her scarlet mouth.

Il va ses ergots dressant
Sur les bras d'elle qu'il serre,   170
Et de son ventre pressant
Contraint la rebelle à terre.
Sous l'oiseau se debat fort,
Le pince et le mord, si est-ce
Qu'au milieu de tel effort
Sentit ravir sa jeunesse.

Le cinabre çà et là
Couloura la vergongneuse:
À la fin elle parla
D'une bouche desdaigneuse: 180
D'où es-tu trompeur volant,
D'où viens-tu, qui as l'audace
D'aller ainsi violant
Les filles de noble race?

Je cuidoy ton cœur, helas!
Semblable à l'habit qu'il porte,
Mais (hé pauvrette) tu l'as
À mon dam, d'une autre sorte.

He rears up on his feet and clasps her arms tightly, and, pressing her with his stomach, forces the rebellious girl to the ground. Beneath the bird she struggles vigorously, pinches him and bites him, but nevertheless in the midst of such efforts she felt her youth being ravished.

Patches of bright cinnabar-red coloured the face of the bashful girl; at last she spoke in a disdainful voice: 'Where are you from, you winged deceiver, where have you come from, you who have the audacity to go about violating the daughters of noble families?

I thought your heart, alas! was like the outward appearance that clothes it, but (oh, poor wretch that I am) it is my misfortune that it is quite different. O you

Ô ciel qui mes cris entens,
190 Morte puissé-je estre enclose
Là bas, puis que mon printemps
Est despouillé de sa rose.

Plus tost vien pour me manger
Ô veufve tigre affamee,
Que d'un oysel estranger
Je sois la femme nommée.
Ses membres tombent peu forts,
Et dedans la mort voisine
Ses yeux ja nouoyent, alors
200 Que luy respondit le Cygne:

Troisiesme Pause

Vierge, dit-il, je ne suis
Ce qu'à me voir il te semble,
Plus grande chose je puis
Qu'un Cygne à qui je resemble:
Je suis le maistre des cieux,
Je suis celuy qui deserre
Le tonnerre audacieux
Sur les durs flancs de la terre.

heavens who hear my cries, may I die and be confined in the Underworld, since my springtime has been despoiled of its rose.

Come and devour me, O you ravenous tigress bereft of your mate, rather than let me be called the wife of an alien bird.' Her limbs drooped limply, and her eyes were already drifting towards an impending death, when the Swan replied to her:
Third Part

'Maiden,' he said, 'I am not what I appear to be; I am capable of much greater things than the Swan I resemble; I am the master of the heavens, I am he who lets loose the fearless thunder over the firm haunches of the earth.

La contraignante douleur
Du tien plus chaud qui m'allume,   210
M'a fait prendre la couleur
De ceste non mienne plume.
Ne te va donc obstinant
Contre l'heur de ta fortune,
Tu seras incontinant
La belle sœur de Neptune:⁵

Et si tu pondras deux œufs
De ma semence feconde,
Ainçois deux triomphes neufs
Futurs ornemens du monde:⁶   220
L'un, deux jumeaux esclorra,
Pollux vaillant à l'escrime,
Et son frere qui aura
Sur tous Chevaliers l'estime:

Dedans l'autre germera
La beauté au ciel choisie,
Pour qui un jour s'armera
L'Europe contre l'Asie.
À ces mots ell' se consent
Recevant telle avanture,   230
Et ja de peu à peu sent
Haute eslever sa ceinture.

'The overpowering pain caused by your warmer body, which sets me on fire, has made me take on the colour of this plumage, which is not my own. So do not go on stubbornly resisting your good fortune; you will become forthwith the sister-in-law of Neptune;

'and moreover with my fertile seed you will lay two eggs, or rather two new glorious triumphs, future ornaments of the world; one will hatch twin boys: Pollux, a valiant wrestler, and his brother, who will be esteemed above all Horsemen;

'inside the other will grow the beauty chosen in heaven, for whose sake one day Europe will take arms against Asia.' At these words she yields, accepting such a fate, and already she feels her girdle gradually rising higher.

60 De l'election de son sepulchre

Antres, et vous fontaines
De ces roches hautaines
Qui tombez contre-bas
    D'un glissant pas:

Et vous forests et ondes
Par ces prez vagabondes,
Et vous rives et bois
    Oyez ma vois.

Quand le ciel et mon heure
Jugeront que je meure,
Ravy du beau sejour
    Du commun jour,

Je defens qu'on ne rompe
Le marbre pour la pompe
De vouloir mon tombeau
    Bastir plus beau:

On the Choice of his Burial Place

Caves, and you fountains, who cascade down from these lofty rocks with a gliding motion,

   and you forests and streams winding through these meadows, and you riverbanks and woods, hear my words.

   When heaven and my time judge that I should die and be snatched away from the beautiful domain of the common light of day,

   I forbid anyone to hew marble, out of a grandiose wish to build me a more beautiful tomb;

94

Mais bien je veux qu'un arbre
M'ombrage en lieu d'un marbre,
Arbre qui soit couvert
      Tousjours de vert.   20

De moy puisse la terre
Engendrer un lierre,
M'embrassant en maint tour
      Tout à l'entour:

Et la vigne tortisse
Mon sepulcre embellisse,
Faisant de toutes pars
      Un ombre espars.

Là viendront chaque année
À ma feste ordonnée   30
Avecques leurs troupeaux
      Les pastoureaux:

Puis ayant fait l'office
De leur beau sacrifice,
Parlans à l'isle ainsi
      Diront ceci:

but rather I want a tree to give me shade instead of a marble monument, a tree forever covered in green.

May the earth engender from me an ivy plant that will enfold me with many twists, twining all about;

and may the spiralling vine adorn my burial place, casting all around a spreading shade.

There every year on my ordained feast day the young shepherds will come with their flocks;

then, after performing the ceremony of their handsome sacrifice, speaking thus to the island, they will say:

Que tu es renommée
D'estre tombeau nommée
D'un, de qui l'univers
        Chante les vers!

40

Et qui onq en sa vie
Ne fut bruslé d'envie,
Mendiant les honneurs
        Des grands Seigneurs!

Ny ne r'apprist l'usage
De l'amoureux breuvage,
Ny l'art des anciens
        Magiciens!

Mais bien à noz campagnes
Fist voir les Sœurs compagnes[1]
Foulantes l'herbe aux sons
        De ses chansons,

50

Car il fist à sa lyre
Si bons accords eslire,
Qu'il orna de ses chants
        Nous et noz champs.

'How renowned you are for being appointed to be the tomb of one whose verses are sung by the whole universe!

'One who never in his life was consumed by envy, or begged for honours from great Lords!

'Nor who revived the use of love potions, nor the arts of the Magicians of old!

'But who instead introduced to our meadows the company of the Sisters trampling the grass to the sounds of his songs,

'for he caused his lyre to select such pleasing chords that he graced with his singing both us and our fields.

La douce manne tombe
À jamais sur ma tumbe,
Et l'humeur que produit
    En May la nuit.   60

Tout à l'entour l'emmure
L'herbe et l'eau qui murmure,
L'un tousjours verdoyant,
    L'autre ondoyant.

Et nous ayans memoire
Du renom de sa gloire,
Luy ferons comme à Pan
    Honneur chaque an.

Ainsi dira la troupe,
Versant de mainte coupe   70
Le sang d'un agnelet
    Avec du laict

Desur moy, qui à l'heure
Seray par la demeure
Où les heureux espris
    Ont leur pourpris.[2]

'Let sweet manna, and the moisture that night produces in May, forever fall on my tomb.

'Let it be enclosed on all sides by grass and by murmuring water, the one always verdant, the other rippling.

'And we, remembering the renown of his glory, will pay honour to him every year as we do to Pan.'

Thus will speak the band of shepherds, as they pour from many a chalice the blood of a young lamb mixed with milk

over me, who at that time will be in the abode where the blessed spirits have their home.

La gresle ne la neige
N'ont tels lieux pour leur siege,
Ne la foudre oncque là
        Ne devala:

Mais bien constante y dure
L'immortelle verdure,
Et constant en tout temps
        Le beau Printemps.

Le soin qui sollicite
Les Rois, ne les incite
Le monde ruiner
        Pour dominer:

Ains comme freres vivent,
Et morts encore suivent
Les mestiers qu'ils avoient
        Quand ils vivoient.

Là là j'oiray d'Alcée
La lyre courroucée,
Et Sapphon qui sur tous
        Sonne plus dous.

Neither hail nor snow have their dwelling in such places, nor did lightning ever strike there,

but most constantly does the everlasting verdure remain there, and constantly so too at all times does lovely Spring.

The troublesome cares that afflict Kings do not drive those spirits to ruin the world in order to dominate it;

instead they live like brothers, and after their death still pursue the trades they plied in their lifetime.

There, O there, I shall hear Alcaeus' warlike lyre, and Sappho, who sings more sweetly than all others.

Combien ceux qui entendent
Les chansons qu'ils respandent,
Se doivent resjouir
      De les ouir?   100

Quand la peine receue
Du rocher est deceue,
Et quand le vieil Tantal'
      N'endure mal?[3]

»La seule lyre douce
»L'ennuy des cœurs repousse,
»Et va l'esprit flatant
      »De l'escoutant.

How greatly must those who listen to the songs that they utter rejoice at hearing them,

when even the torment caused by the boulder is beguiled, and when even old Tantalus suffers no distress?

"The sweet lyre alone drives out affliction from men's hearts, and soothes the mind of the listener."

61 À Guy Pacate

Guy, noz meilleurs ans coulent
Comme les eaux qui roulent
D'un cours sempiternel:
La mort pour sa sequelle
Nous ameine avec elle
Un exil eternel.

Nulle humaine priere
Ne repousse en arriere
Le bateau de Charon,
Quand l'ame nue arrive
Vagabonde en la rive
De Styx et d'Acheron.

»Toutes choses mondaines
»Qui vestent nerfs et veines,
»La Mort egale prend,
»Soient pauvres, ou soient Princes:
Dessus toutes provinces
Sa main large s'estend.

To Guy Pacate

Guy, our best years glide past like waters that roll on with a never-ending movement; death in her train brings with her an everlasting exile for us.

No human prayer can repel and drive back Charon's boat, when the naked soul, aimlessly wandering, reaches the banks of the Styx and the Acheron.

"All earthly things that are endowed with nerves and veins are taken by Death the leveller, be they poor, or be they Princes"; her broad hand spreads over all realms.

La puissance tant forte
Du grand Achille est morte,   20
Et Thersite odieux
Aux Grecs, est mort encores:
Et Minos qui est ores
Le conseiller des Dieux.

»Jupiter ne demande
»Que des bœufs pour offrande:
»Mais son frere Pluton
»Nous demande nous hommes,
»Qui la victime sommes
»De son enfer glouton.   30

Celuy dont le Pau baigne
Le tombeau, nous enseigne
N'esperer rien de haut,
Et celuy que Pegase
(Qui fit sourcer Parnase)
Culbuta si grand saut.[1]

»Las! on ne peut cognoistre
»Le destin qui doit naistre,
»Et l'homme en vain poursuit
»Conjecturer la chose,   40
»Que Dieu sage tient close
»Sous une obscure nuit.

The might of great Achilles, powerful as it was, is dead, and Thersites, hated by
the Greeks, is dead, too; and also Minos, who is now the counsellor of the Gods.

"Jupiter asks only for cattle as an offering; but his brother Pluto asks for us, us
men, who are the sacrificial victims of his voracious hell."

He whose tomb is washed by the river Po teaches us not to aspire to anything
excessive, as does he whom Pegasus (who caused Parnassus to produce a spring)
threw off, inflicting such a great fall.

"Alas! one cannot know the destiny that must come to pass, and man seeks in
vain to divine that which God in his wisdom keeps buried in murky darkness."

Je pensois que la trope
Que guide Calliope,
(Trope mon seul confort)
Soustiendroit ma querelle,
Et qu'indonté, par elle
Je donteroy la mort:

Mais une fiévre grosse
50   Creuse desja ma fosse
Pour me bannir là bas,
Et sa flame cruelle
Se paist de ma mouelle,
Miserable repas.

Que peu s'en faut, ma vie,
Que tu ne m'es ravie
Close sous le tombeau!
Et que mort je ne voye
Où Mercure convoye
60   Le debile troupeau!

Et Alcé, qui les peines
Dont les guerres sont pleines
Va là bas racontant,

I thought that the band of Muses that Calliope leads (the band which is my sole comfort) would uphold my cause, and that, unconquered, with their help I would conquer death;

but a grievous fever is already digging my grave in order to banish me below, and its cruel fire is feeding on my very marrow – a miserable repast.

How very close you are, my life, to being snatched away from me and sealed in a tomb! How very close I am to dying and journeying to where Mercury escorts the frail flock!

And Alcaeus, who roams the Underworld recounting the woes that wars are full

Alcée qu'une presse
Des espaules espesse,
Admire en l'escoutant.

À bon droit Promethée
Pour sa fraude inventée
Endure un tourment tel,
Qu'un aigle sur la roche   70
Luy ronge d'un bec croche
Le poumon immortel.

Depuis qu'il eut robée
La flame prohibée
Pour les Dieux despiter,
Les bandes incognues
De fiévres sont venues
Nostre terre habiter:

Et la Mort despiteuse
Au-paravant boiteuse   80
Fut legere d'aller.
D'ailes mal-ordonnées
Aux hommes non données
Dedale coupa l'air.[2]

of, Alcaeus, marvelled at by a dense throng, pressed shoulder to shoulder, as they listen to him.

Prometheus deservedly, because of the crime he devised, endures a torment whereby on the rock an eagle gnaws his indestructible lungs with its hooked beak.

After he had stolen the forbidden fire in order to defy the Gods, hitherto unknown troops of fevers came to inhabit our earth;

and defiant Death, which used to come with halting steps, became swiftly moving. With badly fashioned wings, which men are not permitted to possess, Daedalus cut a course through the air.

La maudite Pandore
Fut forgée, et encore
Astrée s'en-vola,
Et la boete feconde
Peupla le pauvre monde
De tant de maux qu'il a.[3]

Ah! le meschant courage
Des hommes de nostre âge
N'endure par ses faits,
Que Jupiter estuye
Sa foudre, qui s'ennuye
De voir tant de mesfaits.

Accursed Pandora was created, and moreover Astraea took flight, and the fertile box populated the poor world with the many ills it now is home to.

Oh! by their deeds the evil-hearted men of our age prevent Jupiter from sheathing his thunderbolt, for he is incensed at seeing so many misdeeds.

62 'Bel aubepin fleurissant'

Bel aubepin fleurissant,
    Verdissant
Le long de ce beau rivage,
Tu es vestu jusqu'au bas
    Des longs bras
D'une lambrunche sauvage.

Deux camps de rouges fourmis
    Se sont mis
En garnison sous ta souche:
Dans les pertuis de ton tronc   10
    Tout du long
Les avettes ont leur couche.

Le chantre Rossignolet
    Nouvelet,
Courtisant sa bien-aimée,
Pour ses amours alleger
    Vient loger
Tous les ans en ta ramée.

'Lovely hawthorn, blossoming'

Lovely hawthorn, blossoming, flourishing greenly along this lovely riverbank, you are clad from top to toe in the long tendrils of a wild vine.

Two armies of red ants are garrisoned beneath your roots; in the cracks down the length of your trunk the bees make their home.

The Nightingale, youthful little songster, when he is wooing his beloved, in order to ease the pain of love takes up residence every year in your leafy boughs.

Sur ta cime il fait son ny
       Tout uny
De mousse et de fine soye,
Où ses petits esclorront,
       Qui seront
De mes mains la douce proye.

Or vy gentil Aubepin,
       Vy sans fin,
Vy sans que jamais tonnerre,
Ou la coignée, ou les vents,
       Ou les temps
Te puissent ruer par terre.

On your topmost branch he makes his nest, smoothly finished with moss and fine silk, where his little ones will hatch, which will become the sweet prey of my hands.

So live, dear Hawthorn, live everlastingly, live without thunder, or the axe, or winds, or time ever being able to dash you to the ground.

63 'Pourquoy comme une jeune poutre'

Pourquoy comme une jeune poutre
De travers guignes-tu vers moy?
Pourquoy farouche fuis-tu outre
Quand je veux approcher de toy?

Tu ne veux souffrir qu'on te touche:
Mais si je t'avoy sous ma main,
Asseure toy que dans la bouche
Bien tost je t'aurois mis le frain.

Puis te voltant à toute bride
Je dresserois tes pieds au cours, 10
Et te piquant serois ton guide
Dans la carriere des amours.

Mais par l'herbe tu ne fais ores
Que suivre des prez la fraicheur,
Pource que tu n'as point encores
Trouvé quelque bon chevaucheur.

'Why, like a young filly'

Why, like a young filly, do you glance sidelong at me? Why do you, as if untamed, bolt when I try to come near you?

You will not let anyone touch you; but if I could lay hands on you, you can be sure that I would very soon have put the bit in your mouth.

Then, making you twist and turn at speed, I would teach you to gallop, and, spurring you on, I would be your trainer in the riding school of love.

But at present, wandering over the grass, all you do is seek the freshness of the meadows, because you have not yet found a good rider.

64 À sa Muse

Plus dur que fer j'ay finy cest ouvrage,
Que l'an dispos à demener les pas,
Que l'eau rongearde, ou des freres la rage,[1]
Qui rompent tout, ne ru'ront point à bas.
Le mesme jour que le dernier trespas
M'assoupira d'un somme dur, à l'heure
Sous le tombeau tout Ronsard n'ira pas,
Restant de luy la part qui est meilleure.

   Tousjours tousjours, sans que jamais je meure,
10   Je voleray tout vif par l'Univers,
Eternisant les champs où je demeure
De mes Lauriers honorez et couvers:
Pour avoir joint les deux Harpeurs divers[2]
Au doux babil de ma lyre d'yvoire,
Qui se sont faits Vandomois par mes vers.

   Sus donque, Muse, emporte au ciel la gloire
Que j'ay gaignée, annonçant la victoire
Dont à bon droit je me voy jouyssant:
Et de Ronsard consacre la memoire,
20   Ornant son front d'un Laurier verdissant.

To his Muse

I have finished this work, more durable than iron, which the years eager to sweep away our steps, which water's eroding force or the brothers' fury will not hurl down to perdition, although these things destroy everything. On the very day when death will finally put me to sleep in a heavy slumber, at that moment the whole of Ronsard will not go to the grave, since the better part of him will survive.

Evermore, evermore, without ever dying, I shall soar, a living spirit, through the Universe, immortalizing the fields where I live, which I have glorified and adorned with my Laurels, having united in the sweet murmur of my ivory lyre the two quite different Bards, who now belong to Vendôme through my poetry.

Come then, Muse, carry aloft to the heavens the glory I have won, proclaiming the victory that is rightfully mine to enjoy; and consecrate the memory of Ronsard, garlanding his brow with verdant Laurel.

LE BOCAGE ROYAL

65 Discours du Verre

Ceux que les Sœurs aimeront plus que moy,
Comme un d'Aurat, d'un vers digne de toy
Feront sçavoir aux nations lointaines
De tes vertus les louanges hautaines:
Quant est de moy, je n'oseroy, Brinon,
Sur mon espaule eslever ton renom
Pour engarder que la mort ne l'enterre:
Il me suffist si l'honneur d'un seul verre
Lequel tu m'as pour estreines donné,
Est dignement en mes vers blasonné.   10

Ô gentil verre, oseroy-je bien dire
Combien je t'aime, et combien je t'admire?
Tu es heureux, et plus heureux celuy
Qui t'inventa pour noyer nostre ennuy!
Ceux qui jadis les Canons inventerent,
Et qui d'enfer le fer nous apporterent,
Meritoient bien que là bas Rhadamant
Les tourmentast d'un juste chastiment:

ROYAL MEDLEY

Discourse on a Glass

Those whom the Sisters love more than me, people such as Dorat, will broadcast the exalted praises of your virtues to distant nations in verse worthy of you. As far as I am concerned, I shall not dare, Brinon, to hoist your reputation on to my shoulder to ensure that death does not bury it. It is enough for me if the honour of a single glass, which you gave me as a New Year present, is worthily celebrated in my verses.

O noble glass, shall I really dare to tell how much I love you, and how much I admire you? You are blessed, and even more blessed is he who invented you to drown our sorrows! Those who in earlier times invented Cannons, and those who brought us iron from the Underworld, thoroughly deserved to be tortured down there, justly punished by Rhadamanthus; but the inventor who, with a lively mind,

Mais l'inventeur, qui d'un esprit agile
Te façonna, fust-ce le grand Virgile,
Ou les Nochers qui firent sans landiers
Cuire leur rost sur les bords mariniers,[1]
Meritoient bien de bailler en la place
De Ganymede à Jupiter la tasse,
Et que leur verre aussi transparent qu'eau
Se fist au ciel un bel Astre nouveau.
  Non, ce n'est moy qui blasme Promethée
D'avoir la flame à Jupiter ostée:
Il fist tres bien: sans le larcin du feu,
Verre gentil, jamais on ne t'eust veu,
Et seulement par les bois les Fougeres
Eussent servy à nos vieilles Sorcieres.[2]
Aussi vrayment c'estoit bien la raison
Qu'un feu venant de si bonne maison
Comme est le ciel, fust la cause premiere,
Verre gentil, de te mettre en lumiere,
Toy retenant comme celestiel
Le rond, le creux, et la couleur du ciel:
Toy, dy-je toy, le joyau delectable
Qui sers les Dieux et les Rois à la table,
Qui aimes mieux en pieces t'en-aller
Qu'à ton Seigneur la poison receler:

fashioned you, whether it was great Virgil, or the Sailors who cooked their roast without trivets on the seashores, that inventor thoroughly deserved to offer the cup to Jupiter in place of Ganymede, and to have the glass, which is as transparent as water, made into a beautiful new Star in the sky.

No, I am not one to blame Prometheus for stealing the flame from Jupiter: he did very well. Without the theft of fire, noble glass, we should never have seen you, and the Ferns in the woods would have been of use only to our old Witches. So it was truly altogether appropriate that fire, coming from such a good home as the sky, should be the original cause, noble glass, of bringing you to light, since like something celestial you retain the roundness, the concavity and the colour of the sky; you, I say, you, delightful jewel who serve the Gods and Kings at table, who prefer to shatter into pieces rather than to conceal poison from your Lord; you, companion of joyful

Toy compagnon de Venus la joyeuse,
Toy qui guaris la tristesse espineuse,
Toy de Bacchus et des Graces le soin,
Toy qui l'amy ne laisses au besoin,
Toy qui dans l'œil nous fais couler le somme,
Toy qui fais naistre à la teste de l'homme
Un front cornu,[3] toy qui nous changes, toy
Qui fais au soir d'un Crocheteur un Roy.   50

    Aux cœurs chetifs tu remets l'esperance,
La verité tu mets en evidence,[4]
Le laboureur songe par toy de nuict
Que de ses champs de fin or est le fruict:
Et le pescheur qui ne dort qu'à grand'peine,
Songe par toy que sa nacelle est pleine
De poissons d'or, et le dur Bucheron
Ses fagots d'or, son plant le vigneron.

    Mais contemplons de combien tu surpasses,
Verre gentil, ces monstrueuses tasses,   60
Et fust-ce celle horrible masse d'or,
Que le vieillard Gerinean Nestor
Boivoit d'un trait, et que nul de la bande
N'eust sceu lever, tant sa panse estoit grande.[5]

Venus, you who cure irksome sadness, you the concern of Bacchus and the Graces; you who do not abandon your friend in need; you who cause slumber to glide into our eyes; you who cause horns to sprout on a man's head; you who cause us to change; you who make a Porter into a King in the evening.

    You restore hope to the faint-hearted, you reveal the truth, through you the ploughman dreams at night that the fruits of his fields are pure gold; and through you the fisherman, who finds it difficult to sleep, dreams that his little boat is full of fish of gold, the rugged Woodcutter that his logs are of gold, the wine grower his vine.

    But, noble glass, let us contemplate how far you surpass those monstrous goblets, and even that fearsome mass of gold that the old Gerenian, Nestor, drained in one draught, which none of his band could have lifted, so great was the capacity of its belly.

Premierement devant que les tirer
Hors de leur mine, il faut plus deschirer
L'antique mere, et cent fois en une heure
Craindre le heurt d'une voute mal-seure:
Puis quand cest or par fonte et par marteaux
70   Laborieux, s'arrondist en vaisseaux,
Tout cizelé des fables poëtiques,
Et buriné de medailles antiques,
Ô Seigneur Dieu! quel plaisir ou quel fruict
Peut-il donner? sinon faire de nuict
Couper la gorge à ceux qui le possedent,
Ou d'irriter quand les peres decedent,
Les heritiers à cent mille procez,
Ou bien à table, apres dix mille excez,
Lors que le vin sans raison nous delaisse,
80   Faire casser par sa grosseur espaisse
Le chef de ceux qui n'agueres amis,
Entre les pots deviennent ennemis?
Comme jadis apres trop boire firent
Les Lapithois, qui les monstres desfirent
Demy-chevaux:[6] Mais toy verre joly,
Loin de tout meurtre, en te voyant poly,
Net, beau, luisant, tu es plus agreable
Qu'un vaisseau d'or, lourd fardeau de la table:

First of all, before these goblets are pulled out of their mine, it is necessary to rip apart their ancient mother earth again, and to fear a hundred times in an hour the collapse of an insecure roof; then when this gold, by casting and by diligent hammering, is rounded into vessels, chased all over with poetic fables, and engraved with ancient medallions, O Lord God, what pleasure or profit can it give, except to cause those who possess it to have their throats cut in the night, or to infuriate heirs with a hundred thousand lawsuits after their fathers have died, or else at table, after ten thousand excesses, when wine deprives us of reason, to smash with its heavy weight the skulls of those who, though formerly friends, become enemies in their cups? Just as long ago the Lapiths did, when, after drinking too much, they slaughtered the monsters who were half-horse. But you, pretty glass, who are remote from all murder, when I see you polished, clean, beautiful, gleaming, you are more attractive than a vessel of gold, that heavy burden of the table; and if you were not

Et si n'estois aux hommes si commun
Comme tu es, par miracle un chacun   90
T'estimeroit de plus grande value
Qu'un diamant, ou qu'une perle eslue.

C'est un plaisir que de voir r'enfrongné
Un grand Cyclope à l'œuvre embesongné,[7]
Qui te parfait de cendres de fougere,
Et du seul vent de son haleine ouvriere.

Comme l'esprit enclos dans l'univers
Engendre seul mille genres divers,
Et seul en tout mille especes diverses,
Au ciel, en terre, et dans les ondes perses: 100
Ainsi le vent par qui tu es formé,
De l'artizan en la bouche enfermé,
Large, petit, creux ou grand, te façonne
Selon l'esprit et le feu qu'il te donne.[8]

Que diray plus? par espreuve je croy
Que Bacchus fut jadis lavé dans toy,
Lors que sa mere attainte de la foudre,
En avorta plein de sang et de poudre:[9]
Et que dés lors quelque reste de feu
Te demeura: car quiconques a beu   110

so commonly possessed by men as you are, miraculously everyone would estimate your value as higher than a diamond, or a choice pearl.

It is a pleasure to see toiling at his creation a huge, frowning Cyclops, who is bringing you to perfection out of fern ash, with the wind of his creative breath alone.

Just as the animating spirit infused into the universe engenders alone a thousand different genera, and alone a thousand different species in all, in the sky, on earth, and in the azure waves, just so the wind by which you are formed, which is enclosed in the mouth of the craftsman, fashions you to be wide, small, hollow or large, according to the amount of spirit and fire that he gives you.

What more shall I say? From experience I believe that long ago Bacchus was washed in you, when his mother, struck by the thunderbolt, miscarried him covered with blood and dust, and that since then some vestige of fire has remained in you; for anyone who has drunk a draught from you, throughout his life the more he

Un coup dans toy, tout le temps de sa vie
Plus y re-boit, plus a de boire envie,
Et de Bacchus tousjours le feu cruel
Ard son gozier d'un chaud continuel.
   Je te salue heureux Verre propice
Pour l'amitié, et pour le sacrifice:
Quiconque soit l'heritier qui t'aura
Quand je mourray, de long temps ne voirra
Son vin ne gras ne poussé dans sa tonne:
Et tous les ans il voirra sur l'Autonne
Bacchus luy rire, et plus que ses voisins
Dans son pressouer gennera de raisins:
Car tu es seul le meilleur heritage
Qui puisse aux miens arriver en partage.

120

drinks of it, the more he wants to drink, and the cruel fire of Bacchus forever burns his throat with a continual heat.

   I salute you, blessed Glass favourable to friendship and sacrificial libations; whoever he may be who will inherit you when I die, he will not soon see his wine grow thick or cloudy in its cask; and every year in Autumn he will see Bacchus smiling on him, and he will crush more grapes in his wine-press than his neighbours; for you are alone the best legacy that can come to my heirs as their allotted share.

LES MASCARADES, COMBATS
ET CARTELS

66 Cartel pour le combat à cheval, en forme de balet

Ces nouveaux Chevaliers par moy vous font entendre[1]
Que leurs premiers ayeuls furent fils de Meandre,
À qui le fleuve apprit à tourner leurs chevaux
Comme il tourne et se vire et se plie en ses eaux.
   Pyrrhe en telle façon sur le tombeau d'Achille
Feit une danse armée, et aux bords de Sicile
Enée en decorant son pere de tournois,
Feit sauter les Troyens au branle du harnois,
Où les jeunes enfans en cent mille manieres
Meslerent les replis de leurs courses guerrieres.   10
   Pallas qui le conduit, a de sa propre main
Façonné leurs chevaux, et leur donna le frein,
Mais plustost un esprit, qui sagement les guide
Par art, obeissant à la loy de la bride.[2]

MASQUERADES, TOURNAMENTS
AND CHALLENGES

Challenge for a Mounted Tournament, in the Form of a Ballet

These Knights now making their entrance inform you, through me, that their earliest ancestors were the sons of Meander, who were taught by the river to turn their horses just as it turns and twists and winds in its waters.

In this fashion Pyrrhus executed an armed dance over the tomb of Achilles, and Aeneas on the shores of Sicily, honouring his father with tournaments, directed the Trojans to perform the armed movements of a war dance in which young boys interlaced the windings of their warlike gallops in a hundred thousand ways.

Pallas, who is guiding them, has schooled the horses with her own hand and given them the bit, or rather a mind, which guides them wisely with artful skill, and makes them obey the rule of the bridle.

Tantost vous les voirrez à courbettes danser,
Tantost se reculer, s'approcher, s'avancer,
S'escarter, s'esloigner, se serrer, se rejoindre
D'une pointe allongée, et tantost d'une moindre,
Contrefaisant la guerre au semblant d'une paix,
20   Croisez, entrelassez de droit et de biais,
Tantost en forme ronde, et tantost en carrée,
Ainsi qu'un Labyrinth, dont la trace esgarée
Nous abuse les pas en ses divers chemins,
    Ainsi qu'on voit danser en la mer les Dauphins,
Ainsi qu'on voit voler par le travers des nues
En diverses façons une troupe de Grues.
Or pour voir nostre siecle, où preside Henry,
En toute discipline honnestement nourry,
Où la perfection de tous mestiers abonde,
30   Autant qu'il est parfaict et le plus grand du monde,
Ces Centaures armez à nostre âge incognus,
Au bruit d'un si haut Prince en France sont venus
Pour les peuples instruire, et les rendre faciles
Autant que sous le frein leurs chevaux sont dociles.
Et faire de son nom tout le monde ravir,
Afin que toute-chose apprenne à le servir.

Now you will see them curvetting as they dance, now retreating, moving closer, advancing, moving apart, moving away, coming together, meeting in an elongated point and now in a shorter one, simulating war in a show of peace, criss-crossing, intersecting, in straight or oblique lines, now in a circular figure and now in a square one, just like a Labyrinth whose confusing trail leads our steps astray by its diverse paths,

just like the Dolphins we see dancing in the sea, just like a company of Cranes we see forming diverse patterns as they fly through the clouds. Now these armed Centaurs, who were unknown to our age, have been drawn to visit our century, which is reigned over by Henry, who is honourably educated in every discipline, and in whom perfection in all skills abounds, so perfect and supreme is he in the world; for hearing of the fame of such a noble Prince they have come to France to instruct the people, and make them as amenable as their horses are docile to the bit, and to ensure that all the world is entranced by the glory of his name, so that all things will learn to serve him.

67 La Mort de Narcisse, en forme d'elegie
À Jean Daurat, son precepteur

Sus, dépan, mon Daurat, de son croc ta Musette,
Qui durant tout l'hyver avoit esté muette,
Et loin du populace allons ouyr la vois
De dix mille oiselets qui se plaignent és bois.

    Ja des monts contre-val les tiedes neiges chéent,
Ja les ouvertes fleurs par les campaignes béent,
Ja l'espineux rosier desplie ses boutons
Au lever du Soleil, qui semblent aux tetons
Des filles de quinze ans, quand le sein leur pommelle,
Et s'eleve bossé d'une enfleure jumelle.   10

    Ja la mer gist couchée en son grand lit espars,
Ja Zephyre murmure, et ja de toutes pars
Calfeutrant son vaisseau, le Nocher hait le sable,
Le pastoureau le feu, et le troupeau l'estable,
Qui desire dés l'Aube aller brouter les prez
Costoyez des ruisseaux aux Naiades sacrez.

THE ELEGIES

The Death of Narcissus, in the Form of an Elegy
To Jean Dorat, his Tutor

Come now, Dorat my friend, take down from their hook your pipes, which have been silent all winter long, and let us go far away from the masses to hear the voices of ten thousand little birds uttering their laments in the woods.

    Now melting snow is sliding down from the mountains, now blossoming flowers are fully open in the countryside, now as the Sun rises the thorny rose bush unfurls its buds, which resemble the nipples of fifteen-year-old girls, when their breasts swell like apples, and develop roundly in twin mounds.

    Now the sea lies outstretched in its large, spacious bed, now Zephyr whispers, and now, caulking his vessel all round, the Boatman spurns the sandy shore, the shepherd boy his fireside and the flock the fold, because it desires to go at Dawn to browse in the meadows bordered by the streams sacred to the Naiads.

Ja l'arbre de Bacchus[1] rampe en sa robbe neuve,
Se pend à ses chévreaux, et ja la forest veuve
Herisse sa perruque, et Cerés du Ciel voit
20   Desja crester le blé qui couronner la doit:
Ja pres du verd buisson, sur les herbes nouvelles,
Tournassent leurs fuseaux les gayes pastourelles,
Et d'un long lerelot aux forests d'alentour
Et aux prochaines eaux racontent leur amour.

    Ceste belle saison me remet en memoire
Le Printemps où Jason, espoinçonné de gloire,
Esleut la fleur de Grece, et de son aviron
Baloya, le premier de Tethys le giron:
Et me remet encor la meurtriere fontaine
30   Par qui le beau Narcis aima son ombre vaine,
Coulpable de sa mort: car pour trop se mirer
Sur le bord estranger, luy convint expirer.

    Une fontaine estoit nette, claire et sans bourbe,
Enceinte à l'environ d'un beau rivage courbe
Tout bigarré d'esmail: là le rosier pourpré,
Le glayeul, et le lis, à Junon consacré,
À l'envi respiroyent une suave haleine,
Et la fleur d'Adonis,[2] jadis la douce peine

Now the plant of Bacchus in its new garments begins to spread, and it is hung on the horns of his goat-kids, and now the bare forest begins to put forth its leafy tresses, and from the Heavens Ceres sees that the corn which is to furnish her crown is already forming ears; now beside the green bushes, on the newly sprung grass, merry young shepherdesses rapidly turn their spindles, and with a long hey-nonny-nonny they tell their love to the surrounding forests and the nearby waters.

This lovely season recalls to my mind the Spring when Jason, spurred on by love of glory, selected the flower of Greek heroes, and became the first to sweep his oars over the bosom of Tethys; and it also recalls the murderous pool that led beautiful Narcissus to fall in love with his empty reflection, which was guilty of his death: because he gazed too long at himself on the alien water's edge, he was condemned to perish.

It was a pool, pure, clear and unsullied, encircled around by a lovely curving bank, enamelled all over in many hues; there the crimson rose bush, the gladiolus and the lily sacred to Juno vied with each other in exhaling their perfumed breath,

De la belle Venus, qui chetif ne sçavoit
Que le destin si tost aux rives le devoit,   40
Pour estre le butin des vierges curieuses
À remplir leurs cofins des moissons amoureuses.

   Nulle Nymphe voisine ou bœuf ou pastoureau,
Ny du haut d'un buisson la cheute d'un rameau,
Ny sangler embourbé n'avoyent son eau troublée.

   Or' le Soleil avoit sa chaleur redoublée,
Quand Narcisse aux beaux yeux, pantoisement lassé
Du chaud, et d'avoir trop aux montaignes chassé,
Vint là pour estancher la soif qui le tourmente.
Mais las! en l'estanchant une autre luy augmente: 50
Car en beuvant à front, son semblant apperceut
Sur l'eau representé, qui fraudé le deceut.

   Helas que feroit-il, puis que la destinée
Luy avoit au berceau ceste mort ordonnée?
En vain son ombre il aime, et simple d'esprit croit
Que ce soit un vray corps, de son ombre qu'il voit,
Et sans avoir raison sottement il s'affolle,
Regardant pour-neant une menteuse idole:

and so, too, did the flower of Adonis, who was once the source of sweet sorrow to lovely Venus, and who, poor unfortunate, did not know that fate destined him so soon for the meadows, to become the booty of maidens anxious to fill their baskets with an amorous harvest.

No Nymph from the neighbourhood, or any cattle, or a shepherd, nor a branch falling from the top of a shrub, nor any mud-caked boar had disturbed its waters.

Now the Sun had redoubled its warmth, when beautiful-eyed Narcissus, out of breath and exhausted from the heat, and from hunting for too long in the mountains, came there to quench the thirst that was torturing him. But alas! as he was quenching it, another thirst grew within him; for while drinking, face down, he caught sight of his likeness pictured in the water, which deluded and deceived him.

Alas, what could he do, since from his cradle destiny had ordained this death for him? In vain he loves his reflection, and in his simplicity he believes that it is a real body, this reflection of his that he can see, and, losing his reason, foolishly he falls madly in love, gazing to no avail at a deceitful image; he admires himself, and,

Il admire soy-mesme, et sur le bord fiché,

60 Bée en vain dessus l'eau, par les yeux attaché.

Il contemple son poil, qui, renversé se couche
À rebours sur sa face, il voit sa belle bouche,
Il voit ses yeux ardents, plus clairs que le Soleil,
Et le lustre rosin de son beau teint vermeil:
Il regarde ses doigts et sa main merveillable,
Et tout ce dont il est luy-mesmes admirable.

Il se prise, il s'estime, et, de luy-mesme aimé,
Allume en l'eau le feu dont il est consumé:
Il ne sçait ce qu'il voit, et de ce qu'il ignore

70 Le desir trop goulu tout le cœur lui devore,
Las! et le mesme abus qui l'incite à se voir,
Luy nourrist l'esperance, et le fait decevoir.

Quantes-fois pour-neant, de sa lévre approchée,
Voulut toucher son ombre, et ne l'a point touchée?
Quantes-fois pour-neant de soy-mesmes épris,
En l'eau s'est voulu prendre, et ne s'est jamais pris?

Leve, credule enfant, tes yeux, et ne regarde
En vain comme tu fais, une idole fuyarde:

---

rooted to the spot on the bank, in vain he peers longingly into the water, unable to tear his eyes away.

He contemplates his hair, which falls forward the wrong way over his face, he sees his beautiful mouth, he sees his burning eyes, brighter than the Sun, and the rosy glow of his beautiful pink complexion; he looks at his fingers, and his wonderful hand, and everything for which he himself is admired.

He appreciates himself, he values himself, and, beloved of himself, he kindles in the water the fire by which he is consumed; he does not know what he sees, and his excessively voracious desire for what he does not know devours his whole heart, alas! and the same delusion that impels him to look at himself nurtures his hope, and causes him to be deceived. How many times, to no avail, lowering his lips, did he wish to touch his reflection, and fail to touch it? How many times, to no avail, enamoured of himself, did he wish to be embraced in the water, and fail ever to be embraced?

Raise your eyes, you naive child, and do not gaze in vain at a fleeting image, as

Ce que tu quiers, n'est point: si tu verses parmi
L'onde un pleur seulement, tu perdras ton ami: 80
Il n'a rien propre à soy, l'image presentée
Que tu vois dedans l'eau, tu l'as seul apportée,
Et la remporteras avecques toy aussi,
Si tu peux sans mourir te remporter d'ici.

    Ny faim, ny froid, ny chaud, ny de dormir l'envie
Ne peurent retirer sa miserable vie
Hors de l'eau mensongere, ains, couché sur le bord,
Ne fait que souspirer sous les traits de la mort:
Ne sans tourner ailleurs sa simple fantasie,
De trop se regarder ses yeux ne ressasie,   90
Et par eux se consume: à la fin s'elevant
Un petit hors de l'eau, tend ses bras en avant
Aux forests d'alentour, et plein de pitié grande,
D'une voix casse et lente, en plourant leur demande:

    Qui, dites moy, forests, fut onques amoureux
Si miserablement que moy, sot malheureux?
Hé vistes-vous jamais, bien que soyez agées
D'une infinité d'ans, amours si enragées?
Vous le sçavez, forests: car mainte et mainte fois
Vous avez recelé les amans sous vos bois.   100

you are doing. What you seek does not exist; if you drop a single tear into the pool, you will lose your beloved. He has nothing that is his own, and the likeness you see revealed in the water, you alone brought it here, and you will take it away with you, too, if you can take yourself away from here without dying.

    Neither hunger, nor cold, nor heat, nor the desire to sleep could pluck his wretched life from the deceiving water, but on the contrary, lying at the edge of the pool, he does nothing but sigh, in the agonies of death. He does not divert elsewhere his naive fancy, for his eyes have not had their fill of gazing at himself, and because of them he is perishing. In the end, raising himself away from the water a little, he stretches his arms out to the forests all round, and, full of great sadness, in a feeble, faltering voice, weeping, he asks them,

    'Tell me, forests, who was ever so miserably in love as I am, poor foolish wretch? Oh, have you at any time seen, even though you have lived to an infinite age, any loves so frenzied? You know this, you forests, for many and many a time you have concealed lovers in your thickets.

Ce que je voy, me plaist, et si je n'ay puissance,
Tant je suis desastré, d'en avoir jouyssance,
Ny tant soit peu baiser la bouche que je voy,
Qui ce semble, me baise et s'approche de moy.

Mais ce qui plus me deult, c'est qu'une dure porte,
Qu'un roc, qu'une forest, qu'une muraille forte
Ne nous separe point, seulement un peu d'eau
Me garde de jouyr d'un visage si beau.

Quiconque sois, enfant, sors de l'eau, je te prie:
110   Quel plaisir y prens-tu? ici l'herbe est fleurie,
Ici la torte vigne à l'orme s'assemblant
De tous costez espand un ombrage tremblant:
Ici le verd lierre, et la tendrette mousse
Font la rive sembler plus que le sommeil douce.

À peine il avoit dit, quand un pleur redoublé
(Qui coula dedans l'eau) son plaisir a troublé:

Où fuis-tu? disoit-il : celuy qui te supplie,
Ny sa jeune beauté, n'est digne qu'on le fuye.
Las! demeure: où fuis tu? les Nymphes de ces bois
120   Ne m'ont point desdaigné, ny celle qui la vois

'What I see delights me, yet so ill-starred am I that I do not have the power to possess it, nor can I place the lightest of kisses on the mouth I see, which seems to reach out to me and kiss me.

'But what pains me most is that it is not a solid gate, or a rock, or a forest, or a fortified wall that separates us, but that only a little water prevents me from joyfully possessing such a beautiful countenance.

'Whoever you are, child, come out of the water, I beseech you; what pleasure do you find there? Here the grass is covered with flowers, here the twining vine unites with the elm to spread its quivering shade on all sides; here green ivy and tender young moss make the bank seem sweeter than slumber.'

Scarcely had he finished speaking when repeated tears (which dropped into the pool) disturbed his pleasure.

'Where are you fleeing to?' he said. 'Neither the person who implores you nor his youthful beauty deserves to be fled from. Alas! stay; where are you fleeing to? The Nymphs in these woods have never spurned me, nor she who sends her voice

Fait retentir és monts d'une complainte lente,[3]
Et si n'ont point jouy du fruit de leur attente.
Car alors de l'amour mon cœur n'estoit espoint,
Pour aimer maintenant, ce qui ne m'aime point.

Las! tu me nourrissois tantost d'une esperance:
En l'onde tu tenois la mesme contenance
Que baissé je tenois: si mes bras je pliois,
Tu me pliois les tiens: moy riant, tu riois,
Et autant que mon œil de pleurs faisoit espandre,
Le tien d'autre costé autant m'en venoit rendre.   130
Si je faisois du chef un clin tant seulement,
Un autre clin ton chef faisoit également:
Et si parlant j'ouvrois ma bouchette vermeille,
Tu parlois, mais ta voix ne frappoit mon oreille.

Je cognois maintenant l'effet de mon erreur,
Je suis mesme celuy qui me mets en fureur,
Je suis mesmes celuy, celuy mesmes que j'aime,
Rien je ne voy dans l'eau que l'ombre de moy-mesme.

Que feray-je chetif? pri'ray-je, ou si je doy
Moy-mesme estre prié? je porte avecques moy   140
Et l'amant et l'aimé, et ne sçaurois tant faire,
Las! que de l'un des deux je me puisse desfaire.

echoing round the mountains with a lingering lament, yet they did not enjoy the fruits of their expectations. For then my heart was not pierced by love, leaving me to love now one who loves me not.

'Alas! a moment ago you nourished my hopes: your face in the water wore the same expression that mine wore when I leant down; if I folded my arms, you folded yours in return; when I smiled, you smiled, and as many tears as my eyes shed, so many did you for your part give back to me. If I simply nodded my head, your head nodded back as well; and if I opened my pretty red mouth to speak, you would speak, but your voice did not reach my ear.

'Now I know the consequence of my error: I am the very one who makes me mad with love, I am the very one, the very one I love; what I see in the water is nothing but the reflection of myself.

'What shall I do, wretched as I am? Shall I beseech him, or must I myself be beseeched? I carry with me both the lover and the beloved, and alas! there is nothing I can do to free myself from one of the two.

Mais seray-je tousjours couché dessus le bord
Comme un froid simulachre, en attendant la mort?
Ô bien-heureuse mort, haste toy je te prie,
Et me tranche d'un coup et l'amour et la vie,
À fin qu'avecques moy je voye aussi perir
(Si c'est quelque plaisir) ce qui me fait mourir.

    Il avoit achevé, quand du front goute à goute
150   Une lente sueur aux talons luy degoute,
Et se consume ainsi que fait la cire au feu,
Ou la neige de mars, qui lente peu à peu
S'escoule sur les monts de Thrace ou d'Arcadie,
Des rayons incertains du Soleil attiedie.

    Si bien que de Narcis qui fut jadis si beau,
Qui plus que laict caillé avoit blanche la peau:
Qui de front, d'yeux, de bouche, et de tout le visage
Resembloit le portrait d'une Adonine image,
Ne resta seulement qu'une petite fleur,
160   Qui d'un jaune safran emprunta la couleur,
Laquelle n'oubliant sa naissance premiere,
Suit encore aujourd'huy la rive fontainiere,

'But shall I remain forever lying on the bank like a cold effigy, waiting for death? O blessed death, hasten, I beseech you, and with a single blow sever both my love and my life, so that I may see also perishing with me (indeed this is some comfort) that which is causing my death.'

He had finished, when drop by drop from his forehead sweat slowly drips down to his feet, and he is consumed like wax in a fire, or snow in March, which little by little slowly melts on the mountains of Thrace or Arcadia in the fitful rays of the Sun as it warms up.

With the result that of Narcissus, who was once so beautiful, whose skin was whiter than milk curds, whose forehead, eyes, mouth and whole face resembled the portrayal of an image of Adonis, there remained only a little flower, which assumed the colour of saffron yellow, and which, mindful of its first origin, still haunts today

Et tousjours pres des eaux apparoist au Printemps,
Que le vent qui tout soufle, abat en peu de temps.
Aux arbres la Nature a permis longue vie:
Ceste fleur du matin ou du soir est ravie.
Ainsi l'ordre le veut et la necessité,
Qui dès le premier jour de la nativité
Allonge ou raccourcist nos fuseaux, et nous donne
Non ce que nous voulons, mais cela qu'elle ordonne.   170

the banks of pools, always appearing near water in Spring, and which the wind, that blows everything away, destroys in a short time. Nature has granted trees a long life; this flower is ravaged in a morning or an evening. This is the will of the order of things and of necessity, which from the first day of our birth lengthens or shortens our life-thread and gives us, not what we want, but what it ordains for us.

68 Elegie XIII

Nous fismes un contract ensemble l'autre jour,
Que tu me donnerois mille baisers d'amour,
Colombins, tourterins, à lévres demi-closes,
À souspirs souspirans la mesme odeur des roses,
À langue serpentine, à tremblotans regars,
De pareille façon que Venus baise Mars,
Quand il se pasme d'aise au sein de sa Maistresse.
Tu as parfait le nombre, helas! je le confesse:
Mais Amour sans milieu, ami d'extremité,
Ne se contente point d'un nombre limité.
    Qui feroit sacrifice à Bacchus pour trois grapes,
À Pan pour trois aigneaux? Jupiter, quand tu frapes
De ton foudre la terre, et poitrissant en l'air
Une poisseuse nue enceinte d'un esclair,
Ta majesté sans nombre eslance pesle-mesle
Pluye sur pluye espaisse et gresle dessus gresle,
Sur champs et sur forests, sans regarder combien.
Un Prince est indigent, qui peut nombrer son bien.

10

Elegy XIII

We made a contract together the other day that you would give me a thousand loving kisses, pigeon-like, turtle-dove-like, with parted lips, with sighs sighing the very scent of roses, with snake-like tongue, with fluttering glances, in the same way as Venus kisses Mars, when he swoons with pleasure on the breast of his Mistress. You have completed the number, alas! I admit it; but Love, knowing no middle way, loving extremes, is not satisfied with a limited number.

Who would make a sacrifice to Bacchus for only three bunches of grapes, or to Pan for only three lambs? Jupiter, when you strike the earth with your thunderbolt, moulding in the air a pitch-black cloud pregnant with lightning, your majesty hurls down pell-mell and without number rain upon torrential rain and hail upon hail, on fields and forests, without looking to see how many. A Prince is poverty-stricken

À ta maison celeste appartient l'abondance.
En terre ma Maistresse a semblable puissance. 20
   Toy Deesse cent fois plus belle que n'estoit
Celle qu'aux bords de Cypre une Conque portoit,
Pressurant les cheveux de sa teste immortelle
Encores tous moiteux de la mer maternelle,[1]
Tu ne devrois conter les baisers savoureux
Que tu donnes trop chiche à ton pauvre amoureux.
Si tu ne contes point les soucis ny les peines
Ny les larmes qui font de mes yeux deux fontaines,
Tu ne devrois conter les biens que je reçoy,
Non plus que moy les maux que je souffre pour toy. 30
Car ce n'est la raison de donner par mesure
Tes baisers quand des maux innombrables j'endure.
Donne moy donc au lict, ensemble bien unis,
Des baisers infinis pour mes maux infinis.

---

if he can number his possessions. Abundance is characteristic of your celestial mansion. On earth my Mistress is likewise bountifully supplied.

You, Goddess a hundred times more beautiful than she who was borne to the shores of Cyprus on a Shell, wringing out the hair of her immortal head, still wet from the sea that gave her birth, you should not count the delicious kisses that you bestow too stingily on your poor lover. If you do not count the cares or the sorrows or the tears that make my eyes into two fountains, you ought not to count the blessings I receive, any more than I count the ills I suffer for you. For it is not reasonable for you to give a measured quantity of kisses when I endure innumerable ills. So in bed, as we lie close together, give me an infinite number of kisses in exchange for my infinite ills.

69 À Philippes Des-Portes, Chartrain. Elegie
[Pièce ajoutée en 1587]

Nous devons à la Mort et nous et nos ouvrages:
Nous mourons les premiers, le long reply des âges
En roulant engloustist nos œuvres à la fin:
Ainsi le veut Nature et le puissant Destin.

  Dieu seul est eternel: de l'homme elementaire
Ne reste apres la mort ny veine ny artere:
Qui pis est, il ne sent, il ne raisonne plus,
Locatif descharné d'un vieil tombeau reclus.

  C'est un extreme abus, une extreme folie
10 De croire que la Mort* soit cause de la vie:
Ce sont poincts opposez autant que l'Occident
S'oppose à l'Orient, l'Ourse au Midy ardent.

  L'une est sans mouvement, et l'autre nous remue,
Qui la forme de l'ame en vigueur continue,
Nous fait ouyr et voir, juger, imaginer,
Discourir du present, le futur deviner.

To Philippe Desportes of Chartres. Elegy [Added in 1587]

We must pay to Death both ourselves and our achievements; we die first, and finally the long ages as they roll by swallow up our works in the folds of time; such is the will of Nature and mighty Destiny.

  God alone is eternal: of man, who is composed of the elements, neither vein nor artery remains after death. What is worse, he does not feel, he does not reason any longer, but is the desiccated tenant of an old, sealed tomb.

  It is an immense error, an immense madness, to believe that Death* gives rise to life; these are points as opposed to each other as West is opposed to East, and the Great Bear to the blazing South.

  The one is without motion, and the other, which preserves the form of the soul in vigour, makes us move, makes us hear and see, judge, imagine, discuss the present and divine the future.

Les morts ne sont heureux, d'autant que l'ame vive**
Du mouvement principe, en eux n'est plus active.
L'heur vient de la vertu, la vertu d'action:
Le mort privé du faire est sans perfection.[1]   20

    L'heur de l'ame, est de Dieu contempler la lumiere:
La contemplation de la cause premiere
Est sa seule action: contemplant elle agist:
Mais au contemplement l'heur de l'homme ne gist.

    Il gist à l'œuvre seul, impossible à la cendre
De ceux que la Mort faict soubs les ombres descendre.
C'est pourquoy de Pluton les champs deshabitez
N'ont polices ny loix ny villes ny citez.

    Or l'ouvrage et l'ouvrier font un mesme voyage,
Leur chemin est la Mort. Athenes et Carthage,   30
Et Rome qui tenoit la hauteur des hauteurs,
Sont poudre maintenant comme leurs fondateurs.

    Pource les Grecs ont dit que, glout de faim extreme
Saturne devoroit ses propres enfans mesme.
Le general est ferme et ne fait place au temps,
Le particulier meurt presque au bout de cent ans.

The dead are not happy, inasmuch as the life-giving soul,** the principle of movement, is no longer active in them. Happiness comes from virtue, virtue from action; a dead man, deprived of activity, is without perfection.

The happiness of the soul consists of contemplating the light of God; contemplation of the first cause is its only action: in contemplating it is acting; but the happiness of a man does not lie in contemplation.

It lies in works alone, which are impossible for the ashes of those whom Death sends down to the shades. That is why the realm of Pluto, with no living inhabitants, has neither governance, nor laws, nor towns, nor cities.

Now the work and the workman make the same journey; their road is Death. Athens and Carthage, and Rome, which occupied the height of heights, are dust now like their founders.

For this reason the Greeks said that Saturn, ravenous with extreme hunger, even devoured his own children. That which is of a genus is stable and does not yield to time; that which is of a species dies after about a hundred years.

Chacun de son labeur doit en ce Monde attendre
L'usufruit seulement, que present il doit prendre
Sans se paistre d'attente et d'une eternité,***
40   Qui n'est rien que fumée et pure vanité.

Homere, qui servit aux neuf Muses de guide,
S'il voyait aujourd'huy son vaillant Eacide,
Ne le cognoistroit plus, ny le docte Maron
Son Phrygien Enée.[2] Ainsi le froid giron
De la tombe assoupist tous les sens de nature,
Qui sont deus à la terre et à la pourriture.

Nous semblons aux Toreaux, qui de coutres trenchans,
À col morne et fumeux, vont labourant les champs,
Sillonnant par rayons une germeuse plaine,
50   Et toutefois pour eux inutile est leur peine:
Ils ne mangent le bled qu'ils ont ensemencé,
Mais quelque vieille paille, ou du foin enroncé.[3]

Le belier Colonnel de sa laineuse troupe,
L'eschine de toison pour les autres se houpe:
Car le drap, bien que sien, ne l'habille pourtant:
L'homme, ingrat envers luy au dos le va portant
Sans luy en sçavoir gré. Ainsi nostre escriture
Ne nous profite rien: c'est la race future

Each person must expect to receive in this World only the usufruct of his labours, which he must take in the present, without nourishing himself with expectations and hopes of eternity,*** which is nothing but smoke and pure illusion.

Homer, who served the nine Muses as their guide, if he were to see today his valiant hero, the grandson of Aeacus, would no longer recognize him, nor would learned Maro recognize his Trojan Aeneas. Thus does the cold womb of the grave numb all the natural senses we must repay to the earth and to decay.

We are like Bulls, with their forlorn, steaming necks, who till the fields with keen-edged ploughshares, tracing furrows on the fertile land, and yet for them their toil is fruitless: they do not eat the wheat they have sown, but only some old straw, or bramble-infested hay.

The Ram, Colonel of his woolly flock, sprouts fleece over his backbone for others, for the cloth, although it is his, nevertheless does not clothe him: man, showing no gratitude towards him, wears it on his back without giving him any thanks. Likewise

Qui seule en jouyst toute, et qui juge à loisir
Les ouvrages d'autruy, et s'en donne plaisir,   60
Rendant comme il luy plaist nostre peine estimée.

    Quant à moy, j'aime mieux trente ans de renommee,
Jouyssant du Soleil, que mille ans de renom
Lors que la fosse creuse enfouyra mon nom,
Et lors que nostre forme en une autre se change.
»L'homme qui ne sent plus n'a besoin de louange.

    Il est vray que l'honneur est le plus grand de tous
Les biens exterieurs qui sont propres à nous,
Qui vivons et sentons: les morts n'en ont que faire,
Toutefois le bien faire est chose necessaire,   70
Qui profite aux vivans, et plaist aux heritiers.

    Les fils, de leurs ayeuls racontent volontiers
Les magnanimes faicts: la louange illustrée
D'un acte vertueux ne fut jamais frustrée
De son digne loyer, soit futur ou present.

    Le Ciel ne donne à l'homme un plus riche present
Que l'ardeur des vertus, les aimer et les suivre,
Un renom excellent, bien mourir et bien vivre.

---

our writing brings us no profit: it is the future generation that alone enjoys it all, and that judges at leisure the works of others, and takes pleasure from them, distributing approval for our pains as it pleases.

As for me, I would rather have thirty years of renown while I enjoy the Sun than a thousand years of fame when the hollow grave has buried my name, and when our present form changes into another. "A man who no longer feels anything has no need of praise."

It is true that honour is the greatest of all external blessings that are peculiar to us, who live and feel; the dead have no use for it, but nevertheless doing good is a necessary thing, which benefits the living, and pleases our heirs.

Sons gladly recount the noble deeds of their ancestors; such fame, illustrated by a virtuous act, has never been deprived of a fitting recompense, whether future or present.

Heaven gives man no richer present than this: that he shall have a passion for virtue, that he shall love it and pursue it, have an excellent reputation, die well and live well.

Des-Portes, qu'Aristote amuse tout le jour,
80   Qui honores ta Dure, et les champs qu'à l'entour
Chartres voit de son mont, et panché les regarde,
Je te donne ces vers, à fin de prendre garde
De ne tuer ton corps desireux d'acquerir
Un renom journalier qui doit bien-tost mourir:
Mais happe le present d'un cœur plein d'allegresse,
Cependant que le Prince, Amour, et la jeunesse
T'en donnent le loisir, sans croire au lendemain.
Le futur est douteux, le present est certain.

Annotations de l'autheur

* *Que la Mort soit cause de la vie.* Contre les Pythagoriques, qui pensoient qu'apres la mort nos ames revenoient en autres corps, et mesmes és bestes.
** *Les morts ne sont heureux.* C'est l'opinion d'Aristote qui est faulse: car les morts qui meurent en Dieu, sont heureux parfaitement.
*** *D'une eternité.* Contre les Poëtes qui ne promettent autre chose à eux mesmes et aux autres par leurs vers, que l'eternité.

Desportes, you who are engrossed in Aristotle all day long, who honour your river Eure, and the fields round about, which Chartres can see from its hill as it gazes steadily down at them, I give to you these lines, to warn you to take care not to kill your body out of a wish to acquire an ephemeral reputation that must soon die. Instead, grasp the present with a heart full of joyfulness, while the King, Love and youth give you the opportunity, without putting your faith in the morrow. The future is doubtful, the present is certain.

Author's Notes

* Against the Pythagoreans, who thought that after death our souls returned in other bodies, and even in animals.
** This is the opinion of Aristotle, which is erroneous, for the dead who die in God have perfect happiness.
*** Against Poets who promise themselves and others, through their verse, nothing less than eternity.

LES HYNNES

70 Hynne de Calays et de Zethés

[...]
  Là Zethe et Calays les derniers du bateau
Sortirent pour dormir au premier front de l'eau,
Ausquels de tous costez comme deux belles ondes
Les cheveux d'or flottaient dessus les ailes blondes,   150
Et pleins de liberté s'entremesloient dedans
Les plumes pesle-mesle à l'abandon des vents.

  Telle troupe d'Heros, l'eslite de la Grece,
Accompaignoient Jason d'un cœur plein d'allegresse
Qui toute nuict couchez sur le rivage nu
Dormirent jusqu'au poinct que le jour fut venu.

  Aussi tost que du jour l'aube fut retournée,
Voicy venir au bord le mal-heureux Phinée
Qui plus qu'homme mortel enduroit de torment:
Car le pauvre chetif n'estoit pas seulement   160
Banny de son pays, et une aveugle nue
N'estoit (ô cruauté!) dessus ses yeux venue

THE HYMNS

Hymn to Calais and Zetes

[...]
  There Zetes and Calais disembarked last of all from the ship, to sleep at the very edge of the sea. All around them their golden hair floated like two lovely waves over their pale wings, and, totally unrestrained, mingled with the feathers in confusion, at the mercy of the winds.

  Such was the band of Heroes, the flower of Greece, that accompanied Jason with hearts full of high spirits and, lying on the bare shore, slept all night long until the break of day.

  As soon as the day had dawned, see the hapless Phineus come down to the shore, he who suffered more torment than any mortal man; for not only was the poor wretch banished from his own land, and not only (O such cruelty!) had a cloud of

Par le vouloir des Dieux, qui lui avoient osté
(Pour trop prophetiser) le don de la clarté:
Mais à tous ses repas les Harpies cruelles
Demenans un grand bruit et du bec et des ailes,
Luy pilloient sa viande, et leur griffe arrachoit
Tout cela que Phinée à sa lévre approchoit,
Vomissant de leur gorge une odeur si mauvaise,
170   Que toute la viande en devenoit punaise.
    Tousjours d'un craquetis leur maschoire cliquoit,
Tousjours de palle faim leur bec s'entrechoquoit.
Comme la dent d'un Loup, quand la faim l'espoinçonne
De courre apres un Beuf, la maschoire luy sonne,
Et béant et courant et faisant un grand bruit
Fait craqueter sa gueule apres le Cerf qui fuit:
Ainsi bruyoient les dents de ces monstres infames,
Qui du menton en haut sembloient de belles femmes,
De l'eschine aux oiseaux, et leur ventre trembloit
180   De faim, qui de grandeur un bourbier resembloit,
Et pour jambes avoient une acrochante griffe
En escailles armée, ainsi qu'un Hippogrife.[1]

blindness settled upon his eyes by the will of the Gods, who had taken from him
(because he had prophesied too much) the gift of clear vision, but also at all his meals
the cruel Harpies, making a loud noise with both beaks and wings, pillaged his
food, and their claws snatched everything Phineus was about to put into his mouth,
as they spewed from their throats a stench so loathsome that all the food became
foul.

    All the time their jaws clattered with a cracking sound, all the time their beaks
clashed together in their pallid hunger. Just as the teeth of a Wolf make its jaw
resound, when hunger drives it to hunt an Ox, or when, opening wide its throat
and running and making a great noise, it makes its mouth clatter while pursuing a
fleeing Stag, just so rattled the teeth of these vile monsters, which from the chin up
seemed like beautiful women, but which had backs like birds; and their stomachs,
which in size resembled a swamp, shivered with hunger, and for legs they had
hooked claws armoured with scales like a Hippogriff.

Ce chetif ne vivoit que de petits morceaux
Qui tomboient infectez du bec de ces oiseaux,
Et fust mort de douleur sans la ferme esperance
Qu'il avoit de trouver quelque jour delivrance
Par les fils Boreans, que le noble Jason
Devoit par là conduire allant à la Toison.

Aussi tost que Phinée au rivage ouyt bruire
Les Princes esveillez au siflet du navire,   190
Il se leva du lict ainsi qu'un songe vain,
Appuyant d'un baston sa tremblotante main,
Et tastonnant les murs sortit hors de sa porte
D'un pied foible et recreu, lequel à peine porte
Le corps vieil et moisy, l'eschine de son dos
Ne monstroit aux voyans qu'une carcasse d'os
Sous une peau crasseuse, et sa perruque dure
Comme poil de cheval se herissoit d'ordure.

Luy sortant de sa chambre affoibly des genous
Se trainoit vers le bruit bronchant à tous les coups: 200
Or' un estourdiment tout le cerveau luy serre,
Ore tout à la ronde il pensoit que la terre
Chancelloit dessous luy, et ores il dormoit
Accablé d'un sommeil qui son chef assommoit.[2]
[. . .]

This poor wretch lived only on little crumbs that fell, contaminated, from the beaks of these birds, and he would have died of misery without the steadfast hope he had of finding himself delivered one day by the sons of Boreas, who would be brought here by noble Jason in his quest for the Golden Fleece.

As soon as Phineus heard noises on the shore from the Princes, who had been awakened by the ship's whistle, he rose from his bed like an empty dream; supporting his shaking hand with a stick, and groping along the walls, he went out of his door on feeble, flagging feet, which could scarcely carry the mouldering old body; the spine of his back revealed to the onlookers only a carcass of bones beneath a grimy skin, and his hair, coarse as horsehair, was stiff with filth.

Coming out of his room, on weakened knees, he dragged himself towards the noise, stumbling at every step. Now dizziness gripped his entire brain, now he felt that the earth all around was reeling beneath him, and now he slept, overcome by a slumber that stupefied his mind. [. . .]

Ainsi parloit Phinée, et ja dessus le sable
Les valets de ce Prince avoient dressé la table
La chargeant à foison l'un sur l'autre de plats,
De ces meschans oiseaux le dernier repas.

Là Zethe et Calays en une chaire ornée
De gazons firent soir le malheureux Phinée,
Le priant de manger, et de jetter bien loin
Aux ondes et au vent sa famine et son soin.
Aussi tost que ses doigts toucherent la viande,
330   On entendit en l'air ceste troupe gourmande
Criailler d'un grand bruit, comme on oit dans un bois
Pres le bord de la mer une confuse vois
Des Palles et Butors, quand un larron ils trouvent
Qui remarque leurs nids et leurs femmes qui couvent.

Puis en fondant du ciel sans les appercevoir
(Ainsi qu'un foudre ardent qui prompte se laisse choir
S'esclattant d'un grand bruit) dessus luy se percherent,
Et de leurs becs crochus la viande arracherent
Hors de ses vuides mains, haletant une odeur
340   Qui empuantissoit des Chevaliers le cœur.
Là quelque peu de temps en mangeant sejournerent,
Et comme tourbillons en l'air s'en retournerent.

Thus spoke Phineus, and already on the sand the servants of the Prince [Jason] had set up the table, piling it plentifully with dishes, one upon another, which were to be the last meal of those evil birds.

There Zetes and Calais made the unfortunate Phineus sit on a seat adorned with grassy turf, inviting him to eat, and to cast far away to the waves and the wind his ravenous hunger and his worries. As soon as his fingers touched the food, that gluttonous troop was heard in the air uttering loud screeches, just like the raucous cries of Shovelers and Bitterns heard in a wood by the sea, when they find a thief eyeing their nests and their mates as they sit on their eggs.

Then, swooping down from the sky without being noticed (like a fiery bolt of lightning that suddenly hurtles down, exploding with a loud crash), they perched on top of him, and with their hooked beaks they tore the food out of his empty hands, exhaling a stench that sickened the stomachs of the Knightly Heroes. There they remained eating for some little time, and then departed again like whirlwinds

Lors Zethe et Calays happerent leurs boucliers,
Dont l'acier reluisoit comme des Astres clairs,
Puis de leur gaine large à cloux d'or diaprée
Tirerent brusquement leur flamboyante espée,
Commandant aux valets d'un pied prompt et leger
Rapporter sur la table encores à manger.
À peine à peine estoient les viandes servies,
Que voicy derechef les friandes Harpies   350
Tourner dessus la table, et de leur bec pillard
Ravissant la viande, affamer le vieillard.

   Zethes du premier coup son aile ne remue,
Ny Calays la sienne: ains ainsi qu'une Grue
Avance une enjambée, ou deux ou trois avant
Qu'abandonner la terre et se donner au vent:
Ainsi deux ou trois pas en sautant enjamberent
Les enfans d'Aquilon, puis en l'air s'esleverent
Pendus dedans le Ciel, secouant d'un grand bruit
Les ailes, que leur pere entre deux airs conduit   360
Pour leur donner vitesse: autrement par trop lentes
N'eussent jamais attaint les Harpies volantes,
Qui de legereté les foudres egaloient,
Venant ou retournant à l'heure qu'elle' alloient

into the air. Thereupon Zetes and Calais snatched up their shields, whose steel shone like bright Stars, and then from their broad scabbards studded with gold nails they quickly drew their flashing swords, ordering the servants to move briskly and nimbly, and bring some more food to the table. Scarcely, scarcely had the food been served, when the voracious Harpies are here again, wheeling above the table, and condemning the old man to starvation by snatching the food with their plundering beaks.

   To begin with, Zetes does not spread his wings, nor does Calais; instead, in the same way as a Crane moves one stride forward, or two or three, before abandoning the earth and giving itself up to the wind, in the same way the sons of the North Wind strode forward with two or three jumping steps, then rose into the air, soaring in the Sky, noisily flapping their wings, as their father carried them along between two currents of air to give them speed: otherwise they would have been far too slow and would never have caught up with the flying Harpies, which were as swift as lightning, as they flew up or down in order to devour the meals of blind Phineus,

Devorer les repas de l'aveugle Phinée
Condamné par les Dieux à telle destinée.
Les Preux desur le bord s'arresterent béans,
Accompaignans des yeux ces grands Monstres fuyans
Tant qu'ils peuvent en l'air, ayans l'ame surprise
370   Du desir de sçavoir la fin de l'entreprise.

    Ainsi que deux Faucons qui parmy l'air s'en vont
Hautains apres leur proye, et volent front à front,
Ces Chevaliers voloient, secouant en la dextre
L'espée, et le bouclier en l'autre main senestre.

    Les Monstres en voyant leurs ennemis ailez,
Tournant autour du bord ne s'en sont en-volez
Guieres haut dedans l'air: sans plus leur volerie
Ressembloit au Milan qui l'aile ne deplie:
Mais quand sifler l'espée ils ouyrent au vent
380   Des freres, qui de pres les alloient poursuivant,
Ils doublerent le vol, et de leurs gueules pleines
Rendirent les morceaux pour voler plus hautaines,
Comme on voit un Heron sa gorge descharger
Quand il sent le Faucon, pour estre plus leger:

who had been condemned by the Gods to such a fate. The Valiant Heroes on the shore stood open-mouthed, their eyes following in the air as long as they could those huge fleeing Monsters, their souls seized by the desire to know the end of the adventure.

Like two Falcons that travel on high through the air, and fly side by side in pursuit of their prey, these Knightly Heroes flew, brandishing in their right hands their swords, and their shields in their left hands.

On seeing their winged enemies, the Monsters, wheeling around the shore, flew to no great height in the sky; their hovering flight was exactly like that of a Kite whose wings are not beating; but when they heard swishing through the air the swords of the brothers, who were pursuing them very closely, they quickened their flight, and spat the morsels out of their crammed mouths in order to fly higher, just as we see a Heron empty its crop, in order to be lighter, when it senses the presence of a Falcon. Now the Harpies soar in the Sky, now in packs they descend

Ores dedans le Ciel les Harpies se pendent,
Ores plus bas en l'air à pelotons descendent,
Et ores en laissant pres de terre ramer
Les ailes vont razant les plaines et la mer.[3]

    Comme un liévre pressé d'une importune suite
De chiens par mainte ruze entre-coupe sa fuite   390
Maintenant d'un destour, maintenant d'un retour,
Pour tromper les chasseurs amusez à l'entour:
Tout ainsi ces oiseaux de ruzes et d'entorces
Errant puis çà puis là, mettoient toutes leurs forces
De tromper ces guerriers, qui sans fin ne repos
Haletant les suivoient, et leur pendoient au dos,
Tousjours du fer tranchant martelant sur leurs plumes:
Mais autant eust valu frapper sur des enclumes:
Car jamais nulle playe à la chair ne prenoit,
Et du coup sur l'espée aucun sang ne venoit.   400

    Ainsi que les bateurs qui frappent dans une aire
Par compas les presens de notre antique mere,
L'aire faict un grand bruit, le fleau qui se roidist,
Contre le bled battu dedans l'air rebondist:
Ainsi ces Boreans à grands coups d'alumelles
Chamailloient sur le chef, sur les flancs, sur les ailes,

lower in the air, and now, their wings beating close to the ground, they skim over the meadows and the sea.

As a hare, hard pressed by the hot pursuit of hounds, interrupts its headlong flight with many ruses, now by turning aside, now by turning back, to give the slip to the huntsmen who are distracted elsewhere, just so did those birds, with ruses and twisting turns, ranging hither and thither, put all their strength into giving the slip to these warriors, who, without ceasing or resting, followed them, gasping for breath, and harried them closely, continually striking hammer blows against their feathers with the keen-edged steel; but it would have been as much use to strike at anvils, for never did any wound damage their flesh, and no blood appeared on the swords as a result of the blows.

Just like threshers who rhythmically beat the gifts of our primeval mother on the threshing floor, and just as the floor resounds with a loud noise, and the flail becomes rigid and rebounds from the threshed grain into the air, just so these sons of Boreas with heavy blows from their swords pounded the monsters' heads, sides and wings,

D'un coup suivy menu: le dos en gemissoit,
Et sans playe l'espée en hault rejalissoit.[4]
[...]

 Dedans le champ de Mars dessous un joug d'acier
D'une chaisne de fer il vous faudra lier
Deux toreaux dont les pieds sont d'airain, et la gorge
Resemble une fournaise où le feu se regorge.[5]

 Comme deux grands soufflets qu'un mareschal boiteux[6]
À sa forge ententif, comble d'esprit venteux,
Puis haut puis bas tirant et repoussant l'haleine
Du vent en ses soufflets, dont leur poictrine est pleine,
Avecques un grand bruit fait ronfler ses fourneaux:
580 Ainsin en reniflant les nez de ces toreaux
Jettent à pelotons une flame allumée
Par ondes noircissante en obscure fumée,
Deçà delà rouez à l'abandon du vent:
Mais à force de mains courbé sur le devant
Tirant encontre-bas leurs cornes par outrance,
Vous les ferez broncher à genoux sur la panse
Dontez dessous le joug, et fendant les sillons
Les picquerez aux flancs à grands coups d'aiguillons.

with frequent rapid blows; their backs groaned from the buffeting, and the swords recoiled without inflicting a wound.
[...]

 [Phineus speaks:] 'In the field by the temple of Mars, using a chain of iron, you must harness under a yoke of steel two bulls whose hooves are of bronze, and whose throats resemble a furnace spewing forth fire.

 'Just as a lame blacksmith, busy at his forge, inflates two enormous bellows with animating wind, and then, now high, now low, drawing the breath of the wind into and expelling it from his bellows, whose lungs are full of it, makes his furnaces roar with a loud noise, in the same way the nostrils of these bulls as they snort emit bursts of fiery flame, which comes in waves and turns into a dense black smoke, tossed this way and that at the mercy of the wind; but by leaning over from in front and by using the strength of your hands to pull their horns down violently, you will force them on to their knees and on to their bellies, subjugating them beneath the yoke, and as you plough the furrows you will prod their flanks with sharp jabs of the goad.

Semant en laboureur la fertile contrée
Des dents d'un grand serpent: comme d'une ventrée   590
Les mottes enfantront en lieu de blez germez
Une fiere moisson de Chevaliers armez.

On ne voit point la nuict tant d'estoiles flambantes
Driller au firmament, quand les nues pendantes
Ont desvoilé le Ciel, comme en ce champs de Mars
Vous voirrez flamboyer d'escus et de soudars,
De harnois, de boucliers, de picques, et de haches,
Et de clairs morions crestez de longs panaches.

Cet escadron voudra desur vous se ruer:
Mais d'un revers d'espée il le faudra tuer,   600
Ou le rendre mutin d'une civile guerre:
Les uns desja tous grands marcheront sur la terre,
Les autres à grand' peine auront le chef sorty:
Aux uns le corps en deux sera demy-party,
Du col jusqu'au nombril ayant estre et figure,
Et du nombril aux pieds ce sera terre dure:

Les autres mani'ront les jambes en à-bas,
Qui n'auront point encor d'espaules ny de bras:
Et les autres du chef donneront cognoissance,
Levant la motte en hault, de leur prompte naissance.   610

'When like a farmer you sow the fertile land with the teeth of a huge serpent, the clods of earth, as if giving birth, will bring forth, instead of shoots of corn, a fearsome harvest of armed Warriors. There are not so many blazing stars to be seen sparkling in the firmament at night, when the looming clouds have unveiled the Sky, as there are to be seen blazing on this field of Mars shields and soldiers, harnesses, bucklers, pikes and axes, and gleaming helmets with long plumes on their crests.

'This battalion will try to hurl themselves at you, but you must kill them with a slash of your sword, or else make them rise up rebelliously in a civil war. Some, already fully grown, will be walking on the earth, while others will scarcely have their heads above the ground; some will have their bodies divided in two, from neck to navel having being and form, while from navel to feet they will be solid earth.

'Others, who do not yet have shoulders or arms, will have movement lower down, in their legs; and others will give notice of their imminent birth, by raising the clods aloft with their heads.

Comme un homme duquel le champ est en debat,
De bon matin s'esveille, et de sa faulx abat
En haste la moisson toute verte tombée:
Il sie à toutes mains: la faucille courbée
Ne pardonne aux sillons: en la mesme façon
Vous trancherez soudain la guerriere moisson
Des hommes terre-nez qui ne feront que d'estre,
Et sentiront la mort aussi tost que le naistre:
Les sillons de leur sang à grands flots ondoyront,
620   Les uns dessus le front, les autres tomberont
Renversez sur le dos, les autres de cholere
En trepignant mordront les mottes de leur mere:
Et les autres tranchez autant qu'iceux adonc
Esleveront le corps: la moitié de leur tronc
Coulera dans le Phase aux poissons la pasture,
Et l'autre engressera les champs de pourriture.

Par charmes vous pourrez endormir le serpent
Qui couve sous le ventre en largeur un arpent,
De crestes perruqué, à qui jamais le somme
630   Tant soit peu, jour ne nuict les paupieres n'assomme:
Il a le chef horrible, il a les yeux ardans,
Sur la maschoire large il a trois rangs de dents,

'Just as a man whose ownership of a field is in dispute gets up early in the morning, and with his scythe hastily cuts down the harvest, which is laid low while still green, he hacks with might and main, and the curved sickle does not spare the furrows; in the same way you will promptly fell the warrior harvest of the earth-born men who are just coming into existence, and who will experience death at the same time as birth; the furrows will flow with their blood in streaming floods. Some will fall on to their faces, others will be pitched on to their backs; others, drumming their feet in rage, will bite the clods of their mother earth, and others, felled like them, will then raise their bodies; one half of their trunks will slide into the river Phasis to become food for fishes, and the other will fertilize the fields by decaying.

'By magical charms you will be able to lull to sleep the serpent, which, as if hatching eggs, covers with its belly an acre in area; its head is crowned with crests, its eyelids are never in the slightest made drowsy by slumber, day or night. Its head is hideous, its eyes blazing, its vast jaw has three rows of teeth, and its tongue,

Et sa langue en sifflant sible d'une voix telle,
Que les petits enfans se mussent sous l'aisselle
De leur mere en tremblant, quand luy faisant un bruit
Garde la Toison d'or et veille toute nuict.

 Comme on voit bien souvent (quand un Pasteur qui
   garde
Ses troupeaux dans un bois, et laisse par mesgarde
Choir en un chesne creux quelque tizon de feu,
La flame en tournoyant s'augmente peu à peu   640
Dés le commencement, puis le feste s'allume,
Puis toute la forest s'embraze et se consume)
Un repli de fumée entre-suivi de pres,
Puis un autre et un autre, et puis un autre apres
Se voute en ondoyant: ainsi de ceste beste
Le dos se va courbant de la queue à la teste
De plis longs et tortus: toutefois prenez cœur,
Un seul enchantement vous en fera veinqueur,
Et gaignerez la peau de fils d'or en-noblie,
Puis vous retournerez veinqueurs en Thessalie.[7] 650
[. . .]

hissing, utters such a loud whistling sound that small children tremble and hide their faces in their mothers' laps, as it noisily guards the Golden Fleece and watches all night long.

 'Just as quite often (when a Shepherd, who is guarding his flocks in the woods, carelessly lets fall in a hollow oak some spark of fire, the flame, swirling about, grows little by little from its beginning, then the treetop catches fire, then the whole forest blazes up and is consumed) you see a curl of smoke, and then in quick succession, another and another, and then another after them arches and undulates, just so this beast's back curves from its tail to its head in long, twisted coils. Nevertheless, take heart: a single spell will render you victorious over it, and you will win the fleece that is enriched with gold threads, and then you will return victorious to Thessaly.'

 [. . .]

71 Les Daimons
À Lancelot Carle

Carle, de qui l'esprit recherche l'Univers,
Pour gage d'amitié je te donne ces vers,
Afin que ton Bordeaux, ta rive et ta Garonne
Flottant contre ses bords ta louange resonne,
Et ton nom par la France autant puisse voler
Que ce vers qui s'en-vole aux habitans de l'air.
En ta faveur, mon Carle, il est temps que j'envoye
Ma Muse extravaguer par une estroitte voye
Laquelle des François aux vieux temps ne fut pas
10   (Tant elle est incogneue) empreinte de leurs pas,
Afin d'estre promeue au mystere admirable
Des Daimons, pour t'en faire un present venerable:
L'argument est fort haut, mais un esprit ne peut
Trouver rien de fascheux, si la Muse le veut.[1]

Quand l'Eternel bastit le grand palais du Monde,
Il peupla de poissons les abysmes de l'onde,
D'hommes la terre, et l'air de Daimons, et les cieux
D'Anges, à celle fin qu'il n'y eust point de lieux

The Daemons
To Lancelot Carle

Carle, whose mind seeks to understand the Universe, to you I give these lines as a token of friendship, so that your Bordeaux, your shores and your river Garonne, lapping against its banks, may resound with your praise, and so that your name may fly throughout France as freely as this poem, which takes its flight to the inhabitants of the air. My dear Carle, it is time I did you the favour of sending my Muse exploring along a narrow path that was not marked by the footprints of the French in olden times (so little is it known), in order that she may be elevated to the wondrous mystery of the Daemons, to make you a valuable present of them. The subject is very exalted, but no mind can find anything offensive if it is willed by the Muse.

When the Eternal Being built the great palace of the World, he peopled with fish the depths of the seas, and with men the earth, the air with Daemons, and the heavens with Angels, with the intention that there should be no empty places in the

Vuides en l'Univers, et selon leurs natures
Qu'ils fussent tous remplis de propres creatures.   20
Il mist aupres de luy (son plaisir le voulut)
L'escadron precieux des Anges qu'il eslut
Pour citoyens du ciel, qui sans corps y demeurent,
Et francs de passions non plus que luy ne meurent:
Esprits intelligens plus que les nostres purs,
Qui cognoissent les ans tant passez que futurs,
Et tout l'estat mondain, comme voyant les choses
De pres au sein de Dieu, où elles sont encloses.
En l'estage de l'air dessous la Lune espars,
Air gros espais brouillé qui est de toutes pars   30
Tousjours remply de vents, de foudres et d'orages,
Il logea les Daimons au milieu des nuages,
Leur place destinée, ayans un corps leger,
L'un de feu, l'autre d'air, à fin de voyager
Aisément par le vague, et ne tomber en terre:
Et pesant quelque peu, à fin que leur corps n'erre
Trop haut jusques au ciel, abandonnant le lieu
Qui leur est destiné par le vouloir de Dieu.

Universe, and that, in accordance with their natures, all parts should be filled with their own particular creatures. He placed beside himself (his pleasure willed it) the precious host of Angels whom he elected to be citizens of heaven, and who dwell there, without bodies, and who, being free from passions, like him do not die. They have intelligent minds, purer than ours, which know equally the years that are past and those to come, and the whole state of the universe, since they see all things at close range in the bosom of God, wherein they are enclosed.

In the layer of the air that lies beneath the Moon, heavy, thick, murky air that from all quarters is always pervaded by winds, lightning and thunderstorms, he housed the Daemons among the clouds, their destined place, as they have light bodies; one has a body of fire, another of air, so that they can travel easily through the void and not fall to earth; and yet they have some little weight, so that their bodies do not stray too high up towards the heavens, abandoning the place that is destined for them by the will of God.

Ne plus ne moins qu'on voit l'exercite des nues
40   En un temps pluvieux egalement pendues
D'un juste poids en l'air, marcher ainsi qu'il faut,
Ny descendre trop bas, ny s'eslever trop haut:
Et tout ainsi qu'on voit qu'elles mesmes se forment
En cent divers portraits, dont les vents les transforment
En Centaures, serpens, oiseaux, hommes, poissons,
Et d'une forme en l'autre errent en cent façons:
Tout ainsi les Daimons qui ont le corps habile,
Aisé souple dispost à se muer facile,
Changent bien tost de forme, et leur corps agile est
50   Transformé tout soudain en tout ce qu'il leur plaist:
Ores en un tonneau grossement s'eslargissent,
Ores en peloton rondement s'estrecissent,
Ores en un chévron les voirriez allonger,
Ores mouvoir les pieds, et ores ne bouger.
Bien souvent on les voit se transformer en beste
Tronque par la moitié, l'une n'a que la teste,
L'autre n'a que les yeux, l'autre n'a que les bras
Et l'autre que les pieds tous velus par-à bas.
   Les autres sont entiers, et à ceux qu'ils rencontrent,
60   En forme de serpens et de dragons se monstrent,
D'orfrayes, de chouans, cheveches, de corbeaux,

Exactly as we see the battalion of clouds in rainy weather hanging evenly in the air with their due weight, marching just as they should, neither descending too low nor rising too high; and just as we see them forming themselves into a hundred diverse figures, and being transformed by the winds into Centaurs, serpents, birds, men, fish, and drifting from one form into another in a hundred ways; just so do the Daemons, whose bodies are nimble, lithe, supple, lively and readily transmuted, very quickly change their form, and their agile bodies are transformed quite abruptly into anything they please: now they swell out hugely into a barrel, now they shrink roundly into a little ball, now you might see them lengthening like a meteor, now shifting their feet, and now not moving at all. Very often we see them transform themselves into an animal that has been cut in half; one has only a head, another only eyes, another only arms and another only feet with soles completely covered with hair.

Others are whole, and to those they meet they appear in the form of serpents or

De boucs, de mastins noirs, de chats, loups et taureaux,
Et prennent les couleurs à tels corps convenables,
Pour mieux representer leurs feintes vraysemblables:[2]
En la façon qu'on voit Iris se figurer
Des rayons du Soleil, qui la vient peinturer
De trois couleurs pourveu que l'opposée nue
Où l'image se fait, soit et creuse et menue:
Autrement l'Arc-en-ciel n'auroit impression.

    Mais le Daimon la prend de sa propre action   70
Et de sa volonté, en la maniere mesme
Que soudain nostre joue en craignant devient blesme
De son propre vouloir, et toute rouge alors
Que la honte luy peint la peau par le dehors:[3]
En ce point les Daimons masquez de vaines feintes,
Donnent aux cœurs humains de merveilleuses craintes.
Car ainsi que l'air prend et reçoit à l'entour
Toute forme et couleur ce-pendant qu'il est jour,
Puis les rebaille aux yeux qui de nature peuvent
En eux les recevoir, et qui propres se treuvent: 80
Tout ainsi les Daimons font leurs masqueures voir
À nostre fantaisie apte à les recevoir:
Puis nostre fantaisie à l'esprit les r'apporte
De la mesme façon et de la mesme sorte

dragons, of sea eagles, screech owls, little owls, and crows, of goats, black dogs, cats, wolves and bulls, and they take on the colours appropriate to such bodies, the better to perform their plausible pretences: in the same way as we see Iris materializing from the rays of the Sun, as he comes to paint her in three colours, provided that the cloud facing him, on which the image is created, is both hollow and thin; otherwise the Rainbow would make no impression.

  But the Daemon takes on his appearance by his own action and by his own will, in the same way as, when we are afraid, our cheeks suddenly of their own volition turn pale, or turn bright red when shame outwardly paints their skin: in this manner, the Daemons, under the mask of illusory disguises, fill human hearts with the utmost dread. For just as the air takes and receives from all around every shape and colour, provided there is daylight, then passes them on to the eyes, which by their nature are able to receive them, and which are fitted for the task, just so do the Daemons make their disguises visible to our imagination, which is designed to receive them.

Qu'elle les imagine en dormant, ou veillant:
Et lors une frayeur va nos cœurs assaillant,
Le poil nous dresse au chef, et du front goute à goute
Jusqu'à bas des talons la sueur nous degoute.

    Si nous sommes au lict, n'osons lever les bras,
90   Ny tant soit peu tourner le corps entre les draps:
Adonq nous est advis que nous voyons nos peres
Morts dedans un linceul, et nos defunctes meres
Parler à nous la nuict, et que voyons en l'eau
Quelqu'un de nos amis perir dans un bateau:
Il semble qu'un grand Ours tout affamé nous mange,
Ou que seuls nous errons par un desert estrange
Au milieu des Lions, ou qu'au bois un volleur
Nous met pour nostre argent la dague dans le cœur.[4]

    Souvent à l'improuveue on les voit apparoistre,
100   Tellement qu'on les peut facilement cognoistre
Comme Achille cogneut Minerve qui le print
Par le poil de la teste, et son courroux retint:
Mais eux bien peu de temps de leur forme jouyssent,
Et tout soudain en rien elles s'esvanouyssent,
Comme si de couleurs les ondes on teignoit,
Ou si l'air et le vent de couleurs on peignoit:

Next our imagination conveys them to our mind, in the same fashion and in the same way as it conceives them while we are asleep or awake. Then terror assails our heart, the hair of our head stands on end, and from our forehead, drop by drop, right down to our feet, the sweat drips from us.

If we are in bed, we dare not raise our arms, nor make the slightest movement of our body between the sheets; then we seem to see our dead fathers in their shrouds, and our deceased mothers speaking to us in the night, and to see one of our friends perishing in a boat on the water; it seems as if a huge, ravenous Bear is devouring us, or as if we are wandering alone in a strange desert surrounded by Lions, or as if in a wood a robber is plunging his dagger into our heart for our money.

Often we see them appear without warning, in such a manner that we can easily recognize them, just as Achilles recognized Minerva, who grasped him by the hair of his head, and checked his wrath. But they retain their shapes for a very short time, and then in an instant these vanish away to nothing, just as if the waves were being dyed with colours, or as if the air and the wind were being painted with

Car leur corps n'est solide et apte de nature
À retenir long temps une prise figure.

    Les uns vivent en l'air de respirations,
Les autres plus grossiers d'evaporations,   110
À la façon de l'huistre:[5] aussi le sacrifice
Du sang des animaux leur est doux et propice.
Ils sont participans de Dieu et des humains:
De Dieu comme immortels, des hommes comme pleins
De toutes passions: ils desirent, ils craignent,
Ils veulent concevoir, ils aiment et desdaignent:
L'air compose leur corps, ains leur masque commun:
Dieu loin de la matiere (ouvriere d'un chacun
Qui respire icy bas) n'est qu'une simple essence,
D'un meslange agencé nos corps prennent naissance.   120
    Or deux extremitez ne sont point sans milieu:
Les deux extremitez sont les hommes et Dieu:
Dieu qui est tout-puissant de nature eternelle,
Les hommes impuissans de nature mortelle.
Des hommes et de Dieu les Daimons aërins
Sont communs en nature, habitans les confins
De la terre et du ciel, et dans l'air se delectent,
Et sont bons ou mauvais tout ainsi qu'ils affectent:

colours, for their body is not solid and by nature capable of holding for long any appearance it assumes.

    Some of them live in the air on exhalations, others of coarser constitution live on vapours, like the oyster, and moreover they find the sacrifice of animal blood agreeable and beneficial. They partake of the nature of both God and human beings: of God in that they are immortal, of humans in that they are filled with every passion: they desire, they fear, they wish to procreate, they love and hate; their body, or rather the appearance they usually assume, is composed of air; God, far removed from matter (which constitutes each of us who breathes here below), is simply pure essence, whereas our bodies are born from a balanced mixture.

    Now two extremities must have a mid-point. The two extremities are men and God: God who is all-powerful and eternal by nature, and men who are powerless and mortal by nature. The Daemons of the air share in the nature of men and God, inhabiting the confines of earth and heaven, and they take delight in the air, and are

Les bons viennent de l'air jusques en ces bas lieux
130 Pour nous faire sçavoir la volonté des Dieux,
Puis r'emportent à Dieu nos faicts et nos prieres,
Et détachent du corps nos ames prisonnieres
Pour les mener là-haut, à fin d'imaginer
Ce qui se doit sçavoir pour nous endoctriner.
Ils nous monstrent de nuict par songes admirables
De nos biens de nos maux les signes veritables.
D'eux vient la Prophetie, et l'art qui est obscur
De sçavoir par oiseaux augurer le futur.
Hannibal sceut par eux d'un de ses yeux la perte:
140 Tullin se vit par eux la perruque couverte
D'un feu presagieux: par eux l'Aigle se mit
Sur le chef de Tarquin qui grand Roy le predit.[6]

  Les mauvais au contraire apportent sur la terre
Pestes, fiévres, langueurs, orages et tonnerre:
Ils font des bruits en l'air pour nous espoventer,
Ils font aux yeux humains deux Soleils presenter,
Ils font noircir la Lune horriblement hideuse,
Et font pleurer le Ciel d'une pluye saigneuse:
Bref, tout ce qui se fait en l'air de monstrueux
150 Et en terre çà bas, ne se fait que par eux.

good or bad just as they choose. The good ones come down from the air to these
lower regions to inform us of the will of the Gods, then carry back to God our deeds
and our prayers, and they free our imprisoned souls from our bodies to take them
up to heaven, so that we may have a vision of what we need to know to become
learned. By night, through amazing dreams, they show us the true signs of the good
and the ill that will befall us. From them comes Prophecy, and the mysterious art of
augury that makes it possible to foretell the future by means of birds. It was through
them that Hannibal knew that he would lose one of his eyes; it was through them that
Servius Tullius saw his head encircled by a prophetic fire; through them the Eagle
settled on the head of Tarquin, thus predicting that he would be a great king.

 The bad ones, on the other hand, afflict the earth with plagues, fevers, languishing
sicknesses, storms and thunder; they cause noises in the air to terrify us, they cause
two Suns to appear to human eyes, they cause the Moon to turn black and become
horribly hideous, and cause the Sky to rain tears of blood. In short, everything
monstrous that occurs in the air and on earth here below occurs only through them.

Les uns vont habitant les maisons ruinées,
Ou des grandes citez les places destournées
En quelque carrefour, et hurlent toute nuit
Accompagnez de chiens, d'un effroyable bruit.[7]
Vous diriez que cent fers ils trainent par la rue,
Esclatant une voix en complaintes aigue,
Qui resveillent les cœurs des hommes sommeillans,
Et donnent grand' frayeur à ceux qui sont veillans.
 Les autres sont nommez par divers noms, Incubes,
Larves, Lares, Lemurs, Penates, et Succubes,   160
Empouses, Lamiens, qui ne vaguent pas tant
Que font les aërins:[8] sans plus vont habitant
Autour de nos maisons, et de travers se couchent
Dessus nostre estomac, et nous tastent et touchent:
Ils remuent de nuict bancs, tables et treteaux,
Clefs, huys, portes, buffets, licts, chaires, escabeaux,
Ou comptent nos tresors, ou jettent contre terre
Maintenant une espée, et maintenant un verre:
Toutefois au matin on ne voit rien cassé,
Ny meuble qui ne soit en sa place agencé.   170
 On dit qu'en Norovegue ils se louent à gages
Et font comme valets des maisons les mesnages,

Some take up residence in derelict houses, or in the deserted parts of big cities, at some crossroads, and, accompanied by dogs, howl all night long with a dreadful noise. You would think they were dragging a hundred iron chains down the street, shouting out in a voice shrill with complaints, which rouse the hearts of slumbering men and instil great terror into those who are awake.

Others are called by various names, Incubi, Larvae, Lares, Lemures, Penates, Succubi, Empousas, Lamias, and do not travel around as much as the Daemons of the air. They merely take up residence around our houses, and lie across our stomachs, and feel and fondle us. By night they move benches, tables and trestles, keys, doors, gates, dressers, beds, chairs, stools, or count our money, or hurl to the ground now a sword and now a glass. Nevertheless, in the morning we do not find anything broken, nor any furniture that is not in its place.

It's said that in Norway they hire themselves out for wages, and do the housework like servants; they look after the horses, they go and draw the wine, they cook the

Ils pensent les chevaux, ils vont tirer le vin,
Ils font cuire le rost, ils serencent le lin,
Ils filent la fusée, et les robbes nettoyent
Au lever de leur maistre, et les places baloyent.

    Or qui voudroit narrer les contes qu'on fait d'eux,
De tristes, de gaillards, d'horribles, de piteux,
On n'auroit jamais fait: car homme ne se treuve
180   Qui tousjours n'en raconte une merveille neuve.

    Les autres moins terrains sont à part habitans
Torrens fleuves ruisseaux les lacs et les estans,
Les marais endormis et les fontaines vives,
En forme de Sereine apparoissant aux rives.

    Tant que les aërins ils n'ont d'affections,
Aussi leur corps ne prend tant de mutations:
Ils n'aiment qu'une forme, et volontiers icelle
Est du nombril en haut d'une jeune pucelle
Qui a les cheveux longs, et les yeux verts et beaux,
190   Contre-imitans l'azur de leurs propres ruisseaux.
Pource ils se font nommer Naiades, Nereides,
Les filles de Thetis, les cinquante Phorcides,
Qui errent par la mer sur le dos des Dauphins,
Bridans les Esturbots, les Fouches, et les Thins,

roast, they card the flax, they spin the thread, and clean the clothes for when their master rises, and sweep the rooms.

Now anyone who wanted to recount the tales that are told about them, be they sad ones, merry ones, horrible ones, or pitiful ones, would never be done, for there is no one who is not forever relating a fresh marvel about them.

Others, less earthbound, live in seclusion in torrents, rivers, streams, in lakes and ponds, in stagnant marshes and bubbling springs, appearing on their banks in the guise of Sirens.

They do not have emotions, as those that dwell in the air do, and so their bodies do not undergo so many mutations: they favour only one form, and this is usually that of a young girl from the navel up, with long hair and lovely green eyes, reflecting the azure of their own streams. For this reason, they are called Naiads, Nereids, daughters of Thetis, the fifty daughters of Phorcys, who range over the sea on the backs of Dolphins, harnessing Turbot, Seals, and Tunny fish, sometimes borne

Aucunefois vagant tout au sommet des ondes,
Aucunefois au bas des abysmes profondes.[9]

   Ils ont le mesme esprit que les autres Daimons,
Les uns pernicieux, les autres doux et bons:
Ils font faire à la mer en un jour deux voyages,[10]
Ils appaisent les flots, ils mouvent les orages,   200
Ils sauvent les bateaux, ou font contre un rocher
Perir quand il leur plaist, la nef et le nocher.

   Neptune le Daimon voulut noyer Ulysse,
Leucothoé luy fut à son danger propice:
L'Egyptien Protée attaché d'un lien,
Par sa fille trahy, enseigna le moyen
Au chetif Menelas de retourner en Grece,
Qui tout desesperé se rongeoit de tristesse.[11]

   Ils se changent souvent en grands flambeaux ardans
Pendus dessus une eau, pour conduire dedans   210
Le passant fourvoyé trompé de leur lumiere,
Qui le meine noyer dedans l'onde meurdriere.

   Les uns ayant pitié des hommes et des naux,
Esclairent sur le mast, comme deux feux jumeaux,
Et tirent la navire et les hommes de peine,
Nommez le feu sainct Herme, ou les freres d'Heleine.[12]

---

hither and thither on the very crest of the waves, sometimes in the very depths of the abysses of the sea.

They have the same characters as the other Daemons, some malevolent, others amiable and kindly. They cause the sea to travel back and forth twice a day, they calm the waves, they stir up storms, they save boats, or, when they feel so inclined, they destroy both ship and sailor, dashing them against a rock.

The Daemon Neptune tried to drown Ulysses, but Leucothea proved benevolent to him, in his time of danger; Egyptian Proteus, fastened with bonds as a result of his daughter's betrayal, told the unfortunate Menelaus how he could return to Greece, when, in the depths of despair, he was racked by sorrow.

They often change into huge flaming torches hovering over a stretch of water, ready to lure into it the passer-by who has lost his way and is deluded by their light, which leads him to drown in the murderous waters.

Some, taking pity on men and ships, shine on the mast, like two twin fires, and pull ship and men out of difficulty. These are called St Elmo's fire or Helen's brothers.

Les autres moins subtils, chargez d'un corps plus gras
Et plus materiel, habitent les lieux bas,
Et ne changent jamais de la forme qu'ils tiennent:
220   Car point d'affections de changer ne leur viennent
Non plus qu'à la souriz qui dans un trou se tient,
Et rien en souvenir que manger ne luy vient.

Si sont-ils toutefois de meschante nature:
Car si quelqu'un devalle en un puis d'aventure,
Ou va par avarice aux minieres de fer,
D'or de cuivre ou d'argent ils viennent l'estoufer,
Et serrant son gosier sans haleine le tuent.

Aucunefois sous terre engloutissent et ruent
Les peupleuses citez et leurs murs trebuchans:
230   Ils font trembler la terre, ils crevassent les champs,
Et d'une flamme ardente au profond de Tartare
Allument le mont d'Etne et Vesuve et Lipare.

Aucunefois transis d'excessive froideur,
Laissent les lieux terreins pour chercher la chaleur,
Non celle du Soleil, car elle est trop ardante,
Mais le sang temperé d'une beste vivante:
Et entrent dans les porcs, dans les chiens, dans les loups,
Et les font sauteller sur l'herbe comme fouls.

Others, less ethereal by nature, weighed down by a body more solid and more earthy, inhabit the nether regions, and never change the shape they have, for no desire for change occurs to them, any more than it does to a mouse that stays in its hole, and thinks of nothing except eating.

However, they are evil-natured, for if someone chances to fall into a well, or out of greed goes into mines for iron, gold, copper or silver, they come to suffocate him, and, gripping his throat so that he cannot breathe, they kill him.

Sometimes they cast down and bury underground the densely populated cities and their tottering walls; they make the earth shake, they make cracks appear in the fields, and with a fiery flame from the depths of Tartarus they set alight Mount Etna and Vesuvius and Lipari.

Sometimes, numbed with extreme cold, they leave subterranean regions to seek heat, not the heat of the Sun, for that is too scorching, but the warm blood of a live animal, and they take possession of pigs, or dogs, or wolves, and make them cavort on the grass like mad things.

Les autres plus gaillards habitent les montagnes,
Les taillis, les forests, les vaux et les campagnes, 240
Les tertres et les monts, et souvent dans un bois
Ou dans le creux d'un roc, d'une douteuse vois
Annoncent le futur, non qu'au parfait cognues
Toutes choses leur soient ains que d'estre venues:
Mais eux qui par long âge experimentez sont
Aux affaires du monde, et qui plus que nous ont
L'esprit aërien, plustost que nous advisent
(Nous qui mourons trop tost) le futur qu'ils predisent:
Toutefois la prudence et l'advis peut donner
Aux hommes craignans Dieu pouvoir de deviner. 250

Les uns aucunefois se transforment en Fées,
En Dryades des bois, en Nymphes et Napées,
En Faunes, en Sylvains, en Satyres et Pans,
Qui ont le corps pelu marqueté comme fans:
Ils ont l'orteil de bouc, et d'un chevreul l'oreille,
La corne d'un chamois, et la face vermeille
Comme un rouge Croissant, et dansent toute nuit
Dedans un carrefour, ou pres d'une eau qui bruit.[13]

Ils craignent tous du feu la lumiere tres-belle:
Et pource Pythagore ordonna que sans elle 260

Others, more active, inhabit mountains, copses, forests, valleys and plains, knolls and hills, and often, in a wood or in the hollow of a rock, with ambiguous words they foretell the future; not that all things are perfectly known to them before they have happened, but they, who by virtue of their long existence have become experienced in the affairs of the world, and who have minds more ethereal than ours, perceive sooner than we do (we who die too soon) the future they predict. However, prudence and wisdom may give to God-fearing men the power of divination.

Some on occasion transform themselves into Fairies, into Dryads of the woods, into Nymphs and Napaeae, or into Fauns, Silvans, Satyrs and Pans, who have hairy bodies dappled like fawns. They have the feet of a goat, the ears of a deer, the horns of a chamois, and a rubicund face like a red Crescent moon, and they dance all night long at a crossroads, or near a murmuring brook.

They are all afraid of the most beautiful light of fire, and for this reason Pythagoras

On ne priast les Dieux: mais plus que les flambeaux
Ny que les vers charmez ils craignent les couteaux,
Et tremblant vont fuyant s'ils voyent une espée,
De peur de ne sentir leur liaison coupée:
Ce que souventefois j'ay de nuict esprouvé,
Et rien de si certain contre eux je n'ay trouvé.[14]
D'un poinct nous differons: quand le fer nous incise,
Nostre chair est long temps avant qu'estre reprise,
Des Daimons à l'instant: ainsi que qui fendroit
270   L'air, ou le vent, ou l'eau, qui tost se reprendroit.
Que diray-je plus d'eux? ils sont pleins de science,
Quant au reste impudens, et pleins d'outrecuidance,
Sans aucun jugement: ils sont follets, menteurs,
Volages, inconstans, traistres et decepteurs,
Mutins, impatiens, qui jamais n'apparoissent
À ceux qui leur nature et leurs abus cognoissent:
    Mais s'ils sentent un homme abandonné d'espoir
Errer seul aux deserts, le viendront decevoir,
Ou tromperont les cœurs des simplettes bergeres
280   Qui gardent les brebis, et les feront sorcieres.

ordained that without this light prayers should not be said to the gods; but more than of flaming torches or magic incantations they are afraid of knives, and they tremble and take flight if they see a sword, for fear they may feel their sinews severed. I have confirmed the truth of this many times at night, and I have found nothing so effective in protecting myself against them. We differ from them in one respect: when the steel pierces us, our flesh is very slow to heal, whereas Daemons heal instantly, just as if one were to cleave the air, or the wind, or water, which would quickly become whole again. What more shall I say about them? They possess great knowledge, but on the other hand they are rude, full of presumption, and lacking in any judgement; they are fatuous, lying, fickle, inconstant, treacherous and deceitful, rebellious, impatient; and they never appear to those who are aware of their nature and their deceptions.

But if they sense that a man is abandoned by hope and is wandering alone in a desolate place, they will approach and lead him astray, or they will delude the hearts of simple shepherdesses who are watching their sheep, and turn them into witches.

Si tost que leurs cerveaux sont abusez et pris
Des folles vanitez de ces meschans espris,
Elles cuident pousser ou retenir les nues,
Et les rivieres sont par elles retenues:
Elles tirent la Lune, et les espics crestez
Sont par elle d'un champ dans un autre arrestez,
Et par elles souvent la foudre est retardée:
Telles furent jadis Circe, Thrace, Medée,
Urgande, Melusine,[15] et mille dont le nom
Par effects merveilleux s'est acquis du renom.　　　　290
Au reste, ils sont si sots et si badins qu'ils craignent
Les charmeurs dont les poincts et la voix les contraignent
À leur faire service, et les tiennent fermez
Ou dedans des mirouers, ou des anneaux charmez,
Et n'en osent sortir enchantez d'un murmure,
Ou d'une voix barbare, ou de quelque figure.[16]
　Aucunesfois malins entrent dedans nos corps,
Et en nous tourmentant nous laissent presque morts,
Ou nous meuvent la fiévre, ou troublans nos courages
Font nos langues parler de dix mille langages.　　　　300

As soon as their brains are deceived and entrapped by the foolish vanities of these evil spirits, they claim that they can drive clouds over the sky or hold them back, and that by their agency the rivers cease to flow; that they can draw down the moon, and that by their agency tall stalks of corn are transported from one field into another, and that by their agency the lightning is often held in check. Such in times past were Circe, Thrace, Medea, Urgande, Melusine, and a thousand others whose names have become famous for their miraculous deeds. Moreover, the Daemons are so foolish and so silly that they are afraid of magicians, who by their magical marks and their utterances force the Daemons to serve them, and keep them imprisoned either in mirrors, or in enchanted rings, so that they dare not come out, being under a spell cast by a muttered charm, or by a meaningless incantation, or by some symbolic figure.

Sometimes, maliciously, they creep into our bodies, and by tormenting us leave us almost dead, or they infect us with fevers, or disturbing our minds make our tongues speak in ten thousand languages. But if someone chides them in the name

Mais si quelcun les tence au nom du Tres-Puissant,
Ils vont hurlant criant tremblant et fremissant,
Et forcez sont contraints d'abandonner la place:[17]
Tant le sainct nom de Dieu leur est grande menace!
Auquel nom[18] seulement les Anges ne sont pas
Flechissans les genoux, mais nous et ceux d'embas,
Toute essence immortelle, et tout ce qu'on voit naistre,
Comme au nom du Seigneur de toute chose maistre.

    Ô Seigneur Eternel en qui seul gist ma foy,
310   Pour l'honneur de ton nom, de grace donne moy,
Donne moy que jamais je ne trouve en ma voye
Ces paniques terreurs: mais ô Seigneur envoye
Loin de la Chrestienté dans les pays des Turcs
Ces Larves ces Daimons ces Lares et Lemurs,
Ou sur le chef de ceux qui oseront mesdire
Des chansons que j'accorde à ma nouvelle lyre.

of the Almighty, they start to howl, shriek, tremble and shake, and are forcibly constrained to abandon their position; so powerful is the threat posed to them by the holy name of God! At his name not only do the Angels bend the knee, but we ourselves and those below, every immortal being, and everything that is born, kneel to the name of the Lord, the master of all things.

    O Eternal Lord in whom alone resides my faith, for the glory of thy name, by thy grace grant me, grant me this: that I may never encounter in my way these panic terrors, but, O Lord, send these Larvae, these Daemons, these Lares and Lemures far away from Christendom into the lands of the Turks, or upon the heads of those who dare to speak ill of the songs that I set to the music of my new lyre.

72 Hynne du Ciel
À Jean de Morel, Ambrunois

Morel, qui pour partage en ton ame possedes
Les plus nobles vertus, thresor dont tu ne cedes
À nul de nostre siecle, ou soit en equité,
Soit en candeur de mœurs, ou soit en verité,
Qui seul de nos François de mes vers pris la charge
Couverts de ta faveur, comme Ajax sous sa targe
Couvroit l'archer Teucer, que les Troyens pressoyent
De traits, qui sur le dos du boucler se froissoyent:
    Ce-pendant qu'à loisir l'Hynne je te façonne
Des Muses, pren en gré ce Ciel que je te donne,   10
À toy digne de luy, comme l'ayant cognu
Long temps avant que d'estre en la terre venu,
Et qui le recognois, si apres la naissance
Quelque homme en eut jamais çà-bas la cognoissance.[1]
    Ô Ciel rond et vouté, haute maison de Dieu,
Qui prestes en ton sein à toutes choses lieu,

Hymn to the Sky
To Jean Morel of Embrun

Morel, you whose soul is endowed with the noblest virtues, treasures in which you are second to none in our century, whether in justice, whether in purity of morals, or whether in truthfulness, you who alone of our fellow Frenchmen championed my verses, protecting them by your favour, just as Ajax protected Teucer the archer with his shield, when the Trojans were assailing him with arrows, which shattered against the surface of the buckler,

while I am fashioning for you at my leisure a Hymn to the Muses, graciously accept meanwhile this Hymn to the Sky, which I give to you, you who are worthy of it, as you knew the heavens for a long time before coming to earth, you who retain the knowledge of them still, if any man after birth ever had any knowledge of them here below.

O round and vaulted Sky, lofty dwelling of God, you who afford a place to all

Et qui roules si tost ta grand' boule esbranlée
Sur deux essieux fichez, que la vistesse ailée
Des aigles et des vents par l'air ne sçauroyent pas
En volant egaler le moindre de tes pas:
Tant seulement l'esprit de prompte hardiesse
Comme venant de toy, egale ta vistesse.
Ô Ciel viste coureur, tu parfais ton grand tour
D'un pied jamais recreu, en l'espace d'un jour!
Ainçois d'un pied de fer, qui sans cesse retourne
Au lieu duquel il part, et jamais ne sejourne
Trainant tout avec soy, pour ne souffrir mourir
L'Univers en paresse à faute de courir.[2]

    L'esprit de l'Eternel, qui avance ta course
Espandu dedans toy, comme une vive source
De tous costez t'anime, et donne mouvement,
Te faisant tournoyer en sphere rondement
Pour estre plus parfait: car en la forme ronde
Gist la perfection qui toute en soy abonde.[3]

    De ton branle premier des autres tout divers,
Tu tires au rebours les corps de l'Univers,
Bandez en resistant contre ta violence,
Seuls à part demenant une seconde dance:

---

things in your bosom, and so swiftly roll your huge spinning ball on its two fixed poles that the winged speed of eagles and of the winds in the air as they fly could not equal the slowest of your movements, only the mind in its bold rapidity equals your speed, since it comes from you. O Sky, you who run so speedily, you complete your long cycle in the space of a day, with a never-tiring foot! On the contrary, you have feet of iron, which ceaselessly return to their point of departure, and never pause, pulling everything along with them, in order not to let the Universe die in idleness by failing to keep running.

The spirit of God the Eternal, which, diffused within you, drives your course, like a lively stream animates you through and through, and gives you your motion, making you rotate as a sphere, in a circle, in order to attain perfection, for in a circular form lies perfection, which is wholly complete in itself.

With your first dancing movement, which is quite different from all the others, you pull the various bodies of the Universe in the opposite direction, though they strain to resist your power, separately performing a second dance by themselves, one

L'un deçà, l'autre là, comme ils sont agitez
Des mouvements reiglez de leurs diversitez.   40
Ainsi guidant premier si grande compagnie,
Tu fais une si douce et plaisante harmonie,
Que nos luts ne sont rien au pris des moindres sons
Qui resonnent là haut de diverses façons.[4]

    D'un feu vif et divin ta voute est composée,
Non feu materiel dont la flame exposée
Çà bas en nos fouyers mangeroit affamé
De toutes les forests le branchage ramé:
Et pource tous les jours il faut qu'on le nourisse
Le repaissant de bois, s'on ne veut qu'il perisse.   50
Mais celuy qui là haut en vigueur entretient
Toy et tes yeux d'Argus, de luy seul se soustient
Sans mendier secours: car sa vive etincelle
Sans aucun aliment se nourrit de par-elle:
D'elle mesme elle luit, comme fait le Soleil,
Temperant l'Univers d'un feu doux et pareil
À celuy qui habite en l'estomac de l'homme,
Qui tout le corps eschaufe et point ne le consomme.[5]

    Qu'à bon droit les Gregeois t'ont nommé d'un beau nom![6]
Qui bien t'avisera, ne trouvera sinon   60

---

this way, another that way, according to how they are propelled by the ordered movements of their diverse natures. Thus you, the first conductor of so great a company, make such a sweet and pleasing harmony that our lutes are nothing in comparison to the least sounds that resound on high in diverse ways.

Your vault is composed of a living, divine fire, not a physical fire, whose flame, seen on our hearths here on earth, would hungrily devour the boughs and branches of all the forests, which makes it necessary to nourish it every day, feeding it with wood, if one does not want it to die. But the fire that on high maintains you and the eyes of Argus in vigorous existence sustains itself from its own resources without seeking assistance, for its lively spark nourishes itself by its own action without any sustenance. Unaided it shines, as the Sun does, tempering the Universe with a gentle fire like that which is present in a man's stomach, and which heats the whole body and does not consume it.

How right the Greeks were to name you with a beautiful name! Anyone who

En toy qu'un ornement, et qu'une beauté pure,
Qu'un compas bien reglé, qu'une juste mesure,
Et bref, qu'un rond parfait: dont l'immense grandeur,
Hauteur, largeur, biais, travers et profondeur
Nous monstrent en voyant un si bel edifice,
Combien l'esprit de Dieu est rempli d'artifice,
Et subtil artizan, qui te bastist de rien
Et t'accomplist si beau, pour nous monstrer combien
Grande est sa Majesté, qui hautaine demande
70   Pour son Palais royal une maison si grande.[7]

    Or ce Dieu tout puissant, tant il est bon et dous,
S'est fait le citoyen du monde comme nous,
Et n'a tant desdaigné nostre humaine nature,
Qu'il ait outre les bords de ta large closture
Autre maison bastie, ains s'est logé chez toy,
Chez toy, franc de soucis, de peines et d'esmoy,
Qui vont couvrant le front des terres habitables,
Des terres, la maison des humains miserables.[8]

    Si celuy qui comprend doit emporter le pris
80   Et l'honneur sur celuy qui plus bas est compris,
Tu dois avoir l'honneur sur ceste masse toute,
Qui tout seul la comprens dessous ta large voute,

---

contemplates you will find in you nothing but elegance and pure beauty, a well-ordered proportion, a just measure, in short, a perfect circle, whose immense size, height, breadth, diagonals, transverse measurements and depth all show us, as we behold such a beautiful construction, how greatly God's spirit is filled with artistry, for, being a skilful artisan, he built you out of nothing and created you with such beauty, to show us how great is his Glory, which majestically insists on such a large dwelling for his royal Palace.

    Now, this almighty God is so good and kind that he became a citizen of the universe like us, and did not so despise our human nature that he built another dwelling beyond the limits of your wide bounds, but took up residence within you, within you the sky, who are free from the cares, sorrows and worry that cover the face of the inhabited earth, the earth which is the home of suffering humanity.

    If that which contains must win the prize and the honour over that which is contained below, you must have the honour over this whole mass, as you and you

Et en son ordre à part limites un chacun:
Toy, qui n'as ton pareil, et ne sembles qu'à un
Qu'à toy, qui es ton moule et la seule modelle
De toy-mesme tout rond, comme chose eternelle.

    Tu n'as en ta grandeur commencement ne bout,
Tu es tout dedans toy, de toutes choses tout,
Non contraint, infini, fait d'un fini espace,
Dont le sein large et creux toutes choses embrasse   90
Sans rien laisser dehors: et pource c'est erreur,
C'est un extreme abus, une extreme fureur
De penser qu'il y ait des mondes hors du monde.
Tu prens tout, tu tiens tout dessous ton arche ronde
D'un contour merveilleux la terre couronnant,
Et la grand' mer qui vient la terre environnant,
L'air espars et le feu: et bref, on ne voit chose
Ou qui ne soit à toy, ou dedans toy enclose,
Et de quelque costé que nous tournions les yeux,
Nous avons pour object la closture des Cieux.[9]   100

    Tu mets les Dieux au joug d'Anangé la fatale,
Tu depars à chacun sa semence natale,

---

alone contain it under your broad vault, and set limits for each part individually with its own ordered position; you, who have not your equal, and resemble only one thing, namely yourself, you who are your own mould and the only model for yourself, completely round, like things eternal.

    In your immensity you have neither beginning nor end, you are altogether contained in yourself, of all things all, unconstrained, infinite, though made of finite space, you whose broad and hollow bosom enfolds all things without leaving anything outside; and for this reason it is a mistake, it is a flagrant error, a flagrant delusion to think that there are other worlds outside this world. You gather everything within you, you hold everything beneath your round arch, crowning the earth with a wondrous curving outline, and you hold also the vast sea that surrounds the earth, the wide spreading air, and fire; and, in short, we see nothing that either does not belong to you or is not enclosed within you, and whichever way we turn our eyes, we have as the object of our gaze the enclosing Heavens.

    You subjugate the Gods to the yoke of Anange, ineluctable fate; you allot to each

La nature en ton sein ses ouvrages respend:
Tu es premier chaisnon de la chaisne qui pend:[10]

    Toy comme fecond pere, en abondance enfantes
Les Siecles, et des ans les suites renaissantes,
Les mois et les saisons, les heures et les jours
Ainsi que jouvenceaux jeunissent de ton cours
Frayant sans nul repos une orniere eternelle,
Qui tousjours se retrace et se refraye en elle:
Bref, te voyant si beau, je ne sçaurois penser
Que quatre ou cinq mille ans te puissent commencer.[11]

    Sois Saint de quelque nom que tu voudras, ô Pere,
À qui de l'Univers la nature obtempere,
Aimantin, varié, azuré, tournoyant,
Fils de Saturne, Roy tout-oyant, tout-voyant,
Ciel grand Palais de Dieu, exauce ma priere:
Quand la mort desli'ra mon ame prisonniere,
Et celle de Morel, hors de ce corps humain,
Daigne les recevoir, benin, dedans ton sein
Apres mille travaux: et vueilles de ta grace
Chez toy les reloger en leur premiere place.[12]

entity the seed that engenders it, in your bosom nature spreads forth its works; you are the first link in the chain that is suspended.

Like a fertile father, you give birth to the Centuries in abundance; and the cycles of years that are reborn, the months and seasons, the hours and the days are ever youthful, rejuvenated by your course, and, never resting, create an eternal track, which continuously retraces and recreates itself; in short, seeing you so beautiful, I cannot believe that you were begun only four or five thousand years ago.

Holy Father, whatever the name you choose to be called by, you whom the Universe by its nature obeys, you who are magnetic and adamantine, diverse, azure, spinning, son of Saturn, all-hearing and all-seeing King, Sky the great Palace of God, hear my prayer: when death releases my imprisoned soul, and that of Morel, from this human body, grant in your kindness that you will receive them into your bosom after a thousand labours, and by your grace take them to live with you again in their first home.

73 Hynne de l'Autonne
À Claude de l'Aubespine

Le jour que je fu né, Apollon qui preside
Aux Muses, me servit en ce monde de guide,
M'anima d'un esprit subtil et vigoureux,
Et me fist de science et d'honneur amoureux.

    En lieu des grans thresors et des richesses vaines
Qui aveuglent les yeux des personnes humaines,
Me donna pour partage une fureur d'esprit,
Et l'art de bien coucher ma verve par escrit.

    Il me haussa le cœur haussa la fantaisie,
M'inspirant dedans l'ame un don de Poësie,   10
Que Dieu n'a concedé qu'à l'esprit agité
Des poignans aiguillons de sa Divinité.

    Quand l'homme en est touché il devient un Prophete,
Il predit toute chose avant qu'elle soit faite,
Il cognoist la nature et les secrets des Cieux,
Et d'un esprit bouillant s'eleve entre les Dieux.

Hymn to Autumn
To Claude de l'Aubespine

On the day that I was born, Apollo, who presides over the Muses, acted as my guide
in this world, animated me with a penetrating and active mind, and made me love
knowledge and honour.

    Instead of the great treasures and the worthless riches that dazzle the eyes of
human beings, he gave me as my birthright the fury of inspiration, and the art of
skilfully putting my lively imaginings into writing.

    He exalted my heart and exalted my imagination, inspiring my soul with a gift
for Poetry, which God has granted only to those minds spurred by the sharp goads
of his Divinity.

    When a man is affected by this gift he becomes a Prophet, he predicts everything
before it happens, he knows the nature and the secrets of the Heavens, and with his
mind in a ferment he is raised aloft among the Gods.

Il cognoist la vertu des herbes et des pierres,
Il enferme les vents, il charme les tonnerres:
Sciences que le peuple admire et ne sçait pas
20   Que Dieu les va donnant aux hommes d'ici bas,
Quand ils ont de l'humain les ames separées,
Et qu'à telle fureur elles sont preparées
Par oraison, par jeusne et penitence aussi,
Dont aujourd'huy le monde a bien peu de souci.

   Car Dieu ne communique aux hommes ses mysteres
S'ils ne sont vertueux devots et solitaires,
Eslongnez des tyrans, et des peuples qui ont
La malice en la main et l'impudence au front,
Brulez d'ambition et tourmentez d'envie,
30   Qui leur sert de bourreau tout le temps de leur vie.

   Je n'avois pas quinze ans que les monts et les bois
Et les eaux me plaisoyent plus que la Court des Rois,
Et les noires forests en fueillages voutées,
Et du bec des oiseaux les roches picotées:
Une valée un antre en horreur obscurci,
Un desert effroyable estoit tout mon souci:
   À fin de voir au soir les Nymphes et les Fées,
Danser dessous la Lune en cotte par les prées,

He knows the powers of plants and stones, he imprisons the winds, he casts a spell on the thunder: arts that the people admire, unaware that God gives them to men here on earth, when their souls are separated from what is human, and when they have been prepared for this fury of inspiration through prayer, through fasting and repentance also, matters for which the world cares very little today.

For God does not reveal his mysteries to men if they are not virtuous, devout and solitary, far removed from tyrants, and from peoples who have the weapons of hatred in their hands and effrontery on their faces, burning with ambition and tormented by envy, which is their torturer all the days of their life.

I was not yet fifteen years old when the mountains and the woods and the waters pleased me more than the Court of Kings, and the dark forests with their leafy vaults, and the rocks pecked by the beaks of birds, a valley, a cave full of gloomy horror, a fearsome wilderness, these were all I cared for;

so that, my mind given to fantastical imaginings, I might see in the evenings Nymphs and Fairies in their petticoats, dancing in the meadows beneath the Moon,

Fantastique d'esprit: et de voir les Sylvains
Estre boucs par les pieds, et hommes par les mains,   40
Et porter sur le front des cornes en la sorte
Qu'un petit aignelet de quatre mois les porte.

   J'allois apres la danse, et craintif je pressois
Mes pas dedans le trac des Nymphes, et pensois
Que pour mettre mon pied en leur trace poudreuse
J'aurois incontinent l'ame plus genereuse:
Ainsi que l'Ascrean qui gravement sonna
Quand l'une des neuf Sœurs du Laurier luy donna.

   Or je ne fu trompé de ma jeune entreprise:
Car la gentille Euterpe ayant ma dextre prise,   50
Pour m'oster le mortel, par neuf fois me lava
De l'eau d'une fontaine[1] où peu de monde va,
Me charma par neuf fois, puis, d'une bouche enflée
(Ayant dessus mon chef son haleine soufflée)
Me herissa le poil de crainte et de fureur,
Et me remplist le cœur d'ingenieuse erreur,
En me disant ainsi: Puis que tu veux nous suivre,
Heureux apres la mort nous te ferons revivre
Par longue renommée, et ton los en-nobli
Accablé du tombeau n'ira point en oubli.   60

and see Sylvan Deities, with feet like goats' and hands like men's, who have horns on their foreheads like the ones a little four-month-old lamb has.

I followed the dance, and fearfully pressed my steps into the prints of the Nymphs, and I thought that by placing my feet in their dusty tracks my soul would immediately become more noble, just like that of Ascrean, who uttered solemn poetry when one of the nine Sisters presented him with Laurel.

Now I was not disappointed in my youthful projects, for kindly Euterpe, taking my right hand, in order to cleanse me of all that was mortal, washed me nine times in the water of a fountain frequented by few people, cast a spell on me nine times, then, her mouth filled with air (exhaling her breath over my head), she made my hair stand on end in fear and the fury of inspiration, and imbued my heart with artful madness, saying to me, 'Since you wish to follow us, we shall make you live happily again after your death through an enduring renown, and your illustrious glory will not go down to oblivion, overwhelmed by the grave.

Tu seras du vulgaire appellé frenetique,
Insensé furieux farouche fantastique,
Maussade mal-plaisant: car le peuple médit
De celuy qui de mœurs aux siennes contredit.

Mais courage, Ronsard, les plus doctes Poëtes,
Les Sibylles Devins Augures et Prophetes,
Huez siflez moquez des peuples ont esté:
Et toutefois, Ronsard, ils disoyent verité.

N'espere d'amasser de grans biens en ce monde:
70 Une forest un pré une montaigne une onde
Sera ton heritage, et seras plus heureux
Que ceux qui vont cachant tant de thresors chez eux:
Tu n'auras point de peur qu'un Roy de sa tempeste
Te vienne en moins d'un jour escarbouiller la teste,
Ou confisquer tes biens: mais tout paisible et coy
Tu vivras dans les bois pour la Muse et pour toy.

Ainsi disoit la Nymphe, et de là je vins estre
Disciple de Dorat, qui long temps fut mon maistre,
M'apprist la Poësie, et me monstra comment
80 On doit feindre et cacher les fables proprement,
Et à bien desguiser la verité des choses
D'un fabuleux manteau dont elles sont encloses:

'By the common people you will be called frenetic, insane, frenzied, frightening, fantastical, sullen, disagreeable, for the masses revile those whose ways are contrary to their own.

'But take courage, Ronsard, the most learned Poets, the Sibyls, Seers, Augurs and Prophets have been jeered at, hissed at and derided by the masses; and yet, Ronsard, they were speaking the truth.

'Do not hope to amass great wealth in this world: a forest, a meadow, a mountain, a stream, these will be your heritage, and you will be happier than those who hide such a store of treasure in their homes. You will have no fear that a King will come like a raging whirlwind and in less than a day crush your head, or confiscate your wealth, but instead you will live in the woods, for the Muses and for yourself, in peace and quiet.'

Thus spoke the Nymph, and as a result I became a disciple of Dorat, who was for a long time my master, who taught me Poetry, and showed me how to imagine and conceal fables appropriately, and how to mask the true nature of things by

J'appris en son escole à immortaliser
Les hommes que je veux celebrer et priser,
Leur donnant de mes biens,[2] ainsi que je te donne
Pour present immortel l'Hynne de ceste Autonne.[3]
[. . .]

    Ainsi dist la nourrice, et l'Autonne sur l'heure
S'en-alla dedans l'Antre où le monstre demeure.   170

    Elle trouva le vent tout pantois et lassé
D'avoir la mer d'Afrique et ses sablons passé,
Et ja pour s'endormir avoit plié ses ailes
Depuis le bas des flancs jusqu'au haut des aisselles:
Tout ainsi qu'un Faucon laisse fourcher en crois
Les siennes sur le dos quand il se perche au bois.

    Ce vent humide et chaud gisoit à la renverse
Estendu sur le dos d'une longue traverse
Au beau milieu de l'antre (horrible chose à voir):
Meints fleuves du menton comme d'un entonnoir   180
Luy couloyent à ses pieds, et sa teste chenue
Estoit de tous costez couverte d'une nue,
Qui de-çà qui de-là sur le dos luy rendoit
Des vapeurs qu'en volant par le monde espandoit.

veiling them in a fabulous mantle. At his school I learned to immortalize the men I wish to celebrate and honour, giving them some of my own wealth, just as I give you as an immortal present this Hymn to Autumn. [. . .]

So said the nurse, and Autumn at once went into the Cave where the monster Auton lives.

She found the wind utterly breathless and exhausted from crossing the sands and the sea of Africa, and already, preparing to sleep, he had folded his wings from the lowest part of his sides up to his shoulders, just as a Falcon crosses its wings one over the other on its back when it perches in the wood.

This warm, damp wind was lying flat, stretched out at full length on his back, right across the middle of the cave (a horrible sight): many rivers flowed from his chin down to his feet, as if from a funnel, and his hoary head was covered all over by a cloud, which, now on this side, now on that, formed on his back vaporous fogs that he spread over the world as he flew.

Son antre s'estuvoit d'une chaleur croupie,
Moite lasche pesante ocieuse assoupie,
Ainsi qu'on voit sortir de la gueule d'un four
Une lente chaleur qui estuve le jour.

    Là sur un peu de paille à terre estoit couchée
190   Une lice aboyant jusqu'aux os deseichée:
Les voisins d'alentour (qui paistre la souloyent)
La vieille Maladie en son nom l'appelloyent.
Elle avoit un grand rang de tetaces tirées
Longues comme boyaux, par le bout deschirées,
Que d'un muffle affamé une engence de maux
Luy suçoyent tout ainsi que petits animaux,
Qu'elle (qui doucement sur sa race se veautre)
De son col retourné lechoit l'un apres l'autre,
Pour leur former le corps en autant de façons
200   Qu'on voit dedans la mer de sortes de poissons,
De sablons sur la rade, et de fleurs au rivage
Quand le jeune Printemps descouvre son visage.

    Là comme petits loups les caterres couvoit,
Et là la fiévre quarte et tierce se trouvoit,
Enflures flux de sang langueurs hydropisies,
La toux ronge-poumon, jaunisse pleuresies,

His cave was humid with a sluggish, dank, listless, heavy, indolent, drowsy heat, just as we see emerging from the mouth of an oven a torpid heat that makes the air humid.

There on the ground, on some straw, lay a barking bitch, emaciated, no more than skin and bone; her neighbours round about (who used to feed her) called her by the name of Old Disease. She had a lengthy row of drooping dugs, as long as intestines, and lacerated at the ends. A litter of maladies were sucking at these with ravenous muzzles, just like little animals, which she (gently sprawling over her offspring), turning her head, licked one after the other, in order to shape their bodies in as many different ways as we can see sorts of fish in the sea, grains of sand on the shore, and flowers on the riverbanks when youthful Spring unveils his face.

There she nurtured catarrhs like wolf cubs, and there quartan and tertian fevers were to be found, as well as swellings, haemorrhages, consumptions, dropsies, lung-destroying coughs, jaundices, pleurisies, lethargies, plagues, carbuncles,

Lenteurs pestes charbons tournoyement de cerveau,
Et rongnes dont l'ardeur fait allumer la peaù.

    Ceste vilaine et sale et monstrueuse osture,
Bien qu'elle soit d'un part, n'est pas d'une nature,   210
L'une croist en un jour, l'autre en demande trois,
L'une en demande sept, et l'autre veut un mois,
L'autre est vieille en une heure, et l'autre ne peut croistre.

    Or si tost qu'ils sont grans, pour eux-mesmes se paistre
La mere oste leur voix et leurs langues, à fin
D'aller sans dire mot loger chez le plus fin.[4]
[...]

    De là se fist porter au Palais de l'Esté,
Que Cerés festoyoit en pleine majesté.

    Triptoleme faisoit (pour le doux benefice
Du beau froment donné) à Cerés sacrifice,
Où la blonde Déesse en appareil estoit
Avecques son mary l'Esté qu'elle traitoit,
Et tenoit en dansant au milieu de la feste,
Du pavot en la main, des espics sur la teste.   310

---

giddiness of the brain, and scabies, which sets the skin on fire with its heat.

    This ugly, filthy and monstrous troop, although it belongs to a single litter, is not of a single nature; one grows in a day, another requires three, one requires seven days, and another needs a month, another is old in an hour, and another cannot grow at all.

    Now, as soon as they are mature, in order that they can find their own food, their mother takes away their voices and tongues, so that by not making a sound they can take up residence with even the shrewdest people. [...]

    From there she had herself transported to the Palace of Summer, whom Ceres was entertaining most majestically.

    Triptolemus (in return for the kind gift of fine wheat that he had been given) was making an offering to Ceres, in the place where the golden-haired Goddess, in her finest clothes, was with her husband, Summer, for whom she was giving the banquet, and whom she clasped as they danced in the middle of the festivities, with poppies in her hand and ears of corn on her head.

Ce-pendant ceste garse entra dans le Chasteau:
Dedans la bassecourt elle vit meint rateau,
Meinte fourche, meint van, meinte grosse javelle,
Meinte gerbe, toison de la moisson nouvelle,
Boisseaux poches bissacs de grans monceaux de blé
En l'aire çà et là l'un sur l'autre assemblé:
Les uns battoyent le grain dessus la terre dure,
Les autres au grenier le portoyent par mesure,
Et sous les tourbillons les bourriers qui voloyent
320   Pour le jouet du vent, parmi l'air s'en-alloyent.

Elle entra dans la salle, et au croc vit pendantes
(Faites comme en tortis) de grans flames ardantes,
Dont l'Esté s'affubloit pour mieux se bragarder,
Quand son pere venoit de pres le regarder:
Elle prist finement deux rayons de son frere
Pour en parer son chef, puis alla voir sa mere.[5]

Le Palais magnifique où Nature habitoit,
Sur piliers Phrygiens elevé se portoit:
Les voûtes estoyent d'or, d'or estoit la closture,
330   Et d'argent affiné la haute couverture:
Là cent portes estoyent toutes faites d'aymant:
En-contre les parois reluist meint diamant,

Meanwhile that girl Autumn entered the Castle; within the courtyard she saw many a rake, many a fork, many a winnowing basket, many a large bundle of corn, many a sheaf, those fleecy shearings of the new harvest, and bins, bags, sacks, great piles of wheat on the threshing floor, massed here and there one on top of another. Some men were beating the grain on the hard earth, others were taking it in regular batches to the granary, and in the swirling gusts the chaff, becoming the plaything of the wind, flew about and took off through the air.

She entered the hall, and saw hanging from a hook huge blazing flames (interwoven as in a garland), which Summer used to wear to make himself look more splendid, when his father came to look at him from close quarters. She slyly took two rays of flame from her brother to adorn her head, then she went to see her mother.

The magnificent Palace where Nature lived was borne high on pillars of Phrygian marble; the vaulted ceilings were of gold, of gold, too, were the outer walls, and of refined silver the lofty roof; there were a hundred doors, entirely made of adamant;

Meint rubi, meint saphir, que le boiteux manœuvre[6]
A luy-mesme attachez, ingenieux chef-d'œuvre.

   Là sont d'âge pareils cent jeunes jouvenceaux,
Beaux vermeils crespelus aux mentons damoiseaux,
Aux coudes retroussez, et cent Nymfes vermeilles
Toutes d'âge de face et de beautez pareilles,
Qui ont l'un apres l'autre, et en toute saison
La charge et le souci d'une telle maison.   340
Ils portent en la main de grans cruches profondes,
L'une verse à longs flots la semence des ondes,[7]
L'autre coule le plomb, l'autre espuise du sein
Des antres de Pluton les rivieres d'estain,
L'autre les ruisseaux d'or, l'autre affine le cuivre,
L'autre le vif argent qui veut tousjours se suivre,
L'autre cherche le soulfre, et l'autre est diligent
De fouiller les conduits du fer et de l'argent.

   Là sont dedans des pots sur des tables, encloses
Avec leurs escriteaux les semences des choses,   350
Que ces jeunes garçons gardent, à celle fin,
Que ce grand Univers ne prenne jamais fin,
Les semans tous les ans d'un mutuel office,
À fin qu'en vieillissant le Monde rajeunisse,

along the inner walls shone many a diamond, many a ruby and many a sapphire, which the lame craftsman himself had fixed there, an ingenious masterpiece.

   There are found a hundred youths of like age, handsome, fresh-faced, curly-headed, with beardless chins, and sleeves rolled up, together with a hundred fresh-faced Nymphs, all alike in age, in face and in beauty; these, one after the other and in all seasons, take on the responsibility and care of such a mansion. They carry in their hands large, deep pitchers. One pours out in long streams the seeds of the waves, another casts lead, another draws tin from the rivers deep within Pluto's caves, another draws gold from the streams, another refines copper, another quicksilver, which always tries to chase itself, another seeks sulphur, and another is assiduous in mining the seams of iron and silver.

   There, in labelled pots on tables, are enclosed the seeds of all things, which these young boys watch over with the object that this great Universe shall never end, since they sow them every year, for their mutual benefit, so that as it ages the World is

Que l'air ait ses oiseaux, et la mer ses poissons,
Et la terre ses fleurs de diverses façons.[8]

    Si tost que la Nature eut apperceu sa fille,
Fuy (dit-elle) d'ici, tu perdras ma famille,
Fuy-t'en de ma maison: tu seras en tes ans
360   La perte et le malheur de mes autres enfans:
Tu perdras tout cela que la bonne froidure
De l'Hyver germera: tout ce que la verdure
Du Printemps produira, et tout ce qui croistra
De meur et de parfait quand l'Esté paroistra:
Tu feras escouler les cheveux des bocages,
Chauves seront les bois, sans herbes les rivages,
Par ta main Phthinopore,[9] et dessus les humains
Maligne respandras mille maux de tes mains.

    L'Autonne en larmoyant s'en estoit en-allée
370   Quand elle ouit un bruit au fond d'une vallée,
Et s'approchant de pres, elle vit un grand Roy
Que deux Tigres portoyent en magnifique arroy:
Ses yeux estinceloyent tout ainsi que chandelles,
Ses cheveux luy pendoient plus bas que les aisselles,
Sa face estoit de vierge, et avoit sur le front
Deux petits cornichons comme les chévreaux ont:

rejuvenated, and the air has its birds, the sea its fish, and the earth its flowers of various sorts.

As soon as Nature noticed her daughter, she said, 'Leave here quickly, you will destroy my family, leave my house; you will be in your time the destruction and affliction of my other children; you will destroy everything that the beneficial cold of Winter will germinate, everything that the verdant freshness of Spring will produce, and everything ripe and perfect that will grow when Summer appears. You will make the leafy tresses of the copses drop, the woods will be bald, the riverbanks without vegetation, because of your Decay-engendering hand, and malevolently from your hands you will spread a thousand ills over the human race.'

Autumn had gone away in tears, when she heard a noise at the far end of a valley, and, drawing near, she saw a great King riding on two Tigers in splendid array; his eyes were shining just like candles, his hair hung down below his shoulders, his face was girlish, and on his brow he had two little horns such as goat-kids have; his lips

Ses lévres n'estoyent point de barbe crespelées,
Son corps estoit bouffi, ses cuisses potelées,
Jeunesse et Volupté luy servoyent de voisins,
Et tenoit en sa main deux grapes de raisins.   380

   Devant ce Roy dansoyent les folles Edonides,
Les unes talonnoyent des Pantheres sans brides,
Les autres respandoyent leurs cheveux sur le dos,
Les autres dans la main branloyent des javelos
Herissez de lierre et de fueilles de vigne:
Silene au rouge nez sans mesure trepigne
Monté dessur son asne, et comme tout donté
De vin laisse tomber sa teste d'un costé:
Les Satyres cornus, les Sylvains pieds-de-chevre
Font un bruit d'instrumens: l'un qui enfle sa lévre   390
Fait sonner un hau-bois, et l'autre tout autour
De la brigade fait resonner un tabour.

   Si tost que Bacchus vit Autonne la pucelle,
Venus luy fist descendre au cœur une etincelle
Par les yeux envoyée, et tout soudainement
Il devint amoureux, et si ne sceut comment.[10]
[...]

were not adorned with a curling beard, his body was corpulent, his thighs plump,
Youth and Pleasure were his escorts, and he held in his hand two bunches of grapes.

In front of this King danced the frenzied Bacchants. Some rode Panthers without
bridles, others had their hair loose over their backs, others brandished in their hands
javelins bristling with ivy and vine leaves. Red-nosed Silenus cavorts out of control,
mounted on an ass, and, as if totally overcome by wine, lets his head droop to one
side; horned Satyrs and goat-footed Sylvan Deities noisily play instruments; one,
bulging out his lips, makes sounds on a flute, and another, weaving around the
company, makes a drum resound.

As soon as Bacchus saw the maiden Autumn, Venus sent down into his heart a
spark issuing from her eyes, and he instantly, but without knowing how, fell in love.
[...]

74 La Harangue de tres-illustre prince François, duc de Guise, aux soldats de Metz.

Dediee à Charles, cardinal de Lorraine, son frere

[...]
 Et quand ja les tortis de serpentes tranchées[1]
Furent gros de soldats, et de piques couchées
Du long contre leur flanc prest à donner l'assaut:
Lors ton frere de Guise eslancé d'un plein saut   30
Sur le rempart cognu, plein d'effroyable audace
Desfiant leurs canons s'arma devant leur face.
Il prist ses beaux cuissots, et ses gréves encor,
Gréves faites d'argent, et jointes à cloux d'or:
D'or les boucles estoient, où sourdoient eslevées
Mille croisettes d'or au burin engravées:
Sur le ply du genou erroit un grand serpent,
Qui des tortis brisez de son ventre rampant
Faisoit le mouvement de ceste genouliere,
Le bordant de sa queue en lieu de cordeliere.   40

THE POEMS

Exhortation of the Most Illustrious Prince, François, Duke of Guise, to the Soldiers at Metz.
Dedicated to Charles, Cardinal of Lorraine, his Brother

[...]
 And now when the maze of tortuous trenches was packed with soldiers, who had their pikes levelled at full length by their sides, ready to attack, then your brother Guise, leaping with one great bound on to the famous rampart, and full of awesome boldness, braving their cannons, put on his armour in full view of the enemy. He took his fine cuisses, and then his greaves, greaves made of silver and fastened together by rivets of gold; of gold, too, were the buckles, from which a thousand little crosses of gold stood out in relief, engraved with a burin; round the bend of his knee there curled a huge serpent, which, with the rippling coils of its slithering belly, formed the hinge of this genouillere, and with its tail girdled the border like a cord.

Il a d'un corselet son corps environné
De fils d'or et d'argent par lignes rayonné
Opposez l'un à l'autre, et dedans ceste armeure
Vivoit (miracle grand!) une riche engraveure.
　　Aupres du hausse-col le Pape Urbain estoit
En blanche barbe peint qui grave admonestoit
Les Rois Chrestiens de faire aux Sarrazins la guerre
Et de Hierusalem le saint Royaume acquerre:
Sa robe estoit de pourpre et à replis bossus,
50　　Son roquet cramoisi luy pendoit par-dessus:
Dessous à plis ondez faict d'une toile blanche
Son sourpelis couloit jusqu'au bas de la hanche.
Vis à vis de ce Pape engravez en or fin
Tressailloient d'allegresse Eustace, Baudouin,
Et le Comte de Flandre, et faisoient de leur teste
Un signe d'obeyr à si juste requeste.[2]
　　Là le Duc Godefroy d'un art laborieux
Embossé dans l'acier, vendoit devotieux
Verdun, Mets et Buillon, et d'un brave courage
60　　Ainsi qu'une tempeste amenoit un orage
De soldats tous armez: le fer qui gemissoit
Sous le pied des chevaux, d'effroy s'y herissoit.

He covered his body with a breastplate, which had lines of gold and silver wire
radiating outwards, in opposite directions, and on this armour (a wondrous marvel)
a rich engraving sprang to life.

Beside his gorget Pope Urban was depicted with a white beard, gravely urging
Christian Kings to make war on the Saracens and to conquer the holy Kingdom of
Jerusalem. His vestment was purple with swelling folds, his crimson rochet hung
down over it; billowing underneath, his surplice, made of white linen, flowed down
below his hips. Opposite this Pope, engraved in fine gold, Eustache, Baudouin and
the Count of Flanders quivered with joy, and nodded their heads as a sign of
obedience to such a just request.

There, embossed in the steel with painstaking artistry, Duke Godefroy was selling,
out of piety, Verdun, Metz and Bouillon, and, like a hurricane, with valiant courage
was leading a storming troop of soldiers, all armed; even the iron shoes that groaned
beneath the hooves of the horses shuddered in fright.

Autour du corselet dessus les feintes plaines
De l'Ocean vaguoient trois cens navires pleines
De Chevaliers croisez: d'autre costé le bord
Du payen Corborant rougissoit de la mort.[3]

Là, veincus s'eslevoient en graveure bossée
Les grands murs d'Antioche, et les murs de Nicée,
Ceux de Tyr et Sidon, et là ce Godefroy
De toute la Judée estoit peint comme Roy.　　　　70

Puis il saisit apres sa merveilleuse targe
Forte massive dure en rondeur aussi large
Qu'est un Soleil couchant, où du fils d'Aristor[4]
Estoient gravez les yeux en cent estoiles d'or.

Deux couleuvres d'acier dos à dos tortillées
Trainant dedans le fer leurs traces escaillées
Couroient le long du bord, qui d'un col replié
Resembloient de couleur à cest Arc varié
Que Jupiter attache au milieu des nuages
En voute pour servir aux hommes de presages.　　　　80

Around the breastplate, on the simulated expanses of the Ocean, sailed three hundred ships full of crusader Knights; opposite, the shores of the pagan Corborant were stained red with death.

There, in embossed metalwork, rose the great walls of Antioch, the walls of Nicaea, and those of Tyre and Sidon, all of them conquered, and there this Godefroy was depicted as King of all Judaea.

Then Guise grasped next his wondrous shield, which was strong, solid and hard, as broad as a setting Sun, with its circular shape, and on it the eyes of Arestor's son were engraved as a hundred golden stars.

Two grass-snakes of steel, entwined back to back and trailing in the iron their scaly tracks, glided along the rim; with their coiling necks they resembled in colour that multi-hued Bow that Jupiter fixes as an arch amid the clouds to serve as a portent to men.

Du milieu de l'escu Gorgone s'eslevoit
Borgnoyant renfrongné, qui trois testes avoit
Naissantes d'un seul col, et de chacune teste
Grongnante, vomissoit la foudre et la tempeste.

Là comme Roy de Naple, estoit emburiné
Charles Comte du Maine, et le bon Roy René,
Et tous les vieux combats que la maison Lorraine
A faits sur le tombeau de l'antique Seraine.[5]

Apres il s'afubla d'un morion brillant
90　　Comme un long trac de feu, qui des champs va pillant
Les espics desja meurs, lors que parmy les plaines
Des laboureurs fraudez le Ciel gaste les peines.

Haletant dans l'acier, Anthée fut empreint
Sur le haut de la creste horriblement estreint
Des bras courbez d'Hercule,[6] et luy qui se travaille
D'eschapper hors du ply de si dure tenaille,
Enfle ses nerfs en vain, et tout acravanté
Encor' sur un genouil, mal-seur se tient planté,
Puis tout à coup il tombe, et de sa gueule bée
100　　Desgorge un panonceau. Puis il print son espée
Au flambant émery: le fourreau fut d'un os
D'Elephant Indien, marqueté sur le dos

From the middle of the shield, scowling and glowering, a Gorgon reared up, who had three heads springing from a single neck, and from each growling head it spewed forth thunder and storms.

There, as King of Naples, was engraved Charles, Count of Maine, and good King René, and all the old battles that the house of Lorraine fought in the place where the ancient Siren is buried.

After that he donned a helmet, gleaming like a long streak of fire that ravages the corn already ripe in the fields, when, in the countryside, the Heavens lay waste the labours of the cheated ploughmen.

Antaeus was stamped into the steel on the top of the crest, gasping for breath, gripped violently in an armlock by Hercules, and, struggling to escape from the jaws of such a cruel vice, he strains his sinews in vain; the breath crushed out of him, he still supports himself unsteadily on one knee, then suddenly falls, and from his gaping mouth he disgorges the plumes of the helmet. Then Guise took up his sword, which was burnished to a fine lustre with emery; the scabbard was made

De barbillons courbez, et sa dague guerriere
Plus que l'astre de Mars espandoit de lumiere.

   Apres qu'il eut de fer tout son corps revestu,
Branlant la pique au poing, aguisa la vertu
De ses nobles soldats, et d'un cœur magnanime
Par ces vers Tyrteans au combat les anime:[7]

   Sus, courage, Soldats, sus, sus, monstrez vous or'
De la race d'Hercule, et de celle d'Hector.   110
Hercule, apres avoir l'Espaigne surmontée
Vint en Gaule espouser la Royne Galatée
Dont vous estes yssus: puis le Troyen Francus
Seul heritier d'Hector quittant les murs veincus
D'Ilion, vint en France, et la race Troyenne
Mesla cent ans apres avec l'Herculienne.[8]
[...]

   Non, je n'ignore pas qu'une belle victoire
D'âge en âge coulant n'eternize la gloire
Des hommes combatans, soient jeunes, ou soient vieux,
Et de terre enlevez ne les envoye aux cieux.   150
Mais certes Enyon la guerriere Déesse
Cent fois plus que les vieux estime une jeunesse

---

from the tusk of an Indian Elephant, patterned on the back with hooked barbs, and his warlike dagger radiated more light than the planet Mars.

After he had clad his whole body in armour, wielding a pike in his hand, he sharpened the courage of his worthy soldiers, and noble-heartedly spurred them on to battle with these lines by Tyrtaeus:

'Fight, take courage, Soldiers, fight, fight, show now that you belong to the race of Hercules, and to that of Hector. After conquering Spain, Hercules came to Gaul to marry Queen Galatea, from whom you are descended; then the Trojan Francus, sole heir of Hector, leaving the vanquished walls of Ilium, came to France, and a hundred years later the Trojan race mingled with the Herculean race.
[...]

'No, I am not unaware of the fact that a fine victory, passed on from age to age, renders immortal the glory of the combatants, whether they are young or whether they are old, and, detaching them from the earth, dispatches them to the heavens. But indeed Enyo, the warrior Goddess, values a hundred times more than the old

Qui brusle de combatre, et qui ne fait encor'
A l'entour du menton que jaunir d'un poil d'or.
Ceste jeunesse-là mordant ses lévres d'ire,
Et grinçant de fureur à soy-mesmes inspire
Une ame valeureuse, et s'ente dans le cœur
Je ne sçay quel effort qui desdaigne la peur.
Ceste jeunesse-là tousjours brave s'essaye
160   De se voir entre-ouvrir l'estomac d'une playe,
Combatant la premiere, et mieux voudroit se voir
Mourir de mille morts qu'au dos la recevoir.
C'est vergongne de voir couché sur la poulsiere
Un jeune homme fuyant navré par le derriere,
Ayant le dos béant d'ulceres apparens!
Celuy vrayment honnit ses fils et ses parens,
Longue fable du peuple, et la cruelle Parque
Passe son nom et luy dans une mesme barque:[9]
Mais celuy qui premier s'opposant à l'effort
170   Des vaillans ennemis, meurt d'une belle mort,
Tenant encor' au poing sa pique vangeresse:
À l'heure qu'on l'enterre, une dolente presse
Chantant du trespassé la gloire et les valeurs,
Reschaufe le corps froid d'une tiede eau de pleurs.

the young men who are burning to fight, and whose chins are still acquiring the yellow of golden hair. These young men, biting their lips in wrath and gnashing their teeth in fury, themselves inspire valour in their souls, and graft into their hearts an energy that scorns fear. These young men, ever courageous, put themselves to the test by visualizing their stomachs ripped open by a wound while fighting in the front rank, and they would rather see themselves die a thousand deaths than receive the wound in their back. It is shameful to see a young man lying in the dust, struck down from behind as he fled, his back gaping with plainly visible injuries! Such a man truly dishonours his sons and his family, becoming the subject of an enduring popular fable, and the cruel Fate consigns his name and himself to one and the same boat; but the man who, in the front rank, while resisting the efforts of the valiant enemy, dies a glorious death, still grasping in his fist his avenging pike; at the moment when he is buried a grieving throng singing of the glory and the valorous deeds of the deceased warms the cold body with the tepid water of tears.

Jamais des masles cueurs les louanges ne meurent,
Et les fils de leur fils tousjours louez demeurent
Comme Dieux au vulgaire, et tousjours renommez
Demeurent leurs tombeaux de mille fleurs semez.

Si quelcun de la troupe en combatant evite
La mort cent fois cherchée, et qu'ensemble il incite   180
Son prochain compaignon à choquer vivement,
Ou vrayment à mourir l'arme au poing bravement,
Le peuple par la rue honorera sa face,
Petits et grands assis debout luy feront place
L'honorant comme un Dieu, et n'aura son pareil,
Premier en la bataille, et premier au conseil.

Le couard au contraire enlaidy d'une honte
Ne sera rien sinon un populaire conte,
Et peut-estre bany de son pays natif,
Pour sa couardeté vagabond et fuitif,   190
Portant ses fils au col d'huis en huis ira querre
Son miserable pain en quelque estrange terre,
Et de haillons vestu, et privé de bon-heur
N'osera plus hanter les gens dignes d'honneur:
Et sa race à jamais, fust elle decorée
De nobles bisayeux, sera des-honorée.

'Never do the praises of manly hearts die, and the sons of their sons, forever praised, continue to be like Gods to the common people, and their tombs, forever renowned, continue to be strewn with a thousand flowers.

'If, while fighting, one among the troop eludes the death he has sought a hundred times, and if at the same time he urges his nearest comrade in arms to strike vigorously, or indeed to die bravely with his weapon in his hand, the people in the streets will honour him; the humble and the great, those sitting and those standing, all will defer to him, honouring him like a God, and, first in the battle and first in the council, he will have no equal.

'The coward, in contrast, besmirched by shame, will be no more than a popular tale, and, banished perhaps from his native land to become a wandering fugitive on account of his cowardice, carrying his sons on his shoulders, he will go from door to door, begging a miserable crust of bread in some strange land; and, clad in rags, deprived of happiness, he will no longer dare to frequent people who are worthy of honour, and his family, even were it distinguished by noble ancestors, will be forever dishonoured.

Pource faites-vous preux: bien qu'il soit ordonné
Du naturel destin que tout ce qui est né
Vestu d'os et de nerfs, soit quelque jour la proye
200   De la Mort mange-tout, et que mesmes à Troye
Achille et Sarpedon, enfans des Dieux, n'ont pas
Non plus que fist Thersite, evité le trespas.

   Mouron, mouron, Amis, il vaut mieux pour defendre
Nous et nostre pays l'ame vaillante rendre,
L'ame vaillante rendre au dessus du rempart
D'un grand coup de canon faussez de part en part,
Ou d'un grand coup de pique accourcir nostre vie,
Que languir vieux au lict mattez de maladie.

   Courage donc Soldats, ne craignez point la mort:
210   »La mort ne peut tuer l'homme vaillant et fort:
La mort tant seulement par les combats vient mordre
Je ne sçay quels couhards qui n'osent tenir ordre.
Tenez doncque bon ordre, et gardez vostre ranc,
Pressez l'un contre l'autre, et collez flanc à flanc,
Pied contre pied fiché, et teste contre teste
Bataillez bravement, et creste contre creste.
Tienne le canonnier le canon comme il faut
Droitement contre ceux qui viendront à l'assaut:

'Therefore show your prowess, although it is ordained by natural destiny that everything that is born and has the vesture of bones and sinews will one day become the prey of all-devouring Death, and although even Achilles and Sarpedon, the children of Gods, did not escape extinction at Troy, any more than did Thersites.

'Let us die, let us die, my Friends, it is better to yield up our valiant souls in the defence of ourselves and our country, to yield up our valiant souls upon the rampart, pierced through and through by a violent cannon shot, or else to have our lives cut short under a violent blow from a pike, than to languish in our beds, old and debilitated by disease.

'Courage then, Soldiers, do not be afraid of death. "Death cannot kill a man who is valiant and brave." In combat death comes to savage only those cowards who dare not remain in their battle order. Therefore remain in good battle order, and keep to your ranks, press one against another, stay close side by side, foot braced against foot, and head against head, crest against crest, battle bravely. The cannoneer shall hold the cannon in the correct way, directly against those who come to assail us; in

Bref que chacun de vous à son estat regarde,
Le halebardier tienne au poing sa halebarde,   220
La pique le piquier, et le harquebutier
Couché plat sur le ventre exerce son mestier.[10]
[. . .]

short, each of you shall attend to his own function, the halberdier shall hold in his
hand his halberd, the pikeman his pike, and the arquebusier, lying flat on his
stomach, shall exercise his craft.'
[. . .]

75 La Lyre
À Jean Belot, Bordelois, Maistre des Requestes du Roy

Belot parcelle ains le tout de ma vie,
Quand je te vy, je n'avois plus envie
De voir la Muse, ou danser à son bal,
Ou m'abreuver en l'eau que le cheval
D'un coup de pied fist sourçoyer de terre.[1]
    Peu me plaisoit le Laurier qui enserre
Les doctes fronts, le Myrte Paphien
Ny la fleur teinte au sang Adonien,[2]
Ny tout l'esmail qui le Printemps colore,
Ny tous ces jeux que la jeunesse honore:
Mais au contraire et malade et grison
J'aimois au feu l'aise de ma maison,
Aux plus gaillars quittant la Poësie
Que j'avois seule en jeunesse choisie
Pour soulager mon cœur qui bouillonnoit
Quand de son trait Amour l'aiguillonnoit,
Comme venin glissé dedans mes veines,
Entre-meslant un plaisir de cent peines.

The Lyre
To Jean Belot of Bordeaux, the King's Master of Appeals

Belot, you who are a part, or rather the whole, of my life, when I first saw you, I had lost my desire to see the Muse, or join in her dance, or quench my thirst with the water that the horse, striking the ground with his hoof, caused to spring forth.

    I found little pleasure in the Laurel that binds learned brows, or the Myrtle of Paphos, or the flower that is dyed with the blood of Adonis, or all the enamelled colours that embellish the Spring, or all those sports that young men value; but, on the contrary, being both ill and grey-haired, I loved the comfort of my fireside at home, leaving Poetry to those who are more vigorous, poetry that I had chosen to the exclusion of all else in my youth, to soothe my heart, which was in ferment when Love pierced it with his arrow, like a poison seeping into my veins, intermingling one pleasure with a hundred pains.

Je ne faisois allegre de sejour,
Fust au coucher fust au lever du jour,   20
Qu'enter planter et tirer à la ligne
Le sep tortu de la joyeuse vigne
Qui rend le cœur du jeune plus gaillard,
Et plus puissant l'estomac du vieillard.

    Cerés nourrist, Bacchus resjouist l'homme:
C'est pour cela que Bon-Pere on le nomme.

    Or pour-autant que le pere Evien[3]
A bonne part au mont Parnasien,
Tousjours portrait au temple des neuf Muses
Pour ses vertus en nos ames infuses,   30
Comme Prophete et Poëte vineux
Je l'honorois d'artifice soigneux,
Ne cultivant, ou fust jardin ou prée,
Devant le sep de la vigne sacrée.
Il a rendu salaire à mon labeur,
De sa fureur me remplissant le cœur.
Car comme dit ce grand Platon, ce sage,
Quatre fureurs brulent nostre courage,
Bacchus, Amour, les Muses, Apollon,
Qui dans nos cœurs laissent un aiguillon   40
Comme freslons, et d'une ardeur secrete
Font soudain l'homme et Poëte et Prophete.[4]

Enjoying this time of leisure, I did nothing, either at sunset or at break of day, except graft, plant, and tie into line the twisted stem of the joyous vine, which makes a young man's heart more spirited, and an old man's stomach stronger.

Ceres feeds man, and Bacchus gladdens him: it is for that reason that he is called Good Father.

Now, inasmuch as this father Euhius has an important place on Mount Parnassus and is always depicted in the temple of the nine Muses on account of his powers, which he infuses into our souls, I, as a wine-loving Prophet and Poet, honoured him with painstaking artistry, cultivating the sacred plant of the vine in preference to either garden or meadow. He paid wages for my labour, filling my heart with his inspiring fury. For, as great Plato, that wise man, says, four furies kindle our spirit, those of Bacchus, Love, the Muses and Apollo, which, like hornets, leave their sting in our hearts, and at once, with a secret ardour, make a man both Poet and Prophet.

Je voy par là que Poëte je suis
Plein de fureur: car faire je ne puis
Un trait de vers, soit qu'un Prince commande,
Soit qu'une Dame ou l'Ami m'en demande,
Et à tous coups la vérve ne me prend:
Je bée en vain, et mon esprit attend
Tantost six mois, tantost un an, sans faire
50   Vers qui me puisse ou plaire ou satisfaire.

J'attens venir (certes je n'en ments point)
Ceste fureur qui la Sibylle espoint:[5]
Mais aussi tost que par long intervalle
Dedans mon cœur du Ciel elle devalle,
Colere, ardant, furieux, agité,
Je tremble tout dessous la Deité.

Or comme on voit ces ruisseaux qui descendent
Du haut des monts, et flot sur flot se rendent
À gros bouillons en la vallée, et font
60   Une riviere et aguisent son front,
(Et c'est pourquoy les Peintres qui les feignent
Fleuves-Taureaux, au front cornu les peignent)
Fumeux bruyans escumeux et venteux,
Et de leur corne ouvrent au devant eux

From this I see that I am a Poet when filled with fury, for I cannot compose a single line of verse, whether a Prince commands me, or a Lady or Friend asks me, and the enthusiasm does not come to me at all times: I hunger for it in vain, and my mind waits sometimes six months, sometimes a year, without producing a line capable of pleasing or satisfying me.

I wait (truly I tell no lie) for that fury to come which excites the Sibyl, but, as soon as it comes down from Heaven into my heart after a long interval, I tremble all over under the influence of the Deity, raging, impassioned, frenzied, stirred.

Now, like the streams that we see flowing down from the tops of the mountains, and running into the valley, wave upon wave in gushing torrents, and forming a river and shaping it into a surging head (and that is why Painters represent them as Bull-Rivers, painting them with horns on their heads), seething, clamorous, foaming

Un chemin d'eau sans que rien les empesche,
Pour s'emboucher ou dans la rive fresche
D'un prochain fleuve, ou au bord reculé
Du vieil Neptune au rivage salé.

    Ainsi je cours à course desbridée
Lors que la vérve en moy s'est desbordée,   70
Impetueux sans raison ny conseil.

    Elle me dure ou le tour d'un Soleil,
Quelquefois deux, quelquefois trois, puis morte
Elle languist en moy de telle sorte
Qu'une herbe fait languissant pour un temps:
Puis dessus terre elle vit au Printemps,
Par son declin prenant force et croissance,
Et de sa mort une jeune naissance.

    Quand la fureur me laisse, tout soudain
Plume et papier me tombent de la main: 80
Du tout je semble à la forte Commere,
Laquelle (ayant d'une tranchée amere
Jetté son Part) fuit de son lit: ainsi
Je fuy la chambre, oubliant le souci
De ceste ardeur qui me tenoit en serre,
Et lors du Ciel je devalle en la terre,

and storming, and with their horns opening ahead of them a watery track, unimpeded by any obstacle, pouring out either between the fresh banks of a larger river nearby, or on to the briny strand on the remote shore of old Neptune,

in the same way, when that enthusiasm overflows within me I race at a headlong run, impetuous, without reason or reflection.

It remains with me either for a single turn of the Sun, or sometimes two, sometimes three, then, dying, it languishes within me in the way a plant does, languishing for a time; then, rising above the ground, it comes to life in Spring, from its decline taking strength and growth, and from its death a youthful birth.

When the fury leaves me, pen and paper fall abruptly from my hand; I am exactly like a strong Mother, who (having given birth to her Infant in agonizing labour) quickly leaves her bed: thus do I quickly leave my room, forgetting the pain of this fervour, which held me imprisoned, and then from Heaven I come down to earth,

Ah! et en lieu de vivre entre les Dieux,
Je deviens homme à moy-mesme odieux.

Mais quand du tout ceste ardeur se retire,
90   Je ne sçaurois ny penser ny redire
Les vers escrits et ne m'en souvient plus.

Je ne suis rien qu'un corps mort et perclus,
Dont l'ame vole autre part esbranlée,
Laissant son hoste aussi froid que gelée,
Et m'esbahis de ceux ausquels il est
Prompt de verser des vers quand il leur plaist.

Le grand Platon en ses œuvres nous chante
Que nostre esprit comme le corps enfante,
L'un des enfans qui surmontent la mort,
100 L'autre des fils qui doivent voir le port
Où le Nocher tient sa Gondolle ouverte
À tous venans, riche de nostre perte.[6]

Ainsi tous deux conçoivent, mais il faut
Que le sang soit jeune gaillard et chaud:
Car si le sang chaude vigueur ne baille
À tels enfans ils ne font rien qui vaille.

Lors que Pallas sortoit hors du cerveau
De Jupiter, Vulcan prist un couteau
Dont il ouvrit à Jupiter la teste:
110 Adonc Pallas sortit à la grand' creste,

oh! and, instead of living among the Gods, I become a man, hateful to myself.

But when this fervour departs altogether, I can neither create nor repeat the verses I have written, and I can no longer recollect them.

I am nothing but a dead and palsied body, whose soul, greatly disturbed, flies elsewhere, leaving its host as cold as ice, and I am amazed by those who find it easy to pour out poetry whenever they like.

Great Plato in his works tells us that our mind, like our body, gives birth, the former to children who vanquish death, the latter to sons who must see the harbour where the Ferryman keeps his Boat ready for all comers, growing rich by our loss.

Thus they both conceive, but our blood must be young, lively and hot, for if the blood does not impart hot vigour to such children, they do nothing of any value.

When Pallas was emerging from the brain of Jupiter, Vulcan took a knife, and with it cut open Jupiter's head; then Pallas emerged, with a large crest, and a helmet

Au chef armé, ayant d'un grand pavois
Le bras chargé et le corps d'un harnois:
Les Muses sœurs furent les sages-femmes.

    Quant à Vulcan, c'est l'ardeur de nos ames
Qui nous eschaufe, et ouvre vivement
De l'esprit gros le meur enfantement:
Quant à Pallas qui sort de la cervelle,
C'est de l'esprit l'œuvre toute nouvelle
Que le penser luy a fait concevoir:
Les Muses sont l'estude et le sçavoir.   120

    Or mon cerveau qui le labeur desdaigne,
Estoit en friche et devenu brehaigne
Sans enfanter, ou soit qu'il fust lassé
De trop d'enfans conceus au temps passé,
Soit qu'il cherchast le repos solitaire:
Il m'asseuroit de jamais plus ne faire
Ryme ny vers ny prose ny escrit
Donnant repos à mon fantaste esprit.[7]
[. . .]

    D'or est l'archet, les chevilles encor
Ont le bout d'or, le haut du coude est d'or,
Tout à l'entour meinte lame d'yvoire
Est engravée ou d'une vraye histoire   270

on her head, her arm covered with a large shield, and her body with a suit of armour; the sister Muses acted as midwives.

As for Vulcan, he represents the fervour of our souls that heats us, and he vigorously opens the way for the pregnant mind to bring forth its fully developed child; as for Pallas, who emerges from the brain, she represents the totally new work of the mind, which thought has made it conceive; the Muses represent study and knowledge.

Now my brain, which scorns toil, was uncultivated and had become barren, no longer bearing children, either because it was exhausted after conceiving too many children in the past, or because it was seeking rest and solitude; it assured me that it would never again produce rhyme or verse or prose or any writing, thus giving my fantastical mind a rest. [. . .]

Of gold is the bow, the ends of the tuning pegs, too, are of gold, the top of the angular neck is of gold, and all round many an ivory panel is engraved either with

Ou de portraits plaisans et fabuleux,
Dont ceste Lyre a le ventre orgueilleux.[8]

   Les plus hauts Dieux en festin delectable
Y sont assis: au milieu de la table
Est Apollon, qui accouple sa vois
Au tremblotis de l'archet et des doits.

      En le voyant, vous diriez qu'il accorde,
Frappant son Luth, ceste vieille discorde
D'entre Pallas et le Roy de la mer
Deux puissans Dieux, qui vouloyent surnommer
De leur beau nom les naissantes Athenes.[9]

   Tous deux au bord des Attiques arenes
Se presentoyent parrains de la Cité:
L'une en courroux et au front despité,
À la grand' targe, à la poitrine armée,
Fist sortir hors de la terre germée
Un Olivier, qui la motte haulsoit
Du haut du chef et de terre croissoit
En se formant: puis chargé de fueillage,
De fleurs et fruits couvroit tout le rivage,
Signe de Paix: Neptune plus ardent
Deux et trois coups frappant de son Trident,

a true story or with pleasing pictures of fables, which the belly of this Lyre proudly displays.

The highest Gods are seated there at a delightful banquet: at the middle of the table is Apollo, who unites his voice with the trilling of the bow and the fingers.

If you saw him, you would say that by playing the Lute he brings into accord that old discord between Pallas and the King of the sea, two powerful Gods, who both wanted to name the newborn city of Athens with their own admirable names.

On the sandy coast of Attica they both offered themselves as godparents of the City. One, incensed, and with an angry countenance, with her large shield and armoured breast, caused an Olive Tree to spring from the fruitful earth; growing from the earth as it took shape, it pushed up the clods with the top of its head, then, heavy with foliage, flowers and fruit, it covered the whole seashore, a sign of Peace. Neptune, more fervent, striking the ground two and three times with his Trident,

Faisoit semblant de faire issir de terre
Un grand coursier instrument de la Guerre,
Aux larges crins dessus le col espars,
Qui hannissant frappoit de toutes pars
D'un son aigu toute la rive verte
Chaude du vent de sa narine ouverte.

    Au naturel dans l'yvoire attaché
Vit un Marsye au corps tout escorché,   300
Qui de son sang fait un fleuve en Phrygie,
Punition d'oser sa chalemie
Plus que le luth d'Apollon estimer.

    Vous le verriez lentement consommer
Mort dans l'yvoire, et d'une face humaine
N'estre plus rien qu'une large fontaine.

    En l'engraveure Apollon qui s'estoit
Un peu courbé, luy-mesme se chantoit:
Comme les rocs bondissans par la voye
Traçoyent ses pas, maçon des murs de Troye,   310
Et comme au bruit de ses nerfs bien tendus
Mille rochers de leur bon gré fendus
Suivoyent du luth la corde non commune,
Où dix à peine alloyent apres Neptune,

appeared to make issue from the earth a huge charger, an instrument of War, with a thick mane spreading over its neck, whose neighing buffeted with an ear-piercing sound all the green shore on all sides, and warmed it with the wind from its flaring nostrils.

Realistically depicted on the ivory panel, Marsyas lives, his body completely flayed, and with his blood forms a river in Phrygia, as a punishment for daring to prize his flute more highly than Apollo's lute.

You could see him in the ivory slowly perishing, then dead, and, losing his human face, becoming nothing but a copious fountain.

In the engraving Apollo, leaning forward slightly, was singing about himself: how the stones leaping up along the way marked his steps, as he built the walls of Troy, and how a thousand rocks, splitting apart of their own accord at the sound of his taut strings, followed the incomparable chords of the lute, whereas scarcely ten went with Neptune, a God who had coarse manners and ways, while the other was

Un Dieu grossier de mœurs et de façons,
L'autre le Roy des vers et des chansons:[10]
(Miracle estrange) encores depuis l'heure
Le son conceu dans les pierres demeure,
Qui va sonnant sous les coups du marteau,
320   Quand le maçon pour orner un château,
En les taillant les frappe d'artifice,
Honneur de luy et de son edifice.

   Cest Apollon de Dieu fait un Pasteur,
Aux bords d'Amphryse allume tout son cœur
Du jeune Admete, ah! et pour luy complaire
Gardoit ses bœufs aux piés-tors sans salaire,
Entre-rompant ses beaux vers blandissans
Dessous le cri des taureaux mugissans.[11]

   Pres Apollon main-à-main y sont peintes
330   Les corps tous nuds des trois Charites jointes
Suivant Venus, et Venus par la main
Conduit Amour, qui tire de son sein
Des pommes d'or, et comme une sagette
En se jouant aux Charites les jette
À coup perdu: puis au sein il se pend
D'une des trois, et la baise en enfant.

the King of poetry and song; (strange miracle) ever since that time the sound engendered in the stones remains, and resounds under the blows of the hammer when the mason, to embellish a castle, skilfully strikes them as he shapes them, to bring honour to him and to his building.

This Apollo, on the banks of the Amphrysus, changed from a God into a Shepherd, has his whole heart ablaze for young Admetus, oh! and to please him he tended his cloven-hooved cattle without wages, breaking off his beautiful honeyed poetry because of the clamour of the bellowing bulls.

Beside Apollo are painted the totally naked bodies of the three Graces linking hand in hand, following Venus, and Venus leads by the hand Love, who pulls golden apples from the folds of her garments, and, out of playfulness hurls them randomly, like arrows, at the Graces; then he clings to the bosom of one of the three, and kisses her like a child.

Sur l'autre yvoire, où les cordes s'attachent
Et d'ordre egal dessus la lyre marchent,
Vit un Bacchus potelé gros et gras,
Vieil-jouvenceau, tenant entre ses bras   340
Un vase plein qui tout enrichi semble
S'enorgueillir de cent fruits tous ensemble,
Fruits qui passoyent les lévres du vaisseau
En gros trochets: ainsi qu'au renouveau
Un beau guinier par gros trochets fait naistre
Son fruit touffu, pour ensemble nous paistre,
Et les oiseaux qui frians de son fruit,
Autour de l'arbre affamez font un bruit.

    Là mainte figue, ornement de l'Autonne,
Est peinte au vif, et tout ce que Pomonne   350
De tous costez verse de larges mains
Dessus les champs pour nourrir les humains.

    Là le Raisin de joyeuse rencontre,
Là le Concombre au ventre enflé s'y montre:
Et la Chastaigne au rempart espineux.
Là fut la Pêche au goust demi-vineux,
Et le Pompon aux costes separées,
Et les Citrons ayans robbes dorées.

On the other piece of ivory, where the strings are attached and stride in measured order over the lyre, Bacchus springs to life, podgy, plump and fat, an aged youth, holding in his arms a full vase, which in its cornucopian abundance seems to take pride in a hundred fruits all together, fruits that overflow the lips of the vessel in large clusters, just as in spring a fine sweet-cherry tree brings forth its thick-set fruit in large clusters, to feed us and also the birds, which, being famished, and very fond of its fruit, create a hubbub around the tree.

There are painted as if living many a fig, ornament of Autumn, and everything that Pomona on every side pours out with generous hands over the fields to nourish humans.

There the Grape with joyful countenance, there the Cucumber with swelling belly shows itself, and the Chestnut with its prickly defences. There was the Peach with its wine-like taste, and the Melon with its divided ribs, and the golden-robed

360

Là fut le Glan fils des Chesnes ombreux,
La Meure teinte au sang des amoureux,[12]
L'Abricot froid, la Poire pepineuse,
Le Coin barbu, la Framboise areneuse,
Et la Cerise aux malades confort,
Et le Pavot qui les hommes endort,
Et la Cormeille au dur noyau de pierre,
La Corme aussi qui le ventre resserre,
Avec la Fraize au teint vermeil et beau
Semblable au bout d'un tetin Damoiseau:
Et par sur tout de Pampre une couronne

370

Qui du vaisseau les lévres environne.

Entre la guerre et la Paix est ce Dieu,
Ny l'un ny l'autre, et si tient le milieu
De tous les deux, ensemble pour la lance,
Ensemble propre à conduire une danse.
Bas à ses pieds un mont est elevé,
Où Mercure est en l'yvoire engravé,
Qui tient au poing sa baguette dorée
De deux serpens enlacez honorée.
Sa capeline est riche d'ailerons,

380

Ses patins ont deux ailes aux talons,
Qui vont portant ce courrier Atlantide
Plustost que vent par le sec et l'humide,

Lemons; there was the Acorn, son of the shady Oaks, the Mulberry dyed with the blood of the lovers, the cold Apricot, the pip-filled Pear, the bearded Quince, the sand-loving Raspberry, and the Cherry, comforter of invalids, and the Poppy, which makes men drowsy, and the Dogberry with its hard stony kernel, the Sorb, too, which gives you stomach cramps, together with the Strawberry with its beautiful rosy complexion, just like the tip of a Virginal nipple; and over the whole a garland of Vine branches, which surrounds the lips of the vessel.

Between War and Peace stands this God, being neither the one nor the other, and thus he occupies the middle way between the two, as well fitted for the lance as he is well fitted to lead a dance. Down by his feet a mountain is raised, where Mercury is engraved in the ivory, holding in his hand his gilded staff graced with two interlaced snakes. His hat is adorned with little wings, his sandals have two wings on the heels, which carry this messenger, a descendant of Atlas, faster than the wind

Ou soit qu'il tombe aux enfers odieux,
Ou soit qu'il monte au Ciel siege des Dieux.[13]

    Il va suivant d'un gentil artifice
Une Tortue errant par le Cytise
Herbe odorante, et luy froissant les os
Son dur rempart luy arrache du dos,
Mange sa chair, et laisse sa coquille
Pendre long temps au croc d'une cheville   390
Pour la secher aux rayons du Soleil.

    Puis attachant par un art nompareil
D'un ordre egal les tripes bien sechées
Du haut en bas à la coque attachées
D'un animal marche-tard ocieux,
Fist une lyre au son delicieux,
Au ventre creux, aux accords delectables,
Le seul honneur des temples et des tables,
Et des bons Dieux le plaisir le plus pront,
Quand le Nectar leur eschaufe le front.   400

    Apollon vit aupres de ceste image,
Au cœur bouffi, à la poignante rage
De voir ses bœufs aux gros jarrets courbez,
Au large front, estre ainsi desrobez

over dry land and water, whether he descends to the odious Underworld, or whether he ascends to the Heavens, the seat of the Gods.

With clever cunning he is pursuing a Tortoise wandering through the clover, a sweet-smelling plant, and, crushing its bones, he tears the hard rampart from its back, eats its flesh, and leaves the shell hanging on a hooked peg for a long time, to let it dry in the rays of the Sun.

Then, he attaches with unparalleled skill and in measured order the well-dried guts, attaching them to the top and bottom of the shell, and out of a slow-moving, sluggish animal he made a lyre with an exquisite sound, with a hollow belly and delightful harmonies, the highest honour of both temples and tables, and the most spontaneous pleasure of the good Gods, when they grow heated from the effects of Nectar.

Beside this image Apollo comes to life, with his heart swelling in a passionate rage at the sight of his cattle, with their huge, bent hocks and broad heads, stolen

D'un art subtil: Mercure qui desire
Jeune larron, d'Apollon flatter l'ire,
En contre-eschange à ses bœufs, luy donna
Son instrument sur lequel il sonna
Long temps apres les enfans de la Terre
410   Pied contre-mont accablez du tonnerre.[14]

    Peu leur servit les trois monts amassez,
Vains monuments sur leurs corps renversez:
Exemple vray que ceux qui veulent prendre
Guerre à leur Roy, autant doivent attendre
De traits soulfrez aux bords Charanteans,
Que les Geans aux sablons Phlegreans.[15]
[. . .]

from him by ingenious craft; Mercury, the young thief, wishing to soften Apollo's wrath, in exchange for his cattle gave him his instrument, to which Apollo would sing much later of the children of the Earth hurled down head over heels by the thunderbolt.

  The three mountains they had piled up were of little avail, worthless monuments demolished on top of their bodies; this true example shows that those who want to make war on their King must expect as many sulphurous arrows on the banks of the Charente as the Giants on the sands of Phlegra. [. . .]

76 Le Chat
À Remy Belleau, Poëte

Dieu est par tout, par tout se mesle Dieu,
Commencement, la fin et le milieu
De ce qui vit, et dont l'ame est enclose
Par tout, et tient en vigueur toute chose,
Comme nostre ame infuse dans nos corps.
    Ja dés long temps les membres seroyent morts
De ce grand Tout, si ceste ame divine
Ne se mesloit par toute la machine,
Luy donnant vie et force et mouvement:
Car de tout estre elle est commencement.   10
    Des Elemens et de ceste ame infuse
Nous sommes nez: le corps mortel qui s'use
Par trait de temps des Elemens est fait:
De Dieu vient l'ame, et comme il est parfait
L'ame est parfaite, intouchable immortelle,
Comme venant d'une essence eternelle:
L'ame n'a donc commencement ny bout,
Car la partie ensuit tousjours le tout.[1]

The Cat
To Rémy Belleau, Poet

God is in everything and in everything God is diffused, the beginning, end and middle of all that lives, whose soul is enclosed in everything, and who maintains all things in vigour, like our soul, which is instilled into our bodies.

    The parts of this great Whole would have died long since, if that divine soul were not diffused throughout the whole mechanism of the universe, giving it life and strength and movement, for it is the origin of all being.

    From the Elements and from this instilled soul we are born: our mortal body, which wears out in the course of time, is made from the Elements; the soul comes from God, and as he is perfect the soul is perfect, intangible, immortal, because it comes from an eternal essence; our soul, therefore, has neither beginning nor end, for the part always imitates the whole.

Par la vertu de ceste ame meslée
20   Tourne le Ciel à la voûte estoilée,
La mer ondoye, et la terre produit
Par les saisons herbes, fueilles et fruit:
Je dy la terre, heureuse part du monde,
Mere benigne, à gros tetins feconde,
Au large sein: De là tous animaux,
Les emplumez, les escadrons des eaux:
De là, Belleau, ceux qui ont pour repaire
Ou le rocher ou le bois solitaire,
Vivent et sont: et mesmes les metaux,
30   Les diamans, rubis Orientaux,
Perles, saphirs ont de là leur essence,
Et par telle ame ils ont force et puissance,
Qui plus qui moins selon qu'ils en sont pleins:
Autant en est de nous, pauvres humains.

Ne vois-tu pas que la sainte Judée
Sur toute terre est plus recommandée
Pour apparoistre en elle des esprits
Remplis de Dieu de Prophetie épris?

Through the power of this diffused soul the Sky with its starry vault turns, the waves of the sea rise and fall, and the earth produces in their seasons plants, foliage and fruit: the earth, I say, that blest realm of the world, a kindly mother, fertile, with large breasts and a generous bosom. From this soul all animals, the feathered creatures, the legions of the waters, from it, Belleau, those creatures that have for their lair either rock or lonely wood, all take life and have their being; and even metals, diamonds, Oriental rubies, pearls and sapphires draw their essence from it, and from this soul they have strength and vigour, some more, some less, according to how fully they are imbued with it. The same applies to us, poor humans.

Do you not see that holy Judaea is most highly esteemed above all other lands because in her there appeared spirits filled with the Godhead and fired with Prophecy?

Les regions, l'air et le corps y servent,
Qui l'ame saine en un corps sain conservent: 40
Car d'autant plus que bien sain est le corps,
L'ame se monstre et reluist par dehors.

  Or comme on voit qu'entre les hommes naissent
Augurs, devins, et prophetes qui laissent
Un tesmoignage à la posterité
Qu'ils ont vescu pleins de divinité:
Et comme on voit naistre ici des Sibyles
Par les troupeaux des femmes inutiles.

  Ainsi voit-on prophetes de nos maux
Et de nos biens, naistre des animaux,   50
Qui le futur par signes nous predisent,
Et les mortels enseignent et avisent.
Ainsi le veut ce grand Pere de tous
Qui de sa grace a toujours soin de nous.

  Pere il concede en ceste terre large
Par sa bonté aux animaux la charge
De tel souci pour ne douter de rien,
Ayant chez nous qui nous dit mal et bien.

  Regions, air and body, which maintain a healthy mind in a healthy body, are favourable to prophecy, for the more the body is truly healthy, the more the soul becomes visible and shines forth on the outside.

  Now just as we see that among men there are born augurs, seers and prophets, who leave to posterity a testimony that they have lived filled with the divine spirit; just as we see Sibyls born here among the droves of worthless women;

  in the same way we see animals born to be prophets of our good and bad fortune, which predict the future for us by signs, and inform and warn mortals. Such is the will of this great Father of all, who by his grace always cares for us.

  On this wide earth, he, as Father, in his goodness grants to animals the responsibility for such a task, so that we may fear nothing, having among us creatures which

De là sortit l'escolle de l'Augure
60   Merquant l'oiseau, qui par son vol figure
De l'advenir le prompt evenement,
Ravi de Dieu: et Dieu jamais ne ment.

    En nos maisons ce bon Dieu nous envoye
Le coq, la poule et le canard et l'oye,
Qui vont monstrant d'un signe non obscur,
Soit ou mangeant ou chantant, le futur.

    Herbes et fleurs et les arbres qui croissent
En nos jardins prophetes apparoissent:
Mien est l'exemple et par moy je le sçay,
70   Enten l'histoire et je te diray vray.

    Je nourriçois à la mode ancienne
Dedans ma court une Thessalienne,
Qui autrefois pour ne vouloir aimer
Vit ses cheveux en fueille transformer,
Dont la verdure en son Printemps demeure.[2]

    Je cultivois ceste plante à toute heure,
Je l'arrosois, la cerclois et bechois
Matin et soir: la voyant je pensois
M'en faire au chef une belle couronne:

tell us good and bad tidings. This gave rise to the school of Augury, with its observation of birds, which by their flight prefigure imminent future events, being inspired by God; and God never lies.

This good God sends into our homes the cock, the hen, the duck and the goose, which reveal the future to us by clear signs, either by their eating or their singing.

Plants, flowers and the trees that grow in our gardens show themselves to be prophets; here is my own example, which comes from my personal experience. Listen to the story and I shall tell you the truth.

In my courtyard I cultivated in the old manner a Thessalian, who in bygone days, because she refused to love, saw her hair transformed into leaves, which remain evergreen as in Spring.

I used to tend this plant at all hours, I watered it, I dug and hoed round it morning and evening. As I looked at it, I was planning to make a beautiful crown from it

L'homme propose et le Destin ordonne: 80
Cruel Destin à mon dam rencontré,
Qui m'a de l'arbre et de mon soin frustré.

   J'avois la plante au poinct du jour touchée,
Une heure apres je la vis arrachée
Par un Démon: une mortelle main
Ne fist le coup: le fait fut trop soudain.

   Une heure apres je vy la plante morte
Qui languissoit contre terre, en la sorte
Que j'ay depuis languy dedans mon lit:
Et me disoit, Le Démon qui me suit   90
Me fait languir, comme une fiévre quarte
Te doit blesmir: en pleurant je m'escarte
Loin de ce meurdre, et soudain repassant
Je ne vy plus le tige languissant,
Esvanouy comme on voit une nue
S'esvanouir sous la clairté venue.

   Deux mois apres un cheval qui rua,
De coups de pied l'un de mes gens tua,
Luy escrageant d'une playe cruelle
Bien loin du test la gluante cervelle.   100

for my head; but man proposes and Destiny commands, cruel Destiny, which I encountered to my misfortune, and which cheated me of the tree and all my care.

I had attended to the plant at daybreak, but one hour later I saw it uprooted by a Demon; a mortal hand did not strike the blow: the deed was done too suddenly.

One hour later I saw the dying plant languishing on the ground, in the same way as I have since languished in my bed, and it said to me, 'The Demon that pursues me is making me languish, just as a quartan fever will turn you pale.' Weeping, I moved far away from this murder, and then immediately returning I could no longer see the languishing sapling, which had vanished just as we see a cloud vanish with the arrival of bright skies.

Two months later a bucking horse killed one of my men with blows of its hooves, crushing his skull with a cruel wound and strewing his glutinous brains far and wide.

Luy trespassant m'appelloit par mon nom,
Me regardoit, signe qui n'estoit bon:
Car je pensay qu'un malheureux esclandre
Devoit bien tost dessus mon chef descendre,
Comme il a fait: onze mois sont passez
Que j'ay la fiévre en mes membres cassez.

   Mais par-sus tous l'animal domestique
Du triste Chat a l'esprit prophetique,
Et faisoyent bien ces vieux Egyptiens
De l'honorer, et leurs Dieux qui de chiens
Avoyent la face et la bouche aboyante.

   L'ame du Ciel en tout corps tournoyante
Les pousse, anime, et fait aux hommes voir
Par eux les maux ausquels ils doivent choir.
Homme ne vit qui tant haysse au monde
Les Chats que moy d'une haine profonde:
Je hay leurs yeux, leur front et leur regard,
Et les voyant je m'enfuy d'autre part
Tremblant de nerfs de veines et de membre',
Et jamais Chat n'entre dedans ma chambre,
Abhorrant ceux qui ne sçauroyent durer
Sans voir un Chat aupres eux demeurer.
Et toutefois ceste hideuse beste
Se vint coucher tout aupres de ma teste,

As he was dying he gazed at me and called me by my name, which was not a good sign; for I thought that a disastrous accident would very soon befall me, as it has: for these eleven months past I have had a fever in my enfeebled limbs.

But more than all others that domestic animal the melancholy Cat has a prophetic spirit, and those ancient Egyptians were right to honour it, as well as their Gods who had the faces and barking mouths of dogs.

The soul of Heaven, which circulates through each body, stirs these creatures, animates them, and causes man to see, through them, the evils that are in store for him. There is not a man in the world who hates Cats as much as I do, with a deep-seated hatred: I hate their eyes, their face and their stare, and when I see them I beat a hasty retreat, with my nerves, veins and limbs trembling, and never do I allow a Cat to enter my bedroom, having a horror of those people who cannot bear not to have a Cat living beside them. Yet nevertheless this hideous beast came and

Cherchant le mol d'un plumeux oreiller
Où je soulois à gauche sommeiller:
Car volontiers à gauche je sommeille
Jusqu'au matin que le coq me resveille.

　Le Chat cria d'un miauleux effroy:
Je m'esveillay comme tout hors de moy,　　　　130
Et en sursaut mes serviteurs j'appelle:
L'un allumoit une ardante chandelle,
L'autre disoit qu'un bon signe c'estoit
Quand un Chat blanc son maistre reflatoit:
L'autre disoit que le Chat solitaire
Estoit la fin d'une longue misere.

　Et lors fronçant les plis de mon sourci,
La larme à l'œil je leur respons ainsi:
Le Chat devin miaulant signifie
Une fascheuse et longue maladie,　　　　140
Et que long temps je gard'ray la maison,
Comme le Chat qui en toute saison
De son seigneur le logis n'abandonne,
Et soit Printemps soit Esté soit Autonne,
Et soit Hyver, soit de jour soit de nuit,
Ferme s'arreste et jamais ne s'enfuit,
Faisant la ronde et la garde eternelle
Comme un soldat qui fait la sentinelle,

---

lay close beside my head, seeking the softness of a feather pillow, where I was accustomed to sleep on my left side; for I habitually sleep on my left side through to morning when the cock wakes me up.

　The Cat wailed with a fearful mewing; I woke up, completely beside myself, and, startled, I called my servants; one lit a bright candle, another said that it was a good sign when a white Cat rubs against its master, another said that the solitary Cat meant the end of a long period of misery.

　And then, knitting my wrinkled brows, with tears in my eyes, I answered them with these words, 'The prophetic Cat by mewing signifies a long and distressing illness, and that I shall have to stay indoors for a long time, like the Cat which does not leave its owner's house whatever the season, and, whether it be Spring or Summer or Autumn or Winter, whether by day or by night, never steals away, but steadfastly remains there, doing sentry duty and ceaselessly mounting guard like a

Avec le Chien et l'Oye, dont la vois
150   Au Capitole annonça les Gaulois.[3]

     Autant en est de la tarde Tortue
Et du Limas qui plus tard se remue,
Porte-maisons, qui tousjours sur le dos
Ont leur palais, leur lict et leur repos,
Lequel leur semble aussi bel edifice
Qu'un grand chasteau basti par artifice.
L'homme de nuit songeant ces animaux,
Peut bien penser que longs seront ses maux:
Mais s'il songeoit une Grue ou un Cygne,
160   Ou le Pluvier, cela luy seroit signe
De voyager: car tels oiseaux sont pront':
À tire d'aile ils reviennent et vont
En terre, en l'air sans arrester une heure.

     Autant en est du Loup qui ne demeure
En son bocage et cherche à voyager:
Aux maladifs il est bon à songer:
Il leur promet que bien tost sans dommage
Sains et guaris feront quelque voyage.

     Dieu qui tout peut, aux animaux permet
170   De dire vray, et l'homme qui ne met

soldier posted as sentinel, with the Dog and the Goose, whose cries on Capitol Hill warned of the arrival of the Gauls.'

The same is true of the tardy Tortoise and of the Snail, which moves even more tardily, house-carrying creatures that always have their palaces on their backs, with their beds and places to rest, and these seem to them edifices as beautiful as a great castle built with artistry. A man dreaming at night of these animals may truly think that his troubles will be prolonged; but if he dreamed of a Crane or a Swan or a Plover, that would be a sign that he would travel, for such birds are swift: with rapid wings they come and go, on earth and in the air, without stopping for an hour.

The same is true of the Wolf, which does not stay in its copse, but seeks to travel; it is a good thing for the sick to dream of a wolf: it promises them that soon, unharmed, restored and healthy, they will go travelling.

God, who can do everything, permits animals to tell the truth, and a man who

Creance en eux est du tout frenetique:
»Car Dieu par tout en tout se communique.
　Mais quoy? je porte aux forests des rameaux,
En l'Ocean des poissons et des eaux,
Quand d'un tel vers, mon Belleau, je te flate,
Qui as traduit du vieil poëte Arate
Les signes vrais des animaux certains,
Que Dieu concede aux ignorans humains
En leurs maisons, et qui n'ont cognoissance
Du cours du Ciel ny de son influence　　　　　　　180
Enfans de terre: ainsin il plaist à Dieu
Qui ses bontez eslargist en tout lieu:
Et pour aimer sa pauvre creature,
A sous nos pieds prosterné la nature
Des animaux, autant que l'homme est fait
Des animaux l'animal plus parfait.

does not place credence in them is altogether deranged: "For God makes himself known through everything and in everything."

But what am I saying? I am taking branches to the forests, fish and water to the Ocean, when I treat you to lines like this, Belleau my friend, you who have translated the work of the old poet Aratus on the truthful signs of reliable animals. God allows such animals in the homes of ignorant humans, because, being children of the earth, they themselves have no knowledge of the movement of the Heavens, nor of their influence. Such is the pleasure of God, who bestows his good gifts in every place, and, out of love for his poor creation, has humbled the animal world beneath our feet, since man is made the most perfect animal among the animals.

77 L'Ombre du Cheval

Amy Belot, que l'honneur accompagne,
Tu m'as donné non un cheval d'Espagne,
Mais l'ombre vain d'un cheval par escrit
Que je comprens seulement en esprit.
Je ne le puis ny par les yeux comprendre
Ny par la main: il ne se laisse prendre,
Chose invisible, et fantôme me fuit,
Ainsi qu'on voit en nos songes de nuit
Se presenter je ne sçay quels images
10   Sans corps, sans mains, sans bras et sans visages,
Qui çà qui là revolent haut et bas.
Plus pour les prendre on allonge les bras,
Plus vont fuyant, et volages nous laissent
Béans en l'air apres elles qui naissent
De vent leger et comme vent s'en-vont.
    Sans plus à l'homme un desir elles font
De les happer: ton cheval ce me semble
Ton cheval non, mais l'ombre leur resemble,
Que seulement en dormant j'apperçoy:
20   Car autrement ton cheval je ne voy.

The Shade of a Horse

Belot, my friend, you who are attended by honour, have given me, not a Spanish horse, but the spectral shade of a horse that exists only in writing, which I can apprehend only in my mind. I can apprehend it neither with my eyes nor with my hand: an invisible thing, it does not allow itself to be grasped, and phantom-like it flees from me, just as we see in our dreams by night certain images appear without bodies, without hands, without arms and without faces, which fly hither and thither, up and down. The more we stretch out our hands to grasp them, the more they flee, and, being ephemeral, these images, which are born of the empty wind and which, like the wind, fade away, leave us gazing into the air after them open-mouthed.

    At once they instil in men the desire to seize them; your horse, it seems to me, no, not your real horse, but its shade, resembles those images, which I can behold only while asleep; for in no other way can I see your horse. The more I present myself

Plus en songeant ton cheval je me donne,
Plus il me trompe, et fuit sur la Garonne
Aux crins espars, au jarret souple et pront,
À l'estomac refait, au large front,
À la grand' queue, à la drillante oreille,
Et hannissant bien souvent il m'esveille,
Ou bien je l'oy, ou je le pense ouir,
Puis comme idole en l'air s'esvanouir.

    C'est un cheval que je nourris sans peine:
Il ne luy faut ny paille ny aveine,   30
Il ne me faut ny acheter du foin,
Ny des valets pour en avoir le soin,
Bride ne mors, selle ny estrivieres:
Il n'a souci d'herbes ny de rivieres.

    Bref, ce n'est pas le cheval de Sejan,
Lequel donnoit à son maistre mal-an,
Ny le cheval à l'eschine si forte
Qui le surnom du teste de bœuf porte,
Ny le cheval qui conduit faussement
Trompa les Rois, quand son hannissement   40
(Pour la jument qu'il vit à la traverse)
Fist son seigneur le Monarque de Perse.[1]

---

with your horse in my dreams, the more it eludes me, and flees over the Garonne with a streaming mane, a supple and rapid leg, a firm stomach, a broad head, a long tail and a twitching ear; and very often it wakes me up by neighing, and either I hear it, or I think I hear it, and then it vanishes into the air like a spectre.

It is a horse that I have no difficulty in feeding: it needs neither straw nor oats, I do not need to buy hay, nor to have grooms to look after it, nor bridle, nor bit, nor saddle nor stirrup leathers; it does not care about grass or rivers.

In short, it is not the horse of Sejus, which brought its master bad luck, nor is it the horse that was so strongly built that it bore the name of ox-head, nor the horse that tricked the Kings by being cunningly led so that its neighing (provoked by the mare that it saw on a side path) made its master Monarch of Persia.

Ce n'est, Belot, ce bon cheval Bayard
Qui aux combas panadoit si gaillard,
De qui Renault pressoit la courbe eschine:
Mais ton cheval, fantôme, ne chemine.[2]

    C'est le cheval du gentil Pacolet,
Qui dedans l'air s'en-voloit tout seulet,
Faisant service à Mogis, dont les charmes
50   Faisoyent honneur aux Dames et aux armes.[3]
Il vole en l'air, boit en l'air, d'air se paist:
C'est un corps d'air, l'air seulement luy plaist
Et la fumée et le vent et le songe,
Et dedans l'air seulement il s'allonge.

    Les beaux coursiers viste-pieds de Junon
Vivent ainsi: ils ne mangent sinon
Qu'air, qu'ambrosie: ou quand ils ont grand erre
Conduit du Ciel leur Royne en nostre terre,
Mangent un peu de lottes dans les prez
60   Qu'à sa grandeur Samos a consacrez.[4]

    Ainsi se paist le dos-ailé Pegase,
Et le cheval de l'Aurore qui passe
Ceux du Soleil: ainsi nourrist les siens
Minerve et Mars par les prez Thraciens.

It is not, Belot, that good horse Bayard, which pranced so proudly in battle, and whose curving back was gripped by Renaud; in contrast your horse, ghost-like, does not go anywhere.

It is like worthy Pacolet's horse, which flew off into the air all alone, doing service to Mogis, whose spells did honour to Ladies and to weapons. It flies in the air, drinks in the air and feeds on air; it is a body of air, air alone delights it, together with smoke and wind and dreams, and only in the air does it lie down.

The beautiful, swift-footed steeds of Juno live in the same way: they eat nothing but air or ambrosia; or when they have speedily conveyed their Queen from the Heavens to our earth, they eat a little lotus in the meadows that Samos has consecrated to her greatness.

Wing-backed Pegasus feeds in the same way, and so does Aurora's horse, which outstrips those of the Sun; in the same way Minerva nourishes hers, and Mars his in the Thracian meadows. In the same way yours nourishes itself without pasture, for

Ainsi le tien se nourrist sans pasture:
Car c'est, Belot, un cheval en peinture,
Qui me sert plus quand je suis à sejour,
Songeant au lit, qu'il ne me sert le jour.

 La chaude Afrique en certaine contrée
A des jumens, qui en tournant l'entrée   70
De leur nature au vent Zephyrien,
Sur le Printemps vont concevant de rien:
Le tien venteux est yssu de la race
De ces jumens, qui mesme le vent passe.[5]

 On dit qu'Ulysse autrefois prist le vent:
Mais ton cheval, Belot, est si mouvant,
Si fretillant, qu'il ne veut pas permettre
Qu'en ses longs crins les doigts on puisse mettre,
Et du fin Grec la main ne le prendroit:
Car tel cheval jamais ne l'attendroit.[6]   80

 Aurois-tu leu (ô teste rare et chere)
Dedans les vers du fantastique Homere,
Qu'un des chevaux d'Achille s'avança,
Et le trespas à son maistre annonça?[7]

---

it is, Belot, a horse in a painting, which serves me better when I am at rest, dreaming in bed, than it serves me in the daytime.

 In a certain area of hot Africa there are mares that, by turning the opening of their generative organs towards Zephyr's wind, in the Spring conceive from nothing; your speedy horse, which outpaces even the wind, is born of the race of these mares.

 They say that once upon a time Ulysses captured the wind; but your horse, Belot, is so lively, so restless, that it will not allow anyone to lay a finger on its flowing mane, and even the hand of that cunning Greek would not have been able to capture it; for a horse like this would never stand still long enough.

 Have you perhaps read (O you dear, rare person), in the poetry of that fantastical Homer, that one of Achilles' horses came forward and warned his master of impending death?

Tu crains, voyant ma longue maladie,
Que ton cheval en parlant ne me die
Prophetizant quelque funebre mot:
Garde le bien, je n'en veux point, Belot.

Mon cher ami, j'ay bien voulu t'escrire
90   Ces vers raillards pour mieux te faire rire
Apres ta charge, et le souci commun
De conceder audience à chacun,
Haut-elevé au throne de Justice,
Aimant vertu et chastiant le vice.

Dieu, qui sous l'homme a le monde soumis,
À l'homme seul le seul rire a permis
Pour s'esgayer, et non pas à la beste
Qui n'a raison ny esprit en la teste.

»Il faut du rire honnestement user
100 »Pour vivre sain, non pour en abuser:
Car volontiers on jette à gorges pleines
Le ris qui naist des actions vilaines.

Le ris est fils d'un acte vergongneux:
On ne rit point d'un geste vertueux,

Seeing my lengthy illness, you are afraid that your horse may speak to me and prophetically utter some doom-laden words; keep it with you, I do not want it, Belot.

My dear friend, I very much wanted to write these light-hearted lines for you, to make you laugh more heartily after your duties, and your regular task of granting audience to all comers, when you are raised up high on the seat of Justice, favouring virtue and punishing vice.

God, who has subordinated the world to man, has granted laughter alone to man alone for his enjoyment, and not to animals, which have neither reason nor mind in their heads.

"We must use laughter honourably, in order to live healthily, not to abuse it"; for we burst freely into full-throated laughter when it is provoked by ignoble actions.

Laughter is born of a shameful act; we do not laugh at a virtuous deed, but instead

Mais on l'admire: ainsi tu pourras rire
De ma folie, et de t'oser escrire
Je ne sçay quoy qui est encor plus vain
Que ton cheval qui n'a selle ny frain.

admire it; so you will be able to laugh at my folly, and at my daring to write you something that is even more insubstantial than your horse, which has neither saddle nor bit.

78 Gayeté [Pièce retranchée en 1584]

Jaquet aime autant sa Robine
Qu'une pucelle sa poupine:
Robine aime autant son Jaquet
Qu'un amoureux fait son bouquet.
Ô amourettes doucelettes,
Ô doucelettes amourettes,
Ô couple d'amis bien-heureux,
Ensemble aimez et amoureux!
Ô Robine bien-fortunée
10 De s'estre au bon Jaquet donnée!
Ô bon Jaquet bien-fortuné
De s'estre à Robine donné!
Que ny les robes violettes,
Les ribans, ny les ceinturettes,
Les brasselets, les chaperons,
Les devanteaux, les mancherons
N'ont eu la puissance d'espoindre
Pour macreaux ensemble les joindre.
Mais les rivages babillars,
20 L'oisiveté des prez mignars,
Les fontaines argentelettes
Qui attrainent leurs ondelettes

A Frolic [Suppressed in 1584]

Jaquet loves his Robine as much as a little girl loves her doll; Robine loves her Jaquet
as much as a lover loves his posy. O sweet little love affairs, O love affairs so sweet,
O happy pair of friends, both loved and loving! O Robine, most fortunate to have
given herself to good Jaquet! O good Jaquet, most fortunate to have given himself
to Robine! Neither violet gowns, ribbons, nor sashes, bracelets, bonnets, aprons, nor
sleeves had the power to excite her and act as pimps to bring them together.

Instead, babbling river banks, the idleness of delightful meadows, silvery springs,
which lead their ripples along a little mossy channel from the hollow of a verdant

Par un petit trac mousselet
Du creux d'un Antre verdelet,
Les grands forests renouvellées,
Le solitaire des vallées
Closes d'effroy tout à l'entour
Furent cause de telle amour.

   En la saison que l'Hyver dure,
Tous deux pour tromper la froidure,   30
Au pied d'un chesne my-mangé
De main tremblante ont arrangé
Des chenevotes, des fougeres,
Du chaume sec et des bruyeres,
Des buchettes et des brochars,
Et souflans le feu de deux pars
Chaufoient à fesses acroupies
Le cler degout de leurs roupies.

   Apres qu'ils furent un petit
Des-angourdis, un appetit   40
Se vint ruer en la poitrine
Et de Jaquet et de Robine.

   Robine tira de son sein
Un gros quignon buret de pain,
Qu'elle avoit fait de simple aveine
Pour tout le long de la sepmaine:

Cave, large forests continually reborn, the loneliness of valleys fearsomely enclosed all around, these were the cause of this love.

   In the season when Winter persists, in order to escape the cold, at the foot of a half-eaten oak, with shivering hands, the two of them arranged hemp stalks, bracken, dry straw and heather, logs and sticks, and, blowing the flames from both sides, squatting down on their haunches, they warmed the shining dewdrops on the ends of their noses.

   After they had thawed out a bit, appetite came surging into the breasts of both Jaquet and Robine.

   Robine pulled out from her bosom a large chunk of brown bread, which she had made from plain oats to last the whole week; and, rubbing it with cloves of garlic,

Et le frottant contre des aux,
En esternuant des naseaux
De l'autre costé reculée
50 Mangeoit à part son esculée.

 D'autre costé Jaquet espris
D'une faim enragée, a pris
Du ventre de sa panetiere
Une galette toute entiere
Cuitte sur les charbons du four,
Et blanche de sel tout autour,
Que Guillemine sa marraine
Luy avoit donné pour estraine.
Comme il repaissoit, il a veu
60 Guignant par le travers du feu
De sa Robine recourssée
La grosse motte retroussée,
Et son petit cas barbelu
D'un or jaunement crespelu,
Dont le fond sembloit une rose
Non encor' à demy-déclose.

 Robine aussi d'une autre part
De Jaquet guignoit le tribart,
Qui luy pendoit entre les jambes
70 Plus rouge que les rouges flambes

and sneezing through her nostrils, she moved away to one side, and by herself began eating her bowlful.

On the other side Jaquet, seized by a ravenous hunger, took from the belly of his pouch a whole untouched pancake, cooked over the coals of an oven, and white with salt all over, which Guillemine, his godmother, had given him for a New Year present. While he was eating, peering across the fire, he saw Robine with her skirt hitched up, and her huge pussy exposed, and her little lips bearded with gold that curled yellowly, deep within which was what looked like a rose not yet half open.

Robine, too, was peering from the other side at Jaquet's tool, which was hanging down between his legs, redder than the red flames that she was carefully fanning.

Qu'elle attisoit soigneusement.
Apres avoir veu longuement
Ce membre gros et renfrongné,
Robine ne l'a desdaigné,
Mais en levant un peu la teste
A Jaquet fist ceste requeste:
    Jaquet (dit-ell') que j'aime mieux
Ny que mon cœur ny que mes yeux,
Si tu n'aimes mieux ta galette
Que ta mignarde Robinette,   80
Je te pri' Jaquet, chouze moy
Et mets la quille que je voy
Dedans le rond de ma fossette.
    Helas! (dit Jaquet) ma doucette,
Si plus cher ne t'est ton grignon
Que moy Jaquinot ton mignon,
Approche toy mignardelette
Mignardelette doucelette,
Mon pain, ma faim, mon appetit,
Pour mieux t'embrocher un petit.   90
     À-peine eut dit qu'elle s'approche,
Et le bon Jaquet qui l'embroche
Fist trepigner tous les Sylvains
Du dru maniment de ses reins.

After eyeing at length this huge, louring member, Robine did not scorn it, but, raising her head a little, she made this request to Jaquet:

   'Jaquet' (she said) 'that I love more than my heart or my eyes, unless you love your pancake more than your darling Robinette, I beg you, Jaquet, do it to me and thrust that rod I can see into my round hole.'

   'Alas!' (said Jaquet) 'my little sweetie, unless your crust is dearer to you than me, Jaquinot, your beloved, come here, you little darling, little darling, little sweetie, my bread, my hunger, my appetite, so it's easier for me to skewer you for a while.'

   No sooner had he spoken than she approached, and good Jaquet, skewering her, made all the Sylvans excitedly drum their feet at the vigorous movement of his loins.

Les boucs barbus qui l'aguetterent,
Paillards, sur les chévres monterent,
Et ce Jaquet contr'aguignant
Alloient à l'envy trepignant.
  Ô bien-heureuses amourettes,
Ô amourettes doucelettes!
Ô couple d'amans bien-heureux,
Ensemble aimez, et amoureux!
Ô Robine bien-fortunée
De s'estre au bon Jaquet donnée!
Ô bon Jaquet bien-fortuné
De s'estre à Robine donné!
Ô doucelettes amourettes,
Ô amourettes doucelettes!

100

The bearded billy goats that watched him, lecherous creatures, mounted the nanny goats, and peering over at Jaquet vied with him in drumming their feet.

O happy love affairs, O love affairs so sweet! O happy pair of lovers, both loved and loving! O Robine, most fortunate to have given herself to good Jaquet! O good Jaquet, most fortunate to have given himself to Robine! O sweet little love affairs, O love affairs so sweet!

EPITAPHES DE DIVERS SUJETS

79 Epitaphe de François Rabelais [Pièce retranchée en 1578]

Si d'un mort qui pourri repose
Nature engendre quelque chose,
Et si la generation
Est faite de corruption,
Une vigne prendra naissance
De l'estomac et de la pance
Du bon Rabelais, qui boivoit
Toujours ce-pendant qu'il vivoit,
   Car d'un seul trait sa grande gueule
Eust plus beu de vin toute seule,   10
L'epuisant du nez en deux cous,
Qu'un porc ne hume de lait dous,
Qu'Iris de fleuves,[1] ne qu'encore
De vagues le rivage more.

   Jamais le Soleil ne l'a veu,
Tant fust-il matin, qu'il n'eust beu,
Et jamais au soir la nuit noire,
Tant fust tard, ne l'a veu sans boire,
Car alteré, sans nul sejour,
Le gallant boivoit nuit et jour.   20

EPITAPHS ON VARIOUS SUBJECTS

Epitaph for François Rabelais [Suppressed in 1578]

If Nature engenders something from a dead man who lies rotting, and if generation comes from corruption, a vine will be born from the stomach and belly of our worthy Rabelais, who drank constantly while he was alive,
   for with a single swig his great gob would by itself have drunk more wine, draining it, nose first, in two shakes, than a pig drinks sweet milk, or than Iris drinks rivers, or than the tawny shore drinks waves.
   Never, however early in the morning, did the Sun see him when he had not been drinking, and never in the evening, however late, did black night see him not drinking, for, being parched, the good fellow drank night and day without a break.

Mais quand l'ardente Canicule
Ramenoit la saison qui brule,
Demi-nus se troussoit les bras,
Et se couchoit tout plat à bas
Sur la jonchée entre les tasses,
Et, parmi des escuelles grasses
Sans nulle honte se touillant,
Alloit dans le vin barbouillant
Comme une grenouille en la fange:
30 Puis yvre chantoit la louange
De son ami le bon Bacchus,
Comme sous luy furent vaincus
Les Thebains, et comme sa mere
Trop chaudement receut son pere,
Qui en lieu de faire cela,
Las! toute vive la brula.[2]

Il chantoit la grande massue,
Et la jument de Gargantue,
Le grand Panurge, et le païs
40 Des Papimanes ébaïs,
Leurs loix, leurs façons et demeures,
Et frere Jean des Antoumeures,
Et d'Episteme les combas.[3]
Mais la Mort, qui ne boivoit pas,

But when the blazing Dog Days brought round the burning season, he rolled up his sleeves, leaving his arms half bare, and lay spread-eagled on the rush-strewn floor amid the drinking vessels, and without any shame, becoming filthy among greasy dishes, he wallowed in the wine like a frog in the mire; then, drunk, he sang the praises of his friend, good Bacchus, recounting how the Thebans were subjugated by him, and how his mother was visited by his father too hotly, who instead of doing it to her, burned her alive, alas!

He sang of the great club and the mare of Gargantua, of great Panurge, and the land of the credulous Papimanes, their laws, their ways and their homes, and of Jean des Entommeures, and of Epistemon's battles. But Death, who was not a

Tira le beuveur de ce monde,
Et ores le fait boire en l'onde
Qui fuit trouble dans le giron
Du large fleuve d'Acheron.
   Or toy, quiconques sois, qui passes,
Sur sa fosse répen des taces,   50
Répen du bril et des flacons,
Des cervelas et des jambons:
Car si encor dessous la lame
Quelque sentiment a son ame,
Il les aime mieus que des lis,
Tant soyent ils fraichement cueillis.[4]

drinker, hauled the drinker out of this world, and now makes him drink from the water that flows murkily into the bosom of the wide river Acheron.

Now, you who pass by, whoever you may be, hang drinking vessels over his grave, hang some sparkling wine there, and some bottles, sausages and hams; for, if beneath his tombstone his soul still has some feeling, he prefers these to lilies, however freshly they are picked.

DISCOURS DES MISERES DE CE TEMPS

80 *Continuation du Discours des Miseres de ce temps*
À la Royne Catherine de Medicis

Ma Dame, je serois ou du plomb ou du bois,
Si moy que la Nature a fait naistre François,
Aux races à venir je ne contois la peine
Et l'extreme malheur dont nostre France est pleine.

Je veux de siecle en siecle au monde publier
D'une plume de fer sur un papier d'acier,
Que ses propres enfans l'ont prise et dévestue,
Et jusques à la mort vilainement batue.

Elle semble au marchand, accueilli de malheur,
Lequel au coing d'un bois rencontre le volleur,   10
Qui contre l'estomac luy tend la main armée,
Tant il a l'ame au corps d'avarice affamée.

Il n'est pas seulement content de luy piller
La bourse et le cheval: il le fait despouiller,
Le bat et le tourmente, et d'une dague essaye
De luy chasser du corps l'ame par une playe:

DISCOURSE ON THE MISERIES OF THE TIME

Continuation of the Discourse on the Miseries of the Time
To Queen Catherine de Medicis

Your Majesty, I would be made of lead or of wood, if I, whom Nature caused to be born French, did not recount to generations to come the suffering and extreme misfortune that fill our land of France.

I want to proclaim to the world from century to century, with a pen of iron on paper of steel, the fact that her own children have seized her and stripped her bare, and brutally beaten her to the point of death.

She is like a merchant, overtaken by misfortune, when he meets a robber in a lonely forest, who, having such a greedily avaricious soul within his body, strikes him in the stomach with a weapon in his hand.

He is not content simply to plunder his victim's purse and his horse: he makes him strip, beats him and tortures him, and with a dagger tries to drive his soul out

Puis en le voyant mort se sou-rit de ses coups,
Et le laisse manger aux mastins et aux loups.
Si est-ce que de Dieu la juste intelligence
20   Court apres le meurtrier et en prend la vengence:
Et dessus une roue (apres mille travaux)[1]
Sert aux hommes d'exemple et de proye aux corbeaux.
Mais ces nouveaux Chrestiens qui la France ont pillée,
Vollée assassinée à force despouillée
Et de cent mille coups tout l'estomac batu
(Comme si brigandage estoit une vertu)
Vivent sans chastiment, et à les ouïr dire,
C'est Dieu qui les conduit et ne s'en font que rire.
      Ils ont le cœur si haut si superbe et si fier,
30   Qu'ils osent au combat leur maistre desfier.
Ils se disent de Dieu les mignons: et au reste
Qu'ils sont les heritiers du Royaume celeste:[2]
Les pauvres insensez! qui ne cognoissent pas
Que Dieu pere commun des hommes d'ici-bas
Veut sauver un chacun, et qu'à ses creatures
De son grand Paradis il ouvre les clostures.

of his body through a wound; then, seeing him dead, he laughs at his injuries, and
leaves him to be eaten by dogs and wolves. Nevertheless, God's righteous judgement
pursues the murderer and visits vengeance on him; and, stretched on the wheel
(after a thousand torments), he serves to men as an example and as prey to the crows.
But these new-fangled Christians, who have plundered, robbed, assassinated and
forcibly stripped France, and beaten her all over her body with a hundred thousand
blows, they live without punishment (as if banditry was a virtue), and, to hear them
speak, they are following God's orders, and they do nothing but laugh about their
actions.

      Their hearts are so haughty, so arrogant and so proud that they have the temerity
to challenge their master to a battle. They say that they are God's favourites, and,
moreover, that they are the inheritors of the heavenly Kingdom: poor mad fools!
They do not realize that God, the father common to all men here on earth, desires
to save each person, and that he opens the gates of his great Paradise to all his

Certes beaucoup de vuide et beaucoup de vains lieux
Et de sieges seroyent sans ames dans les Cieux:
Et Paradis seroit une plaine deserte,
Si pour eux seulement la porte estoit ouverte.   40

    Or ces braves vanteurs controuvez fils de Dieu,
En la dextre ont le glaive et en l'autre le feu,
Et comme furieux qui frappent et enragent,
Vollent les temples saints et les villes saccagent.

    Et quoy? brusler maisons, piller et brigander,
Tuer assassiner par force commander,
N'obeir plus aux Rois amasser des armées,
Appellez-vous cela Eglises reformées?

    JESUS que seulement vous confessez ici
De bouche et non de cœur ne faisoit pas ainsi: 50
Et saint Paul en preschant n'avoit pour toutes armes
Sinon l'humilité les jeusnes et les larmes:
Et les Peres Martyrs aux plus dures saisons
Des Tyrans ne s'armoyent sinon que d'oraisons:
Bien qu'un Ange du Ciel à leur moindre priere
En soufflant eust rué les Tyrans en arriere.[3]

creatures. Indeed, much empty space and many vacant places and dwellings would be devoid of souls in Heaven, and Paradise would be a deserted wasteland, if the door was opened for them alone.

Now, these boastful braggarts, who pretend to be sons of God, have a sword in their right hand and fire in the other, and, like madmen who lash out and go berserk, they rob holy temples and sack towns.

What? Burning houses, plundering and pillaging, killing, assassinating and dominating by force, no longer obeying Kings, raising armies, is this what you call reformed Churches?

JESUS, whom you acknowledge only with your mouths and not with your hearts, did not act like this; and Saint Paul, when he preached, had only humility, fasting and tears as his weapons; and the first Christian Martyrs, in the harshest periods of Tyranny, armed themselves only with prayers, even though at their least entreaty an Angel from Heaven would have overthrown and blown away the Tyrants.

Par force on ne sçauroit Paradis violer:
JESUS nous a monstré le chemin d'y aller.
Armez de patience il faut suivre sa voye,
60 Non amasser un camp, et s'enrichir de proye.[4]
[. . .]

Vous ressemblez encore à ces jeunes viperes,
Qui ouvrent en naissant le ventre de leurs meres:
Ainsi en avortant vous avez fait mourir
La France vostre mere en lieu de la nourrir.[5]

  De Beze,[6] je te prie escoute ma parolle
Que tu estimeras d'une personne folle:
S'il te plaist toutefois de juger sainement,
Apres m'avoir ouy tu diras autrement.

  La terre qu'aujourd'huy tu remplis toute d'armes
100 Et de nouveaux Chrestiens desguisez en gendarmes
(Ô traistre pieté!) qui du pillage ardans
Naissent dessous ta voix tout ainsi que des dents
Du grand serpent Thebain les hommes qui muerent
Le limon en couteaux desquels s'entretuerent,
Et nez et demy-nez se firent tous perir,
Si qu'un mesme Soleil les vit naistre et mourir.[7]

We cannot violate Paradise by force: JESUS has shown us the way to enter it. Armed with patience, we must follow his path, not raise an army and enrich ourselves with spoils. [. . .]

You resemble also those young vipers, which split open the bellies of their mothers when they are born: in the same way, by your aborted birth, you have brought about your mother France's death, instead of nurturing her.

De Bèze, I beseech you, listen to my words, which you will assume are those of a mad person; if, however, you are willing to judge sanely, after you have heard me you will change your opinion.

This land, which today you have totally filled with weapons and (O treacherous piety) with new Christians disguised as men of war, who are born under the influence of your voice with a burning desire to plunder, just as from the teeth of the huge Theban dragon sprang men who transmuted clay into knives with which they killed each other, and, whether born or only half-born, caused each other to perish, to a man, so that a single passage of the Sun witnessed their birth and death;

Ce n'est pas une terre Allemande ou Gothique,
Ny une region Tartare ny Scythique:
C'est celle où tu nasquis, qui douce te receut,
Alors qu'à Vezelay ta mere te conceut: 110
Celle qui t'a nourry, et qui t'a fait apprendre
La science et les arts dés ta jeunesse tendre,
Pour luy faire service et pour en bien user,
Et non, comme tu fais, à fin d'en abuser.

   Si tu es envers elle enfant de bon courage,
Ores que tu le peux, rens-luy son nourrissage,
Retire tes soldars, et au Lac Genevois
(Comme chose execrable) enfonce leurs harnois.

   Ne presche plus en France une Evangile armée,
Un CHRIST empistollé tout noirci de fumée,   120
Qui comme un Mehemet va portant en la main
Un large coutelas rouge de sang humain.[8]
Cela desplaist à Dieu, cela desplaist au Prince:
Cela n'est qu'un appast qui tire la province
À la sedition, laquelle dessous toy
Pour avoir liberté, ne voudra plus de Roy.
[. . .]

this land is not Germanic or Gothic, nor is it a Tartar or Scythian region: it is the
land where you were born, which gently received you when your mother conceived
you in Vézelay; the land that nurtured you, and that taught you science and the arts
from your tender youth, so that you would render her service and use her well, and
not abuse her, as you do.

   If you are a good-hearted child to her, now, while you can, repay her for her
nurturing, withdraw your soldiers, and throw their armour (a hateful thing) into
Lake Geneva.

   Cease preaching in France a Gospel of arms, a gun-toting CHRIST all blackened
with smoke, who, like Sultan Muhammad, carries in his hand a huge cutlass red
with human blood. That displeases God, that displeases the King, that is only a bait
to lure this realm into sedition, so that, under your influence and wanting to be free,
it will no longer accept a Monarch. [. . .]

Un jour en te voyant aller faire ton presche,
Ayant dessous un reistre une espée au costé:[9]
Mon Dieu, ce dy-je lors, quelle sainte bonté!
Ô parolle de Dieu d'un faux masque trompée,
140   Puis que les Predicans preschent à coups d'espée!
Bien tost avec le fer nous serons consumez,
Puis qu'on voit de couteaux les Ministres armez.

    Et lors deux Surveillans qui parler m'entendirent,
Avec un haussebec ainsi me respondirent:
    Quoy? parles-tu de luy? qui seul est envoyé
Du Ciel pour r'enseigner le peuple desvoyé?
Ou tu es un Athée, ou quelque benefice
Te fait ainsi vomir ta rage et ta malice,
Puis que si arrogant tu ne fais point d'honneur
150   À ce Prophete sainct envoyé du Seigneur!
    Adonc je respondi, Appellez-vous Athée
Celuy qui dés enfance en son cœur a gardée
La foy de ses ayeuls? qui ne trouble les lois
De son païs natal les peuples ny les Rois?
Appellez-vous Athée un homme qui mesprise
Vos songes contrefaits les monstres de l'Eglise?

One day, seeing you, de Bèze, on your way to preach your sermon, with a sword at your side beneath your greatcoat, 'Good heavens,' I said at this, 'what holy goodness! O word of God, you are belied by a false mask, when Pastors preach with the aid of the sword! We shall soon be destroyed by steel, when we see Ministers armed with knives.'

And then two Elders who heard me speak answered me thus, with a sneer,

'What? Do you mean him? The man who alone is sent from Heaven to guide the people who have strayed from the path? Either you are an Atheist, or else it is for the sake of some benefice that you spew out your rage and your malevolence, since you are so arrogant that you do not pay honour to this holy Prophet sent by the Lord!'

Then I answered, 'Do you call an Atheist a man who from his childhood has kept in his heart the faith of his ancestors? Who does not flout the laws of his native land, nor its people, nor its Kings? Do you call an Atheist a man who scorns your deformed and monstrous nightmare visions of the Church? Who believes in one

Qui croit en un seul Dieu, qui croit au sainct Esprit,
Qui croit de tout son cœur au Sauveur JESUS-CHRIST?
Appellez vous Athée un homme qui deteste
Et vous et vos erreurs comme infernale peste?　　　　　160
Et vos beaux Predicans, qui subtils oiseleurs
Pipent le simple peuple, ainsi que basteleurs,
Lesquels enfarinez au milieu d'une place
Vont jouant finement leurs tours de passe-passe:
Et à fin qu'on ne voye en plein jour leur abus,
Soufflent dedans les yeux leur poudre d'oribus?[10]

　　Vostre poudre est crier bien haut contre le Pape,
Deschiffrant maintenant sa tiare et sa chape,
Maintenant ses pardons ses bulles et son bien,
Et plus haut vous criez plus estes gens de bien.[11]　　170
[...]

　　Les Apostres jadis preschoient tous d'un accord:
Entre vous aujourd'huy ne regne que discord:
Les uns sont Zvingliens les autres Lutheristes,
Les autres Puritains Quintins Anabaptistes,
Les autres de Calvin vont adorant les pas,
L'un est predestiné et l'autre ne l'est pas,　　　　　230

God alone, who believes in the holy Spirit, who believes with all his heart in the
Saviour JESUS CHRIST? Do you call an Atheist a man who detests both you and
your erroneous beliefs like a plague from hell? And detests your fine Pastors, who,
in the manner of cunning birdcatchers, bamboozle the simple people, like conjurors
with whitened faces who cleverly perform their sleight of hand in town squares,
and who, so that people cannot see their trickery in broad daylight, blow into their
eyes patent powders?

'Your powder consists of clamouring very loudly against the Pope, castigating
now his tiara and his cope, now his pardons, his bulls and his wealth, and the more
loudly you clamour, the worthier you are considered to be. [...]

'The Apostles long ago were all in accord when they preached, but between you
today there reigns only discord: some are Zwinglians, others Lutherans, others
Puritans, Quintins, or Anabaptists, others follow adoringly in the steps of Calvin;
one is predestined, another is not, another insanely adopts the false doctrine of

Et l'autre enrage apres l'erreur Muncerienne,
Et bien tost s'ouvrira l'escole Bezienne.[12]

    Si bien que ce Luther lequel estoit premier,
Chassé par les nouveaux est presque le dernier,
Et sa secte qui fut de tant d'hommes garnie,
Est la moindre de neuf qui sont en Germanie.

    Vous devriez pour le moins pour nous faire trembler,
Estre ensemble d'accord sans vous desassembler:
Car Christ n'est pas un Dieu de noise ny discorde:
240   Christ n'est que charité, qu'amour et que concorde,
Et monstrez clairement par la division
Que Dieu n'est point autheur de vostre opinion.

    Mais monstrez-moy quelqu'un qui ait changé de vie,
Apres avoir suivi vostre belle folie:
J'en voy qui ont changé de couleur et de teint
Hideux en barbe longue et en visage feint,
Qui sont plus que devant tristes, mornes et palles,
Comme Oreste agité des fureurs infernales.

    Mais je n'en ay point veu qui soient d'audacieux
250   Plus humbles devenus plus doux ny gracieux,
De paillards continens, de menteurs veritables,

Munzer, and very soon the school of Bèze will be inaugurated.

'With the result that Luther, who was the first, is now almost the last, supplanted by newcomers, and his sect, which was adorned with so many men, is now the smallest of nine which exist on German soil.

'To make us tremble, you ought at the very least to be in accord with each other, and not split into factions; for Christ is not a God of quarrels or discord; Christ is all charity, love and concord, and by your divisions you show clearly that your opinion does not have its origin in God.

'But show me one person who has changed his life after embracing your fine madness; I see some who have changed their colour and complexion, becoming repulsive, with long beards and hypocritical expressions, and who are sadder, gloomier and paler than previously, like Orestes tormented by the furies from hell.

'But I have not seen any who from being presumptuous have become humbler, gentler or kinder, who have changed from debauched to chaste, from lying to

D'effrontez vergongneux, de cruels charitables,
De larrons aumosniers, et pas un n'a changé
Le vice dont il fut auparavant chargé.[13]
[. . .]

    Achevant ces propos je me retire, et laisse
Ces Surveillans confus au milieu de la presse,   300
Qui disoient que Satan le cœur m'avoit couvé,
Et me grinçant les dents m'appelloient reprouvé.
    L'autre jour en pensant que ceste pauvre terre
S'en alloit (ô malheur!) la proye d'Angleterre,
Et que ses propres fils amenoient l'estranger
Qui boit les eaux du Rhin, à fin de l'outrager:
M'apparut tristement l'idole de la France,
Non telle qu'elle estoit lors que la brave lance
De Henry la gardoit, mais foible et sans confort,
Comme une pauvre femme attainte de la mort.   310
Son sceptre luy pendoit, et sa robbe semée
De fleurs de liz estoit en cent lieux entamée:
Son poil estoit hideux, son œil have et profond,
Et nulle majesté ne luy haussoit le front.[14]

truthful, from shameless to modest, from heartless to generous, from thieving to charitable, and not one has given up the vice that previously possessed him.' [. . .]

    Ending my remarks I withdraw, and leave these Elders covered in confusion in the middle of the crowd, saying that my heart had been hatched by Satan, and, gnashing their teeth in fury, they called me damned.

    The other day, as I was thinking that this poor land (O woe!) was about to fall prey to England, and that her own children were summoning the foreigner who drinks the water of the Rhine to ravage her, there appeared to me the sorrowful spectre of France, not as she used to be when the heroic lance of Henry protected her, but weak and without succour, like a poor woman on the point of death. Her sceptre drooped from her hand, and her gown emblazoned with lilies was torn in a hundred places; her hair was repulsive, her eyes dull and hollow, and there was no semblance of majesty in her bearing.

En la voyant ainsi, je luy dis: Ô Princesse,
Qui presque de l'Europe as esté la maistresse,
Mere de tant de Rois, conte moy ton malheur,
Et dy moy je te pri' d'où te vient ta douleur!

Elle adonc en tirant sa parolle contrainte,
320   Souspirant aigrement, me fit ainsi sa plainte.

Une ville est assise és champs Savoysiens,
Qui par fraude a chassé ses Seigneurs anciens,[15]
Miserable sejour de toute apostasie,
D'opiniastreté, d'orgueil et d'heresie,
Laquelle (en ce-pendant que les Rois augmentoient
Mes bornes et bien loin pour l'honneur combatoient)
Appellant les banis en sa secte damnable,
M'a fait comme tu vois chetive et miserable.

Or mes Rois cognoissans qu'une telle cité
330   Leur seroit, comme elle est, une infelicité,
Deliberoient assez de la ruer par terre:
Mais contre elle jamais n'ont entrepris la guerre:
Ou soit par negligence ou soit par le destin
Entiere ils l'ont laissée, et de là vient ma fin.[16]

Comme ces laboureurs, dont les mains inutiles
Laissent pendre l'hyver un toufeau de chenilles,

Seeing her like this, I said to her, 'O Princess, you who have been almost the mistress of all Europe, mother of so many Kings, recount your misfortunes, and tell me, I beg you, the cause of your distress!'

Thereupon, uttering strangled words and sighing bitterly, she made her complaint to me thus:

'There is a town, situated in the countryside of Savoy, that iniquitously expelled its former Lords, and is now the wretched dwelling of all apostasy, of obduracy, pride and heresy, a town that (during the time when my Kings were extending my boundaries and fighting for honour far from home) invited those banished to join her damnable sect, and caused me to become feeble and wretched, as you see.

'Now, my Kings, realizing that such a city would be a calamity for them, as indeed it is, considered at length whether to crush it utterly; but they never waged war on it: whether through negligence or through fate, they left it intact, and that is the cause of my downfall.

'Compare those farmers whose idle hands allow a cluster of caterpillars to cling

Dans une fueille seiche au feste d'un pommier:
Si tost que le Soleil de son rayon premier
A la fueille eschauffée, et qu'elle est arrousée
Par deux ou par trois fois d'une tendre rosée,   340
Le venin qui sembloit par l'hyver consumé,
En chenilles soudain apparoist animé,
Qui tombent de la fueille, et rampent à grand'peine
D'un dos entre-cassé au milieu de la plaine:
L'une monte en un chesne et l'autre en un ormeau,
Et tousjours en mangeant se trainent au coupeau:
Puis descendent à terre, et tellement se paissent
Qu'une seule verdure en la terre ne laissent.

Alors le laboureur voyant son champ gasté,
Lamente pour neant qu'il ne s'estoit hasté   350
D'estouffer de bonne heure une telle semence:
Il voit que c'est sa faute et s'en donne l'offence.

Ainsi lors que mes Rois aux guerres s'efforçoient,
Toutes en un monceau ces chenilles croissoient:
Si qu'en moins de trois mois telle tourbe enragée
Sur moy s'est espandue, et m'a toute mangée.

Or mes peuple mutins, arrogans et menteurs
M'ont cassé le bras droit chassant mes Senateurs:[17]

to a dry leaf at the top of an apple tree during the winter; as soon as the Sun has warmed the leaf with its first rays, and it has been moistened two or three times with gentle dew, the blight, which seemed to have been destroyed by winter, suddenly springs to life again in the form of caterpillars, which drop from the leaf and with arched backs loop laboriously over the countryside; one climbs an oak tree, another a young elm, and eating all the time they crawl up to the treetops, then come down to the ground, and they feed so vigorously that they do not leave a single trace of greenery in the land.

'Then the farmer, seeing his field laid waste, pointlessly laments that he had not rushed to nip this crop in the bud; he sees that it is his fault, and he blames himself for it.

'In the same way, while my Kings were putting their efforts into fighting wars, all these caterpillars multiplied in hordes, with the result that in less than three months a frenzied throng like this swarmed all over me, and completely devoured me.

'Now, my rebellious, arrogant and perfidious people have broken my right hand

360

Car de peur que la loy ne corrigeast leur vice,
De mes Palais royaux ont bany la Justice:
Ils ont rompu ma robbe en rompant mes citez,
Rendans mes citoyens contre moy despitez:
Ont pillé mes cheveux en pillant mes Eglises,
Mes Eglises, helas! que par force ils ont prises,
En poudre foudroyans Images et Autels,
Venerable sejour de nos saincts immortels.
Contre eux puisse tourner si malheureuse chose,
Et l'or sainct desrobé leur soit l'or de Tholose![18]
[. . .]

by expelling my Senators; for, fearing that the law might punish their crime, they
have banished Justice from the royal Courts of Law; they have ruined my garments
by ruining my cities, turning my citizens against me in anger; they have plundered
my hair by plundering my Churches, my Churches, alas! which they have seized by
force, reducing to rubble Statues and Altars, hallowed dwellings of our immortal
saints. May such a deplorable thing rebound on them, and may the holy gold that
they have looted be to them like the gold of Toulouse!' [. . .]

81 *Discours à G. Des-Autels*

Des-Autels que la Loy et que la Rhetorique,
Et que la Muse suit comme son fils unique,
Je suis esmerveillé que les Grands de la Court
(Veu le temps orageux qui par l'Europe court)
Ne s'arment les costez d'hommes ayans puissance
Comme toy de plaider leurs causes en la France,
Et revenger d'un art par toy renouvelé,
Le Sceptre que le peuple a par terre foulé.
    C'est donques aujourd'hui que les Rois et les Princes
N'ont besoin de garder par armes leurs provinces,   10
Et contre leurs sujets opposer le harnois:
Mais il faut les garder par livres et par lois
Instrumens qui pourront de la tourbe mutine
Appaiser le courage et flatter la poitrine:
Car il faut desormais defendre nos maisons,
Non par le fer trenchant ainsi par vives raisons,
Et d'un cœur courageux nos ennemis abbatre
Par les mesmes bastons dont ils nous veulent batre.

Discourse to G. Des Autels

Des Autels, you who are favoured by the Law and Rhetoric, and by the Muse as if you were her only son, I am amazed (in view of the stormy climate that prevails throughout Europe) that the Great Men of the Court do not arm themselves with men like you at their sides, men who have the power to plead their cause in France, and, by means of an art that has been revived by you, to avenge the Sceptre, which the people have trampled underfoot.

    The fact is that at the present time Kings and Princes do not need to protect their realms with arms and put on armour against their subjects; but they must protect them with books and laws, instruments that can pacify the heart and soothe the breast of the mutinous mob; for in future we must defend our homes, not with the keen-edged sword, but with vigorous reasoning, and with a valiant heart beat down our enemies with the same rods as those with which they mean to beat us.

Ainsi que l'ennemy par livres a seduit
20   Le peuple desvoyé qui faussement le suit,
Il faut en disputant par livres le confondre,
Par livres l'assaillir, par livres luy respondre,
Sans monstrer au besoin nos courages faillis,
Mais plus fort resister plus serons assaillis.

    Si ne voy-je pourtant personne qui se pousse
Sur le haut de la breche et l'ennemy repousse
Qui brave nous assaut, et personne ne prend
La plume et par escrit nostre loy ne defend:
Les peuples ont recours à la bonté celeste,
30   Et à Dieu sans s'ayder recommandent le reste:
Comme gens esperdus demeurent ocieux,
Ce-pendant les mutins se font victorieux.[1]

    Durant la guerre à Troye à l'heure que la Grece
Pressoit contre les murs la Troyenne jeunesse,
Et que le grand Achille empeschoit les ruisseaux
De porter à Thetis le tribut de leurs eaux:[2]
Ceux qui estoient dedans la muraille assiegée,
Ceux qui estoient dehors dans le port de Sigée,[3]
Failloient egalement: mon Des-Autels, ainsi
40   Nos ennemis font faute, et nous faillons aussi.

Just as, by books, the enemy has seduced and led astray the people who mistakenly follow him, in argument we must prove him wrong by books, attack him by books, refute him by books, without revealing hearts failing in the hour of need, but resisting more strongly the more we are attacked.

But I do not see anyone, however, leaping into the forefront of the breach and repelling the enemy who boldly attacks us, and no one takes up the pen and defends our religion by writing; the people turn to the goodness of heaven for aid, and without trying to help themselves commend the rest to God; they remain inert, like people in a daze, while in the meantime the rebels win the victory.

During the Trojan War, at the moment when Greece was harrying the youth of Troy against the walls, and when great Achilles prevented the rivers from carrying to Thetis the tribute of their waters, those who were besieged inside the city walls and those who were outside in the port of Sigeum were equally at fault; Des Autels, my friend, just so do our enemies fall into error, while we are at fault, too. They are

Ils faillent de vouloir renverser nostre empire,
Et de vouloir par force aux Princes contredire,
Et de presumer trop de leurs sens orgueilleux,
Et par songes nouveaux forcer la loy des vieux:
Ils faillent de laisser le chemin de leurs peres,
Pour ensuivre le train des sectes estrangeres:
Ils faillent de semer libelles et placars
Pleins de derisions d'injure et de brocars,
Diffamans les plus grands de nostre Court royale,
Qui ne servent de rien qu'à nourrir un scandale: 50
Ils faillent de penser que tous soient aveuglez,
Que seuls ils ont des yeux que seuls ils sont reiglez,
Et que nous fourvoyez ensuivons la doctrine
Humaine et corrompue et non pas la divine:
Ils faillent de penser qu'à Luther seulement
Dieu se soit apparu, et generalement
Que depuis neuf cens ans l'Eglise est depravée[4]
Du vin d'hypocrisie à longs traits abreuvée:
Et que le seul escrit d'un Bucere vaut mieux,
D'un Zvingle et d'un Calvin (hommes seditieux)   60
Que l'accord de l'Eglise et les statuts de mille
Docteurs poussez de Dieu convoquez au Concile.[5]

at fault in wishing to overthrow our empire, and in wishing to contest by force the
authority of our Princes, and in being presumptuous with their arrogant attitudes,
and flouting the laws of old with dreams of the new; they are at fault in abandoning
the path of their fathers to adopt the ways of foreign sects; they are at fault in
disseminating libellous pamphlets and placards full of mockery, insults and gibes,
which defame the greatest men of our royal Court, and which serve only to foment
scandal; they are at fault in thinking that everyone is blinded, that they alone have
eyes, that they alone are on the right track, and that we have lost our way and
adopted a doctrine which is human and corrupt, and not divine; they are at fault in
thinking that God has appeared only to Luther, and in general that for nine hundred
years the Church has been depraved, having drunk long draughts of the wine of
hypocrisy; and that the writings of Bucer, Zwingli and Calvin (men of sedition) are
alone worth more than the consensus of the Church and the decrees of a thousand
doctors moved by God who are summoned to the Council.

Que faudroit-il de Dieu desormais esperer,
Si luy sans ignorance avoit souffert errer
Si long temps son Eglise? est-il autheur de faute?
Quel gain en reviendroit à sa Majesté haute?
Quel honneur quel profit de s'estre tant celé,
Pour s'estre à un Luther seulement revelé?

Or nous faillons aussi: car depuis sainct Gregoire
70   Nul Pontife Romain dont le nom soit notoire,
En chaire ne prescha: et faillons d'autre-part,
Que le bien de l'Eglise aux enfans se depart.
Il ne faut s'estonner, Chrestiens, si la nacelle
Du bon Pasteur sainct Pierre en ce monde chancelle,
Puis que les ignorans les enfans de quinze ans,
Je ne sçay quels muguets je ne sçay quels plaisans
Ont les biens de l'Eglise et que les benefices
Se vendent par argent ainsi que les offices.[6]

Mais que diroit Sainct Paul, s'il revenoit icy,
80   De nos jeunes Prelats qui n'ont point de soucy
De leur pauvre troupeau, dont ils prennent la laine,
Et quelquefois le cuir: qui tous vivent sans peine,
Sans prescher sans prier sans bon exemple d'eux,
Parfumez decoupez[7] courtisans amoureux,

What hope should we now have of God, if, though not ignorant of the fact, he had allowed his Church to stray for such a long time? Is he capable of falling into error? What gain would accrue to his supreme Majesty? What honour, what profit, from concealing himself for so long, in order to reveal himself to Luther alone?

Now we are at fault as well: for ever since Saint Gregory no Roman Pontiff worthy of renown has preached from the pulpit; and we are at fault moreover in that the wealth of the Church is distributed to children. We must not be surprised, Christians, if the barque of the good Shepherd Saint Peter founders in this world, since ignorant men, fifteen-year-old boys, various young fops and various triflers possess the wealth of the Church, and benefices are sold for money, as are Church offices.

But, if he returned here, what would Saint Paul say about our young Prelates who have no care for their poor flock, from whom they seize their fleece, and sometimes their hide, too; who all live without toil, without preaching, without praying, without setting a good example; perfumed and fashionable, these courtiers,

Veneurs et fauconniers, et avec la paillarde
Perdent les biens de Dieu, dont ils n'ont que la garde?
    Que diroit-il de voir l'Eglise à Jesus Christ,
Qui fut jadis fondée en humblesse d'esprit,
En toute patience en toute obeyssance,
Sans argent sans credit sans force ny puissance,   90
Pauvre nue exilée, ayant jusques aux os
Les verges et les foëts imprimez sur le dos,
Et la voir aujourd'huy riche, grasse et hautaine,
Toute pleine d'escus, de rente et de domaine?
Ses ministres enflez, et ses Papes encor
Pompeusement vestus de soye et de drap d'or?
Il se repentiroit d'avoir souffert pour elle
Tant de coups de baston, tant de peine cruelle,
Tant de banissements, et voyant tel meschef,
Pri'roit qu'un trait de feu luy accablast le chef.   100
    Il faut donc corriger de nostre saincte Eglise
Cent mille abus commis par l'avare Prestrise,
De peur que le courroux du Seigneur tout-puissant
N'aille d'un juste feu nos fautes punissant.

lovers, huntsmen and falconers, who squander on loose living the wealth of God, which is only entrusted to them for safe keeping?

What would he say on seeing the Church of Jesus Christ, which was founded of old on humility of spirit, on perfect long-suffering, on perfect obedience, without money, without resources, without strength or power, poor, naked, exiled, having the marks of rods and scourges cut bone-deep into her back, what would he say on seeing her today, rich, well-fed and haughty, plentifully supplied with gold coins, revenues and estates? Her ministers puffed up, and her Popes furthermore pompously clad in silk and cloth of gold? He would repent of having suffered for her so many beatings, so much cruel pain, so many banishments, and, seeing such a disaster, he would pray that a fiery bolt would crush her head.

We must therefore correct a hundred thousand abuses of our holy Church, committed by the avaricious Priesthood, for fear that the wrath of the almighty Lord will punish our faults with righteous fire.

Quelle fureur nouvelle a corrompu nostre aise?
Las! des Lutheriens la cause est tres mauvaise,
Et la defendent bien: et par malheur fatal
La nostre est bonne et saincte, et la defendons mal.
   Ô heureuse la gent que la mort fortunée
110 A depuis neuf cens ans sous la tumbe emmenée!
Heureux les peres vieux des bons siecles passez,
Qui sont sans varier en leur foy trespassez,
Ains que de tant d'abus l'Eglise fust malade!
Qui n'ouyrent jamais parler d'Œcolampade,
De Zvingle, de Bucer, de Luther, de Calvin:
Mais sans rien innover au service divin
Ont vescu longuement, puis d'une fin heureuse
En Jesus ont rendu leur ame genereuse.
   Las! pauvre France helas! comme une opinion
120 Diverse a corrompu ta premiere union!
Tes enfans qui devroient te garder te travaillent,
Et pour un poil de bouc entre eux-mesmes bataillent,[8]
Et comme reprouvez d'un courage meschant,
Contre ton estomac tournent le fer trenchant.
   N'avions-nous pas assez engressé la campagne
De Flandres de Piedmont de Naples et d'Espagne

What new frenzy has destroyed our well-being? Alas! The Lutherans' cause is very poor, yet they defend it well; and our cause is good and holy, yet, by a fatal misfortune, we defend it poorly.

O happy that race of men whom propitious death has conducted to the tomb these nine hundred years past! Happy those fathers of old in virtuous centuries gone by who perished without wavering in their faith, before the Church fell sick of so many abuses! Who never heard tell of Oecolampadius, of Zwingli, of Bucer, of Luther or of Calvin, but who, without introducing any novelty into the service of God, lived long, and then, rendering up their noble souls, reached a happy end in Jesus.

Alas! Poor France, alas! How greatly has a diversity of opinions corrupted your original unity! Your children, who ought to protect you, torment you instead, and fight between themselves over the hairy skin of a goat, and, like reprobates, with evil hearts, they turn the keen-edged steel against your breast.

Had we not sufficiently fertilized the countryside of Flanders, Piedmont, Naples

En nostre propre sang? sans tourner les couteaux
Contre toy nostre mere, et tes propres boyaux?
Afin que du Grand-Turc les peuples infidelles
Rissent en nous voyant sanglans de nos querelles?   130
Et en lieu qu'on les deust par armes surmonter,
Nous vissent de nos mains nous-mesmes nous donter,
Ou par l'ire de Dieu, ou par la destinée,
Qui te rend par les tiens, ô France, exterminée!

   Las! faut-il, ô destin, que le Sceptre François,
Que le fier Allemant, l'Espagnol et l'Anglois
N'a sceu jamais froisser, tombe sous la puissance
Du vassal qui devroit luy rendre obeyssance?
Sceptre qui fut jadis tant craint de toutes pars,
Qui jadis envoya outre-mer ses soldars   140
Gaigner la Palestine et toute l'Idumée,
Tyr Sydon Antioche, et la ville nommée
Du sainct nom, où Jesus en la Croix attaché
De son precieux sang lava nostre peché:[9]

   Sceptre qui fut jadis la terreur des Barbares,
Des Turcs des Mammelus des Perses des Tartares:[10]
Bref, par tout l'univers tant craint et redouté,
Faut-il que par les siens luy-mesme soit donté?

and Spain with our own blood? Without turning our knives against you, our mother, and your own entrails? For the infidel peoples of the Grand Turk to laugh when they saw us covered in blood from our quarrels? And, when we should have conquered them with weapons, to let them see us defeating ourselves with our own hands, either because of the wrath of God, or because of destiny, which causes you, O France, to be annihilated by your own children?

Alas! Must it come to pass, O destiny, that the Sceptre of France, which the cruel German, the Spaniard and the Englishman have never been able to crush, shall fall under the power of the vassal who ought to render it obeisance? The Sceptre that was once so greatly feared everywhere, that once sent its soldiers overseas to capture Palestine and all Idumaea, Tyre, Sidon, Antioch, and the city named with the holy name, where Jesus, nailed to the Cross, washed away our sin with his precious blood;

the Sceptre that was once the terror of the Barbarians, the Turks, the Mamelukes, the Persians and the Tartars, in short, that was so feared and dreaded throughout the universe, must it come to pass that it shall be subjugated by its own people?

France, de ton malheur tu es cause en partie:
150   Je t'en ay par mes vers mille fois advertie:
Tu es marastre aux tiens et mere aux estrangers,
Qui se mocquent de toy quand tu es aux dangers:
Car sans aucun travail les estrangers obtiennent
Les biens qui à tes fils justement appartiennent.[11]

    Pour exemple te soit ce docte Des-Autels,
Qui à ton los a fait des livres immortels,
Qui poursuivoit en Cour dés long temps une affaire
De bien peu de valeur, et ne la pouvoit faire
Sans ce bon Cardinal,[12] qui rompant le sejour
160   Le renvoya content en l'espace d'un jour.
Voilà comme des tiens tu fais bien peu de conte,
Dont tu devrois au front toute rougir de honte.

    Tu te mocques aussi des Prophetes que Dieu
Choisit en tes enfans, et les fait au milieu
De ton sein apparoistre, afin de te predire
Ton malheur advenir mais tu n'en fais que rire.

    Ou soit que du grand Dieu l'immense eternité
Ait de Nostradamus l'entousiasme excité,
Ou soit que le Demon bon ou mauvais l'agite,
170   Ou soit que de nature il ait l'ame subite,

France, you are in part to blame for your misfortune; I have warned you a
thousand times in my poetry: you are a cruel stepmother to your children and a
mother to foreigners, who mock you when you are in danger; since foreigners
obtain, without working for it at all, the wealth that rightly belongs to your children.

As an example, take the case of this learned Des Autels, who has composed
immortal books to honour you; he had been for a long time engaged in the Courts
in an action that brought him very little advantage, and was unable to bring it to a
conclusion without that good Cardinal, who, putting an end to the delay, sent him
away content in the space of a day. That is how little importance you attach to your
people, for which you ought to blush all over your face for shame.

You also scorn the Prophets whom God chooses from among your children, and
whom he causes to appear within your very bosom, in order to predict the misfortune
that is to befall you, but you only laugh at them.

Whether almighty God in his immense eternity has inspired in Nostradamus a
divine exaltation, or whether a good or bad Demon drives him, or whether by his

Et outre le mortel s'eslance jusqu'aux cieux,
Et de là nous redit des faicts prodigieux,
Ou soit que son esprit sombre et melancolique,
D'humeurs grasses repeu, le rende fantastique:
Bref, il est ce qu'il est: si est-ce toutefois
Que par les mots douteux de sa prophete vois,
Comme un oracle antique, il a dés mainte année
Predit la plus grand part de nostre destinée.[13]
[...]

nature he has an impressionable soul, which transcends mortal limitations and rises up to the heavens, and from there relates to us miraculous facts, or whether his sombre and melancholy spirit, replete with heavy humours, renders him fantastical: in short, he is what he is. However it may be, in the ambiguous words uttered by his prophetic voice, like that of an ancient oracle, he has these many years foretold the greater part of our destiny.
[...]

82 *Remonstrance au peuple de France*

Ô ciel! ô mer! ô terre! ô Dieu pere commun
Des Juifs et des Chrestiens des Turcs et d'un chacun:
Qui nourris aussi bien par ta bonté publique
Ceux du pole Antartiq' que ceux du pole Artique:
Qui donnes et raison et vie et mouvement,
Sans respect de personne à tous egalement:
Et fais du Ciel là-haut sur les testes humaines
Tomber comme il te plaist, les graces et les peines:
　　Ô Seigneur tout-puissant, qui as tousjours esté
Vers toutes nations plein de toute bonté,
Dequoy te sert là haut le trait de ton tonnerre,
Si d'un esclat de feu tu n'en brusles la terre?
Es-tu dedans un throsne assis sans faire rien?
Il ne faut point douter que tu ne sçaches bien
Cela que contre toy brassent tes creatures,
Et toutefois, Seigneur, tu le vois et l'endures!
　　Ne vois-tu pas du Ciel ces petits animaux,
Lesquels ne sont vestus que de petites peaux,
Ces petits animaux qu'on appelle les hommes!
Qu'ainsi que bulles d'eau tu créves et consommes?

Remonstrance to the People of France

O Heaven! O sea! O earth! O God the common father of Jews and Christians, of Turks and of all people, you who nurture with your universal goodness both those from the Antarctic pole and those from the Arctic pole; you who give reason and life and movement without discrimination to all equally, and who from Heaven above shower blessings and punishments on human heads according to your will.

O almighty Lord, who have always been full of all goodness towards all nations, what good is your thunderbolt to you on high, if you do not burn the earth with it in a blaze of fire? Are you sitting on a throne doing nothing? It is not to be doubted that you are well aware of the machinations of your creatures against you, and yet, Lord, you see this and tolerate it!

Do you not see from Heaven these little animals, which are clad only in little skins, these little animals that are called men? Which you burst and destroy like

Que les doctes Romains et les doctes Gregeois
Nomment songe, fumée, et fueillage des bois?
Qui n'ont jamais ici la verité cognue
Que je ne sçay comment par songes et par nue?

   Et toutefois, Seigneur, ils font les empeschez,
Comme si tes secrets ne leur estoyent cachez,
Braves entrepreneurs et discoureurs des choses
Qui aux entendemens de tous hommes sont closes,
Qui par longue dispute et curieux propos
Ne te laissent jouyr du bien de ton repos,   30
Qui de tes sacremens effacent la memoire,[1]
Qui disputent en vain de cela qu'il faut croire,
Qui font trouver ton fils imposteur et menteur:
Ne les puniras-tu souverain Createur?
Tiendras-tu leur parti? veux-tu que l'on t'appelle
Le Seigneur des larrons et le Dieu de querelle?
Ta nature y repugne, aussi tu as le nom
De doux de pacifiq' de clement et de bon:
Et ce monde accordant ton ouvrage admirable
Nous monstre que l'accord t'est tousjours agreable.   40

---

bubbles in water? Which the learned Romans and the learned Greeks call dreams, smoke and the leaves of the forest? Which have never known the truth here on earth, except perhaps through dreams and through a cloud?

   And yet, Lord, they are full of self-importance, as if your secrets were not hidden from them, these bold venturers and inquirers about things that are closed to the understanding of all mortals, these men who with their lengthy disputes and inquisitive questioning prevent you from enjoying the pleasure of your repose, who obliterate the memory of your sacraments, who dispute pointlessly over that which we should believe, who make your Son out to be an impostor and a liar: will you not punish them, supreme Creator? Will you take their part? Do you wish to be called the Lord of scoundrels and the God of quarrels? This is repugnant to your nature; you have a name for being gentle, peace-loving, merciful and kind; and this harmonious world and your wondrous works show us that harmony is always pleasing to you.

Mais qui seroit le Turc le Juif le Sarrasin,
Qui voyant les erreurs du Chrestien son voisin,
Se voudroit baptiser? le voyant d'heure en heure
Changer d'opinion, qui jamais ne s'asseure?
Le cognoissant leger mutin seditieux,
Et trahir en un jour la foy de ses ayeux?
Volontaire incertain, qui au propos chancelle
Du premier qui luy chante une chanson nouvelle?
Le voyant Manichée, et tantost Arrien,[2]
50   Tantost Calvinien tantost Lutherien,
Suivre son propre advis non celuy de l'Eglise?
Un vray jonc d'un estang, le jouet de la Bise,
Ou quelque girouette inconstante, et suivant
Sur le haut d'une tour la volonté du vent?
Et qui seroit le Turc lequel auroit envie
De se faire Chrestien en voyant telle vie?

Certes si je n'avois une certaine foy
Que Dieu par son esprit de grace a mise en moy,
Voyant la Chrestienté n'estre plus que risée,
60   J'aurois honte d'avoir la teste baptisée:
Je me repentirois d'avoir esté Chrestien,
Et comme les premiers je deviendrois Payen.

But what Turk, or Jew, or Saracen, seeing the erring ways of the Christian, his neighbour, would wish to be baptized? Seeing him change his opinion hour by hour, never sure about anything? Knowing that he is capricious, mutinous, seditious, and that he betrays in one day the faith of his ancestors? That he is headstrong, unreliable, and wavers at the suggestion of the first person who sings him a new song? Seeing him a Manichean, and now an Arian, now a Calvinist, now a Lutheran, following his own ideas, not those of the Church? A true reed of the pond, plaything of the North Wind, or some inconstant weathercock, following the will of the wind at the top of a tower? And what Turk would wish to become a Christian, seeing such a way of life?

Indeed, if I did not have an unshakeable faith, which God has placed in me by the grace of his spirit, I would be ashamed at having had my head baptized, seeing that Christianity is no longer anything but a laughing stock; I would repent of having been a Christian, and I would become a Pagan like the first men.

La nuict j'adorerois les rayons de la Lune,
Au matin le Soleil la lumière commune,
L'œil du monde, et si Dieu au chef porte des yeux,
Les rayons du Soleil sont les siens radieux,
Qui donnent vie à tous, nous conservent et gardent,
Et les faits des humains en ce monde regardent.

Je dy ce grand Soleil, qui nous fait les saisons
Selon qu'il entre ou sort de ses douze maisons,   70
Qui remplit l'Univers de ses vertus cognues,
Qui d'un trait de ses yeux nous dissipe les nues,
L'esprit l'ame du monde ardant et flamboyant,
En la course d'un jour tout le Ciel tournoyant,
Plein d'immense grandeur rond vagabond et ferme,
Lequel a dessous luy tout le monde pour terme,
En repos sans repos oisif et sans sejour,
Fils aisné de Nature et le pere du jour.

J'adorerois Cerés qui les bleds nous apporte,
Et Bacchus qui le cœur des hommes reconforte,   80
Neptune le sejour des vents et des vaisseaux,
Les Faunes et les Pans et les Nymphes des eaux,
Et la Terre hospital de toute creature,
Et ces Dieux que l'on feint ministres de Nature.[3]

At night I would worship the rays of the Moon, in the morning the Sun, the universal light, the eye of the world, and if God has eyes in his head, the rays of the Sun are his radiant beams, which give life to all, which preserve and keep us, and watch over the deeds of humans in this world.

This great Sun, I say, who orders the seasons for us according to whether he is entering or leaving his twelve houses of the Zodiac, who fills the Universe with his well-known powers, who with a flash from his eyes disperses the clouds; the spirit, the soul of the world, burning and blazing, traversing the whole Sky in the course of a day, full of immense grandeur, round, wandering yet constant, who has under him the whole world for boundary, at rest yet without rest, at leisure yet not motionless, eldest son of Nature and father of the day.

I would worship Ceres, who brings us corn, and Bacchus, who fortifies the hearts of men, Neptune the abode of winds and vessels, Fauns and Pans and water Nymphs, and the earth, haven for all creatures, and those Gods who are fabled to be the ministers of Nature.

Mais l'Evangile sainct du Sauveur JESUS-CHRIST
M'a fermement gravée une foy dans l'esprit,
Que je ne veux changer pour une autre nouvelle,
Et deussé-je endurer une mort trescruelle.

De tant de nouveautez je ne suis curieux,
90   Il me plaist d'imiter le train de mes ayeux:
Je croy qu'en Paradis ils vivent à leur aise,
Encor qu'ils n'ay'nt suivi ny Calvin ny de Beze.

Dieu n'est pas un menteur abuseur ny trompeur:
De sa sainte promesse il ne faut avoir peur,
Ce n'est que verité, et sa vive parolle
N'est pas comme la nostre incertaine et frivole.

L'homme qui croit en moy (dit-il) sera sauvé:[4]
Nous croyons tous en toy, nostre chef est lavé
En ton nom, ô JESUS, et dés nostre jeunesse
100   Par foy nous esperons en ta sainte promesse.

Et toutefois Seigneur par un mauvais destin
Je ne sçay quel yvrongne apostat Augustin[5]
Nous presche le contraire et tellement il ose,
Qu'à toy la verité sa mensonge il oppose.

But the holy Gospel of our Saviour JESUS CHRIST has firmly engraved in my mind a faith that I am not willing to exchange for a new one, even if I had to endure a most cruel death.

I have no curiosity about so many novelties, I am content to imitate the ways of my forefathers: I believe that they are living serenely in Paradise, even though they did not follow the teachings of either Calvin or Bèze.

God is not a liar, a hypocrite or a deceiver: we need not be afraid to trust his holy promise, it is nothing but the truth, and his living word is not like ours, fickle and capricious.

'A man who believes in me will be saved,' he said. We all believe in you, our heads are sprinkled with water in your name, JESUS, and from our youth, through faith, we place our hopes in your holy promise.

And yet, Lord, by an evil fate, some drunken Augustinian apostate preaches the contrary to us, and he is so presumptuous as to oppose his falsehood to you, who are the truth.

Le soir que tu donnois à ta suitte ton corps,
Personne d'un couteau ne te pressoit alors
Pour te faire mentir et pour dire au contraire
De ce que tu avois deliberé de faire.

Tu as dit simplement d'un parler net et franc,
Prenant le pain et vin: *C'est cy mon corps et sang,*   110
Non signe de mon corps: toutefois ces Ministres,
Ces nouveaux defroquez, apostats et belistres
Desmentent ton parler, disant que tu resvois,
Et que tu n'entendois les mots que tu disois.[6]

Ils nous veulent monstrer par raison naturelle
Que ton corps n'est jamais qu'à la dextre eternelle,
De ton pere là-haut, et veulent t'attacher
Ainsi qu'un Promethée au feste d'un rocher.

Ils nous veulent prouver par la Philosophie
Qu'un corps n'est en deux lieux, aussi je ne leur nie: 120
Car tout corps n'a qu'un lieu: mais le tien ô Seigneur
Qui n'est que majesté que puissance et qu'honneur,
Divin glorifié, n'est pas comme les nostres.

Celuy à porte close alla voir les Apostres,
Celuy sans rien casser sortit hors du tombeau,
Celuy sans pesanteur d'os de chair ny de peau

On the evening when you gave your body to your disciples, no one threatened
you with a knife to make you lie and say the contrary of what you had intended to
say.

You simply said, in plain and sincere words, taking the bread and wine, *This is
my body and my blood,* not the symbol of my body; yet these Ministers, these
new-fangled unfrocked priests, apostates and knaves, gainsay your words, saying
that you were dreaming, and that you did not mean what you were saying.

They want to demonstrate to us by natural reason that your body is never
anywhere but at the eternal right hand of your father on high, and they want to
fasten you to the pinnacle of a rock, like a Prometheus.

They want to prove to us by Philosophy that a body cannot be in two places at
once, and I do not deny it; for each body is in only one place, but yours, Lord, which
is all majesty, all power, and all honour, divine and glorious, is not like ours.

He went through closed doors to see the Apostles; he came forth from the tomb

Monta dedans le Ciel:[7] si ta vertu feconde
Sans matiere apprestée a basti tout ce monde,[8]
Si tu es tout divin tout saint tout glorieux,
130   Tu peux communiquer ton corps en divers lieux.
Tu serois impuissant si tu n'avois puissance
D'accomplir tout cela que ta Majesté pense.

    Mais quel plaisir prens-tu pour troubler ton repos,
D'ouyr l'humain caquet tenir tant de propos?
D'ouyr ces Predicans qui par nouveaux passages
En t'attachant au Ciel, monstrent qu'ils ne sont sages?
Qui pipent le vulgaire et disputent de toy,
Et r'appellent tousjours en doute nostre foy?

    Il fait bon disputer des choses naturelles,
140   Des foudres et des vents, des neiges et des gresles,
Et non pas de la foy dont il ne faut douter:
Seulement il faut croire et non en disputer.

    Tout homme curieux lequel voudra s'enquerre
Dequoy Dieu fit le Ciel les ondes et la terre,
Du Serpent qui parla, de la pomme d'Adam,
D'une femme en du sel, de l'asne à Balaam,

without breaking it open; not weighed down by bones, flesh or skin, he ascended into Heaven; if your abundant might created this whole world without pre-existing matter, if you are all divine, all holy and all glorious, you can communicate your body to diverse places. You would be powerless if you did not have the power to accomplish all that your Majesty wishes.

But what pleasure can you receive from having your peace disturbed by hearing prattling humans uttering so much verbiage? By hearing those Preachers who fix you in Heaven, using new texts, thus demonstrating their lack of wisdom? Who delude the masses and argue about you, and forever cast doubt on our faith?

It is good to argue about natural things, about thunder and wind, snow and hail, but not about our faith, which we must not doubt: we must simply believe, and not argue about it.

Any curious man who wants to ask questions about what God made the Heavens out of, and the waters and the earth, about the Serpent that spoke, about Adam's apple, about a woman turned into salt, about Balaam's ass, about the miracles of

Des miracles de Moyse, et de toutes les choses
Qui sont dedans la Bible estrangement encloses,[9]
Il y perdra l'esprit: car Dieu qui est caché,
Ne veut que son secret soit ainsi recherché.   150

    Bref nous sommes mortels, et les choses divines
Ne se peuvent loger en nos foibles poitrines,
Et de sa prescience en vain nous devisons:
Car il n'est pas sujet à nos sottes raisons.
»L'entendement humain, tant soit-il admirable,
»Du moindre fait de Dieu sans grace n'est capable.

    Mais comment pourroit l'homme avec ses petits yeux
Cognoistre clairement les mysteres des cieux?
Quand nous ne sçavons pas regir nos republiques,
Ny mesmes gouverner nos choses domestiques!   160
Quand nous ne cognoissons la moindre herbe des prez!
Quand nous ne voyons pas ce qui est à nos piez![10]
[. . .]

    Perisse mille fois ceste tourbe mutine
Qui folle court apres la nouvelle doctrine,
Et par opinion se laisse sottement
Sous ombre de piété gaigner l'entendement.

Moses, and about all the things that are mysteriously recorded in the Bible, such a man will lose his mind in the process; for God, who is hidden, does not wish his secrets to be investigated in this way.

In short, we are mortal, and we cannot accommodate divine things in our feeble breasts, and we debate his prescience in vain; for he is not subject to our foolish reasoning. "Human understanding, however admirable it is, without divine grace is not capable of comprehending the smallest act of God."

But how could man with his little eyes understand clearly the mysteries of the heavens? When we cannot rule our states, nor even govern our domestic affairs! When we do not understand the smallest plant of the meadows! When we do not see what is at our feet!
[. . .]

May it perish a thousand times, this rebellious mob that runs madly after the new doctrine, and foolishly allows its judgement to be taken over by dogmatic opinion in the guise of piety.

Ô Seigneur tu devois pour chose necessaire
Mettre l'opinion aux talons et la faire
Loin du chef demeurer, et non pas l'apposer
230   Si pres de la raison, à fin de l'abuser!
Comme un meschant voisin qui abuse à toute heure
Celuy qui par fortune aupres de luy demeure.

Ce monstre qui se coule en nos cerveaux, apres
Va gaignant la raison laquelle habite aupres,
Et alors toute chose en l'homme est desbordée,
Quand par l'opinion la raison est guidée.

La seule opinion fait les hommes armer,
Et frere contre frere au combat animer,
Perd la religion, renverse les grands villes,
240   Les couronnes des Rois, les polices civiles:
Et apres que le peuple est sous elle abbatu,
Lors le vice et l'horreur surmonte la vertu.

Or ceste opinion fille de fantasie,
Outre-vole l'Afrique, et l'Europe et l'Asie
Sans jamais s'arrester: car d'un vol nompareil
Elle attaint en un jour la course du Soleil.

Elle a les pieds de vent, et dessur les aisselles
Comme un monstre emplumé, porte de grandes ailes:

O Lord, you ought of necessity to have located opinion in our heels, and made it dwell far from our heads, instead of placing it so close to reason that it can abuse it! Like a bad neighbour who constantly abuses a person who by chance lives next door to him.

This monster, which infiltrates our brains, takes possession afterwards of our reason, which resides close by, and then everything in man is in turmoil, when reason is controlled by opinion.

Opinion of itself makes men take up weapons, and sets brother against brother in battle; it causes the downfall of religion, it overthrows large towns, the crowns of Kings and civic government; and after the people are subjugated to it, then vice and horror triumph over virtue.

Now this opinion, daughter of fantasy, flies across Africa, Europe and Asia without ever stopping; for with unparalleled powers of flight she completes in one day the course of the Sun.

Her feet speed like the wind, and, like a feathered monster, she sports huge wings

Elle a la bouche ouverte, et cent langues dedans,
Sa poitrine est de plomb, ses yeux prompts et ardans,   250
Tout son chef est de verre, et a pour compagnie
La jeunesse, l'erreur, l'orgueil et la manie.
De ses tetins ce monstre un Vuiclef alaita,
Et en despit du ciel un Jean Hus enfanta,
Puis elle se logea sur le haut de la porte
De Luther son enfant, et dist en ceste sorte:[11]

   Mon fils, il ne faut plus que tu laisses rouiller
Ton esprit en paresse, il te faut despouiller
Cest habit monstrueux, il faut laisser ton cloistre:
Aux Princes et aux Rois je te feray cognoistre,   260
Et si feray ton nom fameux de tous costez,
Et rendray dessous toy les peuples surmontez.
»Il faut oser beaucoup: la Fortune demande
»Un magnanime cœur qui ose chose grande.[12]

   Ne vois-tu que le Pape est trop enflé de biens?
Comme il presse sous soy les Princes terriens!
Et comme son Eglise est toute depravée
D'ambition, de gloire, et d'honneur abreuvée!
Ne vois-tu ses supposts paresseux et poussifs,
Decoupez parfumez delicats et lascifs,   270

on her shoulders; her mouth is open, with a hundred tongues in it, her breast is of lead, her eyes darting and burning, her whole head is of glass, and for companions she has youth, error, pride and mania. At her breast that monster suckled Wycliffe, and to spite the heavens she gave birth to John Hus, then she took up lodgings above the door of her child Luther, and spoke thus:

   'My son, you must no longer let your mind grow rusty in idleness, you must strip off that monstrous habit, you must leave your cloister; I shall make you known to Princes and Kings, and I shall also make your name famous in all quarters, and I shall bring vanquished nations under your power. "One must be very bold: Fortune demands a noble heart that boldly undertakes great things."

   'Do you not see that the Pope is too puffed up with worldly goods? See how he dominates earthly Princes! And how his Church is thoroughly depraved, gorged with ambition, glory and honours! Do you not see his henchmen, slothful and sickly, fashionable, perfumed, foppish and lascivious? They are falconers and huntsmen;

Fauconniers et veneurs, qui occupent et tiennent
Les biens qui justement aux pauvres appartiennent,
Sans prescher sans prier sans garder le troupeau,
Dont ils tirent la gresse et deschirent la peau?

Dieu t'appelle à ce fait: courage je te prie:
Le monde ensorcelé de vaine piperie
Ne pourra resister: tout va de pis en pis,
Et tout est renversé des grands jusqu'aux petits.

La foy la verité de la terre est bannie,
280   Et regnent en leur lieu luxure et gloutonnie:
L'exterieur domine en tout ce monde icy,
Et de l'interieur personne n'a soucy.

Pource je vien du ciel pour te le faire entendre,
Il te faut maintenant en main les armes prendre:
Je fourniray de feu de mesche et de fuzil:
Pour mille inventions j'auray l'esprit subtil,
Je marcheray devant et d'un cri vray-semblable
J'amasseray pour toy le vulgaire muable,
J'iray le cœur des Rois de ma flamme attiser,
290   Je feray leurs citez en deux parts diviser,
Et seray pour jamais ta fidele compagne.

they seize and keep the possessions that rightly belong to the poor, and do not preach, do not pray, do not watch over their flock, whose fat they take and whose skin they rend.

'God calls you to this deed; courage, I beg you; the world, bewitched by specious duplicity, will be unable to stand fast; everything is going from bad to worse, and everything is turned upside down, from the greatest to the smallest.

'Faith and truth are banished from the earth, and in their place lechery and gluttony reign; external appearance is all-important in this world here below, and no one has any concern for what is internal.

'For that reason I have come from heaven to reveal this to you. You must now take up arms; I shall provide you with fire, fuse and flint; my mind will be ingenious in devising a thousand stratagems, I shall march ahead and with a persuasive battle-cry I shall muster for you the fickle masses, I shall proceed to inflame the hearts of Kings with my fire, I shall cause their cities to divide into two factions, and I shall forever be your faithful companion.

Tu feras grand plaisir aux Princes d'Allemagne,
Qui sont marris de voir (comme estant genereux)
Un Evesque Electeur qui domine sur eux:
S'ils veulent qu'en leur main l'election soit mise,
Il faut rompre premier les forces de l'Eglise:[13]
Un moyen plus gaillard ne se trouve sinon
Que de monter en chaire, et d'avancer ton nom,
Abominer le Pape, et par mille finesses
Crier contre l'Eglise, et descrier les Messes.   300

    Ainsi disoit ce monstre, et arrachant soudain
Un serpent de son doz, le jetta dans le sein
De Luther estonné: le serpent se desrobe,
Qui glissant lentement par les plis de sa robe
Entre sous la chemise, et coulant sans toucher
De ce moyne abusé ny la peau ny la chair,
Luy soufle vivement une ame serpentine,
Et son venin mortel vomist en sa poitrine
L'enracinant au cœur: puis faisant un grand bruit
D'escailles et de dents, comme un songe s'enfuit.   310

    Au bruit de ce serpent que les monts redoublerent,
Le Danube et le Rhin en leur course en tremblerent,
L'Allemagne en eut peur, et l'Espagne en fremit:

'You will give great pleasure to the Princes of Germany, who (being of noble birth) resent seeing an Elector-Bishop who has ascendancy over them; if they want the power of election to be placed in their hands, they must first destroy the strength of the Church. There is no more spirited method than to go up into the pulpit, and to promote your name, to abominate the Pope, and by a thousand subtle manoeuvres to cry out against the Church, and to decry the Mass.'

So said this monster, and, suddenly plucking a serpent from her back, she threw it into the bosom of the astounded Luther; the serpent disappears from sight, and, gliding slowly between the folds of his habit, it steals under his shirt, and, sliding along without touching either the skin or the flesh of this deluded monk, it quickly breathes into him a serpent-like soul, and spews its deadly venom into his breast, planting it in his heart. Then, making a great noise with its scales and teeth, it vanishes like a dream.

At the sound of this serpent, re-echoing from the mountains, the Danube and the Rhine trembled in their courses, Germany took fright, and Spain shuddered; France

D'un bon somme depuis la France n'en dormit,
L'Itale s'estonna, et les bords d'Angleterre
Tressaillirent d'effroy comme au bruit d'un tonnerre.

  Lors Luther agité des fureurs du serpent,
Son venin et sa rage en Saxone respand,
Et si bien en preschant il supplie et commande,
320 Qu'à la fin il se voit docteur d'une grand' bande.

  Depuis les Allemans ne se virent en paix:
La mort le sang la guerre et les meurtres espaix
Ont assiegé leur terre, et cent sortes de vices
Ont sans-dessus dessous renversé leurs polices.

  De là sont procedez les maux que nous avons,
De là vient le discord sous lequel nous vivons,
De là vient que le fils fait la guerre à son pere,
La femme à son mary, et le frere à son frere,
A l'oncle le nepveu: de là sont renversez
330 Les conciles sacrez des vieux siecles passez.

  De là toute heresie au monde prist naissance,
De là vient que l'Eglise a perdu sa puissance,
De là vient que les Rois ont le sceptre esbranlé,
De là vient que le foible est du fort violé,

---

never slept in sound slumber from that time on, Italy was petrified, and the shores of England quaked in terror, as if at the sound of thunder.

  Then Luther, stung by the fury of the serpent, spreads his venom and his mad rage throughout Saxony, and in his preaching he entreats and commands so successfully that in the end he becomes the teacher of a large band of followers.

  From that time the Germans have never been at peace. Death, blood, war and frequent murders have beset their land, and a hundred sorts of vice have turned their political systems upside down.

  From this have sprung the evils that we are experiencing, from this comes the discord in which we live, from this it comes about that a son makes war on his father, a wife on her husband, and a brother on his brother, a nephew on his uncle; from this has resulted the overthrow of the sacred councils of ancient centuries past.

  From this all the heresy in the world was born, from this it comes about that the Church has lost its power, from this it comes about that the sceptres of Kings are cast down, from this it comes about that the weak are despoiled by the strong, from

De là sont procedez ces Geans qui eschellent
Le Ciel, et au combat les Dieux mesmes appellent:
De là vient que le monde est plein d'iniquité,
Remply de desfiance et d'infidelité,
Ayant perdu sa reigle, et sa forme ancienne.
[. . .]

    Nous sçavons bien, Seigneur, que nos fautes sont
        grandes,
Nous sçavons nos pechez: mais Seigneur tu demandes
Pour satisfaction un courage contrit,
Un cœur humilié, un penitent esprit.

    Et pource, Seigneur Dieu, ne punis en ton ire
Ton peuple repentant qui lamente et souspire,   360
Qui te demande grace, et par triste meschef
Les fautes de ses Rois ne tourne sur son chef.

    Vous Princes et vous Rois,[14] la faute avez commise
Pour laquelle aujourd'huy souffre toute l'Eglise,
Bien que de vostre temps vous n'ayez pas cognu
Ny senti le malheur qui nous est advenu.

    Vostre facilité qui vendoit les offices
Qui donnoit aux premiers les vaquans benefices,

this have sprung those Giants who scale the heights of Heaven and challenge the Gods themselves to battle; from this it comes about that the world is full of iniquity, filled with distrust and lack of faith, having lost its order and its age-old form.
[. . .]

    We know full well, Lord, that our faults are great, we know our sins; but, Lord, what you ask for in reparation is a contrite spirit, a humbled heart, a penitent soul.

    And therefore, Lord God, in your wrath do not punish your repentant people, who are lamenting and sighing, and who beg for your grace; do not, by a sad calamity, visit the sins of the Kings on their heads.

    You, Princes, and you, Kings, have committed the sin for which the whole Church is suffering today, although in your lifetime you did not experience or feel the misfortune that has befallen us.

    Your indulgence, which sold Church offices, which gave vacant benefices to the

Qui l'Eglise de Dieu d'ignorans farcissoit,
370   Qui de larrons privez les Palais remplissoit,
Est cause de ce mal:[15] il ne faut qu'un jeune homme
Soit Evesque ou Abbé ou Cardinal de Romme:
Il faut bien le choisir avant que luy donner
Une mitre et pasteur des peuples l'ordonner.
   Il faut certainement qu'il ait le nom de Prestre,
Prestre veut dire vieil:[16] c'est à fin qu'il puisse estre
De cent mille pechez en son office franc,
Que la jeunesse donne en la chaleur du sang.
   Si Platon prevoyoit par les molles Musiques
380   Le futur changement des grandes Republiques,
Et si par l'harmonie il jugeoit la cité:[17]
Voyant en nostre Eglise une lasciveté,
On pouvoit bien juger qu'elle seroit destruite,
Puis que jeunes Pilots luy servoyent de conduite.
»Tout Sceptre et tout Empire et toutes regions
»Fleurissent en grandeur par les religions:
»Par elles ou en paix ou en guerre nous sommes:
»Car c'est le vray ciment qui entretient les hommes.

first comers, which stuffed the Church of God with ignoramuses, which filled the Law courts with compliant thieves, that is the cause of this evil. A young man must not become a Bishop or an Abbot or a Cardinal of Rome. A man must be selected carefully before he is given a mitre and invested as shepherd of the people.

He must certainly warrant the name of Priest, and Priest means old; this is so that when he is in office he may be free from a hundred thousand sins that hot-blooded youth is heir to.

If Plato foresaw future changes for great Republics from their languid Music, and if he judged a city from its harmonies, then, seeing lasciviousness in our Church, we could easily deduce that it would be destroyed, since young Pilots were acting as its helmsmen. "Every Sceptre and every Empire and all regions flourish in glory through their religions: through them we are either at peace or at war, for they are the true cement that binds men together."

On ne doit en l'Eglise Evesque recevoir
S'il n'est vieil s'il ne presche, et s'il n'est de sçavoir: 390
Et ne faut eslever par faveur ny richesse
Aux offices publics l'inexperte jeunesse
D'un escolier qui vient de Tholose, devant
Que par longue pratique il devienne sçavant.

    Vous Royne en departant les dignitez plus hautes,
Des Rois vos devanciers ne faites pas les fautes,
Qui sans sçavoir les mœurs de celuy qui plus fort
Se hastoit de picquer et d'apporter la mort,
Donnoient le benefice, et sans sçavoir les charges
Des loix de Jesus-Christ en furent par trop larges,   400
Lesquels au temps passé ne furent ordonnez
Des premiers fondateurs pour estre ainsi donnez.

    Ma Dame, il faut chasser ces gourmandes Harpyes,
Je dy ces importuns dont les griffes remplies
De cent mille morceaux tendent tousjours la main,
Et tant plus ils sont saouls tant plus meurent de faim,
Esponges de la Cour, qui succent et qui tirent,
Plus ils crevent de biens, et plus ils en desirent.

We must not receive into the Church any Bishop if he is not old, if he does not preach, and if he lacks learning; we must not elevate to public offices for reasons of favour or riches the untried youth of a student from Toulouse, before he has become learned through long experience.

Your Majesty, you as Queen, when distributing the highest honours, do not make the errors of the Kings your predecessors, who, without knowing his moral character, used to award a benefice to the man that made most haste in spurring his horse to bring the news of the death of the incumbent. Without appreciating the duties imposed by the laws of Jesus Christ, they were much too liberal with benefices, which were not instituted by the original founders in times past to be awarded like this.

Your Majesty, you must drive away these gluttonous Harpies, I mean these importunate creatures, whose talons, although grasping a hundred thousand morsels, still stretch out for more, and the more gorged they are, the more they are dying of hunger, sponges on the Court, who suck and milk it dry, and the more glutted with wealth they are, the more they desire.

Ô vous doctes Prelats poussez du sainct Esprit,
410   Qui estes assemblez au nom de Jesus-Christ,
Et taschez sainctement par une voye utile
De conduire l'Eglise à l'accord d'un Concile,[18]
Vous mesmes les premiers Prelats reformez vous,
Et comme vrais pasteurs faites la guerre aux loups:
Ostez l'ambition, la richesse excessive,
Arrachez de vos cœurs la jeunesse lascive,
Soyez sobres de table, et sobres de propos,
De vos troupeaux commis cherchez moy le repos,
Non le vostre, Prelats: car vostre vray office
420   Est prescher, remonstrer, et chastier le vice.

Vos grandeurs, vos honneurs, vos gloires despouillez,
Soyez moy de vertus non de soye habillez,
Ayez chaste le corps, simple la conscience:
Soit de nuit soit de jour apprenez la science,
Gardez entre le peuple une humble dignité,
Et joignez la douceur avec la gravité.

Ne vous entremeslez des affaires mondaines,
Fuyez la Cour des Rois et leurs faveurs soudaines,
Qui perissent plus tost qu'un brandon allumé
430   Qu'on voit tantost reluire, et tantost consumé.

O you learned Prelates, moved by the holy Spirit, who are assembled in the name of Jesus Christ and are striving in holiness to lead the Church by a beneficial route to an agreement in the Council, reform yourselves first of all, Prelates, and like true shepherds make war on wolves; eradicate ambition, and excessive riches, pluck youthful lasciviousness out of your hearts, be moderate at table and moderate in speech; seek, I beg you, not your own well-being, Prelates, but that of the flocks entrusted to your care, for your true function is to preach, to remonstrate, and to punish vice.

Strip off your pomp, your honours, your glory, be clothed in virtues, not in silk, have a chaste body, a clear conscience; both by night and by day acquire knowledge, maintain a humble dignity towards the people, and unite mildness with solemnity.

Do not become involved with worldly matters, shun the Courts of Kings and their transitory favours, which perish faster than a burning brand that we see now glowing, now extinguished.

Allez faire la court à vos pauvres ouailles,
Faites que vostre voix entre par leurs oreilles,
Tenez-vous pres du parc et ne laissez entrer
Les loups en vostre clos, faute de vous monstrer.

Si de nous reformer vous avez quelque envie,
Reformez les premiers vos biens et vostre vie,
Et alors le troupeau qui dessous vous vivra,
Reformé comme vous de bon cœur vous suivra.[19]
[. . .]

Que diroit-on de Dieu, si luy benin et doux
Suivoit vostre party, et combatoit pour vous?
Voulez-vous qu'il soit Dieu des meurtriers de ses Papes,
De ces briseurs d'autels de ces larrons de chapes,
Des volleurs de calice? Ha! Prince, je sçay bien
Que la plus grande part des prestres ne vaut rien,
Mais l'Eglise de Dieu est saincte et veritable,
Ses mysteres sacrez, et sa voix perdurable.   660
Prince, si vous n'aviez vostre rang oublié,
Et si vostre œil estoit tant soit peu deslié,
Vous cognoistriez bien tost que les Ministres vostres
Sont (certes je le sçay) plus meschans que les nostres:

Go and pay court to your poor sheep, make sure your voice rings in their ears, stay close to the fold and do not allow the wolves into your pen, as a result of failing to be there.

If you have any desire to reform us, first of all reform your wealth and your lives, and then the flock living under your authority, reformed like you, will gladly follow you. [. . .]

What would we say about God, if he, compassionate and kindly as he is, supported your party, and fought for you? Do you want him to be the God of the murderers of his Popes, of these wreckers of altars, of these robbers of copes, of the thieves of chalices? Oh! Prince, I am well aware that the great majority of priests are worthless, but the Church of God is holy and true, her mysteries sacred, and her voice enduring.

Prince, if you had not forgotten your rank, and if your eyes were in the least clear-sighted, you would very soon realize (indeed, I am certain of this) that your Ministers are more corrupt than ours: in dress they are unpretentious, but they are

Ils sont simples d'habits, d'honneur ambitieux,
Ils sont doux au parler, le cœur est glorieux,
Leur front est vergongneux, leurs ames eshontées:
Les uns sont apostats, les autres sont athées,
Les autres par sur tous veulent le premier lieu:
670   Les autres sont jaloux du Paradis de Dieu,
Le promettant à ceux qui leurs songes ensuivent:
Les autres sont menteurs sophistes qui escrivent
Sur la parole saincte, et en mille façons
Tourmentent l'Evangile, et en font des chansons.[20]

    Dessillez-vous les yeux, Prince tres-magnanime,
Et lors de tels gallans vous ferez peu d'estime:
Recherchez leur jeunesse, et comme ils ont vescu,
Et vous ne serez plus de tels hommes veincu.

    Prince tres-magnanime et courtois de nature,
680   Ne soyez offensé lisant ceste escriture:
Je vous honore et prise, et estes le Seigneur
Auquel j'ay desiré plus de biens et d'honneur,
Comme vostre sujet, ayant pris ma naissance
Où le Roy vostre frere avoit toute puissance.[21]

---

ambitious for honours; they are mild in speech, but their hearts are vainglorious; their countenance is humble, but their souls are shameless; some are apostates, others are atheists, others want the highest position above everyone else, others jealously guard God's Paradise, promising it to those who comply with their delusions, others are liars, sophists who write about the holy word, and torture the Gospel in a thousand ways, and make songs out of it.

Open your eyes, noble-hearted Prince, and then you will have little respect for such splendid fellows; investigate their youth, and how they have lived, and you will no longer be enslaved by such men.

Prince, you who are noble-hearted and gracious by nature, do not be offended when you read these writings. I honour and esteem you, and you are the Lord for whom I have wished the most benefits and honour, being your subject, as I was born where the King your brother held full authority.

Mais l'amour du pays, et de ses loix aussi,
Et de la verité, me fait parler ainsi.[22]
[...]

    But love of my country, and of its laws also, and of the truth makes me speak
thus.
[...]

LES DERNIERS VERS

83 (1)

Je n'ay plus que les os, un Squelette je semble,
Decharné, denervé, demusclé, depoulpé.
Que le trait de la mort sans pardon a frappé,
Je n'ose voir mes bras que de peur je ne tremble.

Apollon et son filz deux grans maistres ensemble,
Ne me sçauroient guerir, leur mestier m'a trompé,
Adieu, plaisant soleil, mon œil est estoupé,
Mon corps s'en va descendre où tout se desassemble.

Quel amy me voyant en ce point despouillé
Ne remporte au logis un œil triste et mouillé,
Me consolant au lict et me baisant la face,

En essuiant mes yeux par la mort endormis?
Adieu chers compaignons, adieu, mes chers amis,
Je m'en vay le premier vous preparer la place.

THE LAST POEMS

(1)

I am nothing but a bag of bones now, I look like a Skeleton, without flesh, without
sinews, without muscles, without substance, which the arrow of death has struck
without mercy; I dare not look at my arms for fear I shall shudder.

Apollo and his son, both great doctors, would not be able to cure me; their craft
has failed me; farewell, delightful sun, my eyes are dimmed, my body is going down
to where all things disintegrate.

What friend, seeing me emaciated to this extent, will not return home with moist
and sorrowful eyes, after comforting me in my bed and kissing my face,

while wiping my eyes, closed by death's sleep? Farewell, my dear comrades,
farewell, my dear friends, I am going ahead to prepare a place for you.

84 (IV)

Ah longues nuicts d'hyver, de ma vie bourrelles,
Donnez moy patience, et me laissez dormir,
Vostre nom seulement, et suer et fremir
Me fait par tout le corps, tant vous m'estes cruelles.

Le sommeil tant soit peu n'esvente de ses ailes
Mes yeux tousjours ouvers, et ne puis affermir
Paupiere sur paupiere, et ne fais que gemir,
Souffrant comme Ixion des peines eternelles.

Vieille umbre de la terre ainçois l'umbre d'enfer,
Tu m'as ouvert les yeux d'une chaisne de fer,
Me consumant au lict, navré de mille pointes:

Pour chasser mes douleurs ameine moy la mort.
Hà mort, le port commun, des hommes le confort,
Viens enterrer mes maux, je t'en prie à mains jointes!

(IV)

Oh, long winter nights, torturers of my life, grant me a respite and let me sleep;
even the thought of you makes me sweat and shake all over my body, so cruel are
you to me.

Sleep with its wings does not, even for the briefest of moments, fan my eyes,
which are always open, and I cannot fasten eyelid upon eyelid, and I can only groan,
suffering eternal agony like Ixion.

Old shadow of the earth, or rather shadow of hell, you keep my eyes open with
an iron chain, ravaging me as I lie in my bed, tormented by a thousand wounds;

bring me death, to drive away my pain. Ah death, our common harbour, comforter
of men, come and bury my afflictions, with clasped hands I beg you!

85 (vi)

Il faut laisser maisons et vergers et Jardins,
Vaisselles et vaisseaux que l'artisan burine,
Et chanter son obseque en la façon du Cygne,
Qui chante son trespas sur les bors Mæandrins.

C'est fait j'ay devidé le cours de mes destins,
J'ay vescu j'ay rendu mon nom assez insigne,
Ma plume vole au ciel pour estre quelque signe
Loin des appas mondains qui trompent les plus fins.

Heureux qui ne fut onc, plus heureux qui retourne
En rien comme il estoit, plus heureux qui sejourne
D'homme fait nouvel ange aupres de Jesuchrist,

Laissant pourrir ça bas sa despouille de boue,
Dont le sort, la fortune, et le destin se joue,
Franc des liens du corps pour n'estre qu'un esprit.

(vi)

We must leave homes and orchards and Gardens, vessels and vases engraved by craftsmen, and sing our obsequies as the Swan does, which sings at its death on the banks of the river Meander.

It is done, I have unwound the thread of my destiny, I have lived, I have made my name very significant, and my pen now flies up to the sky to become a sign, far from the worldly seductions that beguile even the most perceptive of us.

Happy is he who never existed, happier he who returns to the nothingness from which he came, even happier he who from being a man becomes a new angel and dwells with Jesus Christ,

leaving to rot here below his vesture of clay, the plaything of fate, fortune and destiny, and he who is now freed from the bonds of the body to become nothing but a spirit.

Notes

Similar thematic and stylistic features across the selection are pinpointed by a limited number of cross-references. Such references occur at the first mention of the theme or stylistic device and draw attention to comparable characteristics in later poems.

LE PREMIER LIVRE DES AMOURS
(LES AMOURS DE CASSANDRE)

1. (IX: 'Le plus touffu . . .')

The theme of the grieving lover comforted by the solitude of nature is frequent in the verse of Petrarch and his imitators. The association between metamorphosis and passion, and references to painting and portraiture, are structured throughout the entire collection and contribute to its coherence. Line 12 refers to the painter and poet Nicolas Denisot (1515–59). The facing portraits of Ronsard and Cassandre that appear in the opening pages of the 1552 edition may, according to some critics, be the work of Denisot.

2. (XX: 'Je voudroy bien . . .')

This much-admired sonnet is a good example of the tension between the idealized nature of Petrarchism and a repressed desire, which exists throughout the sequence and which gives certain sonnets personal and poetic conviction (cf. poems 4, 5). The mythological references to Jupiter/Danaë (ll. 1–4), to Jupiter/Europa (ll. 5–8) and to Narcissus (ll. 9–11) centre on a common obsession: metamorphosis and the fulfilment of desire. The capitalization of 'Aurore' (l. 13) may denote the presence of an additional mythological figure, for Aurora is often considered by mythographers as a female equivalent of Jupiter because of her regular seductions of beautiful young men.

3. (XXXVI: 'Pour la douleur . . .')

Like a number of sonnets in the cycle, this poem associates Cassandre Salviati with Cassandra of Troy (Xanthus is a river of Troy), and compares the suffering of Ronsard with that of Phoebus Apollo. Throughout the sequence Ronsard places his 'love story' within his native region, the Vendômois (the Loir is a tributary of the much larger river Loire).

4. (XLIII: 'Ores la crainte . . .')

The tension between the idealism of Petrarchism and the articulation of desire manifests itself here, and in the following sonnet, in the juxtaposition of two discordant inspirations, visions and linguistic registers. The quatrains are overwhelmingly Petrarchist in theme (the conflict between fear and hope) and stylistics (antithesis and the metaphor of war), whilst the physical passion of the tercets owes a debt to the Latin erotic poets Ovid and Propertius. The ecstatic death swoon of line 14 is a euphemism for the orgasm.

5. (XLIV: 'Je voudrois estre . . .')

Placed immediately after the previous sonnet to highlight their similarity, this text also strikes an overtly sensual note. Here the tension and the related discrepant items are patterned throughout the poem in alternating lexical clusters of divinity and physical desire. For the references, frequent in Petrarchist verse, to the Underworld punishments of Ixion and Tantalus (ll. 1–4), Prometheus and Sisyphus (ll. 7–8), see Glossary of Names and Places. 'Ambrosie' (l. 14) was the food of the gods.

6. (LII: 'Avant qu'Amour . . .')

The creation of the cosmos from chaos by Eros is found originally in Plato, *Timaeus*. The same idea also appears in Neoplatonist writings (e.g. those of Marsilio Ficino), as indeed does the notion of the perfecting, harmonizing and animating power of love. The allusion to Cupid's bow and the association of arrows with the beloved's eyes (l. 8) are Petrarchist conceits.

7. (LVIII: 'Quand le Soleil . . .')

The battle between love and reason and the accompanying war imagery are features of the poetry of both Petrarch and his early sixteenth-century imitator, Pietro Bembo. The first quatrain evokes night by alluding to the way in which the chariot of the sun-god Phoebus Apollo returns to the Ocean ('le vieillard'), whence it will re-emerge at daybreak.

8. (LIX: 'Comme un Chevreuil . . .')

This poem, imitated from a sonnet by Bembo, falls within the Petrarchist *topos* of the *innamoramento*, the 'first meeting' (cf. poem 23). The French sonnet is superior to its Italian model, especially in the manner in which Ronsard heightens the visual drama of the episode and fuses the two elements of the comparison (lover and roebuck) by a dense and allusive networking of lexical, phonic and rhythmical parallelisms.

9. (XCIV: 'Soit que son or . . .')

The description of the beloved's physical and moral beauty is a recurrent aspect of Petrarchism. This *blason* of Cassandre's hair is indebted to texts of Petrarch and Ariosto, whilst the sexual ambiguity of the poem's closure is a reminiscence of Horace, *Odes*, II, v. The sonnet's strong binary structure opposes lines 1–4 and 9–11 with 5–8, 12–14. For Venus and Adonis, see Glossary of Names and Places. *Adoniser*: an example of Ronsardian neologism.

10. (CXX: 'Franc de raison . . .')

The hunt as an allegory of love occurs in the verse of Petrarch and his imitators. Lines 9–14 allude to the myth of Actaeon.

11. (CXXIX: 'Di l'un des deux . . .')

The antithesis between hope and despair (common in Petrarchist poetry) is woven throughout the entire sonnet and culminates in the epigrammatic last line with the reference to the way that, after their death, Castor and Pollux spent alternate days in Heaven and the Underworld. Line 4 forms part of this same binary scheme by contrasting the spontaneous outpouring of suffering ('lamenter') with pain mediated through artistic convention ('Petrarquiser').

12. (CXXXV: 'Douce beauté . . .')

Originally published in 1569, this sonnet found its definitive place in *Les Amours de Cassandre* in the complete works of 1578, in spite of the fact that neither this poem nor the following 'Stanses' concern Cassandre. The tercets develop an epigram from the *Greek Anthology*, V, 85, recently exploited by Johannes Secundus in an elegy (*Elegiae*, I, v), which Ronsard imitates in 'Stanses'. For similar epicurean utterances, cf. poems 13, 30, 46, 56.

13. Stanses

First published in *Les Meslanges* (1555), this poem was in 1584 placed immediately after the previous sonnet, with which it shares many features. The duplication of syntactical structures and the contrasting behaviour described in stanzas 1 and 2 prepare later antithetical patterns between past and present, beauty and ugliness, life's pleasures and death's decay. Cf. the poem 'To his Coy Mistress' by Andrew Marvell (1620–78).

14. (CLII: 'Lune à l'œil brun . . .')

Selene (the Moon) sent Endymion to sleep on Mount Latmus so that she could the more easily enjoy him without his knowledge. This myth is frequent in Petrarchist poetry; see also *Endymion* by John Keats (1795–1821). The chiasmic pattern of the last tercet and the epigrammatic final line act as strong closural features ('le jour' of line 14 simultaneously alludes to daybreak and to the radiance of Cassandre herself).

15. (CLX: 'Or' que Jupin . . .')

Ronsard skilfully binds together textual reminiscences from diverse sources (Virgil, Horace, Petrarch, du Bellay) to create an original and unified poem on the commonplace Petrarchist theme of the exclusion of the suffering lover from the general happiness of spring. Lines 7–8 allude to Philomela, metamorphosed into a nightingale after her rape by Tereus, king of Thrace (cf. Ovid, *Metamorphoses*, VI).

16. (CLXXII: 'Je veux brusler . . .')

The Platonic theme of the purification of love is here supported by the myth of Hercules ('le fils d'Alcméne') immortalized by fire on Mount Oeta. Neoplatonist motifs here include purification by fire, the release of the soul from its bodily prison, and its ascension to the Ideal World and to the divine archetypal Beauty of which earthly beauty is but a pale and imperfect reflection. Cf. du Bellay, *XIII Sonnetz de l'Honneste Amour*, X.

17. (CLXXIII: 'Mon fol penser . . .')

Adapted from Ariosto (sonnet V: 'Nel mio pensier che così veggio andare'), this text emphasizes the foolishness of divine aspirations by allusion to the disastrous flight of Icarus. Placed immediately after poem 16, this sonnet undercuts the Neoplatonism of the previous poem in an act of deliberate subversion.

18. (CLXXIV: 'Or' que le ciel . . .')

The poetic evocation of winter, and the manner in which the elemental sequence of earth, air and water prefigures the fire/cold opposition of the tercets, compensate for the Petrarchan *topos* of the final lines, where antithesis is conventionally and rather laboriously employed to describe the confused mental state of the lover.

19. (CXCII: 'Il faisoit chaud . . .')

The nocturnal visitation of the beloved in a dream is a familiar theme in Petrarchist poetry, where, however, the evocation remains predominantly chaste, and where the tendency is to focus on the deception of love, on the interface between illusion and reality, and on the transience of happiness. On the other hand, in Ronsard's several dream sonnets of the Cassandre collection, the intensity of desire bestows pleasures denied him in reality, and the dream is perceived as self-fulfilling, as a perfecting of the waking world, and as a moment of heightened ecstasy that transcends time.

20. (CXCIII: 'Ces flots jumeaux . . .')

Inspired from two passages of Ariosto, *Orlando Furioso* (VII, stanza 14; XI, stanza 68), this *blason* of the breasts employs binary patterns to good rhythmical and phonological effect. Feminist analysis of such male-authored *blason*s stresses the manner in which the masculine gaze dominates, fragments and reifies the female body.

LE SECOND LIVRE DES AMOURS
(LES AMOURS DE MARIE)

21. Elegie à son livre

Originally the concluding piece of the *Nouvelle Continuation des Amours* (1556), this elegy was moved to the beginning of the second book of *Amours* in the first collected edition of 1560.

1. In the opening lines (1–32) Ronsard launches his book upon the world with a certain trepidation, given its change of style and tone, and his abandonment of Cassandre.

2. Reference to Petrarch's love for Laura, which supposedly lasted for twenty-one years during her lifetime, and for ten years after her death. In

1553 du Bellay had already published a poem, 'A une Dame', in which he had satirized the thematic and stylistic excesses of Petrarchism.

3. The omitted lines (75–150) continue Ronsard's attack on 'femmes rusees' ('cunning women') with arguments and illustrations typical of traditional anti-feminist literature. However, he argues, if a man should find a sincere and truthful lady who reciprocates his love, she should be treasured as a rare jewel.

4. Reference to Cupid, son of Venus (cf. ll. 177, 182).

5. The Greek poet Pindar was imitated by Ronsard in his *Odes* of 1550 and 1552 (see below, *Les Odes*, and poem 55).

6. Ronsard concludes the elegy (ll. 183–98) by stating that each genre has its appropriate style: the 'grand' style for tragedy, the 'humble' style for love poetry.

22. (II: 'Marie vous avez . . .')

Rustic settings and nature imagery (fruits, flowers, animals, birds) are characteristic of the Marie poems. Peitho (l. 8) is the Greek goddess of persuasion. Lines 12–13 are explained by references in Homer to white-armed Juno and rosy-fingered Dawn.

23. (IV: 'Le vingtiesme d'Avril . . .')

Sporadic Petrarchist features are still present in *Les Amours de Marie*. Here the quatrains are imitated from Petrarch; similarly, the allegory of the *innamoramento* ('first meeting') and the themes of enslavement and entrapment are Petrarchist *topoi*.

24. (IX: 'Marie, qui voudroit . . .')

The Scythians (l. 11) were associated with all that was barbarous and unfeeling.

25. (X: 'Marie, en me tanceant . . .')

A forthright rejection of the Petrarchist principle of fidelity in love.

26. (XIX: 'Marie levez-vous . . .')

Reminiscent of the medieval *aubade*, sung by the troubadour poet to his beloved at dawn. The teasing intimacy of the tone and the manner in which Marie is portrayed, not as a goddess but as a flesh-and-blood person, are very different from the Petrarchist presentation of Cassandre. For the discreet allusion to Philomela (ll. 3–4), see poem 15 and note.

27. (XXVIII: 'Vous mesprisez nature . . .')

The contrast between the activity and animation of nature in spring and the frigidity of the beloved is found in the verse of Petrarch and in the *reverdies* (springtime poems) of the medieval troubadours.

28. (XLIV: 'Marie, baisez-moy . . .')

Written in the style of the *Basia* of the neo-Latin poet Johannes Secundus, which enjoyed widespread popularity in the sixteenth century, this 'kiss-poem' was originally published, like the following 'Amourette', in *Le Second Livre des Meslanges* (1559). Cf. poem 68.

29. Amourette

Adapted from Theocritus, *Idylls*, XXVII, and incorporating echoes from several Latin and neo-Latin poets, this erotic poem captures the breathless excitement of love-play by the perfect harmony of theme, style, rhythm and sound. The graceful and sensual style, reminiscent of Catullus, results here from a diversity of rhythmical effects, from the flirtatious intimacy of conversation, from a suggestive vocabulary (including diminutives and terms of endearment), and from the delicate balancing of lexical, syntactical and phonological items.

30. [VI: 'Je vous envoye un bouquet . . .']

We have reproduced the text of the 1572-3 collected edition for this poem, since it was suppressed in 1578, perhaps because from 1555 Ronsard, whilst never renouncing the decasyllabic line, favoured the alexandrine metre, or perhaps because he felt that this poem duplicated other similar epicurean utterances. One of only twelve decasyllabic sonnets inserted as a group into the alexandrine sonnets of the *Continuation des Amours* (1555), it is imitated from the *Greek Anthology* and from Marullus, whose epigrams to Neaera are the model for a number of the *chansons* ('songs') of the Marie collection.

SUR LA MORT DE MARIE

31. (IV: 'Comme on voit sur la branche . . .')

In this justly renowned sonnet, the freshness, perfume and colour of the perfectly fused rose and woman linger long after the brief allusion to the brutality of death has passed, and the pagan symbols of birth and fertility (milk, flowers) and the sense of plenitude ('plein de') equate life and death within a natural cycle that ensures the survival of beauty.

LE PREMIER LIVRE DES SONNETS
POUR HELENE

32. (III: 'Ma douce Helene . . .')

Like the alternative Helen of Troy myth (see Glossary of Names and Places), this sonnet emphasizes Hélène/Helen's virtue, indicates affinities between Penelope and Helen, and stresses the fragility of identity by playing on her name (e.g. 'Helene'/'haleine') at focal points in the poem. For other exploitations of the alternative Helen legend, cf. poems 38, 39, 45. Line 8 refers to the 'star of Helen', believed by the Ancients to foretell disaster for mariners (cf. the following poem).

33. (VI: 'Dedans les flots d'Amour . . .')

The Petrarchist *topos* of the shipwreck of love is here personalized and rejuvenated by the overt expression of desire and by the sexual allusions to the port the poet seeks to enter. Unlike the standard Petrarchist interpretation, the beacon of Hélène's eyes does not bring salvation but destruction (by her associations in lines 6–8 with 'the star of Helen' (cf. note above) and with a Siren). Line 10 refers to Cupid. 'Surgir' (l. 14) plays on the surname of Hélène de Surgères.

34. (IX: 'L'autre jour que j'estois . . .')

The Petrarchist theme of the 'salut amoureux' ('love's salutation/salvation') and the effects of the beloved's gaze are here anchored ostensibly in the narrative of lived experience (cf. poems 37, 43, 47, 48, 49). However, what principally interests Ronsard is a language of signs (cf. poem 35). For the birth of Helen of Troy and the word play 'signe/Cygne', cf. poems 59, 85 respectively.

35. (XIX: 'Tant de fois s'appointer . . .')

This is one of a number of sonnets, originally published in *Les Amours diverses* (1578), that Ronsard moved into the Hélène cycle in the collected works of 1584 (cf. poems 36, 42, 43). For the rhythmical movement created by repeated syntactical structures and the antithetical patterning of infinitives (here used to evoke the contradictory states of love), cf. poems 47, 66.

36. (xxii: 'Puis qu'elle est tout hyver . . .')

Originally published in *Les Amours diverses* (1578), cf. note above. References to Ronsard's advanced years (he is now in his early fifties) are frequent in this 'autumnal' collection (cf. poems 40, 42, 43, 49, 51). The reproach of line 3 is voiced elsewhere in the cycle.

37. (xxxiii: 'Nous promenant tous seuls . . .')

It was thought that the crocodile (ll. 13–14) attracted people by its weeping and then shed more tears as it devoured its prey. The accusation of hypocrisy is scarcely Petrarchist!

38. (l: 'Bien que l'esprit humain . . .')

Ronsard here defends the primacy of the body and the senses as instruments of knowledge, and rejects the mystical spiritualism of Platonism and its theory of reminiscence. According to Neoplatonist theory, the soul has its origins in God and the Ideal World and does not depend on the bodily senses for its cognitive processes. Imprisoned within the body, it nevertheless recollects things known to it from its previous existence and longs to be reunited with the Ideal World and with perfect knowledge and divine beauty. Hélène appears to have been interested in the Neoplatonist metaphysics of love fashionable at court and in the literary salons and academies. The mention of Ixion, who tried to seduce not the 'real' Juno but a phantom replica substituted by Jupiter, places this sonnet firmly within the illusion/reality frame of the alternative Helen myth. Like a number of others (cf. poems 40, 41, 42, 51), it is constructed on two, rather than the normal three, tercet rhymes (see Glossary of Literary Terms: sonnet).

39. (lx: 'J'attachay des bouquets . . .')

By emphasizing the act of substitution and the dichotomy between the illusory and the real, Ronsard here associates the erotic dream theme with the alternative version of the Helen legend. Contrast the use of the theme in poem 19.

LE SECOND LIVRE DES SONNETS
POUR HELENE

40. (I: 'Soit qu'un sage amoureux . . .')

The images of lines 3–4, 5–6, and the myths of the Moon (Selene)/Pan and Aurora/Tithonus, allusively support the themes of foolishness and old age, whilst the folly of the Platonic flight of the soul is underlined by the mythological reference to the presumption of Icarus (the 'Voleur', drowned in the Aegean) and Phaeton (the 'Charton', burnt by Jupiter's thunderbolt). Lines 9–10 relate the hypocrisy of Plato to an anecdote that recounts how the Greek philosopher fell under the spell of an aged and wrinkled whore.

41. (IX: 'Ny la douce pitié . . .')

Ronsard derives Helen's name not from the Greek word 'to pity', but from the verb 'to ravish, to seize'. The reference to Homer and Ronsard within the opposition between 'fable' and 'histoire au vray' (ll. 5–6) is explained by the 'feigning' role of the poet, whose task is to conceal the truth beneath fictions. Lines 9–10 allude to how Helen, warned in a dream that the Trojan horse contained Greek army chiefs, whispered the names of their beautiful mistresses in an attempt to excite them and make them betray their presence.

42. (XXVI: 'Au milieu de la guerre . . .')

Originally published in *Les Amours diverses* (1578), cf. poem 35 note. Old age, the foolishness of love, personal lawsuits and a farewell to the Muses and their streams of inspiration are set against the backcloth of continuing civil strife, compared here to a Thebaid, a conflict between brothers such as that between Polynices and Eteocles for the succession to Oedipus, king of Thebes. There is a clear parallel with Henri III and his brother François d'Alençon, who were on opposing sides in the Wars of Religion. The 'fleur de lis' ('lilies') was the French royal emblem.

43. (XXXII: 'J'avois esté saigné . . .')

Originally published in *Les Amours diverses* (1578), cf. poem 35 note. Bleeding was a common medical practice used to restore the balance of the four bodily humours. Black blood was a sign of a melancholy disposition that was thought to favour inspiration and a heightened imagination.

44. (XLI: 'Laisse de Pharaon . . .')

Although satire of the court was commonplace in sixteenth-century litera-ture, Ronsard expresses such anti-court sentiments with increasing fre-quency and conviction as he grows older (cf. poems 50, ll. 23–4; 70, note 7; 82, ll. 403–8). The mythological references to Circe and a Siren associate the court with dissimulation and tempting enchantresses, whilst Ronsard, in the persona of Orpheus, proposes to save Hélène/Eurydice from the Underworld of the court. Lines 1–2 refer to the exodus of the Jews from Egypt to the promised land (equated here with the countryside).

45. (XLII: 'Ces longues nuicts d'hyver . . .')

The themes of duplication and deception, the appearance of a phantom beloved in a dream, and the substitution of a false Hélène for the 'real'one, again suggest the alternative Helen myth.

46. (XLIII: 'Quand vous serez bien vieille . . .')

This famous sonnet is both a meditation on the passage of time (note the wide temporal perspective of the verb tenses) and a self-publicizing assertion of the value and glory of Ronsard's name (cf. poem 50, ll. 65–70). It inspired W. B. Yeats's poem 'When you are old and grey and full of sleep' (*The Rose*, 1893). *Ombres myrteux* (l. 10): the myrtle groves of the Underworld reserved for lovers (the myrtle was sacred to Venus: cf. poem 48).

47. (XLIX: 'Le soir qu'Amour vous fist . . .')

The ballet is used to express Ronsard's life-long obsession with patterns and processes of change and movement, and to illustrate the artistic principle of *libre contrainte* (the balance between freedom and constraint, diversity and unity, the fragmentary and the coherent). The Trojan river Meander (l. 8) was renowned for its tortuous course.

48. (LVII: 'De Myrte et de Laurier . . .')

Another example of Ronsard's interest in self-reflexive matters: a confident declaration of his poetic merit and immortality, and a statement of the inspiring power of love (personified as Cupid). The myrtle and laurel were sacred to Venus and Apollo respectively. Ancient poets were crowned with laurel as a mark of honour (cf. poems 75, ll. 6–7; 76, ll. 71–9). Line 8 alludes to the dying poet's metamorphosis into a swan (bird sacred to Apollo) and the flight of immortality (cf. Horace, *Odes*, II, xx). According to Plato

(*Phaedo*, 84e–85b), the song of the dying swan was both beautiful and prophetic (cf. poems 53, 85).

49. (LXV: 'Je ne serois marry . . .')

This sonnet is a playful and ironic commentary on Petrarchist themes (the unattainable beloved as 'Goddess seated in a very high place' and the poet's physical suffering and devotion). Olympus was the home of the gods. Line 11 plays on two meanings of 'court' (royal court and the palace courtyard): in addition to the translation given, Ronsard also voices 'customary complaints about the court' in this sequence (cf. poem 44).

50. Elegie

1. First published in the collected works of 1584, this elegy would have been composed in 1578–9, if the beginning of Ronsard's 'love' for Hélène dates from 1571–2, as most commentators suggest.
2. Ronsard may have recently (re)read Euripides' *Helen*, in view of his familiarity with the alternative Helen legend.
3. Both Charles IX and Henri III were passionately fond of hunting.
4. Ronsard's pronouncements on astrology are ambivalent, although in general terms he seems to have believed that human destinies and future events were written in the stars, but that man was unable to decipher the language.
5. The fountain that Ronsard dedicated to Hélène.

51. (LXXV: 'Je m'enfuy du combat . . .')

Line 7 is explained by Paris' abandonment of the nymph Oenone for Helen and by Jason's desertion of both Hypsipyle and Medea.

SONNETS À DIVERSES PERSONNES

52. (LVII: 'Je vous donne des œufs . . .')

Originally included in *Les Amours diverses* of 1578, this sonnet may well be addressed to Hélène de Surgères in her persona as Helen of Troy. Born from an egg (cf. below, poem 59, note 6), Helen/Hélène would be the appropriate recipient of this sonnet, which fuses cosmology and love in a 'precious' manner much in vogue at court and in the literary salons of the day. Although 'aubin' (l. 7) usually means the white of an egg, most critics agree that Ronsard refers here to the yolk.

53. [LX: 'Vous estes deja vieille . . .']

The text is that of the posthumous 1587 collected edition. Added at the end of the *Sonnets à diverses personnes*, this sonnet and the following one are ironic and wistful commentaries on the relationship between old age and love. For the snake's slough as a motif of rejuvenation (l. 8), cf. poem 59, ll. 59–60. Line 14 is rich in resonance: it alludes to good and bad poets ('Cygne'/'Corbeau'), to the aged poet's beautiful 'swan song' and his flight to immortality, to his associations with Apollo, poetry and prophecy, and to the whitening of his hair.

54. [LXI: 'Que je serois marry . . .']

The text is that of the 1587 edition. Lines 12–14 refer to the custom, on certain days in Cyprus, for young women to prostitute themselves on the seashore in order to earn money for their dowries.

LES ODES

Ronsard's four books of *Odes* were first published in 1550; a fifth book was added in 1552. In a combative preface to the 1550 collection, Ronsard condemns previous French poetry as a 'monstrous error', claims to introduce the ode into France, and boasts of his originality in imitating the Greek poet Pindar and the Latin poet Horace. The odes are predominantly celebratory in tone and content. The most elevated and serious poems glorify poetry and the poetic mission, or treat moral, philosophical and mythological subjects and topics of circumstantial and official importance (homilies to the royal family and potential patrons, accounts of battle victories and court events). The lighter odes (mainly Horatian in inspiration) sing the praises of wine, nature, friendship and love. The lyrical quality of the *Odes* and the Pléiade's design to create a close union between poetry and music are illustrated in the 1552 edition by the inclusion of selected musical settings by leading contemporary composers. In our selection, poems 55 and 56 come from Book I of the 1584 edition, poems 57 and 58 from Book II, poem 59 from Book III, poems 60 to 63 from Book IV and poem 64 from Book V.

55. À Michel de l'Hospital, Chancelier de France

Originally published with music by Claude Goudimel (1520–72), this most famous of Ronsard's Pindaric odes reproduces the triadic form, the celebratory tone, the freely digressive structure, the dense and allusive language, the sublime lyricism, the rhetorical devices and the evocative imagery of his Greek model. The poem is at once a glorification of inspired poetry, a forceful reaffirmation of the tenets of the new school of humanist poets (cf. poem 73, ll. 1–86), and an expression of gratitude to l'Hospital, who had defended Ronsard at court in 1550 against the attacks of Mellin de Saint-Gelais and the followers of Clément Marot. (These poets, still in favour at court at this time, ridiculed in particular Ronsard's obscurity and elevated style.)

1. The lines prior to the extract (1–340) describe the visit of the nine daughters of the mortal Mnemosyne/Memory to their father, Jupiter, who is being entertained by Ocean in the depths of the sea. Impressed by the range and diversity of their songs, which include a cosmological account of the creation of the world from chaos and an epic description of the war between the Gods and the Giants, borrowed from the Greek poet Hesiod, Jupiter begs his daughters to request a gift. Calliope (the future Muse of epic poetry) responds.

2. Lines 341–64: in addition to the gifts of prophecy and incantatory healing, Calliope asks for immortality, knowledge of the cosmic mysteries and the fury of divine inspiration, which separates the soul from the prison of the body and reunites it with the Ideal World, the communion of souls and the Divine Beauty.

3. *monstres boiteux*: specifically, Vulcan.

4. Although 'art' is dismissed here and contrasted with divine inspiration ('sainte fureur'), Ronsard, like his fellow theorist du Bellay, recognizes the fundamental importance of craftsmanship and hard labour in the creative task. Here he is rejecting what he considered to be the artificial excesses and the sterile technical virtuosity of the Grands Rhétoriqueurs.

5. The image of the magnetic chain of inspiration linking Jupiter to Apollo ('fils de Latonne'), and thence to the Muses, poets and the public, is found in Plato, *Ion*, 533d–e, 535e–536b.

6. The four divine furies referred to here are defined by Socrates in Plato, *Phaedrus*, 244a–245b (cf. poem 75, ll. 37–42).

7. The emphasis on the poet's virtue – already prefigured in Epode 13 – and the initiatory process of purification have religious overtones of baptism (cf. Epode 15, where Jupiter's breath is reminiscent of the Holy Spirit).

Such an association of Christian and classical visions is frequent in Ronsard.
8. Intermediary between God and man, the d(a)emon performs the function of a guardian angel in Neoplatonist thought. Cf. poem 71.
9. Periphrasis for Mercury. For Mercury's invention of the lyre, see poem 75, ll. 376-400.
10. The rest of the ode (ll. 511-816) centres on the history of poetry prior to the exile of the Muses in Heaven during the dark Middle Ages. By encouraging the assimilation of Greco-Roman culture, Michel de l'Hospital (the 'guide' of line 498) will ensure that the Muses return to earth with Ronsard and the Pléiade, and that the monster Ignorance is defeated.

56. À sa Maistresse

Originally published in the second edition of *Les Amours* (1553), this celebrated ode to Cassandre develops the commonplace *carpe diem* / *carpe florem* themes of Greco-Roman and neo-Latin poetry. Ronsard will return time and time again to these epicurean themes in poems of exquisite beauty.

57. 'Ô Fontaine Bellerie'

This ode, freely borrowed from Horace, *Odes*, III, xiii, is one of three poems Ronsard dedicates to this fountain, which was situated on his family estate, La Possonnière. The sound, movement and freshness of the fountain are associated with the life-giving properties of Ronsard's verse.
1. In keeping with the classicized vision of Nature in the opening lines, the goat-kid is offered as a sacrifice in honour of the fountain.
2. The midsummer heat of August is accompanied by the appearance of the dog-star, Sirius. 'Canicule' is derived from the Latin word for dog, '*canis*'.
3. *Iô*: exclamation of joy found in ancient literature.

58. 'J'ay l'esprit tout ennuyé'

Published first in *Le Bocage* (1554), this epicurean and Bacchic ode is inspired by poems of Horace and pseudo-Anacreon (a selection of Anacreontic poetry with Latin translation was published in 1554 by Henri Estienne and influenced Ronsard's lighter lyric verse of *Le Bocage* and *Les Meslanges* of 1554-5). Cf. poem 63.
1. Ronsard read this Greek didactic poem of Aratus (*c.* 315-*c.* 240 BC) in 1553-4. Ronsard's fellow poet Rémy Belleau translated a part of the *Phaenomena* (cf. poem 76, especially ll. 173-7).
2. *Orque*: Orcus, another name for Pluto, god of the Underworld.
3. *Corydon*: name (doubtless fictionalized) of Ronsard's servant. Borrowed from Virgil's *Eclogues*.

59. La Defloration de Lede

This mythological narrative poem of the rape of Leda by Jupiter, metamorphosed into a swan, is developed after the manner of the second-century BC Greek bucolic poet Moschus (*Europa*), who provides Ronsard with the idea (but not the detail) of the *ekphrasis* of Part 2 (the description of the decorative painting of Leda's basket). Ronsard's mannerist tendencies are seen, according to some commentators, in the ornate detail and the sensuality of his description.

1. The slough of the snake is often seen by Ronsard as an enviable rejuvenation. Cf. poem 53, l. 8.

2. In classical mythology horses pulled the chariot of the god of the sun from Oceanus, the water believed to surround the entire earth, in the morning, and returned it there in the evening.

3. The flowers alluded to here by periphrasis are the narcissus, the hyacinth (which grew from the blood of the Greek Ajax, who killed himself in anger, having been defeated by Ulysses in the contest for the armour of Achilles), and the heliotrope, which turns towards the sun.

4. When equated with the allegorical figure of Kairos-Occasio (Time as the present opportune moment), Fortune is depicted as being bald except for a forelock of hair. This detail denotes the importance of seizing the present opportunity before it disappears irrevocably: hence the proverbial expression 'to take time by the forelock'.

5. Neptune, god of the sea, is the brother of Jupiter.

6. One egg contains Castor and Pollux; the other contains Helen, whose abduction by Paris was the origin of the Trojan War.

60. De l'election de son sepulchre

This ode is far from being funereal. Thanks to its rhythmical fluidity, its nature imagery evoking protection, abundant growth and movement, and its frequent references to annual ritual and symbols of plenitude and continuity, it is rather a glorification of the immortalizing power of poetry and the triumph of memory over time and death.

1. *les Sœurs compagnes*: the Muses.

2. The 'demeure' of line 74 is that of the Elysian Fields, the abode of those destined for eternal bliss.

3. Allusions to the Underworld punishments of Sisyphus and Tantalus in order to emphasize the therapeutic value of poetry.

61. À Guy Pacate

From a complex interweaving of Horatian reminiscences, Ronsard constructs an original moral and philosophical meditation on mortality, considering death and illness as consequences of archetypal acts of hubris. Guy Peccate (d. 1580) held a number of minor ecclesiastical offices. His nephew, Julien Peccate, was a fellow student of Ronsard in Paris.

1. Periphrastic references to Phaeton and Bellerophon, twin examples of overweening pride and of encroachment on divine prerogatives.
2. Prometheus and Daedalus (ll. 67–84) are further illustrations of the sin of presumption.
3. The departure of Astraea, goddess of justice, from the earth after the Age of Gold is here associated with the evils released into the world from Pandora's box. See Horace, *Odes*, I, iii, 25–40.

62. 'Bel aubepin fleurissant'

Originally published in the *Nouvelle Continuation des Amours* (1556), this ode is renowned for the regularity and musicality of its metre and its picturesque observation of nature.

63. 'Pourquoy comme une jeune poutre'

Included initially in *Les Meslanges* (1555), this poem imitates an ode from Henri Estienne's 1554 selection of Anacreontic verse (cf. poem 58). See also Horace, *Odes*, II, v. The bawdy double meaning of the allegory also has a counterpart in French medieval literature.

64. À sa Muse

The concluding ode in the 1550 collection, this adaptation of Horace's celebrated '*Exegi monumentum*' ('I have finished a monument': *Odes*, III, xxx), is transferred by Ronsard to the end of the five books of odes from the 1567 collected edition onwards as a fitting and assertive monument to the entire section.

1. *des freres la rage*: storms at sea. The twin stars, Castor and Pollux, were supposed to control weather at sea.
2. *les deux Harpeurs divers*: Pindar and Horace. The periphrasis has an alliterative value: it supports the dental pattern [d] of lines 13–14.

LE BOCAGE ROYAL

65. Discours du Verre

Originally dedicated to Ronsard's patron Jean Brinon and published as an elegy in *Les Meslanges* (1555), this *blason* appeared in successive collected editions both in *Les Poëmes* and in *Les Elegies* before finding its definitive place in the second book of the newly constituted *Bocage Royal* of 1584 as a *discours*. Throughout this poem, glass is not only a metonymy for wine (ll. 43–58), but also, through its associations with glass-blowing and the homophonic links between 'verre' (glass), 'vers' (verse), 'uni*vers*' and 'di*vers*', it is a metaphor for invention and textual 'inflation', and for the interplay between diversity and unity, nature and art. *Bocage* (a grove) here denotes a miscellany of poems.

1. Allusion to the fortuitous invention of glass by merchants as recounted by Pliny, *Natural History*, XXXVI, lxv. Virgil is mentioned as an example of artistic inventiveness and as an early prefiguration of the parallel between poetry and glass-making developed later.

2. Fern ash (rich in potassium) was used in glass-making (cf. l. 95). The medicinal and abortifacient properties of ferns alluded to by Pliny, *Natural History*, XXVII, lv, could explain the reference to witches.

3. Horns are a sign of strength and valour here. Bacchus is often described as having horns.

4. Cf. the adage *'in vino veritas'* ('in wine the truth speaks').

5. As narrated in Homer, *Iliad*, XI.

6. For the battle between Lapiths and Centaurs, see Homer, *Odyssey*, XXI; Ovid, *Metamorphoses*, XII.

7. The glass-blower, with his protective transparent mask, is compared to the one-eyed Cyclopes, who, as assistants of Vulcan, made metal armour and ornaments.

8. Ronsard here relates the creative breath of the glass-blower to the cosmological idea of an infused World Spirit as evoked in a well-known passage from Virgil, *Aeneid*, VI.

9. Allusion to the premature birth of Bacchus (cf. poem 79, ll. 30–36). The fashioned glass (described as 'rond' and 'creux' in ll. 38, 103) is equated with a substitute womb, which receives the aborted foetus of Bacchus for the purpose of purification and for the promotion of thirst and inspirational wine.

LES MASCARADES, COMBATS ET CARTELS

66. Cartel pour le combat à cheval, en forme de balet

First published in 1584, this *cartel* (a written challenge to take part in a joust or tournament) is an example of Ronsard's participation in court festivities, often both as poet and theatrical organizer. He demonstrates the creative principle of *libre contrainte* ('free constraint') here by reworking both earlier sonnets of 1578 (poems 35, 47) and a passage of Virgil, *Aeneid*.

1. This line clearly indicates the introduction of a new scene within a wider theatrical programme.

2. Allusion to the golden bridle given by Pallas to Bellerophon to enable him to master the apparently uncontrollable winged horse Pegasus.

LES ELEGIES

First created as a section for the second collected edition of 1567, *Les Elegies* originally drew together diverse pieces from earlier collections. Although the Ronsardian elegy defies precise theoretical definition, it clearly surpasses the restrictive English conception of a 'song of lamentation', and is characterized rather by variety and flexibility of themes and moods. Lyrical and of medium length, Ronsard's elegies express a range of emotions (love remains a prominent subject), and they do so directly and naturally, and without recourse to undue erudition and rhetorical adornment.

67. La Mort de Narcisse, en forme d'elegie

Adapted from Ovid, *Metamorphoses*, III, and originally published in *Le Bocage* in 1554, this piece appeared in *Les Poëmes* in the first collected edition (1560) before being placed in *Les Elegies* in 1567. Some critics have interpreted it in self-reflexive terms to draw attention to Ronsard's constant obsession with poetry itself (see Introduction, section 5).

1. *l'arbre de Bacchus*: ivy.

2. *la fleur d'Adonis*: anemone (cf. poem 75, note 2).

3. Reference to the nymph Echo (Ovid, *Metamorphoses*, III).

68. Elegie XIII

The model for this teasing 'kiss-poem' of 1584 is *Basia*, VI, of Secundus, cf. poem 28 note.

1. Reference to the birth of Venus from the sea off Cyprus. Cf. Botticelli's painting *The Birth of Venus* (*c.* 1485-8).

69. À Philippes Des-Portes, Chartrain. Elegie

This elegy, which first appeared in the posthumous collected edition of 1587 (the text reproduced here), is included exceptionally because of its inherent importance and interest (it is, for instance, the only poem that Ronsard personally annotated). The poem's disenchanted tone, its ambiguities and its deviation from Ronsard's frequent assertions of poetic immortality in favour of an epicurean attitude to fame, are all best read as a defensive, even ironical, commentary on the youthful Desportes's increasing popularity at court and in the literary salons from the mid-1570s onwards.

1. In spite of Ronsard's second note, the influence of Aristotle, and especially the *Nicomachean Ethics*, is evident at this juncture.

2. References to Achilles (grandson of Aeacus) and to Virgil (Publius Vergilius Maro).

3. *enroncé*: a neologism of Ronsard's invention.

LES HYNNES

The majority of Ronsard's *hymnes* were originally published in two books in 1555 and 1556 respectively, and constitute another example both of Ronsard's elevated style and of his divine and social role as interpreter of the world's mysteries. By convention tripartite in structure – dedication, discussion of a single subject, final salutation – Ronsard's *hymnes* are not essentially Christian in design or nature, but are conceived rather after Greek models (the Orphic and Homeric hymns, and especially those of Callimachus). In addition, the influence of the *Hymni naturales* (1497) of the neo-Latin poet Marullus is evident both in Ronsard's overall conception of the genre and, more specifically, in the imitation of certain individual poems (e.g. 'Hynne du Ciel'). Written mainly in alexandrine rhyming couplets as glorifications of important historical and legendary figures or of natural and physical phenomena, the *hymnes* are variously mythological, epic, scientific, philosophical, religious and moral. The vagaries of sixteenth-century spelling are well illustrated by the way in which Ronsard refers to the collection both as 'Hymnes' and 'Hynnes'. In our selection, poems 70-72 are from Book I of the 1584 edition, poem 73 from Book II.

70. Hynne de Calays et de Zethés

The sources for this mythological *hymne*, which recounts an episode from the adventures of Jason and the Argonauts in their quest for the Golden Fleece, are Apollonius of Rhodes and his Latin imitator, Valerius Flaccus. Throughout, Ronsard develops his models by highlighting the presence of the fantastic and the monstrous, and by emphasizing scenes of picturesque descriptive detail and of heightened realism. The opening movements of the poem (ll. 1–146) contain a dedication to Marguerite de France (1553–1615), sister of Henri II and patroness of Ronsard, and a presentation in epic mode of Jason, prince of Thessaly, and the Argonauts. Calais and Zetes, liberators of the blind prophet Phineus, are the sons of Boreas, the north wind.

1. Here, as elsewhere in the poem, Ronsard appeals to the senses of sight, hearing and smell. He also amplifies and elevates his text in true epic fashion with extended Homeric comparisons drawn from the natural world (animals, birds, the threshing of corn, harvesting, fire).

2. In the omitted passage (ll. 205–320), which recalls lines 158–88, Phineus explains to the Argonauts the reason for his punishment and the nature of it. Zetes, moved by the account, offers help. A sacrifice is made to the gods and a meal is prepared as a lure for the Harpies.

3. The restless movement between past and present verb tenses in lines 335–88 dramatizes the action and supports the visual and physical nature of the episode.

4. The omitted lines (409–570) tell how Iris, messenger of the gods, intervenes and forbids the slaughter of the Harpies, who are to be preserved as future instruments of divine punishment. In a series of fantastic and imaginative visions, Phineus foretells the future exploits of the Argonauts.

5. The final prophecy (ll. 571–650) explains how Jason subdues two fire-breathing bulls, yokes them to a plough, overcomes by magical charms the dragon which protects the fleece, and sows its teeth in the ploughed field (an action which results in a harvest of warring soldiers who kill each other in a process symbolizing civil war). The sequence of events is rather confusing. Lines 589–626 become clearer after a reading of lines 627–36.

6. *mareschal boiteux*: Vulcan.

7. In the closing lines (651–720) Phineus's prophecies are followed by the return of Calais and Zetes and the departure of the Argonauts. Ronsard proposes as one possibility an allegorical interpretation to his *hymne*: Jason and the sons of Boreas are 'philosophes constans' (philosopher poets like

Ronsard himself?) who should drive the flatterers and liars of the court (the Harpies) from the rich pickings of the King's table.

71. Les Daimons

Dedicated to Lancelot Carle, Bishop of Riez (c. 1500–68), this poem gives imaginative, and sometimes inconsistent, voice to a catalogue of current views, widely held in the sixteenth century, concerning the origin and nature of d(a)emons, the forms they assume, the process that governs their materialization, their dwelling places, their food, their activities (both beneficent and malicious), and the means by which human beings can control them. Ronsard's principal sources are a Latin translation by Ficino of a treatise on demonology by an eleventh-century Byzantine philosopher, Michel Psellos, and Apuleius, *De deo Socratis*. In the course of subsequent editions Ronsard substantially shortened his text (see below, note 14). Throughout the poem (e.g. ll. 15–38, 121–4, 301–16) Ronsard takes pains to stress his religious orthodoxy by expressing traditional Christian beliefs.

1. From the outset Ronsard stresses the originality of his design (ll. 7–10) and defends his potentially dangerous subject on the ground of the pre-eminence of poetry.

2. This passage (ll. 39–64) is a perfect illustration of the poet's life-long fascination with metamorphosis and mobility, phenomena that he renders by a diversity of rhythmical effects and by patterns of accumulation and repetition (including anaphora).

3. Ronsard seeks to explain the fantastic and the mysterious by rational analogies from human experience (the rainbow, the act of turning pale or blushing).

4. In lines 75–88 Ronsard explains how our imagination ('fantaisie') externalizes its fears and obsessions as if by a psychic secretion, which, transmitted to the d(a)emons, enables them to assume the very form that corresponds to, and reinforces, those fears and obsessions. The nightmarish nocturnal visions of lines 89–98 are thus demonic apparitions occasioned by psychic projections of our terrors.

5. According to certain Neoplatonists (e.g. Ficino), the spiritual energy of the world (the World Soul) circulates in a condensed form in shellfish, including oysters.

6. In Neoplatonic thought d(a)emons, as intermediaries between God and man, were associated with knowledge and divination by such augural processes as cosmic voyages of the mind, prophetic dreams and ornithomancy. The popular examples of Tarquinius and Servius Tullius (fifth and sixth kings of Rome respectively), and Hannibal (who lost the sight of one

eye when marching through the marshes near the river Arno in 217 BC), are all found in Apuleius. For oracular d(a)emons, see also lines 239–50.

7. This description contains an allusion to the demonic activities and the sabbath associated with Hecate. The reference in line 147 is to the moon's eclipse.

8. Ghosts, poltergeists and diverse spirits ('Larves', 'Lares', 'Lemurs'). Some are sexually seductive ('Incubes', 'Succubes'), some one-legged ('Empouses'), some half-woman, half-serpent ('Lamiens'), some familiar and domestic ('Penates', and the gnomes and elves from European folklore referred to in ll. 171–6).

9. Various sea nymphs ('Nereides') and fresh-water spirits ('Naiades'), including those in the form of mermaids and Sirens. Thetis is a marine divinity and the 'Phorcides' are the daughters of the sea god Phorcys.

10. Reference to the tidal ebb and flow.

11. Episodes recounted in Homer, *Odyssey*, IV and V.

12. References to the *ignis fatuus* or 'will-o'-the-wisp' (ll. 209–12) and to St Elmo's fire – electric atmospheric lights which appear on ships' masts in stormy weather (ll. 213–16). The twin stars of the constellation Gemini, Castor and Pollux ('les freres d'Heleine', l. 216), were thought to herald the end of a storm.

13. The link between d(a)emons and fairies, wood spirits and rustic demi-gods (ll. 251–3) was commonplace in contemporary popular belief. Lines 256–7 allude to the ancient practice of painting the faces of gods scarlet.

14. At this point in the 1584 edition Ronsard suppressed thirty-two lines, present in all earlier editions, which recounted a personal encounter with a diabolical hunt, complete with a skeleton on horseback and dogs. These omitted lines are expressed in such realistic detail, and with such a sense of personal witness, that some critics have considered this episode to be genuinely autobiographic. Attacked by Protestants for his excessive cred-ulity in matters of demonology and magic, Ronsard may have excised these lines as an act of circumspection.

15. Sorceresses of ancient mythology and medieval legend.

16. These lines allude to the magical processes that imprison demons within incantatory spells, amulets, talismans and symbolic figures like the pentacle.

17. This account of demonic possession and exorcism leads to a prudent and orthodox Christian conclusion.

18. We have substituted 'nom' for 'non', which appears in the 1584 edition, as 'non' is clearly a misprint.

72. Hynne du Ciel

Ronsard's geocentric world picture is very much that of his time. It is inherited from the medieval tradition and is a synthesis of the ancient cosmological ideas of Ptolemy, Plato, Aristotle and their commentators. For this poem Marullus, *Hymni*, II, 2, *De Caelo*, provides little beyond the basic idea. Ronsard's world system is self-contained and spatially finite: it is composed of a balanced superimposition of the four elements, the seven planets then known, a sphere of fixed stars and, finally, the outer globe of the heaven, the Primum Mobile (Prime Mover). Jean Morel (1511–81), a gentleman of the household of Catherine de Médicis, was an early protector of Ronsard (hence the comparison in ll. 5–8 from Homer, *Iliad*, XII, 362ff.).

1. For Plato and the Neoplatonists knowledge is synonymous with reminiscence. We recollect dimly the perfect knowledge of our former 'existence', when our soul was in communion with the Ideal World.

2. Together with the uniformity, regularity and perfection of circular shape and motion, the self-perpetuating rapidity of the diurnal rotation of the heaven is indicative of the eternal nature of both the universe and time itself.

3. Here the 'esprit de l'Eternel' is equated with an Anima Mundi (an essential feature of Platonic, Neoplatonic and Stoic cosmology). The World Soul is that vital breath, the divine spirit, which first set the Prime Mover in eternal circular movement, and which is infused throughout the cosmos to maintain harmony and ordered beauty.

4. The daily rotation of the Prime Mover is from east to west; the other spheres move in the opposite direction, but they are simultaneously given a second course by the powerful influence of the Prime Mover. In a vision that is at once cosmological and aesthetic, the resulting diversity within unity is that of a balance of variously rotating and perfectly harmonized spheres. The notion of the music of the heavenly spheres has its distant origin in Plato.

5. Here, as elsewhere in his scientific poetry, Ronsard seeks to establish parallels between microcosm and macrocosm in his account of the non-consuming and self-sustaining fire of the outer heaven, the empyrean. The 'yeux d'Argus' (l. 52) are the stars.

6. '*Cosmos*' in Greek signifies 'elegance', 'order'.

7. In a Christianized vision, which sees the perfection of the cosmos as proof of God's omnipotent glory, Ronsard opts for the Old Testament conception of creation *ex nihilo* ('out of nothing': see l. 67). See below, note 11, and poem 82, ll. 127–8.

8. Ronsard places God within the empyrean (there may also be a Christian

allusion in lines 71–5 to the Incarnation). Following ancient cosmology, he draws a distinction between the extra-lunar realm, where all is peace, stability and perfection, and the sub-lunar world inhabited by mortals, which is subject to change, decay and misery.

9. Ronsard develops a brief earlier reference (ll. 15–16) to emphasize the all-encompassing nature of the 'Ciel', and to argue against the plurality of world systems. Lines 96–7 refer to the superimposition of the four elements within the universe.

10. '*Anange*' means 'necessity' in Greek. The 'Gods' here probably refer to the planets named after pagan divinities (Saturn, Venus, etc.). By being subjected to the movement of the Prime Mover, they are in fact subjugated to the yoke of necessity. Line 104 alludes to the Homeric myth of the golden chain on which Zeus suspends the world (*Iliad*, VIII). Ronsard uses the myth here to stress cosmic hierarchy and order, and like Aristotle he traces the links of the chain back to the Unmoved Mover (or God for Christians).

11. Like Plato and Aristotle, Ronsard insists on the fundamental difference between eternity, immutable and unchanging, and time, periodic and mobile in its cyclic return. Lines 111–12 (present in this form for the first time in 1584) would appear to contradict l. 67 with its reference to creation *ex nihilo*. This variant moves Ronsard closer to the Aristotelian position that the universe is eternal, subject neither to instantaneous creation, nor to total destruction. Formed from pre-existing and uncreated matter, it develops and evolves over time.

12. A Christian-Platonic note is heard in the reference to the liberation of the 'imprisoned soul' at death and its reunion with God in the Ideal World, its 'first home'. The son of Saturn (l. 116) is Jupiter.

73. Hynne de l'Autonne

The four seasonal *hymnes* first appeared in 1563. In Ronsard's hymn to Summer, where the seasons are presented as the children of Nature and the Sun, Autumn is described as female, feeble and immature. Allegorical interpretations (sometimes political) have recently been proposed for these four mythological narratives. The lengthy opening section of the hymn to Autumn, with its commentary on the nature and function of poetry, provokes a self-reflexive allegorical reading in which the passage of Autumn from childish sterility to sexual maturity parallels the processes of poetic creativity. Claude de l'Aubespine (died 1567) was one of four 'secrétaires d'État' ('Secretaries of State').

1. The fountain is Hippocrene: Ronsard's poetic initiation is accompanied by ritualistic number symbolism.

2. For these ideas on the nature of poetry and the divine mission of the poet in lines 1–85, see the Introduction, section 1.

3. In the omitted passage (ll. 87–168) the nurse suggests that, as puberty approaches, it is time for Autumn to visit her parents, to put aside childish pursuits, and to become involved in the processes of womanhood by seeking a husband. Auton, the hot and humid south wind ('the monster' of l. 170), will be asked to transport Autumn to see her father, the Sun.

4. Although the enumeration of the progeny of different illnesses and diseases that surround 'Maladie' (ll. 189–216) owes a debt to Folengo, *Macaronicae*, XV, the imaginative detail, the rhythmical richness and the visual copiousness of the description are Ronsard's own poetic contribution. Lines 217–302 recount Autumn's visits first to the Sun, who shrinks from his daughter and refuses to receive her, and subsequently to the palace of her brother Spring. Finding him absent, she steals flowers and moves on to visit Summer.

5. Line 324 refers to the proximity of the Sun to the earth in Summer. In the same way as Autumn had stolen flowers from the palace of Spring, so she takes rays of flame from Summer. She will thus incorporate the dual properties of previous seasons, and will continue the cycle of maturation and germination when fecundated by Bacchus.

6. *le boiteux manœuvre*: Vulcan.

7. Ronsard refers in passing to the ideas of the late seventh-century BC Greek philosopher Thales, for whom water was the primary element, the generative principle activating nature.

8. Throughout his work Ronsard stresses the permanence of Nature's forces by associating her with sexual fertility, regeneration and preservation.

9. *Phthinopore*: word derived from the Greek that emphasizes the destructive role of Autumn in the seasonal cycle prior to her fertilization by Bacchus.

10. Lines 397–470 narrate Bacchus's declaration of love and his union with Autumn. The final salutation underlines the fecundity of Autumn and her integration into the natural rhythm of renewal and abundance.

LES POËMES

Whilst *Les Poëmes* were originally constituted as a separate section in the first collected edition of 1560, the number of books, the contents and the order of individual pieces were constantly modified over the years. *Les Poëmes* do not follow a strictly defined generic model, but rather are characterized by diversity of subject matter, form and tone, as well as by a variety of composition and publication dates. In the 1584 edition *Les Poëmes* were organized in two books: poems 74–7 of our selection are from Book I, poem 78 appeared in Book II of the 1578 collected edition before being suppressed in 1584.

74. La Harangue de [. . .] François, duc de Guise,
aux soldats de Metz [. . .]

Written in 1553 as a circumstantial piece to commemorate the successful defence of Metz against the besieging army of Charles V of Spain (October 1552–January 1553), *La Harangue* falls into two parts: a detailed description of François's armour in Homeric and Virgilian mode (an *ekphrasis*) and an eloquent oration in the grand style addressed to the French army.

1. The omitted lines (1–26) briefly give the historical context and start to describe the martial scene in realistic detail.

2. Lines 45–56 focus on the first crusade (1096–9), of which Urban II was the principal instigator. Eustache and Baudouin were the brothers of Godefroy de Bouillon, the hero of the crusaders, who, legend has it, sold towns in the Lorraine region (ll. 57–9) to finance his expedition. The Guises traced their ancestry back to Godefroy. The Count of Flanders led a contingent of crusaders.

3. Corborant, or Kerbogha, emir of Mossoul, laid siege to the crusaders in Antioch, but was finally defeated in 1098. After the capture of Jerusalem (1099), Godefroy was proclaimed king of the city.

4. Periphrasis for the hundred-eyed Argus.

5. Charles of Anjou, king of Naples, died in 1285. René of Anjou bequeathed to the king of France all claims to the throne of Naples on his death (1480). The original name of Naples was Parthenopia after the Siren Parthenope, who, according to legend, was buried there.

6. The giant Antaeus was invincible only whilst he remained in contact with the earth. Hercules crushed him to death whilst lifting him in the air.

7. The imitation of three war songs by the seventh-century BC Greek poet Tyrtaeus begins here (an edition of Tyrtaeus with Latin translation appeared in 1553). François's exhortation follows a literary tradition (later exploited by Shakespeare in Henry's Agincourt speech in *Henry V*, 1599).

8. Lines 109–16 refer to the mythical ancestry of the French by alluding both to the Gallic Hercules legend and to their Trojan origins (the latter are the subject of Ronsard's unfinished epic, *La Franciade*).

9. Allusions to Charon and the Parcae, or Fates.

10. The address to the royal princes and the soldiers continues in this

nationalistic spirit. The poem closes (ll. 263–92) on a dramatic account of the terror of Charles V faced with the courage of François.

75. La Lyre

This poem of 1569 is at once a meditation on the nature of inspiration, a celebration of poetry and music, and a description of the lyre given to the poet by Jean de Belot (died 1570), a *conseiller* ('magistrate') at the Bordeaux Parlement, who received Ronsard in his house on the banks of the Garonne in April 1565 (cf. below, poem 77). Throughout the poems of 1569 Ronsard refers frequently to his illness and semi-retirement at Saint-Cosme and Croixval during the preceding years. Most of the allusions to mythological stories in this poem have their common source in Ovid, *Metamorphoses*.

1. Hippocrene, the spring of inspiration, created by the horse Pegasus.

2. In classical times poets were awarded a laurel crown as a mark of distinction. The myrtle was sacred to Venus, worshipped at Paphos in Cyprus. Venus made anemones grow from the earth stained with the blood of her beloved Adonis, killed by a wild boar.

3. *pere Evien*: Bacchus.

4. Plato has a rather different account of the four 'madnesses' in *Phaedrus*, ll. 244a–245b.

5. The Cumaean Sibyl – the most celebrated of all Sibyls – prophesied in verse (cf. Virgil, *Aeneid*, VI).

6. See Plato, *Symposium*, ll. 208–9. The 'Nocher' (l. 101) is Charon. Imagery of maternity and conception is structured throughout the poem, and will be echoed later in the allegorical interpretation of the birth of Pallas from Jupiter's head (ll. 107–20), as well as in the belly-like shape of the instrument's sound box (l. 272), from which will be born the superior spiritual children of poetry and music.

7. Lines 129–266 praise the patronage and hospitality of Belot, and recount how his support has inspired Ronsard to write again after a period of creative stagnation. Belot's gift of a lyre is thus symbolic.

8. In the following *ekphrasis* Ronsard does not make a distinction between the lyre and the lute.

9. Lines 277–98 follow Ovid, *Metamorphoses*, VI, in the account of the dispute between Pallas Athene and Neptune over the naming of Athens.

10. According to Homer, Apollo and Neptune collaborated in the building of the walls of Troy (cf. Ovid, *Metamorphoses*, XI). Ronsard attributes to Apollo the power of poetry and song, which is more usually associated with Amphion in the ancient accounts of the construction of Thebes.

11. Apollo looked after the cattle of Admetus, king of Thessaly, on the

banks of the river Amphrysus. 'Bœufs aux piés-tors' (l. 326) is a neologism: one of the ways the Pléiade aimed to enrich the French language was to create new compound words (cf. poem 77, ll. 55, 61).

12. According to Ovid, the mulberry was originally white before it was stained with the blood of Pyramus and Thisbe.

13. The god (l. 371) who is depicted between Neptune/War and Pallas/Peace (cf. ll. 278–98) is Bacchus. As with Bacchus, the caduceus of Mercury (l. 378) symbolizes the balance of opposites. Mercury was a grandson of Atlas (l. 381), the inventor of the lyre (ll. 385ff.), the messenger of the gods, and the conductor of the souls of the dead to the Underworld (l. 383).

14. Having stolen Apollo's cattle, Mercury appeases the god's wrath by giving him the lyre upon which he will later sing of the Gigantomachy (cf. note below).

15. The war between the Giants and the Gods (Gigantomachy), which took place at Phlegra, is here associated with the Catholic victory over the Protestants at the battle of Jarnac (March 1569) near the river Charente. In the final lines (417–28) Ronsard identifies himself with Apollo: both receive lyres which inspire poems.

76. Le Chat

This text of 1569 elaborates a theory of universal signs and presages within a context of Christian and non-Christian elements. Belleau, a member of the Pléiade, was the author of lapidary poems about the powers of precious stones (see ll. 29–33) and the translator of part of Aratus, *Phaenomena*, a long poem about stars, weather signs and the portentous behaviour of animals and birds (see ll. 173–7).

1. Ronsard's prophetic theory of signs seeks to establish links between man and the natural world, and has as its foundation a pantheistic philosophy in which Divine Providence and the World Soul are associated in a manner that some commentators have judged unorthodox in its consequences for the individuality of the human soul.

2. *une Thessalienne*: a laurel tree. Daphne, a native of Thessaly, was metamorphosed into a laurel tree to escape the amorous pursuit of Apollo (cf. Ovid, *Metamorphoses*, I). The personal episodes that Ronsard begins to narrate here, which he interprets as presages of his forthcoming illness (ll. 76–106, 137–50), took place at the priory of Croixval.

3. According to legend, in 387 BC the Romans were warned of the attacking Gauls by the noise of the sacred geese of the temple on Capitol Hill.

77. L'Ombre du Cheval

Originally published in 1569, this poem is a playful and an erudite humanist exercise in paradox and an illustration of how text can be invented from practically nothing (cf. ll. 69–72). The starting point appears to be a drawing or a painting of a horse offered to Ronsard by Belot. The person addressed, the composition date, the allusions to Ronsard's illness of 1568 and the poetic concerns of this text associate it with poem 75. The frequent allusions throughout the poem to 'air' and 'vent' ('wind') play on the rhetorical process of 'in*vent*io' and emphasize the paradoxical way that textual presence is conceived from absence.

1. References (i) to the horse of a certain Cnaeus Sejus, which brought misfortune to his master and to all subsequent owners; (ii) to Bucephalus (Greek for 'ox-head'), the horse of Alexander the Great; (iii) to the horse of Darius, whose neighing, provoked by a ruse, ensured that he was elected king of Persia (reigned 521–486 BC).

2. Bayard (l. 43) was the horse of Renaud of Montauban in the twelfth-century chivalry tale *Les Quatre Fils Aymon*.

3. The dwarf Pacolet (l. 47) invented a wooden horse often mentioned in popular adventure stories. Mogis (l. 49) was a magician in *Les Quatre Fils Aymon* (cf. note above).

4. Hera/Juno is represented in Homer, *Iliad*, V, riding in a magnificent chariot drawn by two horses. Samos was dedicated to Juno. The reference to lotus recalls the episode of the lotus-eaters in *Odyssey*, IX.

5. Detail found in Virgil, *Georgics*, III (like the poet, the mares 'conceive from nothing').

6. This episode is recounted in *Odyssey*, X.

7. Related in *Iliad*, XIX.

78. Gayeté

This bawdy piece is reproduced here in the text of the 1578 collected edition. It first appeared in *Le Livret de Folastries* (1553), a collection attacked by Protestants for its obscenity within the wider context of a condemnation of Ronsard's moral laxity. The rustic setting and the innocent terms of endearment of the opening lines are later parodied and subverted by the *double entendre*s and by the sexually explicit language and imagery.

EPITAPHES DE DIVERS SUJETS

79. Epitaphe de François Rabelais

Our text is that of the 1572–3 collected edition. Although not wholly typical of Ronsard's epitaphs (many of which are circumstantial and official), this comic epitaph, first published in *Le Bocage* (1554) and finally suppressed in 1578, has been included for its intrinsic interest and for the controversy surrounding its interpretation. Various readings have been offered: burlesque, bitterly satirical, eulogistic. Certainly Ronsard focuses more on Rabelais the 'boozer' than Rabelais the humanist, but the tone is far from being mordant or hostile. The genre of the comic epitaph is inherited from the literature of Antiquity (cf. the satirical epitaphs of the *Greek Anthology*), and is found in earlier Italian and French poetry (e.g. Marot's epitaphs).

1. The reference to Iris may allude either to the formation of rainbows from the evaporation of water, or to the river of that name in Asia Minor, which swallows up many tributaries.

2. References to the establishment of the worship of Bacchus in Thebes and to the god's premature birth.

3. Episodes, characters and their attributes in Rabelais's writings.

4. The appeal to the passer-by is a common closural feature of the epitaph in classical literature. Similarly, the comic votive offering of objects appropriate to the vices and weaknesses of the deceased was an aspect of the satirical epitaphs of the *Greek Anthology*.

DISCOURS DES MISERES DE CE TEMPS

80. *Continuation du Discours des Miseres de ce temps*

Following the deaths of Henri II (1559) and François II (1560), and the accession of Charles IX in 1560 (aged 10), Catherine de Médicis had instigated policies of conciliation and compromise in an attempt to ensure national unity and to affirm the authority of the monarchy in the face of the rivalries of the ambitious leaders of powerful noble families (the houses of Guise, Coligny and Bourbon-Condé) intent on exploiting the increasingly violent religious tensions for political and personal ends. The bloody repression of the 'conjuration d'Amboise' of March 1560 (a conspiracy against François II and his ministers, François and Charles de Guise), the failure of the Colloque de Poissy (September–October 1561) to find common ground between Catholic and Protestant theologians, and the massacre of Huguenots at Vassy (March 1562), all underlined the weaknesses of Catherine's policy of reconciliation and made civil war inevitable. The *Continuation du Discours* was composed between July and October 1562: during this period Louis de Condé was at Orléans with Gaspard de Coligny recruiting a Protestant army, including mercenaries from Germany.

1. Allusion to the punishment of Ixion in the Underworld, as well as to a contemporary instrument of torture.

2. Ronsard more frequently refers to the arrogance of the Protestants within a religious perspective, where their theological questioning of doctrine is seen as a challenge to God's prerogatives (cf. poem 82). The charge of sedition and treason (ll. 29-30) has its source in the alleged complicity of Calvinist leaders in the 'conjuration d'Amboise'. Although this is a frequent accusation in Ronsard's polemic poetry (cf. ll. 123-6) and in Catholic propaganda in general, the majority of Protestants professed allegiance to the king. Lines 31-2 allude to the Calvinist doctrines of predestination and election.

3. Biblical echoes are heard throughout the *Discours*. For lines 50 and 55-6, see Matthew 15:7-8 and II Kings 19:35, respectively.

4. In the omitted passage (ll. 61-90) Ronsard associates the violence of Protestant pastors with animals and insects that have biblical resonance (lions, scorpions, locusts). References to animals prefigure the image of caterpillars developed later in the poem (ll. 335-448).

5. Images of birth, nurture, motherhood and matricide are structured throughout the entire poem and culminate later in the allegory of Mother France (ll. 307ff.).

6. Théodore de Bèze (1519-1605) was born in Vézelay (l. 110). Catherine de Médicis considered him a crucial figure in her attempts to reconcile Calvinists and Gallican Catholics.

7. Bèze spent the spring of 1562 recruiting soldiers for the Huguenot army. The allusion is to the dragon killed by Cadmus: from its teeth, sown in the soil, sprang armed soldiers, who began killing each other. The five who survived founded Thebes.

8. Probably a reference to the Turkish Sultan Muhammad II, who captured Constantinople in 1453.

9. Bèze wears the long black coat of a German cavalryman (*reître*).

10. *poudre d'oribus*: dust from a resinous candle claimed by charlatans to have medicinal powers.

11. In the omitted section (ll. 171-224) the hypocrisy, arrogance, envy and ambition of the Protestant preachers are contrasted with the simple faith of the early Christian martyrs.

12. For Ronsard, as for Erasmus, the doctrinal differences between the various Reformed sects are proof of the fundamental error of Protestantism. For Zwingli, Luther, Calvin and Bèze: see Glossary of Names and Places. Thomas Munzer, a leader of the Anabaptists, was opposed by Luther and beheaded by Lutheran troops (1525). Quintin was a spiritual freethinker criticized by Calvin and burnt as a heretic in 1530.

13. In the remainder of this speech (ll. 255–98) Ronsard prays that Louis de Condé will recover his senses and reconvert to Catholicism. He also appeals to his former patron Odet de Coligny, who in 1561 had followed his brothers, Gaspard and François, in defecting to the Protestant cause.

14. In July 1562 rumour was rife that the English, responding to appeals from leading French Protestants, were on the point of invading Normandy. In August, following the breakdown of diplomatic relations between England and France, English forces occupied Le Havre, Rouen and Dieppe. On 20 September 1562 the treaty of Hampton Court was signed between England and the French Huguenots. German mercenaries were being recruited into the Protestant army, although Ronsard conveniently ignores the fact that the Catholic forces also included large numbers of German soldiers. 'Henry' (l. 309) is Henri II, and the 'fleurs de liz' (l. 312) refer to the heraldic lilies of the royal arms of France.

15. Geneva liberated itself from the authority of the Duke of Savoy and abolished the bishopric in 1536.

16. After the 'conjuration d'Amboise' (1560), in which Calvinist leaders had allegedly been implicated, Geneva feared a French invasion. Duke Philibert-Emmanuel of Savoy (1528–80) had tried in vain to elicit the help of France in his plan to reoccupy Geneva.

17. The 'Senateurs' are the 'conseillers des Parlements' (magistrates representing the king in regional assemblies, which were both legal and political).

18. Proverbial expression found in Erasmus, *Adagia*, explained by the fact that Roman troops who had pillaged treasure from a temple in Toulouse in 105 BC had all perished miserably. The remaining lines of the poem (369–408) continue the allegory, giving France's account of the desecration of Catholic churches and tombs, and eulogizing Catherine de Médicis and Charles IX, whose future victory over the Protestants is predicted. Finally France entrusts Ronsard with the mission of recording the 'miseres de ce temps' for future generations.

81. *Discours à G. Des-Autels*

Originally published in the first collected edition of Ronsard's works (1560) and subsequently as a pamphlet in 1562, 1563 and 1564, this poem was composed in the aftermath of the 'conjuration d'Amboise'. The variants of this *discours* reveal Ronsard alternating over the years between a policy of suppression, favoured by the Guises, and a policy of reconciliation. Guillaume des Autels (?1529-81), lawyer and poet, was closely associated with Ronsard and his fellow poets.

1. One of the reasons for the rapid success of Calvinism was the numerous theological treatises, translations of the Bible and polemical texts published in Geneva and circulated in France, whilst Catholic books and propaganda were practically non-existent. In the repression following the 'conjuration d'Amboise', libellous tracts and pamphlets defaming the Guises were published (ll. 47-50).

2. *Thetis*: error for 'Tethys', the Ocean. Achilles made the river Scamander unnavigable by filling it with Trojan corpses.

3. The Greek camp and fleet were based at Sigeum during the Trojan War.

4. According to Reformers like Calvin, the purity of the primitive Church continued only until the sixth century and was followed by corruption and decadence.

5. It was hoped that the Council of Trent, which met from 1545, would favour religious compromise and internal reform; in the event it reaffirmed traditional Catholic doctrines.

6. Criticism of the corruption of the clergy and the abuses of the Church was common both among Protestants and moderate Gallican Catholics (Ronsard continues in this vein to line 104; cf. poem 82, ll. 265-74). Saint Gregory (l. 69) was Pope from 590 to 604.

7. 'Decoupez' refers to the fashion of slashed doublets.

8. Jacob pretended to be his elder brother Esau by covering his face and hands with the skin of a goat-kid, thereby deceiving his father Isaac into giving him his blessing and birthright (Genesis 27).

9. Fear of the Turkish empire and a call for a new crusade are not uncommon in Ronsard's work and in the literature of the period. The periphrasis (ll. 142-4) signifies Jerusalem.

10. General reference to pagans and heathens. The 'Mammelus' were military rulers of Egypt from 1254 to 1811.

11. Ronsard frequently complains about the privileges and public offices

handed out to foreigners (especially Italians) at the court of Catherine de Médicis and her sons.

12. Reference to Charles de Guise, Cardinal de Lorraine. Nothing is known about the 'affaire' (l. 157) in question.

13. The predictions of Nostradamus in *Les Centuries* (1555) were widely believed. In the final lines of the poem (ll. 179–236), Ronsard refers to prophetic astrological signs and portentous events (death of Henri II, the 'conjuration d'Amboise'), which were thought to have been foretold by Nostradamus, and praises the repressive policies of the Guises.

82. *Remonstrance au peuple de France*

The *Remonstrance* (a formal statement of public grievances) was written during the siege of Paris by Huguenot forces under Louis de Bourbon-Condé (November–December 1562). Arguments in the early part of the poem were later developed by Montaigne (*Essais*, II, xii).

1. Luther retained only two of the seven sacraments (baptism and the Eucharist). Calvin reduced the number to one, for he considered the Eucharist to have merely symbolic value. See below, note 6.

2. Early religious heresies. The Persian Mani (third century) proclaimed God and Satan as coeternal forces of Good and Evil. Arius (fourth century) denied the full divinity of Christ.

3. Divinities, like Venus and Cupid, who ensure the survival of species through generation.

4. Christ's words recorded in Mark 16:16.

5. Reference to Luther.

6. Allusion (ll. 110–11) to the events of the Last Supper as recounted in the Gospels. Ronsard reaffirms the traditional Catholic doctrine of transubstantiation (the real presence of Christ in the Eucharist). For Calvin, the bread and the wine are symbolic and commemorative signs only.

7. References to Christ's resurrection, his subsequent appearance to the Apostles and the Ascension.

8. Refers to the creation of the world *ex nihilo*.

9. Episodes from the Bible: the serpent and the apple associated with Adam and Eve (Genesis 2–3); the wife of Lot transformed into a pillar of salt (Genesis 19); the ass that spoke to Balaam (Numbers 22); the miracles performed by Moses before and during the exodus of the Jews from Egypt (Exodus).

10. In the omitted lines (163–222) Ronsard continues to condemn the Protestants who arrogantly debate God's mysteries as if they were the sole

possessors of the truth. He admits that he had been briefly attracted to Calvinism, but had soon realized his error.

11. The Englishman John Wyclif (*c.* 1320–84) and the Czech John Hus (*c.* 1373–1415) were seen as precursors of the Reformation.

12. Opinion's seduction of Luther (ll. 257–64) recalls the Devil's three temptations of Christ.

13. The hereditary Elector-Princes of Germany resented the increasing power of the Catholic Church and its three Elector-Bishops.

14. Ronsard here alludes to kings of an earlier period (cf. ll. 395ff.).

15. Reference to the Concordat of Bologna (1516), which gave French kings the right to nominate bishops and to award Church livings (often sinecures).

16. This refers to the origin of the word 'priest' in the Greek for 'older'.

17. In the *Republic* Plato distinguishes between sweet and martial music (only the latter was allowed in the city state).

18. The Council of Trent (cf. poem 81, note 5).

19. In the omitted passage (ll. 439–652) Ronsard appeals to the judges, nobles, people, merchants and poets to fulfil their duties. More specifically, and in a spirit of conciliation, he addresses a personal plea to Louis de Bourbon-Condé.

20. Allusion to Protestant translations of the Psalms and to the place of singing and music in their worship. For Ronsard, Calvinist austerity and simplicity are hypocritical.

21. Condé's brother, Antoine de Bourbon, king of Navarre (died 1562), was also Duke of Vendôme, where Ronsard was born.

22. In the final phase of the poem (ll. 687–820) Ronsard calls on Condé to stop fighting, praises the Catholic military leaders and troops, and prays for their victory.

LES DERNIERS VERS

Dictated in part by Ronsard from his deathbed and published posthumously in February 1586 (the text reproduced here), this small collection, mainly of sonnets, describes Ronsard's agonizing illness during his final days at the priories of Croixval and Saint-Cosme (November–December 1585).

83. (1: 'Je n'ay plus que les os . . .')

Apollo (ll. 5–6) was associated with medicine and healing. Aesculapius, his son, was the god of medicine. Line 14 echoes Christ's words quoted in John 14: 2–3.

84. (IV: 'Ah longues nuicts d'hyver . . .')

Somnus, the winged god of Sleep, is described as the brother of Death and the son of Night (l. 5). For the Ancients, night was considered as the 'shadow of the earth' (l. 9).

85. (VI: 'Il faut laisser maisons . . .')

The river Meander in Phrygia was renowned for its swans (ll. 3–4). The word play of the rhymes 'Cygne', 'signe', 'insigne' underlines Ronsard's apotheosis as a poet and his metamorphosis into a constellation (l. 7).

How to Read French Poetry

SECTION A: SYLLABIC COUNT

1 French poetry is scanned by the number of syllables in a line. An alexandrine line has twelve syllables, a decasyllabic line has ten syllables. Syllabic count is important as it is associated with the positioning of stress and with rhythm (see section B).

2 Each syllable normally begins with a consonant:

1 2 3 4 5 6 7 8 9 10 11 12
Je/ n'o/se/ voir/ mes/ bras/ que/ de/ peur/ je/ ne/ tremble

3 There are several factors which bear on syllabic count. These are:
(i) The mute 'e' is pronounced *within* the line if it is followed by a word beginning with a consonant ('n'o/*se*' is two syllables), but a mute 'e' is *not pronounced or counted at the end* of the line ('tremble' is one syllable).

(ii) If a word ending in an 'e' is followed by a word beginning with a vowel, the 'e' is not pronounced but elided. Hence in the following line, the last syllables in both 'comme' and 'branche' are elided with the words that follow because these begin with vowels:

1   2   3   4   5   6   7   8   9   10 11 12
Com/m[e] on/ voit/ sur/ la/ bran/ch[e] au/ moy/ de/ May/ la/ rose

(iii) Words like 'ciel' and 'nuit' may count as one or two syllables because of the presence of the semi-vowels [j] and [ɥ]. The best way to determine the syllabic count of such words is to locate several 'normal' lines in the poem, so as to ascertain the number of syllables in these lines, and with them as a model then to work backwards, as it were, to the problematic line.

SECTION B: RHYTHMIC STRESS OR ACCENTUATION

1 The classical alexandrine is normally divided by a breath pause or break (a caesura) into two hemistichs (half-lines) of six syllables each. The caesura in a decasyllabic line normally occurs after either four or six syllables.

2 Each hemistich has a main stress which provides the line with its rhythm. These main stresses occur on the syllable just before the caesura and on the pronounced syllable at the end of the line (the sixth and twelfth syllables). In the following example the caesura is marked \\ and the main stresses //:

//   //

Je/ n'o/se/ voir/ mes/ bras\\ que/ de/ peur/ je/ ne/ tremble

Words receiving the main stress are thus emphasized (or foregrounded): these are often words which are of focal and semantic importance within the line.

3 Deviations from this regular pattern should be studied carefully to ascertain what special effects the poet has achieved.

(a) *Enjambement* occurs when a syntactical unit is carried over and completed in the following line, thus reducing the prominence of the end-rhyme and varying the rhythmic pattern:

comme on voit pesle-mesle
Bondir au temps d'hyver sur l'ardoise la gresle:
Ou dessus une enclume un marteau par compas
Ressauter, quand Vulcan la frappe à tour de bras.

The infinitive 'Ressauter' is given added emphasis by being held over until the following line (this is known as the *rejet*). It also forms a parallel with the infinitive 'Bondir', which also follows an *enjambement*, a feature which in turn helps to draw attention to the common meaning between the two similes.

(b) Additional sense breaks (not necessarily marked by punctuation) can occur within a line, and these result in an increased number of rhythmical stresses and of foregrounded words:

$$// \qquad // \qquad // \qquad //$$
Decharné, denervé, demusclé, depoulpé.

SECTION C: RHYME SCHEMES

Rhyme schemes are categorized in a number of ways:

1 A feminine rhyme (notwithstanding the actual gender of the word) is one which ends in a mute 'e'; a masculine rhyme is one that does not. From the sixteenth century onwards it has been the tradition (which is still widely observed) to alternate masculine and feminine rhymes, that is, to make sure that a masculine pair (or set) of rhymes is followed not by another masculine pair (or set), but by a feminine pair (or set).

2 French poetry distinguishes between *rimes pauvres, rimes suffisantes* and *rimes riches*. The *rime pauvre* is merely assonance (an identity of vowel sound without any pronounced rhyming consonant), e.g. 'chant'/'vent'. A *rime suffisante* has two identical sounds, usually a vowel and one pronounced rhyming consonant, e.g. 'bête'/'fête'. A *rime riche* has at least three common elements, either a vowel plus two pronounced consonants ('espagnol'/ 'rossignol'), or two vowels plus one pronounced consonant ('santé'/'vanté').

3 To determine rhyme patterns, each new rhyme is termed *a*, *b*, *c*, *d*, and so on. *Rimes plates* (rhyming couplets) are structured *aa bb cc*; *rimes embrassées* are organized *abba*, and *rimes croisées* alternate *abab*.

Glossary of Names and Places

Names explained in the Notes do not generally reappear in this Glossary. Only those details necessary for an understanding of the poem are given: fuller information can be found in the reference books mentioned in the Suggestions for Further Reading.

Acheron River of the Underworld.

Achilles Greek hero; killed Hector during the Trojan War.

Actaeon Huntsman who, having inadvertently surprised Diana naked whilst bathing, was transformed into a stag by her and killed by his own hounds.

Adonis Beautiful youth loved by Venus, killed by a wild boar. Venus caused anemones to grow from the blood-stained earth.

Aeneas Hero of Virgil's epic, *Aeneid*, and legendary founder of Rome.

Age of Gold First of four ages of mankind; peaceful and idyllic period with Saturn as ideal king.

Alcaeus Greek lyric poet (lived *c.* 610 BC).

Alexander the Great (356–323 BC) King of Macedonia, educated by Aristotle and founder of a huge empire. He was the only person able to tame and ride his favourite horse, Bucephalus.

Amboise Site of failed Protestant conspiracy against François II (March 1560), which aimed to remove the youthful king from the domination of the Guise dynasty. Provoked the First War of Religion.

Amphion Musician who played the lyre with such beauty that stones moved of their own accord and formed the wall fortifying Troy.

Anacreon Greek lyric poet of mid sixth century BC. Subjects include love, wine and the pleasures of life.

Apollo God of music and poetry, prophecy, medicine and the care of flocks and herds. Sometimes given the epithet Phoebus ('shining'). See **Cassandra of Troy**.

Apollonius Rhodius Alexandrian poet of third century BC. Author of *Argonautica*, an epic poem charting Jason's quest for the Golden Fleece.

Apuleius (born *c*. AD 123) Roman writer, philosopher and orator.

Argus A hundred-eyed giant, killed by Mercury. His eyes were placed by Juno on the tail of the peacock.

Ariosto, Ludovico (1474–1533) Italian poet, best known for his epic *Orlando Furioso*.

Aristotle (384–322 BC) Greek scientist and philosopher, studied under Plato.

Ascrean See **Hesiod**.

Aurora Goddess of Dawn. See **Tithonus**.

Bacchus Identified with Greek Dionysus. Androgynous and double-natured; god of wine, associated with cult of fertility. Was born prematurely when his mother Semele miscarried following the undisguised appearance of his father Jupiter as thunder and lightning. Bacchus was subsequently preserved in Jupiter's thigh to be reborn at the due time.

Baïf, Jean-Antoine de (1532–89) Son of humanist scholar and diplomat, Lazare (1496–1547). Member of Pléiade.

Belleau, Rémy (*c*. 1528–77) Member of Pléiade, best known for *La Bergerie* (1565; augmented 1572).

Bellerophon Tamed the magic winged horse Pegasus thanks to the golden bridle given him by Pallas Athene. Punished by being hurled from Pegasus for his presumption in attempting to ride the horse to the heavens.

Bembo, Pietro (1470–1547) Italian cardinal, humanist and poet; his verse included Petrarchist love poetry.

Bèze, Théodore de (1519–1605) Calvinist theologian, writer and pastor. Fled to Geneva (1548) and succeeded Calvin on his death (1564).

Bourbon, Louis de, prince de Condé (1530–69) A leading Huguenot, adversary of the Guises, uncle of the future Henri IV. Killed soon after being wounded at the battle of Jarnac.

Brinon, Jean (died 1555) Patron of Ronsard, *conseiller* at the Paris Parlement.

Bucer, Martin (1491–1551) Leader of Reform in Strasbourg. Exiled (1549), he died in Cambridge.

Callimachus (*c*. 305–240 BC) Alexandrian poet, scholar and grammarian.

Calliope Muse of epic poetry.

Calvin, Jean (1509–64) French religious Reformer and writer. He finally established his theocratic government in Geneva in 1541.

Cassandra of Troy Daughter of Priam, king of Troy. She was given the gift of prophecy by Apollo, but, as a punishment for refusing his love, she was fated to be disbelieved.

Castor and Pollux Twin brothers of Helen, hatched from an egg after Jupiter, in the form of a swan, seduced Leda. Participated in Jason's quest for the Golden Fleece. Identified with the constellation Gemini, they protected sailors.

Catherine de Médicis (1519–89) Chosen as the wife of the future Henri II as part of the Italian strategy of François Ier. Regent during the minority of Charles IX, she struggled to ensure the survival of the monarchy during the Wars of Religion and in the face of the political rivalries of powerful noble families.

Catullus (c. 84–c. 54 BC) Roman lyric poet, best known for his amatory verse.

Centaurs A tribe of primitive creatures, half-human, half-horse, best remembered for their battle with the Lapiths.

Ceres Corn-goddess.

Charles V (1500–58) King of Spain (1516–56) and Holy Roman Emperor (1519–56); his career was characterized by wars against France and struggles against Reformers and heretics.

Charles IX (1550–74) King of France (1560–74), son of Henri II and Catherine de Médicis.

Charon Ferryman who took the dead across the river Styx.

Coligny, Gaspard de (1519–72) French statesman and soldier; a Protestant military and political leader. Assassinated during the Saint Bartholomew massacre. His brothers, François (1521–69) and Odet, Cardinal de Châtillon (1517–71), were also Protestants; the latter was an important patron of Ronsard.

Cupid God of love, son of Venus. Attributes include bow and arrows, and blindfold (to denote the indiscriminate choice of victim and the irrational nature of love).

Daedalus Legendary inventor and craftsman. See **Icarus**.

Danaë Seduced by Jupiter in the form of a shower of gold.

Desportes, Philippe (1546–1606) French poet whose Petrarchist love poetry became increasingly popular in the 1570s at court and in the literary *salons*.

Dorat, Jean (1508–88) Poet, member of Pléiade, humanist scholar and teacher of Greek and Latin literature at the Collège de Coqueret from 1547 (where Ronsard, du Bellay and Baïf were his pupils).

Du Bellay, Joachim (c. 1522–60) Most important poet of Pléiade after Ronsard. Author of the *Deffence et Illustration de la langue françoyse* (1549), of the first sonnet cycle in French poetry (*L'Olive*, 1549, 1550), and of two major collections of sonnets written during his stay in Rome (1553–7): *Les Antiquitez de Rome* and *Les Regrets* (1558).

Echo A nymph who, when her love for Narcissus was not returned, pined away in grief and left nothing but her echoing voice.

Edoni The Bacchants, Thracian women celebrated for their orgiastic worship of Bacchus.

Erasmus, Desiderius (*c.* 1469–1536) Important Dutch humanist scholar, theologian and satirist who influenced French intellectuals (including Rabelais). Suspected by the diehard theologians of the Sorbonne of complicity with Luther.

Eros See **Cupid**.

Estienne, Henri (1531–98) Humanist printer-scholar who converted to Calvinism. His edition of pseudo-Anacreon (1554) inspired Ronsard's lighter love poetry of the mid 1550s.

Euripides (*c.* 480–406 BC) Greek tragic dramatist.

Europa Seduced by Jupiter metamorphosed as a white bull.

Euterpe Muse of flutes and music.

Ficino, Marsilio See **Plato**.

Folengo, Teofilo (1491–1544) alias Merlin Cocai. Italian burlesque poet.

Furies Goddesses of vengeance and punishment.

Ganymede Carried off by Jupiter to be his cup-bearer.

Giants Rebelled against the Olympian gods, defeated by Jupiter. Associated with the Protestants in Ronsard's *Discours* as an illustration of overweening pride.

Gorgons Three monstrous sisters, the most famous of whom was Medusa. Her appearance was so hideous that anyone who looked at her turned into stone.

Graces Three personifications of beauty and charm, often seen in the company of Venus.

Grands Rhétoriqueurs Group of poets active between 1450 and 1530 whose work, often circumstantial and official in nature, reveals an excessive and mechanistic reliance on rhetorical devices and formal artifices (e.g. elaborate rhyme schemes, word play and alliterative effects).

Greek Anthology Collection of fifteen books of epigrams dating from the sixth century BC, compiled by the tenth-century scholar Cephalas.

Guise Extremely powerful and violently anti-Protestant noble family, promoted by Henri II and François II, restrained by Catherine de Médicis. François (1519–63) took Calais from the English (1558), became military leader of the Catholic forces and was assassinated. His brother Charles, Cardinal de Lorraine (1524–74), was a patron of Ronsard and an important figure at the Colloque de Poissy.

Hannibal (247–183 BC) Great Carthaginian general of the First Punic War between Rome and Carthage.

Harpies Bird-like monsters who seized people or their food; used by gods as instruments of punishment.

Hecate Primitive pre-Greek goddess of the Underworld connected with sorcery and black magic.

Helen of Troy Born from Jupiter's seduction of Leda. Beautiful wife of Menelaus; her abduction by Paris provoked the Trojan War. According to a variant of the myth the real Helen was taken to Egypt during the Trojan War and it was a phantom Helen who accompanied Paris to Troy.

Henri II (1529–59) King of France from 1547, his death in a jousting accident left the monarchy in a weak position because of internal religious and political tensions.

Henri III (1551–89) Elected king of Poland (1573), he returned to France to succeed Charles IX (1574).

Hercules Son of Jupiter and Alcmene, popular Greek hero whose famous exploits (including his twelve labours) derive from his strength and valour. The Gallic Hercules legend traced the origins of the French nation to Hercules, who came to France and married Queen Galatea.

Hesiod Earliest known Greek poet after Homer. Lived in Ascra in Boeotia, where he was given the gift of song by the Muses as he guarded his sheep on the slopes of Mount Helicon.

Hippocrene Spring sacred to the Muses on Mount Helicon, thought to have been produced when the winged horse Pegasus struck the ground with its foot.

Hippogriff Mythical flying horse in medieval romances of chivalry and in Ariosto, *Orlando Furioso*.

Homer Universally regarded by the Ancients as the author of the epic poems the *Iliad* and *Odyssey*, the first dealing with the Trojan War, the second with the wanderings of Odysseus/Ulysses after Troy. The idea of a single author has been contested by scholars.

Horace (65–8 BC) Roman poet, friend of Virgil, whose work was admired and imitated by Ronsard.

Hospital, Michel de l' (*c.* 1505–73) French humanist writer, patron of the Pléiade and Chancellor of France; associated with Catherine de Médicis's policy of conciliation early in the Religious Wars. Played a role in the Colloque de Poissy (1561).

Icarus Son of Daedalus, who made him wings of feathers and wax. Icarus disobeyed instructions by flying too near the sun, thus causing the wax to melt. He fell into the sea and drowned. Example of folly and presumption.

Iris Messenger of the gods and goddess of the rainbow.

Ixion Foiled in his attempt to seduce Juno (Jupiter replaced the real Juno with a cloud made in her image). Suffered eternal punishment in the Underworld by being fixed to a revolving wheel.

Jason Son of Aeson, he assembled an expedition of heroes (Argonauts) and succeeded in his quest for the Golden Fleece with the help of the sorceress-princess Medea, whom he later abandoned.

Juno Roman equivalent of Greek Hera, wife of Jupiter, associated with women, marriage and childbirth.

Jupiter Identified with Greek Zeus, supreme god, father of the Muses. Seducer of Danaë, Leda and Europa in various disguises. Attributes include the thunderbolt. Typical of the period, Ronsard often associates Jupiter with the Christian God.

Leda Seduced by Jupiter in the form of a swan. Helen was born from the union.

Leucothea A sea-goddess who saved Ulysses when his raft was destroyed by Neptune.

Lipari Volcanic island, home of Vulcan.

Luther, Martin (1483–1546) German theologian and Reformer whose writings and campaigns had their greatest effect in France during the thirty years following his original protest at Wittenberg (1517), after which the influence of Calvin was dominant.

Marot, Clément (1496–1544) French poet, with Protestant sympathies, who looks back to the poetic traditions of the late Middle Ages, and forward to the early Renaissance.

Mars Roman god of war, lover of Venus.

Marsyas Finding a flute discarded by Pallas Athene, he challenged Apollo to a musical contest judged by the Muses. The victorious Apollo punished him by tying him to a tree and flaying him alive. His blood was the source of the river Marsyas in Phrygia.

Marullus, Michaelis (c. 1453–1500) Neo-Latin poet whose *Hymni* and *Epigrammata* influenced Ronsard in his collections of 1555–6 (*Les Hymnes* and *Les Amours de Marie*).

Medea Sorceress, princess who helped Jason to win the Golden Fleece. By her magical power, she also rejuvenated Aeson, father of Jason. See also **Jason**.

Medusa See **Gorgons**.

Menelaus Younger brother of Agamemnon, king of Sparta, and husband of Helen.

Mercury Identified with Greek Hermes. Herald and messenger of the gods, inventor of the lyre and guide to the dead. Attributes include winged hat and sandals, and a staff (caduceus).

Minerva See **Pallas Athene**.

Minos King and legislator of Crete. After death, one of three judges of the Underworld.

Montaigne, Michel de (1533–92) Influential French thinker and moralist, author of three books of *Essais*.

Muret, Marc-Antoine de (1526–85) French scholar and pedagogue, poet and dramatist. Wrote commentary on second edition of Ronsard's *Les Amours* (1553).

Muses Nine daughters of Jupiter and Mnemosyne who (under Apollo) preside over poetry and the arts and sciences. Helicon and Parnassus were sacred to them.

Narcissus Beautiful youth who fell in love with his own reflection, pined away and was metamorphosed into the narcissus flower. See **Echo**.

Neptune Brother of Jupiter, and god of the sea. Competed with Pallas over the naming of Athens. With Apollo, built the walls of Troy.

Oecolampadius Real name Johannes Hüszgen (1482–1531). Humanist friend of Erasmus. Reformation leader in Basel.

Orestes Son of Agamemnon and Clytemnestra. Orestes killed his mother's lover, Aegisthus (and, according to some accounts, his mother too), in revenge for the murder of Agamemnon. He was tormented by remorse and pursued by the Furies.

Orpheus Son of Calliope, mythical pre-Homeric poet and musician, he sailed with the Argonauts. He descended into the Underworld, and obtained the release from death of his wife, Eurydice, by charming Pluto with his music. He lost her almost immediately by breaking his vow not to look back at her.

Ovid (43 BC–AD 17/18) Prolific and versatile Roman poet. Many of Ronsard's legends and fables have their source in the *Metamorphoses*.

Pallas Athene Greek goddess of war, patron of arts and crafts, and personification of wisdom (identified with Roman Minerva). Sprang fully armed from the head of her father, Jupiter. See **Bellerophon**; **Neptune**.

Pan Son of Mercury, god of shepherds and herdsmen, represented as having goat's horns, ears and legs. Attempted to seduce Selene with the gift of a magnificent sheep's fleece.

Pandora First woman on earth, created by Jupiter to punish man after Prometheus had stolen fire from the gods and given it to mortals. She brought with her a box containing all known evils and illnesses, which were released into the world when the box was opened, leaving only hope at the bottom.

Parcae The three Fates responsible for spinning, allotting and cutting individual life-threads.

Paris Trojan prince whose abduction of Helen, wife of Menelaus, caused the Trojan War. See also **Helen**.

Parnassus Mountain sacred to Apollo and the Muses.

Pegasus See **Bellerophon; Hippocrene**.

Penelope In Homer, the chaste and faithful wife of Ulysses.

Petrarch, Francesco (1304–74) Italian humanist scholar and writer; most important figure of early Italian Renaissance. His collection of love poetry to Laura (*Canzoniere*) exercised widespread influence on generations of fifteenth- and sixteenth-century European lyric poets.

Phaeton Asked his father, the sun-god Helios, to allow him to drive the chariot of the sun across the heavens for a day. Unable to restrain the horses, he would have destroyed the world by fire had not Jupiter killed him with a thunderbolt. An illustration of hubris.

Phoenix Fabulous Egyptian bird said to set fire to itself every 500 years, which rises miraculously from its ashes, symbolizing death and resurrection.

Pindar (518–438 BC) Greek lyric poet whose odes celebrate victors of athletic games in an elevated style.

Plato (c. 429–347 BC) Athenian philosopher, pupil of Socrates, teacher of Aristotle. The Neoplatonism that pervaded the thought and culture of Renaissance Europe owes a debt to Marsilio Ficino (1433–99), a Florentine priest and humanist who edited and translated Plato, and achieved a synthesis of Platonism and Christianity.

Pléiade Originally, name given to a constellation of seven stars. In French literary history, name traditionally associated with a group of seven French poets active between 1549 and 1589 who, under the leadership of Ronsard, endowed French poetry with a new dignity consistent with humanist principles. Initially called the Brigade, the Pléiade never had the strict organization of a 'school', and its membership changed over the years.

Pliny the Elder (AD 23–79) Roman administrator and writer who died when Vesuvius erupted. Only his *Natural History* survives.

Pluto Ruler of the Underworld.

Poissy Site of a meeting between moderate Catholics and Protestants (1561), who attempted unsuccessfully to reconcile doctrinal differences.

Pollux See **Castor and Pollux**.

Pomona Goddess of fruit and orchards.

Prometheus Punished for stealing fire from the gods and giving it to mortals. He was chained to a rock on Mount Caucasus, and by day an eagle devoured his liver, which was restored during the night in a cycle of endless suffering.

Propertius (*c*. 50–*c*. 16 BC) Roman poet known for his love poetry.

Proserpina Carried off by Pluto; became Queen of the Underworld.

Proteus Minor sea-god, endowed with prophetic gift and able to change shape constantly. Only uttered prophecies if seized firmly. Told Menelaus how to return to Greece after the Trojan War.

Ptolemy (*fl.* AD 127–48) Greek mathematician, astrologer and geographer, whose most celebrated work, his *Geography* and atlas, was the standard work until superseded by the heliocentric world-system of Copernicus in the sixteenth century.

Pyramus and Thisbe Lovers forbidden by parents to meet, who arrange to do so by communicating through a hole in the wall of their adjoining houses. Because of a series of mishaps both lovers die. See Ovid, *Metamorphoses*, IV; Shakespeare, *A Midsummer Night's Dream* (1595–6).

Pyrrhus Also known as Neoptolemus. Son of Achilles.

Pythagoras (*fl. c.* 530 BC) Philosopher and mathematician who believed in the transmigration of souls.

Rabelais, François (1483 or 1494–1553) French humanist, doctor and writer of comic stories of extreme linguistic inventiveness, which conceal serious matters of humanist and evangelical interest.

Rhadamanthus One of the three judges of the dead in the Underworld.

Saint-Gelais, Mellin de (*c*. 1490–1558) Musician and court poet, associated with past poetic tradition. Clashed with Ronsard at court (1550). The two were later reconciled.

Sappho (born *c*. 612 BC) Greek lyric poet from island of Lesbos who was a leading member of a group of women dedicated to the cult of Aphrodite.

Sarpedon Ally of Trojans who distinguished himself by his courage.

Saturn Identified with the Greek Cronos. The metaphor of Time the devourer derives from the way in which Saturn swallowed his children as they were born. Jupiter alone survived. See **Age of Gold**.

Secundus, Johannes (1511–36) Dutch humanist and neo-Latin poet, whose kiss-poems (*Basia*) enjoyed a great vogue in sixteenth-century Europe.

Selene Greek moon-goddess, seducer of Endymion on Mount Latmus. See **Pan**.

Sibyl(s) Inspired prophetesses (the most celebrated being the Sibyl of Cumae).

Silenus Originally a satyr, later a jovial, fat and generally drunk elderly man who rides on a donkey as his legs will not support him. Often seen in the company of Bacchus, he possesses the wisdom inspired by wine.

Sirens Sea nymphs whose beautiful singing had the power to charm and destroy.

Sisyphus Condemned eternally to push a huge stone to the top of a hill in the Underworld, from where it would roll back down again.

Styx River of the Underworld. See **Charon**.

Sylvans Woodland divinities.

Tantalus His punishment in the Underworld was to stand in water up to his chin and to be tempted by food and drink forever just out of his reach.

Tartarus Place of punishment in the Underworld.

Teucer Stepbrother of Ajax, best Greek archer at Troy.

Theocritus (*c.* 300–250 BC) Greek pastoral poet.

Thersites The epitome of cowardice and the only non-heroic character in the *Iliad*.

Thisbe See **Pyramus and Thisbe**.

Tibullus (?48–19 BC) Roman poet, friend of Horace and Virgil.

Tithonus Mortal husband of Aurora, goddess of dawn. She requested of Jupiter that he make Tithonus immortal, but, as she failed also to request eternal youth, he gradually became older, greyer and more decrepit with passing time.

Triptolemus Inventor of the plough and the blessings of agriculture, he is associated with the sowing of the first seeds of wheat.

Tyard, Pontus de (1521–1605) Originally associated with the Lyonnais school of poets, later a member of the Pléiade. Also a writer of philosophical treatises, several of which are Neoplatonic in inspiration.

Ulysses Also known as Odysseus. A principal Greek hero of the Trojan War, famous for his valour, cunning and eloquence. His adventures after Troy are the subject of Homer's *Odyssey*. See **Penelope**.

Valerius Flaccus (1st century AD) Roman author of an unfinished heroic poem (*Argonautica*) about Jason's quest for the Golden Fleece.

Venus Identified with the Greek Aphrodite, goddess of love and beauty. Born from the sea near Paphos, Cyprus. Mother of Cupid, wife of Vulcan, lover of Mars and Adonis.

Virgil (70–19 BC) Roman poet of great distinction whose epic poem, the *Aeneid*, was the principal model for Ronsard's unfinished epic, *La Franciade*.

Vulcan God of fire and metal-working identified with Greek Hephaestus.

Lamed by being thrown from heaven during a quarrel between Jupiter and Juno. Husband of Venus, he trapped her and her lover Mars in a net.

Zwingli, Ulrich (1484–1531) Swiss theologian and Reformer.

Glossary of Literary Terms

allegory Narrative or description in verse or prose in which meaning is symbolically represented, thereby inviting a second, different interpretation. A form of **metaphor** that may be extended over an entire narration (e.g. John Bunyan's *Pilgrim's Progress*, 1678: allegory of the spiritual life of the Christian as a journey towards salvation).

alliteration The repetition of consonants especially at the beginning of words or stressed syllables.

amplification A device in which language is employed to elevate, extend or emphasize.

anaphora The repetition of a word or group of words at the beginning of successive clauses or lines. A process of **foregrounding**.

antistrophe See **strophe, antistrophe, epode**.

antithesis Contrasting ideas expressed by juxtaposition of words having opposite or very different meanings.

apostrophe An exclamatory passage in which a person (sometimes absent or dead), an abstract quality or a thing is addressed as if present and capable of understanding.

assonance The repetition of similar vowel sounds in close proximity.

binary or ternary (patterning) The combination in twos or threes of words or similar syntactic units (often used to accentuate rhythm). E.g. 'Et seul, et seur, loin de chiens et de bruit, /Or' sur un mont, or' dans une valée, /Or' pres d'une onde à l'escart recelée' (poem 8, ll. 5–7).

blason A descriptive poem, such as that which describes the various parts of a woman's body in Petrarchist verse.

carpe diem The phrase ('seize the day') is found in Horace, *Odes*, I, xi, and implies profiting from life while you can. The use of flowers (the rose in particular) as symbols of the beauty and ephemerality of life, accompanied by the appeal to 'gather rosebuds while you may', is what is meant by the *carpe florem* theme.

chiasmus A symmetrical expression in which the order of the first part is reversed in the second part in the formation A ... B/B ... A. E.g. 'Ils sont simples d'habits, d'honneur ambitieux,/Ils sont doux au parler, le cœur est glorieux' (poem 82, ll. 665–6).

circularity The stylistic means by which, at the end of a text, the reader is returned to its opening, either directly or via intermediary features located throughout the text.

closure The manner in which the end of a text (or a division of a text: e.g. a paragraph) is signalled stylistically.

coherence The logic or unity of a text; those stylistic or structural features that bind a text together and make it aesthetically purposeful.

conceit As a literary term, refers to a fanciful and elaborate figurative device intended to delight and surprise by its ingenuity. Many Petrarchist conceits quickly became commonplace. See *topos*.

copiousness Plenitude of thoughts and words. A copious style enriches its subject with an abundance and variety of ornamentation.

deviation The way in which the linguistic features of a text differ, either from what is accepted as the linguistic norm of the language, or from the linguistic and stylistic patterns established within the text itself. A process of **foregrounding**.

ekphrasis Visual description of a work of art or an artefact.

enargeia Vivid representation: those rhetorical features which present a subject as if painted and to be viewed.

epigram A brief, witty statement in verse or prose. Originally an inscription on a monument or statue.

epode See **strophe, antistrophe, epode.**

epyllion Short mythological narrative poem in epic mode.

euphemism The replacement of a harsh and blunt expression by a mild and more agreeable one.

feigning Derived from the Latin *fingere* ('to form, conceive, contrive'). By imitating (rather than reproducing) reality and the truth, the poet is an inventor, a 'liar'.

foregrounding The stylistic processes that draw attention to a word or a syntactical unit, and cause it to stand out from the rest of the text. See **anaphora; deviation; parallelism.**

homonym A word having the same sound and spelling as another, but a different meaning.

homophone A word pronounced the same as another, but with a different spelling and meaning.

humanism In the Renaissance context, refers essentially to the study and assimilation of Greek and Latin writers, philosophers, and rhetoricians.

This revival of classical thought and culture was accompanied by an interest in man, in his dignity and his perfectibility through knowledge.

intertextuality Theory which states that for both writer and reader a text does not exist in isolation, but relates to other texts by its thematic and formal concerns, its references and influences.

invocation Appeal or request for assistance (e.g. for inspiration from the Muses).

lexicon/lexis The vocabulary of a language. Lexical cluster: a grouping of words relating to an area of meaning (a 'semantic field') or to their grammatical function within a given text. Such clusters, operating throughout a text, give it **coherence**.

mannerism A twentieth-century term describing certain aspects of the painting and architecture (mainly Italian) of the period 1520–1600. Often applied to a vision bordering on the excessive and to literary styles characterized by ornateness of language, strange syntax and fantastic imagery.

metaphor Figure of speech whereby one reality is described in terms of another. A comparison is implicit, not overtly stated as in a **simile** by use of 'as' or 'like'. Gives added figurative effect to a text by evoking associations between the two realities concerned.

metonymy Figure of speech that replaces the name of one thing by the name of something else closely associated with it. In poem 65, for example, the material 'glass' is a metonymy both for the physical object, 'a glass', and for its contents, 'wine'.

neo-Latin Use of classical Latin in the work of early modern European writers.

palimpsest Writing material or manuscript on which the initial script has been effaced in order to make way for a second text. Used to refer to the way a writer reworks or rewrites an earlier text in a later one.

paradigm A pattern, example or model.

parallelism The repetition of similar lexical or syntactical items within texts. A process of **foregrounding**.

periphrasis A circuitous, complicated or more allusive expression is used instead of a simple, straightforward term: circumlocution.

personification The attribution of human qualities to inanimate objects.

Petrarchism Term commonly applied both to the love poetry addressed to Laura by Petrarch (1304–74) himself, and to the conventions that developed from the *Canzoniere*'s widespread influence on generations of European poets. The beloved is idealized as an unobtainable goddess and as an icon of perfection. A conception of love based on service and fidelity. The poet's suffering, caused by the woman's coldness, is expressed in conflicting emotional states, often rendered by **antithesis**.

rhetoric The art of speaking and writing well (with persuasion and emotional appeal). For many centuries, rhetoric was a central feature of the school curriculum, and a command of it was considered essential. The rules for oral and written composition were divided into five parts: *inventio* (the discovery and amassing of the relevant material); *dispositio* (the organization of the material); *elocutio* (the choice of the appropriate style – high, middle or low – and the most suitable words, phrases, stylistic devices); *memoria* (how to memorize speeches and make text memorable to the reader or listener); *pronunciatio* (the art of delivering a speech by voice and gesture).

self-reflexivity Used of texts that discuss themselves and define their own creative processes, objectives and concerns.

sententia A maxim or pithy, proverbial statement expressing a general truth.

simile See **metaphor**.

sonnet A fourteen-line poem, originally of Italian invention, comprising two blocks of four lines (quatrains), and two blocks of three lines (tercets). The rhyme schemes of the regular French sonnet as established by the Pléiade are either *abba abba ccdeed* or *abba abba ccdede*.

strophe, antistrophe, epode The lyric stanza form of Greek odes, such as those of Pindar. Originally this triadic form was accompanied by choral song and dance.

topos (plural ***topoi***) A commonplace or stock theme in literature.

Index of Titles and First Lines

In the few cases where our selection does not include the opening line of a poem, the first line of our extract is given, followed by the first line of the poem in brackets. Titles appear in italics.